Comic Spenser

The Manchester Spenser

The Manchester Spenser is a monograph and text series devoted to historical and textual approaches to Edmund Spenser – to his life, times, places, works, and contemporaries.

A growing body of work in Spenser and Renaissance studies, fresh with confidence and curiosity and based on solid historical research, is being written in response to a general sense that our ability to interpret texts is becoming limited without the excavation of further knowledge. So the importance of research in nearby disciplines is quickly being recognised, and interest renewed: history, archaeology, religious or theological history, book history, translation, lexicography, commentary, and glossary – these require treatment for and by students of Spenser.

The Manchester Spenser, to feed, foster, and build on these refreshed attitudes, aims to publish reference tools, critical, historical, biographical, and archaeological monographs on or related to Spenser, from several disciplines, and to publish editions of primary sources and classroom texts of a more wide-ranging scope.

The Manchester Spenser consists of work with stamina, high standards of scholarship and research, adroit handling of evidence, rigour of argument, exposition, and documentation.

The series will encourage and assist research into, and develop the readership of, one of the richest and most complex writers of the early modern period.

General Editors Joshua Reid, Kathryn Walls, and Tamsin Badcoe
Editorial Board Sukanta Chaudhuri, Helen Cooper, Thomas Herron, J. B. Lethbridge, James Nohrnberg, and Brian Vickers

Also available

Literary and visual Ralegh   Christopher M. Armitage (ed.)

Edmund Spenser and the romance of space   Tamsin Badcoe

The early Spenser, 1554–80: 'Minde on honour fixed'   Jean Brink

The art of 'The Faerie Queene'   Richard Danson Brown

A concordance to the rhymes of 'The Faerie Queene'   Richard Danson Brown and J. B. Lethbridge

A supplement of the Faery Queene: By Ralph Knevet   Christopher Burlinson, and Andrew Zurcher (eds)

English literary afterlives: Greene, Sidney, Donne and the evolution of posthumous fame   Elisabeth Chaghafi

A Companion to Pastoral Poetry of the English Renaissance   Sukanta Chaudhuri

Pastoral poetry of the English Renaissance: An anthology   Sukanta Chaudhuri (ed.)

Spenserian allegory and Elizabethan biblical exegesis: A context for 'The Faerie Queene' Margaret Christian

Monsters and the poetic imagination in 'The Faerie Queene': 'Most ugly shapes and horrible aspects' Maik Goth

Celebrating Mutabilitie: Essays on Edmund Spenser's 'Mutabilitie Cantos' Jane Grogan (ed.)

Spenserian satire: A tradition of indirection Rachel E. Hile

Castles and colonists: An archaeology of Elizabethan Ireland Eric Klingelhofer

Shakespeare and Spenser: Attractive opposites J. B. Lethbridge (ed.)

Dublin: Renaissance city of literature Kathleen Miller and Crawford Gribben (eds)

'A Fig for Fortune' by Anthony Copley: A Catholic response to 'The Faerie Queene' Susannah Brietz Monta

Spenser and Virgil: The pastoral poems Syrithe Pugh

The Burley manuscript Peter Redford (ed.)

Renaissance psychologies: Spenser and Shakespeare Robert Lanier Reid

Spenser and Donne: Thinking poets Yulia Ryzhik (ed.)

European erotic romance: Philhellene Protestantism, Renaissance translation and English literary politics Victor Skretkowicz

Rereading Chaucer and Spenser: Dan Geffrey with the New Poete Rachel Stenner, Tamsin Badcoe, and Gareth Griffith (eds)

God's only daughter: Spenser's Una as the invisible Church Kathryn Walls

William Shakespeare and John Donne: Stages of the soul in early modern English poetry Angelika Zirker

Comic Spenser

Faith, folly, and
The Faerie Queene

VICTORIA COLDHAM-FUSSELL

Manchester University Press

Copyright © Victoria Coldham-Fussell 2020

The right of Victoria Coldham-Fussell to be identified as the author of this work has been asserted by her in accordance with the Copyright, Designs and Patents Act 1988.

Published by Manchester University Press
Oxford Road, Manchester M13 9PL
www.manchesteruniversitypress.co.uk

British Library Cataloguing-in-Publication Data
A catalogue record for this book is available from the British Library

ISBN 978 1 5261 3111 9 hardback
ISBN 978 1 5261 6704 0 paperback

First published 2020
Paperback published 2022

The publisher has no responsibility for the persistence or accuracy of URLs for any external or third-party internet websites referred to in this book, and does not guarantee that any content on such websites is, or will remain, accurate or appropriate.

Typeset by Newgen Publishing UK

For my mother

Contents

Acknowledgements		*page* x
List of abbreviations		xii
	Introduction	1
1	Spenser and the comic Renaissance	31
2	Humour and heroism	80
3	Spenser's bawdy; or, Red Crosse's problem with desire	112
4	Laughing at love: *The Faerie Queene* III–IV	137
5	Parody and panegyric	168
	Epilogue: Humour and allegory	193
	Bibliography	206
	Index	227

Acknowledgements

I sincerely thank the following teachers, colleagues, family members, and friends for their valuable feedback on successive drafts of this book: Helen Cooper, Colin Burrow, Andrew Zurcher, Andrew Hadfield, Gavin Alexander, Kathryn Walls, Julian Lethbridge, Kim Coldham-Fussell, Katie Stallard, Vanessa Manhire, Jean Rumball, Miriam Muth, and Tatjana Schaefer. Two anonymous readers helped me to improve my typescript considerably, and I regret that I cannot name them here. I am also very grateful to my copy-editor, Robert Whitelock, for correcting numerous errors in my typescript, and to Matthew Frost and his colleagues at Manchester University Press for their professionalism and warmth.

In particular, I thank Helen Cooper for her support for this project and for her patience and wisdom, Andrew Zurcher for his infectious enthusiasm for Spenser and for finding *The Faerie Queene* funny, and Kathryn Walls for being the best possible mentor – and for inspiring me to read *The Faerie Queene*. As coeditor of this series, Professor Walls engaged with my work critically and constructively, giving me her time even when it was in shortest supply. My correspondence with The Manchester Spenser began under the editorship of Professor Lethbridge, who could not have been a kinder or more humane critic of my work at a time when I needed just such a reader, and I thank him also.

I am grateful for generous financial support from the Cambridge Commonwealth Trust; from Corpus Christi College, Cambridge; and from Victoria University of Wellington, New Zealand.

Finally, I want to thank my family. I am mindful of the practical, emotional, and material support that I have drawn upon over many years. I dedicate this book to my greatest supporter. I also thank my grandmother Doris Plank, who has in many ways facilitated my work,

Acknowledgements xi

and my sisters, Kim and Constance, for giving me help when I needed it. I am also grateful to my father Andrew Coldham-Fussell, for always being interested. Finally, I want to thank my husband Adrian McNabb and my two sons, Guthrie and Louis, for sticking in there when it seemed that this would never be done, and for allowing me (many) periods of necessary selfishness to prepare this book for publication.

Abbreviations

Transcriptions from early printed books are diplomatic with the exception that contractions are expanded, long-*s* changed to 's', and very long titles truncated. Conventions otherwise correspond to modern editions on an individual basis. Quotations from non-English early works are given in their original language first except where an English translation seems more relevant. More recent critical works and classical prose works are given in English. The Bible consulted is the Geneva (1560). I use the following abbreviations for books and journals:

Acts and Monuments	John Foxe, *The Unabridged Acts and Monuments Online* (Sheffield: Digital Humanities Institute, 2011), 1583 edn
ALC	*Ancient Literary Criticism: The Principal Texts in New Translations*, ed. D. A. Russell and M. Winterbottom (Oxford: Oxford University Press, 1972)
Book of the Courtier	Baldassare Castiglione, *The Book of the Courtier*, trans. Sir Thomas Hoby (London: J. M. Dent, 1974 [1928])
Comedy	*Comedy: A Critical Anthology*, ed. Robert W. Corrigan (Boston, MA: Houghton Mifflin, 1971)
Defence	*Sidney's 'The Defence of Poesy' and Selected Renaissance Literary Criticism*, ed. and intro. Gavin Alexander (London: Penguin, 2004)
Discorsi	Torquato Tasso, *Discorsi del poema eroico*, in *Prose*, ed. Ettore Mazzali (Milan: Riccardo Ricciardi, 1959), pp. 487–729

Abbreviations xiii

DS	Dedicatory Sonnets, in *FQ*, pp. 727–35
ECE	*Elizabethan Critical Essays*, ed. G. Gregory Smith, 2 vols (Oxford: Oxford University Press, 1904)
EETS, o.s.	Early English Text Society, original series
ELH	*Journal of English Literary History*
ELR	*English Literary Renaissance*
Folie	Desiderius Erasmus, *The Praise of Folie*, trans. Sir Thomas Chaloner, ed. Clarence H. Miller, EETS, o.s. 257 (London: Oxford University Press, 1965)
Folly	Desiderius Erasmus, *'Praise of Folly' and Letter to Martin Dorp, 1515*, trans. Betty Radice, intro. and notes A. H. T. Levi (London: Penguin, 1971)
FQ	Edmund Spenser, *The Faerie Qveene*, ed. A. C. Hamilton, Hiroshi Yamashita, and Toshiyuki Suzuki (Harlow: Pearson Education, 2001)
GA	Apuleius, *The Golden Ass*, trans. W. Adlington (1566), rev. and intro. S. Gaselee (London: William Heinemann, 1965 [1915])
JEGP	*Journal of English and Germanic Philology*
Of	Ludovico Ariosto, *Orlando furioso*, ed. Lanfranco Caretti (Milan: Riccardo Ricciardi, 1954)
OF	Ludovico Ariosto, *Orlando Furioso*, trans. Sir John Harington (1591), ed. Robert McNulty (Oxford: Clarendon Press, 1972)
LR	'Letter to Raleigh', in *FQ*, pp. 714–18
Met	Ovid, *Metamorphoses*, trans. A. D. Melville, intro. and notes E. J. Kenney (Oxford: Oxford University Press, 1987)
MLS	*Modern Language Studies*
MP	*Modern Philology*
NQ	*Notes and Queries*
OED	*Oxford English Dictionary*
Oxford Handbook of ES	*The Oxford Handbook of Edmund Spenser*, ed. Richard A. McCabe (Oxford: Oxford University Press, 2010)

xiv *Abbreviations*

Pierce Plowman	William Langland, *The vision of Pierce Plowman, nowe the seconde time imprinted*, ed. Robert Crowley (London: R. Grafton, 1550)
PLL	*Papers on Language and Literature*
PMLA	*Publications of the Modern Language Association*
'Preface to Shakespeare'	Samuel Johnson, 'Preface to Shakespeare' (1765), in *Johnson on Shakespeare*, ed. Arthur Sherbo, Vols VII–VIII of *The Yale Edition of the Works of Samuel Johnson*, 23 vols (New Haven: Yale University Press, 1968), Vol. VII, pp. 59–113
Ren&R	*Renaissance and Reformation*
Rhetorique	Thomas Wilson, *Wilson's 'Arte of Rhetorique'* (1560), ed. G. H. Mair (Oxford: Clarendon Press, 1909)
RQ	*Renaissance Quarterly*
SAC	*Studies in the Age of Chaucer*
SAQ	*South Atlantic Quarterly*
SC	Edmund Spenser, *The Shepheardes Calender*, in *The Yale Edition of the Shorter Poems of Edmund Spenser*, ed. William A. Oram, Einar Bjorvand, Ronald Bond, Thomas H. Cain, Alexander Dunlop, and Richard Schell (New Haven: Yale University Press, 1989), pp. 3–215
SEL	*Studies in English Literature, 1500–1900*
Shorter Poems	Edmund Spenser, *The Yale Edition of the Shorter Poems of Edmund Spenser*, ed. William A. Oram, Einar Bjorvand, Ronald Bond, Thomas H. Cain, Alexander Dunlop, and Richard Schell (New Haven: Yale University Press, 1989)
SLI	*Studies in the Literary Imagination*
SN	*Spenser Newsletter*
SP	*Studies in Philology*
SpE	*The Spenser Encyclopedia*, ed. A. C. Hamilton (Toronto: University of Toronto Press, 1990)
Spectator	*Spectator*, ed. G. Gregory Smith, 8 vols (London: J. M. Dent, 1897)

Abbreviations

SR	*Spenser Review*
SSt	*Spenser Studies*
TLS	*Times Literary Supplement*
Traité	Laurent Joubert, *Traité dv ris, contenant son essance, ses causes, et mervelheus effais, curieusemant recerchés, raisonnés & observés* (Paris, 1579)
Treatise	Laurent Joubert, *Treatise on Laughter*, trans. Gregory David de Rocher (Tuscaloosa, AL: University of Alabama Press, 1980)
Var	Edmund Spenser, *The Works of Edmund Spenser: A Variorum Edition*, ed. Edwin Greenlaw *et al.*, 11 vols (Baltimore: Johns Hopkins University Press, 1932–57)
Works of Gascoigne	George Gascoigne, *The Complete Works of George Gascoigne*, ed. John W. Cunliffe, 2 vols (Cambridge: Cambridge University Press, 1907–10)
Works of Malory	Thomas Malory, *The Works of Sir Thomas Malory*, ed. Eugène Vinaver, 2nd edn, 3 vols (Oxford: Clarendon Press, 1973 [1967])

Introduction

> It would obviously be a paradox to find a humorist in Spenser.
>
> Louis Cazamian, *The Development of English Humor*[1]

Spenser's conspicuous ambition and seriousness of purpose in *The Faerie Queene* inhibited recognition of the poem's comic dimension for centuries – from its first publication in 1590 until at least the 1960s. Milton's famous compliment to the 'sage and serious Poet *Spencer*' captures the powerful equation of morality and sobriety that once dominated the critical landscape.[2] Of today, it may be said that irony has largely displaced sobriety as the hallmark of the moralist. In a poem once associated with Protestant and nationalistic 'single-mindedness', we are increasingly appreciative of Spenser's willingness to leave major moral issues in a state of tension.[3] Humour has, as it were, a critical footing. Yet the old view is still deeply influential, shaping our expectations in ways that are often quite unconscious. Spenser's sense of humour remains underexplored and, at

---

1 Louis Cazamian acknowledges comic elements in the minor poems, but finds in the poet of *The Faerie Queene* 'a fervent votary of single-mindedness'; *The Development of English Humor* (Durham, NC: Duke University Press, 1952), pp. 358–62 (p. 358).

2 Milton speaks of 'our sage and serious Poet *Spencer*, whom I dare be known to think a better teacher then *Scotus* or *Aquinas*'; *Areopagitica*, in John Milton, *Complete Prose Works of John Milton*, ed. Don Marion Wolfe, 8 vols (New Haven: Yale University Press, 1953–82), Vol. II: *1643–1648*, ed. Ernest Sirluck (1959), p. 516. There is evidence that Milton appreciated that seriousness in a Christian context does not prohibit humour (see pp. 98–9 below); nevertheless, the dominant sense of his compliment to Spenser has been influential.

3 In contrast to Cazamian (see n. 1 above), Colin Burrow calls the chief delight of *The Faerie Queene* 'elusiveness'; *Edmund Spenser* (Plymouth: Northcote House, 1996), p. 27 n. 1.

2   *Comic Spenser*

crucial moments, missed altogether. Fundamentally, it is undervalued. This book does more than bring a comic perspective to new areas of the poem; it argues that we cannot talk seriously about Christian morality in *The Faerie Queene* without also appreciating the poem's humour. There are many kinds of humour in the Spenserian corpus: wordplay and puns, caricature and grotesquerie, ascerbic satire, naïve and melodramatic narrators, fabliau and mock-epic. And Spenser was magnetically drawn to Ovid, Chaucer, and Ariosto – poets who are celebrated as well as notorious for their humour. In the first half of the twentieth century, a small number of critics turned their attention to these factors, and to the neglected comedic dimension of *The Faerie Queene* in particular. Often approaching this dimension as 'comic relief' requiring emphasis rather than interpretation as such, the tendency of these critics was to survey humorous lines and passages in the poem as an end in themselves.[4] Written in the light of intervening decades, my own study proceeds on the assumption that, as Lauren Silberman has remarked, it is not enough just to notice Spenserian humour; we must 'act critically' on it.[5]

Critical thinking has, to an extent, evolved in this direction. In the wake of Harry Berger's groundbreaking work on Spenserian artifice, self-reflexiveness, and pastiche, a handful of articles in the 1960s and 1970s focused on the contrivances of Spenser's language and on the systemic ironies of his narrative and allegorical techniques.[6] This trend in the direction of sceptical reassessment is still developing, to

---

4 An early acknowledgement of Spenser's use of burlesque and situational comedy may be found in R. W. Church, *Spenser*, 2nd edn (London: Macmillan, 1888), pp. 165, 177, 183–8. Two notes by Charles B. Burke followed five decades later: 'Humour in Spenser', *NQ*, 166 (1934), 113–15; and 'The "Sage and Serious" Spenser', *NQ*, 175 (1938), 457–8. Allan H. Gilbert, Burke's colleague, took up the theme in 'Spenserian Comedy', *Tennessee Studies in Literature*, 2 (1957), 95–104. In an appendix entitled 'Spenser's High Comedy', W. B. C. Watkins argues that Spenser's humour competes with that of the best Elizabethan dramatists: *Shakespeare and Spenser* (Princeton: Princeton University Press, 1950), pp. 293–304. Robert O. Evans, 'Spenserian Humor: *Faerie Queene* III and IV', *Neuphilologische Mitteilungen*, 60 (1959), 288–99 may also be considered as part of this first wave of humour criticism. Evans finds humour in the central books but takes it for granted that the theological and ethical concerns of Books I and II prohibit comic treatment.

5 Lauren Silberman, 'Spenser and Ariosto: Funny Peril and Comic Chaos', *Comparative Literature Studies*, 25 (1988), 23–34 (p. 24).

6 See Martha Craig, 'The Secret Wit of Spenser's Language', in *Elizabethan Poetry: Modern Essays in Criticism*, ed. Paul J. Alpers (New York: Oxford University Press, 1967), pp. 447–72; Judith Petterson Clark, 'His Earnest unto Game: Spenser's Humor in *The Faerie Queene*', *Emporia State Research Studies*, 15 (1967), 13–24, 26–7; J. Dennis Huston, 'The Function of the Mock Hero in Spenser's "Faerie Queene"', *MP*, 66 (1969), 212–17; Lewis

Introduction

the point that irony and humour have been implicated in some of the most fundamental and productive questions in Spenser criticism. How trustworthy are Spenser's narrators, and how postured are his paratexts? Is chivalric romance idealising or provocatively low-brow? When is imitation parodic? What is Spenser's attitude toward sexuality and the body? How sincere is his homage to Elizabeth and her court? These questions have been at the root of a number of ironic interpretations of *The Faerie Queene* in the past two decades. Indicative of this critical trend at its most overt is the volley of articles that appeared between 2002 and 2005 on the subject of Spenserian parody, sparked by Donald Cheney's brief but provocative article on the subject, and continuing most recently in Judith H. Anderson's *Spenser's Narrative Figuration of Women in 'The Faerie Queene'*.[7]

And yet, for all the advances in recent decades, Silberman's gauntlet has not yet been seized as such. Existing work on Spenserian humour is scattered across a broad territory, and is usually ancillary to a distinct

---

H. Miller, Jr, 'The Ironic Mode in Books 1 and 2 of *The Faerie Queene*', *PLL*, 7 (1971), 133–49; Linwood E. Orange, '"All Bent to Mirth": Spenser's Humorous Wordplay', *SAQ*, 71 (1972), 539–47; and William Nelson, *Fact or Fiction: The Dilemma of the Renaissance Storyteller* (Cambridge, MA: Harvard University Press, 1973), Chapter 4. For Berger, see Harry Berger, Jr, *Revisionary Play: Studies in the Spenserian Dynamics* (Berkeley: University of California Press, 1988).

7 Reassessing Spenser's relation to Ariosto, Cheney coins the phrase 'sympathetic parody' to describe Spenser's nuanced imitation of his Italian forebear, and to challenge the assumption that his appropriations of *Orlando furioso* always take the moral high ground; Donald Cheney, 'Spenser's Parody', *Connotations*, 12 (2002), 1–13. In reply, Anthony M. Esolen, 'Highways and Byways: A Response to Donald Cheney', *Connotations*, 13 (2003), 1–4, relates Spenser's playfulness, capacity for chivalric pastiche, and habit of echoing and revising himself to the poet's Christian faith. Richard McCabe's longer essay, 'Parody, Sympathy and Self: A Response to Donald Cheney', *Connotations*, 13 (2003), 5–22, one of the fullest contributions to the subject of Spenser and humour to date, offers a systematic analysis of the proximity of epic and mock-epic, and the many forms of parody (and, more generally, irony) operating in *The Faerie Queene*. In a brief final instalment to the exchange, Lawrence Rhu (who has historically emphasised Spenser's earnest reformation of Ariosto) acknowledges the value of Cheney's amused scepticism, especially as it applies to Arthur's 'altruistic' pursuit of the distressed Florimell; 'On Cheney on Spenser's Ariosto', *Connotations*, 15 (2005), 91–6. Judith H. Anderson's monograph offers a far more in-depth treatment of Spenserian parody, both intertextual and self-reflexive. Having benefited from Anderson's career-long interest in Spenser's playful and parodic side, I regret that my discovery of her study came too late for its findings fully to be taken account of in the present work. Notwithstanding our divergent approaches, Anderson's exploration of Spenser's playful strategies of self-revision and echo, and her general appreciation of the humanising impulse of his sense of humour, at several points speak directly to the findings of this study; Judith H. Anderson, *Spenser's Narrative Figuration of Women in 'The Faerie Queene'* (Kalamazoo: Medieval Institute Publications, 2017).

4 *Comic Spenser*

critical focus, or limited to articles. Moreover, Milton's famous 'sage and serious' remark may be invoked with detachment, but for many it still resonates. Indeed, it is arguably Milton's intended compliment, not the description itself, that has lost most currency. In 2008, Andrew Hadfield was able to declare that *The Faerie Queene* is generally reputed 'worthy and humorless, esoteric and at odds with enjoyment'.[8] While few if any Spenserians would positively lay claim to the latter view, most would acknowledge that the notion of a humourless Spenser is familiar. This study contends that we need to be aware of the insidious effects of this familiarity, and of the extent to which our apprehension of a serious and ambitiously conceived moral vision in *The Faerie Queene* conjures expectations of humourlessness.

The assumption that seriousness and an absence of humour go hand-in-hand is, of course, understandable. Profitability, gravity, and formality are closely entwined concepts in early modern discourse, literary and religious.[9] But the same assumption thrives in our own era. So often we automatically privilege non-comic perspectives as more innately truthful, meaningful, and worthy than comic ones.[10] I shall argue, however, that Spenser's sense of humour is absolutely consistent with his moral and doctrinal preoccupations, and that its operations in *The Faerie Queene* are both central and profound.[11]

As the title of this book indicates, my subject is *The Faerie Queene*. A number of Spenser's shorter poems are notable, and have been noted, for their humour: the shepherds of *The Shepheardes Calender* are engagingly naïve (in comic contrast to the learned pedantry of E. K.'s commentary); *Virgils Gnat* and *Muiopotmos* testify to Spenser's career-long interest in mock-epic; *Mother Hubberds Tale* is a caustic and irreverent satire; and the *Amoretti*, at times bordering on Petrarchan pastiche, provide amusing insights into the lover's psyche. However, while I reinforce these observations in forthcoming chapters, the primary focus of this study is

---

8 Andrew Hadfield, 'Spenser and Jokes', *SSt*, 25 (2010), 1–19 (p. 2).
9 See further Chapter 1.
10 Idiomatic speech is telling in this regard. If something is of great consequence and demands our deepest attention, it is 'no laughing matter'. This phrase dates to the mid-sixteenth century; see *OED*, s.v. 'laughing', *n.*, C2. See further pp. 8–9 and n. 24 below.
11 Few critics have suggested a link between Spenser's humour and his Christian faith. Those who have include C. S. Lewis, *The Allegory of Love* (Oxford: Oxford University Press, 1979 [1936]), p. 356; Esolen, 'Highways and Byways'; Louise Gilbert Freeman, 'Vision, Metamorphosis, and the Poetics of Allegory in the *Mutabilitie Cantos*', *SEL*, 45 (2005), 65–93; and William A. Oram, 'Human Limitation and Spenserian Laughter', *SSt*, 30 (2015), 35–56.

Introduction 5

the role of humour in a poem that proclaims its canonical aspirations. Humour in such a context works 'against the grain' to an intensified degree, and, as the history of Spenser criticism attests, is more likely to be missed, sidelined, or met with puzzlement.

Definitions

Henri Bergson (1859–1941) described the task of theorising laughter as 'a pert challenge flung at philosophic speculation'.[12] If finding something funny feels intuitive, analysing that response can be a tortuous business. Theories of the comic (which for the most part incorporate laughter but also speak to humour more broadly) have roots in discussions of jokes by classical rhetoricians, and, since the early modern period, have evolved within a range of contexts – moral, medical, philosophical, and psychological. Such diversely motivated attempts to encapsulate the essence of humour have been synthesised, by modern historians of comic theory, into three competing schools of thought, commonly referred to as 'superiority theory', 'incongruity theory', and 'relief theory'.[13] Each of these theories is associated with (though not exclusively attributable to) a major figure and intellectual epoch: 'superiority' with Hobbes, 'incongruity' with Kant and Schopenhauer, and 'relief' with Freud. However, although I draw explicitly on these and other theories below, for the purposes of my own analysis a modification of these traditional conceptual divisions has been useful. This is because my task here is not to historicise comic theory or its academic reception, but rather to identify some fundamental principles that have been associated with comic recognition since classical times – in other words, principles that serve to link rather than differentiate the three relatively modern 'schools' of thought. These I summarise as: 'reduction', 'ambiguity', and 'play'.[14]

---

12 Henri Bergson, 'Laughter' ('Le rire' (1900)), trans. Fred Rothwell, in *Comedy: A Critical Anthology*, ed. Robert W. Corrigan (Boston, MA: Houghton Mifflin, 1971), pp. 745–50 (p. 745); henceforth *Comedy*.

13 While superiority theory and relief theory are historically significant, incongruity is now the dominant theoretical model; see John Morreall, 'Philosophy of Humor', in *The Stanford Encyclopedia of Philosophy Archive* (Winter 2016 edn), ed. Edward N. Zalta, https://plato.stanford.edu/archives/win2016/entries/humor/ (accessed May 2019).

14 'Reduction' is more capacious than 'superiority' because, although still reflective of the power of normative social hierarchies to generate humour, it incorporates all bathetic and downward-tending comic gestures without presupposing a particular response (as such 'reduction' may also be integral to both incongruity and relief). 'Ambiguity' captures verbal and visual tensions traditionally encompassed by 'incongruity' while

6 *Comic Spenser*

At a glance, each of these principles is also a comic technique. 'Reduction', that is, may be exemplified by bathos, error, rudeness, and social inferiority. For the most part, these are *things observed* – in contrast to two of the traditional theoretical schools, 'superiority' and 'relief', which are *things experienced*. Fascinatingly, however, it can be a challenge for the comic theorist to maintain a clear distinction between technique (that which elicits comic recognition) and response (the experience of recognising something as comic).[15] My two other conceptual categories, 'ambiguity' and 'play', bring this point into clearer focus. That is, the quality of ambiguity characterises various comic techniques (double meaning, incongruity, tonal inconsistency, for example) but it also characterises our responses to those techniques (confusion, ambivalence, tension). These things are distinct enough in theory, but in practice it is difficult to prise them apart, because a technique is comic only when it is perceived as such. Furthermore, in a literary context 'comic perception' can have multiple points of reference. For example, when a spectator or reader finds something comically ambiguous, their response may reflect their own ambivalence, or, conversely, their perception of ambivalence in the author or narrator or character (or an overlap of these things). In other words, comic recognition can depend upon, and effectively foreground, a dynamic relationship among the spectator or reader, the comic subject, the narrator, and the imagined author. Finally, 'play' broadly alludes to the recreative and pleasure-giving properties of humour and is also classifiable both in terms of technique (fictionality, artifice, nonsense, exaggeration) and response (relief, affirmation, consolation, validation). Again, there is an overlap, and a degree of mutual dependence, between 'play' as the perceived activity of the author, character, or performer on the one hand, and as the province of the reader or spectator on the other.

If the distinction between technique and response is at times difficult to maintain, so too is the distinction between the principles themselves: experientially speaking, 'reduction', 'ambiguity', and 'play' are

---

also, by virtue of pertaining to both objective and subjective states of tension, accessing ambivalence as a response (see further my discussion of comic techniques versus comic responses below). 'Play', as I explain, is a more recent theoretical model canvassing the social functions of the comic, and I draw upon it to foreground the affirmative and pleasurable aspects of humour that are implied, to varying degrees, by all three established theories (i.e. superiority, incongruity, and relief). The element of surprise, also emphasised by theorists of humour, is a potential concomitant of each of the principles I discuss, and is not treated separately.

15 Reflecting this challenge, the three traditional theoretical schools are divided unevenly between technique and response.

Introduction 7

largely interdependent. To give one of thousands of possible examples, the ironic activist battle cry 'the truth will set you free, but first it will piss you off' exemplifies reduction (via linguistic bathos and parodic biblical quotation), out of which arises an ambivalent combination of optimism and cynicism. The intentional starkness of this opposition, achieved through exaggeration and surprise, is essentially playful (which does not mean unserious).[16] For convenience, then, I will elaborate on each principle in turn, treating it like a separate ingredient, before moving, in the second part of this introduction, to the characteristic synthesis of all three principles in the humour of *The Faerie Queene*.

Reduction

Deflation, undercutting, lowering: these are fundamental, powerful generators of humour. The physical body is one of the most universal and timeless of comic themes, especially when its needs and vulnerabilities take precedence over the 'higher' faculties of mind and spirit. Bergson went so far as to say that 'any incident is comic that calls our attention to the physical in a person'.[17] While the lowness of the body is chiefly metaphorical, it is the literally lower regions of the body that dominate in comic situations, especially farcical ones. In such contexts, we also expect to see bodies brought low – for example, tumbling to the ground. Slipping on a banana peel is a twentieth-century cliché that epitomises the comedy of physical vulnerability and of humour's 'downward trajectory'.

The figurative equivalent of slipping on a banana peel is a descent from any perceived height. This may, for example, be linguistic (as in 'the truth will set you free, but first it will piss you off') or social. The cutting down to size of authorities, grandees, and high-mindedness is a prominent function of humour.[18] So too is the foregrounding of low or devalued cultural categories: bodily appetites and various kinds of unattractiveness, error, and disgrace, for example. In the *Poetics*, Aristotle identifies such things as the province of comic drama, so long as their negative consequences are limited. Aristotle takes it for granted that laughter on the stage will always be directed at the preoccupations and

16 Cf. John 8:32: 'the truth shall make you free'.
17 Bergson, 'Laughter', in *Comedy*, p. 748.
18 Freud is unusual in attributing grandeur and elevation to humour, but this is because of what he understands to be its ability to *cut down or reduce* oppressive realities and to assert the 'invulnerability of the ego'; Sigmund Freud, *Art and Literature*, Penguin Freud Library, 14 (London: Penguin, 1990), pp. 428–9 (my italics).

8 *Comic Spenser*

intrigues of low-class people (a rule that the drawing-room comedies of Oscar Wilde happily reversed).[19] Renaissance literary critics often echoed this rule of thumb regarding social class and humour, together with the connection between laughter and ugliness also forged by Aristotle (and Cicero and Quintilian after him).[20] However, comic practice could be far more democratic and wide-ranging than comic theory, as we shall see in Chapter 1.

Comic reduction is at the heart of the aforementioned 'superiority' theory of laughter, associated most notably with Hobbes but also integral to early modern justifications for humour. The essential idea is that when we laugh at others we recognise their limitations and raise ourselves above them.[21] Nevertheless, the lowness of comedy has historically rubbed off on its authors and consumers. Evident in both the *Poetics* and in early modern literary criticism is a further correlation between the ostensibly trivial themes of comedy and the subordinate cultural value of the genre itself. According to Aristotle, 'more dignified [authors] represented noble actions ... of noble men, the less serious those of low-class people'. Elsewhere in the *Poetics*, Aristotle voices the common understanding that 'less vulgar art is superior, and in all cases what is addressed to a superior audience is less vulgar'.[22] Puttenham, too, associated the socially lower subject matter of comic drama ('vnthrifty youthes, yong damsels, old nurses, bawds, brokers, ruffians and parasites') with an audience composed of 'common people'.[23] Today we carefully avoid pejorative conflations of subject matter, audience, and artistic worth (if one of these

---

19 Aristotle, *Poetics*, trans. M. E. Hubbard, in *Ancient Literary Criticism: The Principal Texts in New Translations*, ed. D. A. Russell and M. Winterbottom (Oxford: Oxford University Press, 1972), pp. 85–132 (pp. 94–6); henceforth *ALC*.

20 For Aristotle, ugliness includes ridiculousness. He observes that comedy exaggerates, showing us 'people worse than are found in the world' while limiting negative consequences; see *ibid.*, p. 96. On the influence of Aristotle, Cicero, and Quintilian in establishing ugliness as the object of laughter see Marvin T. Herrick, *Comic Theory in the Sixteenth Century* (Urbana: University of Illinois Press, 1964 [1950]), pp. 37–46 (esp. pp. 37–8) and, for primary sources, p. 35 n. 13 below. Cf. Sidney's remarks on laughter as an expression of scorn in Sir Philip Sidney, *Sidney's 'The Defence of Poesy' and Selected Renaissance Literary Criticism*, ed. and intro. Gavin Alexander (London: Penguin, 2004), pp. 47–8; henceforth *Defence*.

21 For Hobbes's theory of laughter as 'sudden glory' over others see Thomas Hobbes, *The English Works of Thomas Hobbes*, ed. Sir William Molesworth, Bart, 11 vols (London: John Bohn, 1966), Vols III, p. 46; IV, p. 46. On early modern attitudes to humour see Chapter 1.

22 Aristotle, *Poetics*, pp. 94, 131.

23 George Puttenham, *The Arte of English Poesie*, in *Elizabethan Critical Essays*, ed. G. Gregory Smith, 2 vols (Oxford: Oxford University Press, 1904), Vol. II, pp. 1–193 (p. 33); henceforth *ECE*.

Introduction   9

factors is accounted 'low' in some way, it is not assumed that the others must follow suit). Nevertheless, as I noted above, the root assumption that 'that which is important and essential cannot be comical' persists as a tenet of modern culture.[24] It is commonly assumed that a comic perspective is less representative and more radically selective than a non-comic one, and that the truths it reveals are unimportant – indeed, funny *because* unimportant.[25]

The idea that comic works are necessarily lighter in substance or shorter in philosophical reach is, of course, a fallacy. The often involuntary nature of amusement (especially when expressed in laughter) can suggest that the causes and effects of comic material are somewhat self-evident, or, conversely, resistant to analysis. But the psychology of amusement is as complex and profound as is the psychology of suffering: both tap deeply into 'the way the world is' in ways that are revealing and elusive by turns. In the theatre, comedy and tragedy have separate (and, for Aristotle, hierarchical) spheres of jurisdiction – they treat different subjects. But as modes of perception, the comic and the tragic offer alternative perspectives on the same conditions of existence, as the traditional depiction of the laughing philosopher Democritus alongside the weeping philosopher Heraclitus is intended to illustrate. In the words of Mikhail Bakhtin, laughter 'is

---

24 It is a measure of the power of this conviction that it can coexist with esteem for comic art forms and perspectives. Even Bergson, whose essay on laughter seeks to treat his subject with 'the respect due to life', felt compelled to add 'however trivial it may be'; Bergson, 'Laughter', in *Comedy*, p. 745. Mikhail Bakhtin famously (if controversially) dates the onset of this bias to the seventeenth century; *Rabelais and His World*, trans. Hélène Iswolsky (Bloomington: Indiana University Press, 1984), pp. 66–7; cf. p. 78 below. More recently, Derek Brewer has asserted: 'the exaltation of tragedy as a solitary extreme which is alone truly expressive of the human condition is a characteristic of twentieth-century literary theory'; Derek Brewer, ed., *Medieval Comic Tales*, 2nd edn (Cambridge: D. S. Brewer, 1996), p. xvi.

25 The connections among humour, enjoyment, and notional triviality are difficult to tease apart. Dalbir Sehmby proposes that 'the lesser status of all things comical' reflects both the assumption that humour is 'more easily knowable than other, more serious forms of art' and, paradoxically, its unsettling effects; Dalbir Sehmby, 'Comic Nescience: An Experimental View of Humour and a Case for the Cultural Negotiation Function of Humour', in *Developments in Linguistic Humour Theory*, ed. Marta Dynel (Amsterdam: John Benjamins, 2013), pp. 75–102 (pp. 80–1) (see further pp. 11–12 below). Human survival's dependence on toil and the related 'ethical notion that everything man does naturally and without effort is a falsification of true morality' may also cast some light on the cultural devaluation of the comic; see Josef Pieper, *Leisure: The Basis of Culture*, trans. Alexander Dru (London: Faber and Faber, 1952), pp. 37–8. On the Aristotelian tenet that successful comedy depends upon the limitation of negative consequences, see pp. 12, 14–15 below.

10   *Comic Spenser*

one of the essential forms of the truth concerning the world as a whole, concerning history and man'.[26] And, as we shall see in the chapters to come, humour's downward trajectory and fixation upon low cultural categories has significant leverage. Comic reduction can conservatively affirm normative hierarchies – pushing the low lower and the high higher – but it also has an unparalleled power to challenge, if not dismantle, the assumptions that shore up those hierarchies.

Ambiguity

Defined as the 'capability of being understood in two or more ways' (*OED*, 3(a)), ambiguity is a common denominator of a very wide range of comic scenarios, portrayals, and statements. As noted already, the 'capability of being understood in two or more ways' implies something divided in both the comic object and one's response to it. Laurent Joubert, the French physician and prominent Renaissance theorist of laughter, recognised the prevalence of ambivalence as a comic response. His *Traité dv ris* (1579) asserts that conflicted feelings – repulsion and attraction, joy and sadness, for example – are released when we laugh.[27] Such a theory is hardly arcane; most of us will recognise that when we laugh a sense of distance or superiority can be complicated by feelings of identification or empathy, for example. Conflicted responses may also be more cognitive than emotional: for example, we find caricatures funny because they are both close to the truth and patently exaggerated – arguably it is the tension between these simultaneous apprehensions that is comically productive.

Beyond localised examples of emotional or cognitive irresolution, comic ambiguity can have far-reaching, philosophical implications. A refusal to see the world from multiple angles is, essentially, a humourless position. Just so, a willingness to recognise ambiguity and admit confusion is conducive to comic recognition. So often and in so many contexts, laughter registers a fundamental tension between the human drive to make sense of the world (and our countless associated

---

26 Bakhtin, *Rabelais and His World*, p. 66.

27 See Laurent Joubert, *Traité dv ris, contenant son essance, ses causes, et mervelheus effais, curieusemant recerchés, raisonnés & observés* (Paris, 1579), Book I, Chapters 10–14 (pp. 71–90); henceforth *Traité*. For an English translation see Laurent Joubert, *Treatise on Laughter*, trans. Gregory David de Rocher (Tuscaloosa, AL: University of Alabama Press, 1980), pp. 38–45; henceforth *Treatise*. On the classical roots of Joubert's theory, see Erica Fudge, 'Learning to Laugh: Children and Being Human in Early Modern Thought', *Textual Practice*, 17 (2003), 277–94 (pp. 288–93).

Introduction 11

expectations of 'how things should be') and the apparent reluctance of the universe to be known, manipulated, and physically negotiated. This is why dogmatic, fixed, and otherwise inflexible positions regarding 'how things are/must be done' are a prime subject of satire; laughter intuitively acknowledges the other side of the coin.[28]

Some experiences of comic recognition are more ambivalent than others. In his rich theoretical essay on irony and satire, Northrop Frye distinguishes between, on the one hand, 'low-norm satire', which he defines as 'conventional satire on the unconventional', pitched to reinforce shared values, and, on the other hand, a ludic perspective on human affairs that he calls 'quixotic satire', whereby 'the sources and values of the conventions themselves are objects of ridicule'. The latter is fundamentally more sceptical and disorientating than the former. Where the low-norm satirist laughs at socially deviant behaviour and implicitly endorses one or another standard of judgement, the quixotic satirist acknowledges a 'collision between a selection of standards from experience and the feeling that experience is bigger than any set of beliefs about it'.[29] To adapt Frye's formula to my own slight example, one may say that in laughing at the proverbial bad taste of the 1980s, the low-norm satirist passes judgement on the serious-looking people with teased hair, while the quixotic satirist acknowledges the absurd imperatives of fashion itself. Intuition of the limited standards by which we, as human beings, judge the world around us, even in the very moment that we judge, may be described as the linchpin of comic ambivalence at its most profound.

Observing humour's tendency to thrive upon and foster disorientation and interpretative uncertainty in a world that prioritises comprehension, Dalbir Sehmby proposes that this helps to explain the suspicion evoked by humour and 'the lesser status of all things comical'. Both Sehmby and Frye seem to agree that the production of uncertainty (and concomitant rejection or frustration of systematic approaches to knowledge and experience) is both the central 'problem' of humour – the thing that troubles theorists and moralists – and also its most valuable cultural

---

28 A central thesis of Bergson's classic essay on laughter is that 'rigidity is … comic, and laughter is its corrective' (Bergson, 'Laughter,' in *Comedy*, p. 74). See also Schopenhauer on the pleasures of incongruity, pp. 13–14 below.

29 Northrop Frye, *Anatomy of Criticism: Four Essays* (Princeton: Princeton University Press, 1957), pp. 228–9. George Meredith, in his 'An Essay on Comedy' (1877), approaches Frye's concept of the quixotic when he asserts that 'contempt is a sentiment that cannot be entertained by comic intelligence' because part of us always identifies with, and in some sense accepts, the follies we laugh at; *Comedy*, p. 743.

12 *Comic Spenser*

function.[30] Specifically, the value of uncertainty resides in its implicit challenge to dogmatism, reductiveness, and oppression on the one hand, and its fostering of humility, pragmatism, and open-mindedness on the other. Humour's potential seriousness in this respect, its preoccupation with human limitation, casts light on the sometimes surprising proximity of comedy and tragedy. Deep comic ambivalence admits this proximity, introducing elements of pleasure, consolation, and play into the darkest corners of human experience. Although Aristotle dictated that the negative consequences of human limitation must be kept firmly within trivial bounds for comic drama to succeed, in less pliant contexts (such as Shakespearean drama, or indeed real life) the comic may jostle alongside, and comment upon, even the most unflinching acknowledgements of human limitation or failure.[31] As this study will demonstrate, such 'light/ dark' ambivalence toward human agency and the profound humour that is peculiar to it is deeply Spenserian.

Play

Reduction and ambiguity are key comic traits, but only when they are apprehended in a spirit of play. Whole books have been written on the conditions and functions of play, but for our purposes here, its defining characteristic is pleasure. This term may be paraphrased, according to context, as 'fun' or 'affirmation' or 'relief', but I would contend that without a kernel of pleasure, play is not play and humour is not humour. Theorists tend to unite on this point. 'Comedy', wrote Christopher Fry, 'is an escape, not from truth but from despair: a narrow escape into faith. It believes in a universal cause for delight.'[32] For Freud, humour offers an antidote to oppressive realities, and signifies 'not only the triumph of the ego but also [the triumph] of the pleasure principle'. Frye observes that 'in laughter itself some kind of deliverance from the unpleasant, even

30 Sehmby, 'Comic Nescience', pp. 80–1. Cf. Frye, *Anatomy of Criticism*, pp. 229–32. Of relevance here is Bakhtin's theory of carnival, according to which the sphere of popular festivity supplants seriousness and order with humour and chaos, suspending or inverting normative hierarchies (Bakhtin, *Rabelais and His World*, pp. 1–58), and J. Huizinga's *Homo ludens: A Study of the Play-Element in Culture* (London: Routledge & Kegan Paul, 1980 [1949]), according to which play's creativity defies determinism and logic (pp. 3–4, and see further n. 38 below).

31 Aristotle, *Poetics*, p. 96.

32 Christopher Fry, 'Comedy', *Vogue* (January 1951), reprinted in *Comedy*, pp. 754–6 (p. 755).

Introduction   13

the horrible, seems to be very important.[33] The alteration in our brain chemicals when we smile and laugh is now a familiar subject of scientific papers and magazine articles. But reflections on the affirmative aspects of laughter, and, more generally, of amusement, have been a staple of comic and literary theory for centuries. Thomas Deloney, Spenser's contemporary and author of a collection of comic tales (*The Mirrour of Mirth*, 1583), claimed that 'mirth and melody cutteth off care, unburdeneth the mind of sorrow, healeth the grieved heart, and filleth both soul and body with inestimable comfort'. Early modern and medieval examples of this claim could be multiplied here.[34]

Comic theories differ in the degree to which they emphasise the pleasurable aspect of humour and in how they account for it, though a common theme is the sense of validation that attends comic recognition. According to the Hobbesian superiority theory, for example, laughter arises out of feelings of self-worth evoked by the shortcomings of others. Complicating this valid but now marginal theory, modern theorists recognise that the shortcomings of others, where these are comically exaggerated, also allow us in some sense to participate in a refusal to take the self seriously.[35] In other words, comic recognition may 'validate' in opposing ways: by boosting the ego or by suppressing it, by reaffirming social mores and expectations or by momentarily escaping them.

As noted earlier, other major schools of thought are the 'relief theory' associated with Freud and the 'incongruity theory' associated with Kant and Schopenhauer. These theories, which I treat only briefly here, take a different approach to the correlation of humour and pleasure, though validation still plays a role. Relief theory postulates that laughter releases energy that would otherwise be used in tasks of comprehension or, as Freud also argued, repression. Incongruity theory overlaps to some extent with relief theory in that it links the perception of visual, verbal,

---

33 Freud, *Art and Literature*, p. 429; Frye, *Anatomy of Criticism*, p. 46.

34 For *The Mirrour of Mirth* (and Deloney's preface) see P. M. Zall, ed., '*A Hundred Merry Tales' and Other English Jestbooks of the Fifteenth and Sixteenth Centuries* (Lincoln: University of Nebraska Press, 1963), pp. 349–90 (pp. 353–4). For further observations in this vein see V. A. Kolve, *The Play Called Corpus Christi* (London: Edward Arnold, 1966), pp. 124–44; Aron Gurevich, *Medieval Popular Culture: Problems of Belief and Perception*, trans. János M. Bak and Paul A. Hollingsworth (Cambridge: Cambridge University Press, 1988), p. 182; and Bakhtin, *Rabelais and His World*, p. 91.

35 On 'inferiority theory' see Aaron Smuts, 'Humor', in *Internet Encyclopedia of Philosophy*, https://iep.utm.edu/humor/#SH2a (accessed May 2019), section 2(a); and, as cited by Smuts, Robert Solomon, 'Are the Three Stooges Funny? Soitanly!', in *Ethics and Values in the Information Age*, ed. Joel Rudinow and Anthony Graybosch (Belmont, CA: Wadsworth, 2002), pp. 604–10.

14 *Comic Spenser*

or experiential incoherence to pleasure. Exactly where that pleasure originates is a matter of debate. Anticipating Freud, Schopenhauer argued that we enjoy having the facts of sense perception thwart our expectations because the rational mind is a 'troublesome governness', perpetually reminding us of consequences, dangers, and regrets.[36] By contrast, contemporary theorists argue that incongruity affirms, more than it negates, logic: the pleasure of seeing 'why something is wrong' is akin to the intellectual pleasure of puzzle solving.[37] These are opposing ideas but it is possible to imagine a scenario in which both are applicable – a nonsensical children's book, for example, might well provoke pleasure both because 'it breaks the rules' and because 'we know the rules'.

A further theory of humour, one that does not contradict the other theories so much as contexualise them within a social and evolutionary frame, is 'play theory'. Max Eastman observes (with Aristotle) that humour, as a form of play, depends upon the limitation of negative consequences, emotional or otherwise. More specifically, Eastman argues that such safe bounds permit a detached, playful approach to the disappointing or disagreeable – let-downs, unpleasant surprises, apparent aggression, and so forth. In other words, things that might otherwise be perceived as serious or incommodious become sources of pleasure.[38] But it is not simply the case that the limitation of negative consequences permits humour. Equally, humour can impose a limitation on negative consequences, at least as these are perceived, by asserting the admissibility of play in a world of struggles and disappointments. Above I cited the example of Shakespeare, whose tragedies always include humour. In a non-literary illustration of the same principle, Thomas More reportedly shared a joke with the Constable of the Tower as he

---

36 Kant argued that incongruity is displeasing, and that the physical stimulation of laughter reflexively counteracts this displeasure. On the pleasurability of relief and of incongruity, see further Morreall, 'Philosophy of Humor', Sections 3 and 4; and Smuts, 'Humor', 2(b) and (c), both of which resources I am indebted to here.
37 See Morreall, 'Philosophy of Humor', Section 4.
38 Max Eastman, *Enjoyment of Laughter* (London: Hamish Hamilton, 1937), pp. 19, 24–6, 31–2, 43–4. On play theory (which includes ethological approaches) see further Morreall, 'Philosophy of Humor', Section 5; and Smuts, 'Humor', Section 2(d). Another significant contribution to the study of play as a cultural phenomenon is Huizinga's *Homo ludens* (see n. 30 above). Huizinga characterises play as pleasurable and free from constraint ('fun'), and recognises humour as a form of play, although this overlap remains peripheral to his thesis that all human activity, and culture itself, is grounded in play (see pp. 1–27, esp. pp. 3, 5–6).

Introduction 15

mounted the scaffold: 'See me safe up: for my coming down, I can shift for myself.'[39]

The playfulness of humour and its detachment from 'the real world' is inextricable from its low cultural status, but it also has profound ethical value. Previously, I approached the connection between humour and tolerance through the lens of ambivalence. I observed that comic scenarios often tap into, or depend upon, our capacity to hold two ideas in a state of tension, which can in turn be conducive to scepticism and open-mindedness. But pleasure is also conducive to tolerance, and vice versa. Partly, this is intuitive wisdom: I opened this section with a series of impressionistic remarks from comic theorists grappling with the fundamentally affirmative quality of humour: its capacity to convey, through a mood of play, a sense of 'everything is ok', and the way that this counteracts contempt and despair. We know from experience that being made to laugh when we are angry can diffuse our fixation, and that, in turn, being more tolerant increases our aptitude to make or take a joke.

There is a further, chiefly literary, connection between comic pleasure and tolerance. Pleasure is a concern of the humorist in two distinct yet related senses: (1) the pursuit of pleasure is an enduring comic subject; (2) comedy is intended to give pleasure. As an illustration of the first point, it may be said that the only character type more susceptible to satire than the one who seeks gratification in the face of all obstacles is the one who doggedly condemns pleasure (Ben Jonson's comic creation, the hypocritical Puritan Zeal-of-the-Land Busy, brilliantly harnesses the comic potential of both types). There is a connection between (1) and (2), not only because we find pleasure in laughing at the foibles of others, but also because the humorist who satirises unbalanced attitudes to pleasure is also an apologist for pleasure, by virtue of writing comic fiction.[40] Subtly qualifying any satirical denunciation of pleasure as frivolous or immoral are the pleasure-giving properties of the comic text itself. In the early modern period, this sense of audience complicity was grist to the moralist's mill, but it could also be an enriching irony. In *Bartholomew*

---

39 James A. Froude, *History of England*, 10 vols (London: Parker, Son, and Bourn, 1862–6), Vol. II, retrieved from https://babel.hathitrust.org/cgi/pt?id=hvd.hw20o3;view=1up;seq=6 (accessed May 2019), p. 403.

40 Comic or not, fiction is itself an invitation to take pleasure, as R. Rawdon Wilson points out: 'all literature, simply in being literature, must manifest some of the modes of play and game'; 'game', in *The Spenser Encyclopedia*, ed. A. C. Hamilton (Toronto: University of Toronto Press, 1990), pp. 321–3 (p. 321); henceforth *SpE*. Cf. Huizinga, *Homo ludens*, pp. 119–35.

16   *Comic Spenser*

Fair, for example, Jonson develops an analogy between the world of the fair and that of the theatre, both of which hawk their 'ware' to punters. As consumers – humans watching a play for fun – we are reminded to identify with the fairgoers even as we laugh at them.[41] Such tolerant, self-inclusive satire, inclined to rehabilitate pleasure more than to condemn it, is typically Spenserian, as I shall now argue.

Spenserian humour

The Faerie Queene is a bathetic, ambivalent, and playful poem. Approaching the latter two characteristics through the first, this study as a whole may be described as an anatomy of Spenser's pervasive and idiosyncratic art of reduction – the principle of undercutting, contradicting, and parodying that, as Richard McCabe has observed, pervades the poem on 'almost every level'.[42] Key here, I shall argue, is Spenser's double vision of human nature: his Christian, Protestant perception of our potential for good as bestowed by grace on the one hand, and of our innate fallibility, limitation, and vulnerability on the other. The vehicle of Spenser's meditation on human nature, allegorical epic, is uniquely placed to accommodate this ambivalence. First, epic is a self-consciously elevated genre: its classical subject is heroism, or extraordinary valour and virtue. Opportunities for bathos are, by the same token, abundant.[43] Second, allegory is an inherently ambiguous mode; it is conducive to irony and to contradictory interpretation. Its indirection as a mode of representation, moreover, means that it can be visionary – pointing beyond itself – as well as deliberately naïve – a metaphor for the limitations of human sight. These traits are not synonymous with humour, but they certainly create favourable conditions for it.

A conventional argument in favour of allegory (voiced by Spenser's authorial persona in the 'Letter to Raleigh' (LR)) is its didactic usefulness: telling stories is the best way of engaging readers with moral lessons that they might otherwise be bored by (LR, lines 8–10; 21–5). But if allegory elucidates by dramatising abstract ideas, it also 'clowdily enwrap[s]'

---

41   In the 'Induction on the Stage', the stage-keeper describes the play as 'ware' – the word repeatedly used for commodities hawked to fairgoers. One of the attractions of the fair is the puppet show – a parody of the theatre – which is as absurd as the antitheatrical diatribe it incites. The richness of *Bartholomew Fair* lies in its comic ambivalence – its ability, through humour, simultaneously to satirise and to defend recreative entertainments.

42   This study corroborates Richard A. McCabe's observation that 'for every heroic image [in *The Faerie Queene*] there is an unheroic double virtually indistinguishable from the real thing'; McCabe, 'Parody, Sympathy and Self', p. 16.

43   See *ibid.*, pp. 7–8.

Introduction 17

(LR 23), willfully generating ambiguity. As we shall see, Spenser not only accentuates this natural property of allegory (whilst providing a misleading guide to the text in the form of the aforementioned 'Letter'), but also gives us, as companion and interpreter, an unreliable narrator. The tension between the moral aim of instruction and the equally moral aim of obfuscation will emerge, in the course of this study, as a primary generator of irony and humour in *The Faerie Queene*. As a poet with a professed intention to 'fashion a gentleman ... in vertuous and gentle discipline' (LR 8), Spenser occupies a unique position to parody his own project and to challenge its presumptions from within. Indeed, the poem educates its readers in part by critiquing simplistic notions of education – one simplistic notion being that morality offers a stable subject for dissection, another being that seriousness demands a straight face. Spenser tends to be most funny and most morally serious when he is exposing reductive and fixed habits of mind.

To call *The Faerie Queene* 'playful' may sound unhelpfully vague – broadly speaking, all literary fiction is a form of play.[44] But the play element of literature may be foregrounded through an accentuation of literary qualities: for example, generic conventions (culminating in pastiche or parody); puzzle, riddling, or patterning; heightened fictionality (fantasy, coincidence, exaggeration); or ironic narration (unreliability, feigned incompetence, contrived diction). All of these characteristics are recognisably, even intrinsically, Spenserian. Their applications and effects are, of course, wide-ranging, but where comic recognition seems to be invited, one or more of these play characteristics will certainly be operative.

Taken together, the playful qualities of *The Faerie Queene* have a bearing upon one of the poem's central preoccupations. As mentioned above, Spenser implies in his 'Letter to Raleigh' that the pleasures of literary artifice are only superficially important to his moral project. In deference to his more high-minded readers, he implies his own preference for plain sermoning, were it not for the demands of common readers 'these dayes' (LR 8–10; 21–5). For a moment, it sounds as though fiction is a carrot and little more. But *The Faerie Queene* itself offers a more complex meditation on the significance of imaginative and other forms of play in Christian life. The poem suggests, at crucial moments, that a capacity to take pleasure (intellectual, imaginative, bodily) is spiritually essential. Literary play has at least two roles here. First, it has a satirical function. Interpreted as a misleading guide to the text, the 'Letter to Raleigh' is itself a playful undercutting of utilitarian apologies for fiction, and of simplistic

44 See n. 40 above.

18 *Comic Spenser*

allegorical 'keys'. Within the fiction of *The Faerie Queene*, unbalanced attitudes to pleasure (overly indulgent or fearfully puritanical) are often comically represented through a variety of playful means, sometimes overt, sometimes subtle and indirect. Second, the poem as a whole contradicts the utilitarian defence of fiction alluded to in the 'Letter to Raleigh' by engaging us in game whose moral lessons are inseparable from the pleasure of playing. Reading allegorical fiction requires scepticism as well as an open mind – a willingness to question appearances, to accept uncertainty, to be receptive to humour. Literary play is vital to Spenser's moral project because good reading strategies are good life strategies.

The playfulness of *The Faerie Queene* is epitomised by its spirit of bathos. Fascinatingly, this was noted by one of the poem's first readers. In a much-quoted letter to Spenser, Gabriel Harvey described *The Faerie Queene* as '*Hobgoblin* runne away with the Garland from *Apollo*'.[45] 'Hobgoblin' (*OED*, *n*., 1: 'A mischievous, tricksy imp or sprite; another name for Puck or Robin Goodfellow') most obviously invokes the folkloric world of fairy queens and changelings that Spenser cross-pollinates with classical epic. But Harvey's invocation of the proverbial embodiment of mischief and impudence also captures the way *The Faerie Queene* upends its own laureate ambitions, persistently disavowing its proclaimed epic stature. The remainder of this introduction surveys the strategies by which it does so. First I will consider the poem's generic, stylistic, and tonal dissonance, before turning to the crucial role of Spenser's narrator. Finally, I will explain how each chapter draws out the comic agency of Spenserian bathos from a different angle.

Hobgoblin

The Faerie Queene is pervaded by provocative disjunctions. Chivalric romance infiltrates classical epic, and fabliau and burlesque infiltrate chivalric romance. Prince Arthur, inexplicably to many, is twice reminiscent of Chaucer's lampoon knight 'Sir Thopas'.[46] Other unsettling disjunctions are encountered at the level of register, which combines grandiose rhetoric with plain and rustic diction, as well as within the

---

45 'Harvey's Letters and the Preface "To the Cvrteovs Buyer"', in Edmund Spenser, *The Works of Edmund Spenser: A Variorum Edition*, ed. Edwin Greenlaw *et al.*, 11 vols (Baltimore: Johns Hopkins University Press, 1932–57), Vol. X, pp. 441–77 (p. 472); hereafter *Var*. Surely Harvey's tone here is one of witty affront, though Mary Ellen Lamb reads it as more seriously critical; *The Popular Culture of Shakespeare, Spenser and Jonson* (Abingdon: Routledge, 2006), pp. 54–5.

46 See pp. 145–8.

Introduction   19

moral allegory, where a hero's ideal traits are typically belied by human faults, or by the grotesque characters he or she comes into contact with.

Harvey was not the only reader to be confronted by the tonal and aesthetic eccentricities of *The Faerie Queene*. Neoclassical critics were particularly preoccupied with Spenser's unembarrassed use of chivalric romance conventions (monsters, maidens, and marvels) and his archaic diction. Such retrogression was evidently apprehended as comic, though whether Spenser was in control of this comedy is doubtful. Numerous poets of the seventeenth and eighteenth centuries parodied the incidence of the 'low, lewd, and ludicrous' in *The Faerie Queene* (alliteration obviously falling within this camp), and affectionately made fun of Spenser's 'Monsters' and 'Charms' in verse satire – one implication being that such comic recognition was the privilege of a more sophisticated literary age.[47] Abraham Cowley's tribute to William Davenant's *Gondibert* (1651) typifies the satirical vein:

> Methinks Heroick Poesie till now
> Like some fantastique Fairy-land did show;
> Gods, Devils, Nymphs, Witches, and Giants race,
> And all but Man, in Mans best work had place.
> Thou like some worthy Knight, with sacred Arms
> Dost drive the *Monsters* thence, and end the Charms.[48]

Others, however, found much to admire, and assumed that Spenser was in charge of his poem's disjunctive effects. Speaking of the climactic dragon fight of Book I, following which villagers and their children come forth

47 Samuel Johnson spoke of the Elizabethan attraction to medieval romance as evidence that the nation was, in terms of learning and sophistication, still in its infancy; 'Preface to Shakespeare' (1765), in *Johnson on Shakespeare*, ed. Arthur Sherbo, Vols. VII–VIII of *The Yale Edition of the Works of Samuel Johnson*, 23 vols (New Haven: Yale University Press, 1968), Vol. VII, pp. 59–113 (p. 82); henceforth 'Preface to Shakespeare'. Richard Hurd set out to redeem *The Faerie Queene's* 'Gothic' traits by emphasising Spenser's concern for historical accuracy; see Richard Hurd, *Letters on Chivalry and Romance* (1762), Vol. III of *Spenser's 'Faerie Queene': Warton's Observations and Hurd's Letters*, ed. David Fairer, 3 vols (London: Routledge, 2001). '[L]ow, lewd, and ludicrous' is the phrase of the (Spenser-admiring) Romantic poet Leigh Hunt, although it nicely encapsulates neoclassical disapproval; see Greg Kucich, 'The Duality of Romantic Spenserianism', *SSt*, 8 (1987), 287–307 (p. 299). On the Romantic reception of Spenser see further pp. 20–1 below. On neoclassical parody of Spenser see Howard Erskine-Hill, 'Pope', SpE, pp. 555–6; and on neoclassical criticism more generally see p. 57–60 below. On Renaissance ambivalence toward medieval romance, see pp. 62–3 below.

48 William Davenant, *Gondibert* (1651), ed. David F. Gladish (Oxford: Clarendon Press, 1971), p. 270.

Comic Spenser

to prod and marvel at the dragon's dead body, John Upton remarked in 1758, 'this mixture of the dreadful with the comic, the serious and the ridiculous, is much after the manner of Shakespeare, whose genius seems in many respects to resemble Spenser's'.[49] C. S. Lewis was to observe of Faunus's laughter at Diana in the *Mutabilitie Cantos*:

> this intermeddling of the high and low – the poet's eye glancing not only from earth to heaven but from the shapeless, funny gambollings of instinct to the heights of contemplation – is as grave, perhaps even as religious, as the decorum that would, in a different convention, have forbidden it.[50]

A similar sense of the unheroic inclusiveness of Spenser's vision emerges from Graham Hough's assessment of *The Faerie Queene*'s lovers: 'Eros is not to be confined in any particular moral sphere; he haunts the slums and alleyways as well as the heights. And Spenser's idealism is never of a kind that shirks the actual facts of the case.'[51] This apprehension of a profoundly broad-minded moralist – one whose sense of humour is inextricable from that broad-mindedness – echoes the view of those Romantics who praised Spenser's 'extraordinary mixture of light and darkness – of the sublime and the sordid' and his willingness to bring together 'the grotesque and sedate, the lofty and the mean, the sad and the humorous'.[52]

A different view is that Spenser's taste for the discordant, the grotesque, and the humorous arises out of his didactic intent, and his poem's moral dichotomies. This view, still encountered in contemporary criticism, sometimes accompanied the neoclassical emphasis on Spenser's Elizabethan lack of refinement – because the obvious excuse for such 'low' and fantastic elements in an epic poem was the moral argument. The dragon-slaying episode of Book I, Canto xi, is a childish romance fiction, but it is also an apotheosis of evil drawn from Revelation 12:9. Similarly, monsters, whores, hags, braggarts, cuckolds, and seducers belong to the lower moral strata of the poem, travestying epic values, and disjunctions between 'high' and 'low' are straightforwardly hierarchical and didactic.[53]

---

49 *Var* III, p. 306.
50 Lewis, *The Allegory of Love*, p. 356.
51 Graham Hough, *Preface to 'The Faerie Queene'* (London: Duckworth, 1983 [1962]), p. 173.
52 On the Romantic reception of Spenser see Kucich, 'The Duality of Romantic Spenserianism'; the first quotation is from Leigh Hunt, the second from William Roberts; see *ibid.*, pp. 295, 299.
53 See, for example, Frances K. Barasch, 'Definitions: Renaissance, Baroque, Grotesque Construction and Deconstruction', *MLS*, 13 (1983), 60–7: 'moral clarity [in *FQ*] is achieved when ideal creatures come into conflict with grotesque monsters, giants, magicians, hags and spirits'.

Introduction 21

According to this argument, such figures shore up the values they travesty, and 'good' and 'bad' describe different orders of humanity. As Spenser's narrator himself reassures us, 'white seemes fayrer, macht with black attone' (III.ix.2.4). Pope seized upon Spenser's combinations of grotesque and idealised imagery in his parody of *The Faerie Queene*:

> Her Dugs were mark'd by ev'ry Collier's Hand,
> Her Mouth was black as Bull-Dogs at the Stall:
> She scratched, bit, and spar'd ne Lace ne Band,
> And Bitch and Rogue her Answer was to all.

The comedy of Pope's imitation lies in its sudden transition into a conspicuously heroic register:

> All up the silver *Thames*, or all a down;
> Ne *Richmond*'s self, from whose tall Front are ey'd
> Vales, Spires, meandring Streams, and *Windsor*'s tow'ry Pride.[54]

The Romantic view of Spenser's dichotomies was comparatively subversive, and inclined to see the 'low' aspects of the poem as complicating rather than clarifying its ideal images. Leigh Hunt said of Spenser that 'no man, by seeing one thing exquisitely, saw further into its opposite than he did [… He is] at once sacred and seductive'. In Greg Kucich's words, the Romantics were attracted by Spenser's acknowledgement of the 'doubleness of all experience'.[55]

Above I referred to the 'doubleness' of Spenser's Protestant understanding of human nature, its simultaneous corruption and dignity. It is by reference to this fundamental doubleness that I make sense of the poem's wider disjunctive effects, its combinations of the serious and the comic, and its repeated falls from epic height into the realms of the naïve or nostalgic, grotesque or homely. As I shall argue in Chapter 2, for example, the travesty of epic values that we recognise in Book I's lower characters epitomises Red Crosse's chronic sinfulness, and it is theologically crucial – indicative of his capacity for salvation – that we are able to laugh at him. Humour characteristically undercuts *The Faerie Queene*'s apparent optimism as regards human dignity, moral integrity,

54 Alexander Pope, 'The Alley: An Imitation of Spenser' (1727), lines 37–40; 52–4, in Alexander Pope, *The Twickenham Edition of the Poems of Alexander Pope*, ed. Norman Ault and John Butt (London: Methuen, 1953–69), Vol. VI: *Minor Poems* (1964), pp. 43–5.
55 Kucich, 'The Duality of Romantic Spenserianism', p. 295.

22 *Comic Spenser*

and capacity for firm knowledge. But the same scepticism – because it is rooted in Spenser's Christian faith – also mitigates indignation at these shortcomings, displacing moral dogmatism with tolerance, humility, and empathy. Given that Spenser was the author of acerbic moral and political satire and a whole volume of disillusioned complaints on the theme of worldly vanity, these assertions may sound like misguided optimism. As this study contends, however, humour does not (as its notional triviality implies) function by turning a blind eye to hard realities. Like faith, it is capacious enough to acknowledge the very worst that humanity can do, and capable of putting even bile and spleen into a wider perspective.

The narrator

A premise of the following chapters is that our receptiveness to humour in *The Faerie Queene* is largely determined by how we approach the voice of Spenser's narrator. In his seminal study *The Allegory of Love*, Lewis remarked upon Spenser's shifting personae:

> For the study of Spenser himself, I think the most useful thing we can do as a preparative ('Laughing to teach the truth, what hinders?') is to draw up two lists of epithets after the manner of Rabelais. The first would run something like this:
> Elfin Spenser: Renaissance Spenser: voluptuous Spenser: courtly Spenser: Italianate Spenser: decorative Spenser.
> For the second I propose –
> English Spenser: Protestant Spenser: rustic Spenser: manly Spenser: churchwardenly Spenser: domestic Spenser: thrifty Spenser: honest Spenser.
> … It is the measure of his greatness that he deserves the epithets of both lists.[56]

With these contrasting lists Lewis points to a negotiation between licence and discipline in Spenser's art. Although Lewis would seem to imply a division within the poet's own sensibilities, his adjectives (which could be multiplied) also testify to the flexibility and theatricality of Spenser's narrator. The authorial identities themselves are not necessarily comic, though their provisionality can be. This is why some of the most valuable contributions to the subject of Spenser and humour have been generated

---

56 Lewis, *The Allegory of Love*, pp. 320–1. Lewis does not explicitly distinguish between Spenser and his narrator as I am doing, although the distinction is implicit in some of his chosen epithets.

Introduction 23

by close attention to narrative voice; it is also why so much humour in *The Faerie Queene* continues to be missed altogether.[57] Spenser constantly changes the rules of the game: his narrator is a toolbox of voices, veering between naïveté, neutral dependability, and profound wisdom. The reliability or unreliability of the narrator at any given moment is not necessarily obvious. For one reader, the narrator's sorrow will intensify the pathos of a given episode, and his admiration for a particular character will heroically elevate them. Another reader, however, may interpret such bias ironically, and hear pathos tipping into the realm of melodrama and heroic elevation descending (or ascending, as the case may be) into mock epic. Likewise, the narrator's moral pronouncements ('So th' one for wrong, the other striues for right'; I.v.8.1, 9.1) may strike the ear as either authoritative or suspiciously reductive.

Such divisions of perspective are facilitated not only by *The Faerie Queene*, but also by its paratexts. I have mentioned the 'Letter to Raleigh' already; similarly equivocal are the Dedicatory Sonnets. Wayne Erickson discerns in these sonnets a 'lightly ironic and relatively sceptical' voice, where others have characterised the same voice as earnest and optimistic.[58] For the most part, the distinction at issue in these conflicting interpretations does not pertain to the poetic voice itself, so much as to the imagined author behind it. As I observed earlier, comic recognition depends upon the perceived dynamic among the narrator, subject, author, and reader. When Red Crosse is lavished with praise at a particularly ignominious moment in his quest, we do not attribute artful insincerity to the narrator; rather, any irony we perceive derives from our sense of the narrator's distance from 'Spenser'. I have noted, however, that Spenser's distance from his narrator is neither stable nor self-evident; it is subject to change and invites speculation. Our inclinations as speculators, in turn, have a direct bearing on our receptivity to irony and humour in the poem.

The narrator's habits of self-deprecation, and our perception of how these might relate to Spenser's perception of himself and his project, provide an ideal illustration of this point. We are familiar with the idea that the 'humility topos' served numerous purposes in the Renaissance. On one hand, it was conventional for authors to apologise for the idleness

---

57 On irony, parody, and the unreliability of Spenser's narrator see, for example, Miller, 'The Ironic Mode'; Harry Berger, Jr, '"Kidnapped Romance": Discourse in *The Faerie Queene*', in *Unfolded Tales: Essays on Renaissance Romance*, ed. George M. Logan and Gordon Teskey (Ithaca: Cornell University Press, 1989), pp. 208–56; McCabe, 'Parody, Sympathy and Self'; Wayne Erickson, 'The Poet's Power and the Rhetoric of Humility in Spenser's Dedicatory Sonnets', *SLI*, 38 (2005), 91–118; and Oram, 'Human Limitation', pp. 45–50.

58 Erickson, 'The Poet's Power', 96.

24 *Comic Spenser*

of their undertaking and their lack of skill; on the other, it was equally conventional for poetry to be presented (sometimes on the same page) as a channel of divine inspiration, an educator of kings and noblemen, and a conferrer of immortality. There is something of this paradox in the first stanza of *The Faerie Queene*, where Spenser's narrator asserts 'Me, all too meane, the sacred Muse areeds / To blazon broade emongst her learned throng' (Proem I, 1.7–8), which may be translated as: 'although I'm not good enough to write an epic, I am inspired'. The Proems and Dedicatory Sonnets typically make reference to the poet's limitations – conveying his sense of unworthiness or his fatigue in undertaking so great a task – while also, on occasion, undermining the task itself ('these ydle rimes ... / The labour of lost time, and wit vnstayd'; DS 2.7–8). In Spenser's case, such self-deprecation has variously been interpreted as class anxiety, as Protestant awareness of fiction's limitations and dangers, as homage to Chaucer, as *sprezzatura* (feigned carelessness concealing artistic graft and ambition), as flattering deference to patrons and potential critics, and as a cloak for contentious social and political commentary.[59] In other words, self-deprecation may be interpreted as a real authorial impulse, or as wholly artificial and ironic.

In his reading of the Dedicatory Sonnets, Erickson sides with the latter view, but argues that it is not enough to recognise artifice; we must be alert to the 'powerful complexity of the idea of convention itself' in this period, and be able to distinguish between degrees of irony and authorial detachment.[60] When, in the poem's second Dedicatory Sonnet, 'Spenser' abases himself before Lord Burghley, praising the latter's grave eminence as a statesman and dismissing *The Faerie Queene* as 'these ydle rimes', Erickson discerns an intensified irony because the poet's false modesty – here in a particularly ostentatious form – speaks directly to Burghley's real prejudices against poetry. Erickson proposes a distinction between

---

59 On class anxiety see Craig A. Berry, 'Borrowed Armor/Free Grace: The Quest for Authority in *The Faerie Queene* I and Chaucer's "Tale of Sir Thopas"', *SP*, 91 (1994), 136–66 (pp. 138–40). On Spenser's debt to Chaucer see Glenn A. Steinberg, 'Spenser's *Shepheardes Calender* and the Elizabethan Reception of Chaucer', *ELR*, 35 (2005), 31–51; and Anthony M. Esolen, 'The Disingenuous Poet Laureate: Spenser's Adoption of Chaucer', *SP*, 87 (1990), 285–311. On Protestant attitudes to fiction see A. D. Nuttall, 'Spenser and Elizabethan Alienation', *Essays in Criticism*, 55 (2005), 209–25; Nelson, *Fact or Fiction*, pp. 73–91; and, for the classic reading of Elizabethan anxieties about literary pursuits, Richard Helgerson, *The Elizabethan Prodigals* (Berkeley: University of California Press, 1976). On humility as a conventional veil for ambition see William A. Oram, 'Spenser's Audiences, 1589–91', *SP*, 100 (2003), 514–33 (p. 520). On political subtexts see Esolen, 'The Disingenuous Poet Laureate', pp. 285–311.

60 Erickson, 'The Poet's Power', pp. 91, 101.

Introduction   25

the irony of false modesty and the more trenchant irony of parodic *sprezzatura* (what might be called 'false false modesty'). While the sonnet to Burghley arguably has a barb in it, Erickson characterises the tone of the Sonnets as playful, and observes that in dismissing his verse as idle folly, the poet simultaneously flatters his powerful addressees and destabilises the praise he heaps upon them.[61]

I would further argue that the rhetoric of humility playfully (rather than anxiously) destabilises *The Faerie Queene*'s pretentions to elevation more generally. While the humility topos is most visible in the Sonnets and Proems, it is also inscribed into the very language of the poem. Here I am referring to the narrator's archaic and 'rustic' diction. While these registers are not to be equated, they do overlap; as E. K. observes in his Epistle to *The Shepheardes Calender*, 'olde and obsolete words are most used of country folke.'[62] E. K. has a lot of flattering things to say about the dignity, patriotism, and elevating effect of old words, and about the admirable decorum of rural idiom in the mouths of shepherds, but he studiously ignores the most obvious thing about Spenser's language: its naïve inelegance.[63] At a time when Latin was pre-eminent, many considered archaic words to be unrefined and obscure – as Ben Jonson implied with his verdict that Spenser 'writ no Language.'[64] William Webbe commented that Chaucer sounds 'blunte and course to many fine English eares at these dayes', and Thomas Greene was of the opinion that archaic

---

61 *Ibid.*, p. 105.
62 Edmund Spenser, *The Yale Edition of the Shorter Poems of Edmund Spenser*, ed. William A. Oram, Einar Bjorvand, Ronald Bond, Thomas H. Cain, Alexander Dunlop, and Richard Schell (New Haven: Yale University Press, 1989), p. 14 (lines 43–4); henceforth *Shorter Poems*. Spenser's archaism is chiefly characterised by a mix of Middle English borrowings and coinages masquerading as borrowings, while his 'rustic' language pertains to a literary rendering (often with the help of northernisms) of the idiomatic diction of country folk. These registers share stylistic features such as alliteration, syntactical inversion, and grammatical inflections, as well as vocabulary. On the crossover between northern dialect and archaic diction see further Paula Blank, *Broken English: Dialects and the Politics of Language in English Writings* (London and New York: Routledge, 1996), pp. 100, 115–18. See also Dorothy Stephens, 'Spenser's Language(s): Linguistic Theory and Poetic Diction', in *The Oxford Handbook of Edmund Spenser*, ed. Richard A. McCabe (Oxford: Oxford University Press, 2010), pp. 367–84 (henceforth *Oxford Handbook of ES*); and Noel Osselton, 'archaism', in *SpE*, pp. 52–3.
63 E. K. cites Cicero on the nobility of old words and associates their restoration with national pride; *Shorter Poems*, pp. 13–16. On the patriotic use of obsolete words, see Richard Foster Jones, *The Triumph of the English Language* (Stanford: Stanford University Press, 1953), pp. 117–18.
64 Ben Jonson, *Timber; or, Discoveries*, in *Workes* (1640), excerpted in *Spenser: The Critical Heritage*, ed. R. M. Cummings (London: Routledge & Kegan Paul, 1971), p. 294. See also Blank, *Broken English*, pp. 102, 114.

26 *Comic Spenser*

language 'might not be red without great misliking or lothsomnes to the eares'.[65] Moreover, the Count in Castiglione's *Book of the Courtier* points out that the use of obsolete vocabulary sounds a bit silly and affected: 'if I should use in this communication of ours, those auncient Tuskane words ... I believe every man would laugh at me'.[66]

Where E. K. defends the purity of old and dialect words and plays down their ambiguous connotations, Spenser exploits them. In *The Shepheardes Calender*, the shepherds' love-problems and seasonal plights imply a range of authorial agendas, from self-advertisement to political critique. Accordingly, plain-speaking ingenuousness is a source of acute irony. In *The Faerie Queene*, a poem that makes a point of banishing pastoral at the door (Proem I, 1.1–4), archaism and rusticity play off against the poet's ambition and sophistication in an even more provocative way. The Dedicatory Sonnet addressed to Raleigh draws attention to the poem's lack of refinement, calling it 'a rusticke Madrigale', and declaring its style unsavory and rude (DS 14). This is the humility topos, with all the range of possible motives and effects mentioned above, but what is being humbled is, in part, the heroic fiction itself.

When E. K. praises the language of *The Shepheardes Calender*, he invokes the principle of *concordia discors*, comparing the poem to an exquisite painting in which 'daintie lineaments of beautye' are set off by 'rude thickets and craggy clifts': 'Even so doe those rough and harsh termes enlumine and make more clearly to appeare the brightnesse of brave and glorious words.'[67] But in *The Faerie Queene*, the effect of the narrator's archaic and rustic diction is often bathos rather than elevation. As Anthony M. Esolen has pointed out, the fact that Chaucer adopted an amusingly naïve and self-deprecating authorial persona and also happened to be a native speaker of Middle English enhances the humble and comic connotations of Spenser's antiquated diction.[68] On the Chaucerian model, moreover, Spenser's narrator is capable of veering

---

65 William Webbe, *A Discourse of English Poetrie* (1586), excerpted in Derek Brewer, ed., *Chaucer: The Critical Heritage*, 2 vols (London: Routledge & Kegan Paul, 1978), Vol. I, p. 125. Greene's comment appears in his prefatory epistle to the anonymous *Hystorie of the seven wise maisters of Rome* (London, 1576). Both quotations are cited in Glenn A. Steinberg, 'Chaucer's Mutability in Spenser's *Mutabilitie Cantos*', *SEL*, 46 (2006), 27–42 (p. 28).

66 Baldassare Castiglione, *The Book of the Courtier*, trans. Sir Thomas Hoby (London: J. M. Dent, 1974 [1928]), pp. 49–50; henceforth *Book of the Courtier*.

67 *Shorter Poems*, p. 15.

68 Esolen, 'The Disingenuous Poet Laureate', pp. 293–4.

Introduction   27

into crudely unsophisticated territory, with heavy-handed alliteration (Malbecco is a 'cancred crabbed Carle'; III.ix.3.5); jaunty, minstrel-like addresses to the reader ('Then listen Lordings, if ye list to weet'; III.ix.3.1); and crude monosyllables such as 'dugs' and 'rompe'.[69] Anglo-Saxon and dialect vocabulary is often accentuated when we encounter 'bad' characters such as Duessa (with her 'scurfe and filthy scald'; I.viii.47–8) or Despair (whose 'hollow eyne / Lookt deadly dull'; I.ix.35.6–7).

Of course, Spenser's antiquated language has a polite and idealistic side, too. Rather than imitating the diction of country folk, as *The Shepheardes Calender* does, the antiquated vocabulary of *The Faerie Queene* is often drawn from the world of medieval chivalry, giving, as Noel Osselton has put it, 'instant verbal access to an idealized past'.[70] But in *The Faerie Queene*, idealism is a form of pastiche. Typically, nostalgia is tinged with irony, coinciding, for example, with simplistic and naïve definitions of heroism or female virtue, as though Faerie Land were a bygone place and not a spiritual and psychological allegory. Moreover, the poem's archaic language does not always avoid the rustic flavour of *The Shepheardes Calender*. Although Spenser's narrator takes up the 'trumpet sterne' of epic in the first stanza, at critical moments in *The Faerie Queene* the pastoral world restakes its claim on our attention, puncturing the poem's heroic façade and underlining the theatricality and bias of the narrator's competing voices (see especially Chapter 2).

The voice of Spenser's narrator is mercurial, as are the connotations, in any given context, of old and unfamiliar words. The important point for our purposes is that both the narrator's self-deprecation and his diction participate in the poem's wider economy of bathos. But this bathos is not just about contradicting heroic myths, or 'lowering the high'; it is also about 'elevating the low'. I agree with Esolen that Spenser's postured humility, his blending of heroic and unheroic elements, and his ironic allegories are best understood in the light of the paradoxes, reversals, and metaphysical wit at the heart of Christianity, epitomised by Christ's comparison of the Kingdom of God to a mustard seed. In Esolen's words, 'the faith that claims that the last shall be first, that finds its Savior as

---

69 For an interesting note on alliteration and promiscuity see Paul J. Hecht, 'Letters for the Dogs: Chasing Spenserian Alliteration', *SSt*, 25 (2010), 263–85 (p. 270). As Hecht rightly argues, alliteration is a remarkably fluid stylistic feature and bathos is only one of its aspects. The final quotation echoes 'Sir Thopas': 'Listeth, lordes, in good entent' (line 712). All references to Chaucer are to *The Riverside Chaucer*, ed. Larry D. Benson, 3rd edn (Oxford: Oxford University Press, 1988).
70 Noel Osselton, 'archaism', in *SpE*, pp. 52–3 (p. 52).

28   *Comic Spenser*

an unknown carpenter ... may well play the Hobgoblin unseating the Olympian deities'.[71]

The chapters that follow take a selective and non-chronological approach to the books of *The Faerie Queene*, paying closest attention to Books I, III, and IV. While the remaining books also contain a wealth of humour, my focus is deliberate. If holiness and romantic love are among the most revered and inspiring of human pursuits, they are also unparalleled in their capacity to provoke displays of folly. For Spenser, the core tension between ideal and unideal behaviour in two areas so utterly central to his Christian ethos – faith and love – proved to be especially fertile ground for humour, and my focus on the Legends of Holiness, Chastity, and Friendship reflects this. Moreover, the apparent disillusionment expressed by the second installment of *The Faerie Queene* is often compared to the greater sense of heroic possibility and moral optimism conveyed by the earlier books, and by Book I in particular. In their edition of Book VI, Andrew Hadfield and Abraham Stoll are alert to the ways in which humour intersects with moral scepticism and political critique, and their commentary certainly invites further work in this area.[72] My purpose, however, is to show that political satire and comic scepticism regarding humanity's capacity for moral good are as much a feature of Book I as Book VI. 'The Legend of Holiness' possesses an assured narrative trajectory, and is decisive in its celebratory ending, because its scope is eschatological and its heroic agent is divine grace; by contrast, the later books are committed to describing how particular virtues are promoted and embodied, obstructed and impersonated by distinctly human mores and institutions. The redemptive humour of Book I provides a larger context within which to place the follies and moral irresolutions of every book that follows, and it is for this reason – especially in light of its popular reputation as *The Faerie Queene*'s most serious and heroically affirmative book – that I devote two chapters to Spenser's rich and underexplored comic handling of Red Crosse as Christian Everyman.[73]

---

71 Esolen, 'Highways and Byways', p. 4.
72 Edmund Spenser, '*The Faerie Queene*': *Book Six and the Mutabilitie Cantos*, ed. Andrew Hadfield and Abraham Stoll (Indianapolis: Hackett, 2007); see in particular Hadfield's introduction, pp. vii–xviii.
73 As Paul Suttie notes, the earnestness of Book I's design is 'surely the most taken for granted of any [book] in the poem'; 'Edmund Spenser's Political Pragmatism', *SP*, 95 (1998), 56–76 (p. 65).

Introduction   29

Following the historical survey of Chapter 1, which moves Spenser from the sidelines to the centre of the celebrated comic Renaissance, Chapter 2 reflects on the fundamental conflict between heroism and holiness in Book I, and demonstrates Spenser's use of comic strategies to expose the defectiveness of classical heroism in a Christian context. Chapters 3 and 4 highlight Spenser's talent for communicating the comic vulnerability of lovers through acute psychological observation and situational comedy. Chapter 3 revises the traditional assumption that Book I's sexual satire is directed at lust and infidelity, and argues that what it really sends up is bodily shame. Building on this groundwork, Chapter 4 argues that romantic love uniquely testifies to the intersection of sin and redemption in Christian life, and examines the way humour foregrounds this intersection in the central books of the poem. Chapter 5 analyses *The Faerie Queene*'s images of Elizabeth I, and finds that idealisation can be as funny as grotesque caricature. It also argues that Spenser is not above poking fun at himself: in recognition that the poet's ambitions are inextricable from those of his monarch, Spenser's parodic images of Elizabeth often incorporate elements of self-satire. Finally, the epilogue to this study reflects upon the preceding chapters' collective preoccupation with allegory as the foundation of Spenser's comic art, showing it to be a powerful generator of bathos, ambiguity, and pleasure.

In *Spenser's International Style*, a landmark in Spenser studies, David Scott Wilson-Okamura argues that in writing *The Faerie Queene*, Spenser 'wants to write a high-style poem, with "trumpets sterne", and he wants to imitate Virgil'.[74] Aware that *The Faerie Queene* falls conspicuously short of actually being a high-style poem, Wilson-Okamura takes Spenser at his word that the six books we have constitute the first instalment of a projected twelve-book work. He proposes that the unwritten second half would, on the Virgilian model, have been public and epic-tragic (high style) as opposed to private and epic-comedic (the middle style of the present six-book poem).[75] Without disputing Virgil's enormous influence on Spenser or the complex vocabulary of style that Wilson-Okamura so sharply illuminates, my take on the discrepancy between Spenser's

---

74 David Scott Wilson-Okamura, *Spenser's International Style* (Cambridge: Cambridge University Press, 2013), p. 55.

75 Spenser's 'Letter to Raleigh' refers to 'these first twelue books' (lines 19–20). See Wilson-Okamura, *Spenser's International Style*, Chapter 6 (esp. pp. 198–211). Wilson-Okamura understands the narrator's stated commitment to attaining the highest reaches of 'true epic' (in the sense of narrating bloody war in a high style; I.xi.7.1–4) to be a measure of Spenser's ambitions; see pp. 189–96. See further Chapter 2 n. 85 below.

narrator's grand plans and the stylistically ambivalent poem we have is very different. 'Height', I contend, is a useful theatrical illusion, but not an earnest goal, for Spenser.

Spenser's sense of humour, once recognised, cannot be contained or relegated to a specialised area of critical interest. This study is more than a nod to 'the funny bits' in *The Faerie Queene*; it is a proposal that we need to read the poem differently. Receptiveness to humour valuably balances the deep-rooted critical emphasis on Spenser as being subject to, or rendered anxious or frustrated by, the demands and limitations of his text, circumstances, and historical moment. Anxieties and frustrations there surely were, but humour (unlike satire in its angrier guise) thrives upon a certain philosophical and artistic distance from biographical and historical facts. As we shall see, Spenserian humour has a capacity to affirm the licence of the creative imagination, the contradictory experience of being human, and the consolations that wait upon failure and disenchantment.

1

Spenser and the comic Renaissance

Known for its heroic mythology, idealising love poetry, and forth-right didacticism, the Renaissance is sometimes portrayed as a literary Golden Age sandwiched between the unheroic Middle Ages and the mock-heroic eighteenth century. More than a product of modern nostalgia, this reputation for *gravitas* was actively fostered during the period itself: the assumption that seriousness is synonymous with moral and literary value (the latter two things being theoretically equated) is frequently encountered in prefaces and dedications. Elizabethan theorists tell us that epic poetry concerns 'great and excellent persons & things', is characterised by 'grauitie and statelinesse', and should 'erect the mind and lift it up to the consideration of the highest matters'.[1] The seemingly natural partnership of formality and moral seriousness was affirmed in a wide range of contexts other than epic poetry, moreover. Spenser's *Complaints* volume (1591), for example, was advertised to prospective readers as 'meditations of the worlds vanitie; verie *grave and profitable*', adjectives that echo the rhetoric of Protestant piety.[2]

But there is another, diametrically opposite, reputation to consider. The sixteenth century produced a wealth of entertaining and irreverent material fuelled by (and fuelling) the growing book trade – jestbooks, comic plays, witty prose narratives, and voyeuristic exposés of society's criminal underbelly. It also produced a series of comic masterpieces.

---

1 The first two quotations are from Puttenham, *ECE*, Vol. II, p. 43. The third is from Sir John Harington, 'A Preface', in *Orlando Furioso*, trans. Sir John Harington (1591), ed. Robert McNulty (Oxford: Clarendon Press, 1972), p. 3 (line 20); henceforth *OF*.
2 'The Printer to the Gentle Reader', in *Shorter Poems*, p. 223 (lines 14–15; my italics).

32   *Comic Spenser*

Continental works include Erasmus's *Moriae encomium*; Ariosto's *Orlando furioso*; Rabelais's *La vie de Gargantua et de Pantagruel*; and, at the beginning of the seventeenth century, Cervantes's *Don Quixote*.[3] In England, the rise of the public theatre saw comic drama evolve from early Tudor farce to the sophisticated comedies and tragicomedies of Shakespeare and his contemporaries, with ancient Greece and Rome providing a mine of comic templates. Mock-epic, mock-encomium, Menippean satire, Ovidian epyllia, Lucianic dialogue, picaresque novellas, and collections of epigrams and anecdotes were among the diverse literary models to be rediscovered, translated, and imitated. Famously, Bakhtin described the sixteenth century as 'the summit in the history of laughter'.[4]

Speaking of the period's pendulum swings between elevation and bathos, Samuel Johnson observed, 'the reign of Elizabeth is commonly supposed to have been a time of stateliness, formality and reserve, yet perhaps the relaxations of that severity were not very elegant'.[5] The relationship between reserve and relaxation was, in an obvious sense, more complementary than paradoxical, because the period's myths of ideal humanity and civilisation provided fertile ground for life's unheroic realities. Areas of ambition and tension erupted into jokes and caricatures. Looking to the theatre alone, plays are full of rogues and fools empitomising religious hypocrisy and fanaticism (Malvolio, Zeal-of-the-Land Busy), mercantile culture and social mobility (Shylock, Winwife), pretension and pedantry (Jacques, Holofernes, Dogberry), and the unruly body (Falstaff, Ursula). The body is a universal and timeless comic subject, but in this period its consuming, excretory, and sexual aspects empitomised society's anarchic energies as never before.[6]

---

3 First published in 1511, *Moriae encomium* appeared in thirty-six Latin editions by the time of Erasmus's death in 1536, and in Thomas Chaloner's English translation in 1549. Three versions of *Orlando furioso* appeared between 1516 and 1532, and the final revision of 1532 was republished 113 times between 1540 and 1580. Sir John Harington provided the first full English translation in 1591; see Daniel Javitch, *Proclaiming a Classic: The Canonization of 'Orlando furioso'* (Princeton: Princeton University Press, 1991), p. 10. The full set of books under the title *La vie de Gargantua et de Pantagruel* was published in France between 1532 and 1564, with *Pantagruel* first appearing in 1532 and *Gargantua* in 1534. Sir Thomas Urquhart and Pierre (Peter) Le Motteux made the first English translation in 1653, although Rabelais was well known in England before this. *Don Quixote* was published in two parts, in 1605 and 1615, with Thomas Shelton's English translations following in 1612 and 1620.
4 Bakhtin, *Rabelais and His World*, p. 101.
5 'Preface to Shakespeare', p. 72.
6 In the words of Julia Briggs, 'If laughter reveals a society's inner tensions, Tudor audiences must have been childishly preoccupied with bodily control'; *This Stage-Play*

Spenser and the comic Renaissance   33

It has been well observed of the Renaissance that in practice the division between comic and non-comic genres and between 'popular' and 'elite' literary spheres is frequently blurred.[7] It is not unusual for readers to find title pages advertising, for example, 'A Lamentable Tragedie, mixed full of plesant mirth', bawdy puns and Petrarchan parodies infiltrating love sonnets, or collections of obscene tales compiled by humanist scholars and courtiers.[8] Spenser's inclusion of fabliau-esque material (the tale of Malbecco and Hellenore), bawdy jokes (the Squire of Dames's antifeminist tale) and burlesque (the lampoon-knight Braggadochio) within the frame of *The Faerie Queene* is, in this sense, typical of the period.

The Renaissance proclivity for mixing modes was not, however, accepted without objection. I have noted that humour was fuelled by areas of social and political sensitivity; by the same token, humour raised anxieties. The frivolous and potentially anarchic nature of laughter was often emphasised by moralists, by literary critics, and by authors themselves. A capacity to subvert and unsettle is a timeless attribute of humour, but concerns about the right uses of humour were particularly acute during the period in question. First, unprecedented access to comic literary material, both on the page and on the stage, brought humour to the attention of the literary critic. What are the proper bounds of comic representation – when should mirth be indulged, and when eschewed? This was a formal question as well as a moral one. Despite the popularity of hybrid genres such as tragicomedy and epic romance, theorists influenced by Aristotle's *Poetics* understood that genres were supposed to be distinct – and that, moreover, literature's highest reach

World: Texts and Contexts, 1580–1625 (Oxford: Oxford University Press, 1997), p. 282. On bodily control as a Renaissance preoccupation see Norbert Elias, *The History of Manners*, trans. Edmund Jephcott (Oxford: Blackwell, 1978), Chapter 2; and David Hillman, *Shakespeare's Entrails: Belief, Scepticism, and the Interior of the Body* (Basingstoke: Palgrave Macmillan, 2007), p. 60.

7 Although humanist learning and the book trade were closely related developments, on occasion they are associated with polarised spheres of circulation: the educated elite (often associated with manuscript culture) and a popular audience made up of newly literate readers. Yet the period's engagement with the classical past affected all literary genres and reached learned and unlearned audiences alike; conversely, courtly tastes contributed to the demand for entertaining, sensational, and cheaply printed material. See further Garrett Sullivan and Linda Woodbridge, 'Popular Culture in Print', in *The Cambridge Companion to English Literature, 1500–1600*, ed. Arthur F. Kinney (Cambridge: Cambridge University Press, 2000), pp. 265–86.

8 The subtitle is from *The life of Cambises king of Percia* by Thomas Preston (1570), cited by Janette Dillon, 'Elizabethan Comedy', in *The Cambridge Companion to Shakespearean Comedy*, ed. Alexander Leggatt (Cambridge: Cambridge University Press, 2002), pp. 47–63 (pp. 48–9). Jestbook circulation is discussed further below.

34   *Comic Spenser*

was non-comic.[9] In the words of George Gascoigne, 'to entermingle merie jests in a serious matter is an *Indecorum*'.[10] Second, the morality of laughter had been questioned from the Christian viewpoint for centuries, but the upheaval of the Reformation served to intensify the debate. Even as satire was proving an indispensable polemical tool, the impiety of laughter was being newly emphasised.[11] The 'mixed mode' of Spenser's Christian epic – its generic fluidity, its penchant for bathos, and its satirical energy – is, in this sense, both typical of the period and notably provocative.

The remainder of this chapter surveys, under two broad headings, the resources and debates that influenced the character of Renaissance humour, and thus – as I will argue – Spenserian humour. First we will turn our attention to the connections between the comic Renaissance and humanism; second, to medieval influences.

Humanism

The witty gentleman

'Humanist wit' is a familiar conjunction: it encapsulates the Renaissance ideal of the socially-at-ease gentleman who can tell jokes and amusing stories and play with words, and whose schooling in the humanities encompasses a familiarity not only with Virgil and Homer, but also with irreverent authors such as Lucian and Apuleius. Reading the dialogues of Castiglione's handbook fashioning the ideal courtier, one is struck by the prominence of witty remarks and appreciative laughter, and indeed an entire section of the book is devoted to the art of jesting. It is clear that the courtier, in addition to being athletic and learned, also

---

9 For Aristotelian literary criticism, see Torquato Tasso, *Discorsi del poema eroico*, in *Prose*, ed. Ettore Mazzali (Milan: Riccardo Ricciardi, 1959), Book I, pp. 487–729 (pp. 489–513); henceforth *Discorsi* (for an English translation, see *Discourses on the Heroic Poem*, trans. Mariella Cavalchini and Irene Samuel (Oxford: Clarendon Press, 1973), Book I, pp. 10–17; henceforth *Discourses*); and Lodovico Castelvetro, *Castelvetro on the Art of Poetry: An Abridged Translation of Lodovico Castelvetro's 'Poetica d'aristotele vulgarizzata et sposta'*, trans, intro. and notes Andrew Bongiorno, Medieval and Renaissance Texts and Studies, Vol. 29 (Binghamton: State University of New York Press, 1984), pp. 48–9.
10 'Certayne Notes of Instruction', in *The Complete Works of George Gascoigne*, ed. John W. Cunliffe, 2 vols (Cambridge: Cambridge University Press, 1907–10), Vol. I: *The Posies* (1907 [1575]), p. 466; henceforth *Works of Gascoigne*.
11 On Reformation attitudes to humour see further pp. 69–71 below. See also Fudge, 'Learning to Laugh'.

Spenser and the comic Renaissance　　　　35

had to be good at making people laugh.[12] Renaissance scholars were aware that jests and anecdotes had an ancient pedigree. Both Thomas Wilson – described by Gabriel Harvey as 'one of mie best for jesting' – and Castiglione cite Cicero and Quintilian in praising the rhetorical and social uses of humour.[13] Although the compliment is perhaps back-handed, Folly, Erasmus's narrator, is quick to claim kinship with classical rhetoricians: 'in the preceptes of theyr arte, amonges divers other trifles, they have written … largely and exactly, how to provoke laughter in an audience.'[14]

The series of five 'witty and familiar' letters written by Spenser and Harvey and published in 1580 should be considered against this humanist background.[15] Like aphorisms and jokes, letter writing, as anatomised in Renaissance rhetorical handbooks and how-to guides, was a self-conscious classical revival. Far from being personal correspondence that has incidentally found its way into print (as the prefatory epistle would have us believe), the interchange between Spenser and Harvey was evidently an exercise in self-presentation by two aspiring literary men.[16] Peppered with Latin and Greek and references to literary affairs being discussed at court, and with original verse compositions, the letters, as advertised, display their authors' university backgrounds and credentials as witty gentlemen. Part of the appeal of published letters is the illusion of 'listening in' to a private exchange, and Spenser and Harvey include plenty of name-dropping and ambiguous references (including

12　See *Book of the Courtier*, Book II, esp. pp. 121–77.
13　Virginia F. Sterne, *Gabriel Harvey: A Study of His Life, Marginalia, and Library* (Oxford: Clarendon Press, 1979), p. 160. Harvey's comment is from his copy of Wilson's *Arte of Rhetorique* (first published 1553 and revised in numerous editions), which contains a section entitled 'Of deliting the hearers, and stirring them to laughter'; Thomas Wilson, *Wilson's 'Arte of Rhetorique' (1560)*, ed. G. H. Mair (Oxford: Clarendon Press, 1909), pp. 134–8; henceforth *Rhetorique*. In the words of Chris Holcomb, 'early modern rhetoric and courtesy manuals are obsessed with jesting'; *Mirth Making: The Rhetorical Discourse on Jesting in Early Modern England* (Columbia, SC: University of South Carolina Press, 2001), p. 3. For Cicero and Quintilian on wit and humour, see respectively Cicero, *De oratore*, trans. E. W. Sutton and H. Rackham, rev. edn, 2 vols (London: Heinemann, 1959–60 [1948]), Vol. I, 357–419 (Book II, liv–lxxi); and Quintilian, *Institutio oratoria*, trans. H. E. Butler, 4 vols (London: Heinemann, 1953 [1921–2]), Vol. II, pp. 439–501 (Book VI, Chapter 3).
14　Desiderius Erasmus, *The Praise of Folie*, trans. Sir Thomas Chaloner (1549), ed. Clarence H. Miller, EETS, o.s. 257 (London: Oxford University Press, 1965), p. 73; see also p. 91; henceforth *Folie*.
15　See *Var* IX.
16　See Joseph Campana, '*Letters* (1580)', in *Oxford Handbook of ES*, pp. 178–97 (pp. 179–80).

36 *Comic Spenser*

Spenser's use of the pseudonym 'Immerito') to facilitate this pleasure. What is disconcerting for the modern reader of Renaissance epistolary exchanges is the peculiar combination of private and public references and modes of expression. The tone of the letters is by turns affectionate, scolding, baiting, confiding, and boasting – yet it is also highly formal. What is 'familiar' about the Spenser–Harvey letters resides not in the kind of casual informality we might expect today, but in elaborate and self-conscious prose that (though earnestly advertised in the prefatory epistle as material to 'garnish our Tongue') can seem like a facetious game of mutual flattery and tongue-in-cheek rhetorical display. Harvey, for example, teasingly describes Spenser's epistolary style as 'long, large, lauish, Luxurious, Laxatiue'.[17]

If the privacy of the letters is a piece of theatre for a public audience, the reader is nevertheless kept on the outer in trying to gauge the amount and degree of facetious posturing in the exchange. For example, if E. K., the assiduous *Shepheardes Calender* commentator, is (as is often suspected) a persona created by Spenser and Harvey, then Spenser's comment 'Maister E. K. hartily desireth to be commended vnto your Worshippe' becomes a joke accessible, presumably, to only a few.[18] Likewise, it is hard to know just how seriously we are supposed to take the verses attached to the letters; Spenser's *Iambicum trimetrum*, for example, may demonstrate the art of English quantitative verse (the fashion for which is a dominant subject of the letters) but its ponderous depiction of love-sickness – sometimes criticised as inexplicably bad poetry – seems designed to be taken with a grain of salt, which Harvey duly does when he critiques his friend's '*Comicall* Iambicks'.[19]

The ideal of male friendship that Spenser and Harvey embody in these letters is reminiscent of early humanist culture as epitomised by Erasmus and More, two learned literary men who also published 'private' and amusing correspondence. This model evidently continued to exert an influence later in the century. A point to underline is that even as such letters (much like Castiglione's manual for courtiers) relegate humour

---

17 *Var* IX, p. 441.
18 On the identity of E. K. see Thomas H. Cain's introduction to *The Shepheardes Calender* in *Shorter Poems*, pp. 3–10; and D. Allen Carroll, 'The Meaning of "E. K."', *SSt*, 20 (2005), 169–81. For strong disagreement that E. K. is a fabricated persona, see David R. Shore, 'E. K.', in *SpE*, p. 231. On the humour of E. K.'s pedantry see pp. 40–1 below.
19 My italics. The playful nature of the verse is briefly discussed in the *Variorum*, alongside earlier assessments; *Var* IX, p. 225 (see commentary on lines 85–106). The style of *Iambicum trimetrum* is reminiscent of Spenser's *Daphnaida*, a poem that David Lee Miller argues is deliberately bad; 'Laughing at Spenser's *Daphnaida*', *SSt*, 26 (2011), 241–50.

Spenser and the comic Renaissance   37

and play to extemporal and private contexts, they also cement wittiness and ventriloquism as key attributes of the serious courtier poet.

Jestbooks

The wit of Renaissance courtesy books and published letters may be tame (i.e. learned wordplay, literary in-jokes), but the idea that humour ought to be part of the gentleman's repertoire clearly provided a broad licence. Jestbooks are a case in point. These popular story collections featured gullible fools, wily pranksters, and plenty of scatological and sexual jokes, and they were notably fashionable within humanist circles – often circulating in Latin as well as the vernacular.[20] Although many jestbooks derive from medieval folklore and sermon exempla, their learned compilers and readers would have been aware not only of classical authorities on the art of telling jokes (as noted above) but also of ancient works containing scurrilous stories – works including *Margites*, *The Golden Ass*, and the *Satyricon*.[21] Some jestbooks, such as *A Hundred Merry Tales* (1526; compiled by John Rastell, Thomas More's brother-in-law) continued to pay lip service to the medieval exempla tradition by concluding with a superficial moral, while others followed the *Facetiae* of the Italian humanist Poggio Bracciolini (1380–1459) and abandoned any pretext of moral utility beyond implicit warnings about gullibility and foolishness. Over the course of the sixteenth century, jestbooks gradually lost their respectable association with the works of humanists such as Poggio, Erasmus, More, and Skelton to acquire a disreputable status befitting their crude subject matter. Yet they continued to be enjoyed by learned audiences: Elizabeth I apparently listened to stories from *A Hundred Merry Tales* on her deathbed.[22]

---

20 See Stanley J. Kahrl, 'The Medieval Origins of the Sixteenth-Century English Jest-Books', *Studies in the Renaissance*, 13 (1966), 166–83.

21 Only scraps of the pseudo-Homeric *Margites* survive, but the eponymous hero is, judging from a fragment that describes a painful incident involving the funnel of a pot, a naïve blunderer; see Homer, *Homeric Hymns, Homeric Apocrypha, Lives of Homer*, trans. and ed. Martin L. West (Cambridge, MA: Harvard University Press, 2003). Aristotle legitimised the *Margites* as a comic model: '*Margites* bears the same relation to comedy as the *Iliad* and *Odyssey* do to tragedy'; *Poetics*, p. 95. *The Golden Ass* of Apuleius and the *Satyricon* of Petronius are often referred to together as 'Roman novels' and as examples of Menippean satire. Though very different in style, tone, and subject matter, both works are characterised by farcical misadventure and wide-ranging social satire. On *The Golden Ass* see further pp. 42–4 below.

22 Derek Brewer, 'Prose Jest-Books Mainly in the Sixteenth to Eighteenth Centuries in England', in *A Cultural History of Humour: From Antiquity to the Present Day*, ed. Jan Bremmer and Herman Roodenburg (Cambridge: Polity Press, 1997), pp. 90–111

38   *Comic Spenser*

As Hadfield has pointed out, certain marginalia in Harvey's copy of *A merye jeste of a man called Howleglas* prove that Spenser and Harvey, too, enjoyed jestbooks:

> This Howletglasse, with Skoggin, Skelton, and L[a]zarill, given me at London of Mr Spensar XX. Decembris 1[5]78, on condition [I] should bestowe the reading of them over, before the first of Jaunary [imme]diately ensuing: otherwise to forfeit unto him my Lucian in fower volumes.[23]

'Howletglasse', 'Skoggin', and 'Skelton' are all jestbooks; 'L[a]zarill' refers to the Spanish picaresque novel *Lazarillo de Tormes*, which was not far removed from the jestbook world of tricksters and fools (although more complex and grittily descriptive in terms of plot and narration).[24] *Howleglas* is a collection of forty-seven brief tales spanning the birth and death of the titular character, an oddball and petty rogue who travels around under a variety of masters tricking and offending people and, when necessary, running off to reinvent himself. Jestbook humour can be quite unsettling; modern readers, at least, will find it hard to know when to laugh, for example, when they hear how Howleglas tricked a mother into thinking her sick child had been healed, or when he expresses regret on his deathbed that 'when I saw a rich man prick his teeth with his knife, that I had not shitten on the end of it', and that 'I did not drive a wooden wedge in all women's arses that were above 50 years, for they be neither cleanly nor profitable'. Some tales are easier to appreciate, such as the one about the parish play in which the priest casts his mistress as an angel at Christ's tomb. Howleglas directs the simpletons playing the three

---

(p. 91). On early humanist jestbook circulation see also Zall, *A Hundred Merry Tales*, pp. 1–10. On Elizabeth's connection with jestbooks see Sullivan and Woodbridge, 'Popular Culture in Print', p. 274; and Hadfield, 'Spenser and Jokes', p. 5.

23 Hadfield, 'Spenser and Jokes', pp. 5–6; Sterne, *Gabriel Harvey*, p. 228.

24 Diego Hurtado de Mendoza, *Lazarillo de Tormes*, trans. David Rowland (London: Abell Ieffes, 1586). *Howleglas* (an English translation of the medieval *Till Eulenspiegel* first printed in Antwerp around 1510, and read by Harvey in a London edition of *c.* 1528, repr. 1560) and Skelton's *Merie Tales* (1530; repr. 1567) are included in Zall, *A Hundred Merry Tales*. *Merie Tales* is not by Skelton but about him, combining biographical material and popular legend about his witty deeds and sayings. While Skelton is a more learned protagonist than Howleglas, their exploits (often involving wordplay and scatological pranks) overlap in theme and subject matter. Only fragments remain of a sixteenth-century edition of *The iests of Skogyn*, although the later edition, *Scoggins iests* (London, 1626), is, like the two aforementioned works, a series of ostensibly true stories about the experiences of a character in a range of absurd and grotesque situations. On Lucian see pp. 41–2 below.

Spenser and the comic Renaissance 39

Marys: 'When the angel asketh you whom you seek, you may say "The parson's leman with one eye"' (aiming at Howleglas, the offended and partially sighted 'angel' ends up punching one of the Marys).[25]

It is easy to see how the humour of Rabelais, Nashe, and Cervantes corresponds with that of the jestbook tradition of bodily humour, violence, and trickery.[26] But Spenser, too, was influenced: the fox and ape in *Mother Hubberds Tale* bear a distinct family resemblance to jestbook rogues such as Howleglas, and similarly reinvent themselves as they travel about tricking people. Cunning, knavish, or earthy characters in *The Faerie Queene* such as Archimago, Braggadochio, Trompart, Glauce, the Squire of Dames, Hellenore, and Malbecco are also anticipated in the world of the jestbook. Indeed, while the story of Malbecco owes a debt to Chaucer's 'Merchant's Tale' (itself a 'merye tale', according to E. K.), a similar story about a blind husband is retold in *A Hundred Merry Tales*.[27] Hellenore's happy ending with promiscuous satyrs diverges from the story, yet remains distinctly reminiscent of the jestbook tendency to reward cunning and nous, supplanting genuine didacticism with throwaway warnings to naïve husbands.

Jestbooks may have furnished Spenser with more than a catalogue of subhuman characters, moreover. Such stories tend to satirise bodily imperatives *and* make fun of those who would attempt to deny them. As we shall see in Chapters 3 and 4, the extremes of unbridled appetite on the one hand and bodily denial or repression on the other generate profound moral problems in Spenser's allegory, and his heroes' efforts to negotiate these extremes are often comically and irreverently handled.

Wordplay and ventriloquism

Johnson said of Shakespeare, 'a quibble is the golden apple for which he will always turn aside from his career, or stoop from his elevation'. Several generations earlier, Dryden had referred to puns ('Clenches') as 'the most groveling kind of Wit' and as 'the vice of the [Elizabethan] Age'.[28] Although Dryden makes special mention of Jonson and Sidney

---

25 See tales 12, 44, and 9 respectively; Zall, *A Hundred Merry Tales*, pp. 151–237.
26 Brewer 'Prose Jest-Books', p. 102.
27 In the June eclogue of *The Shepheardes Calender*, Colin refers to Tityrus's 'mery tales' (line 87), which E. K. identifies as the *Canterbury Tales*; *Shorter Poems*, p. 117.
28 'Preface to Shakespeare', p. 74; Dryden, *Defence of the Epilogue; or, An Essay of the Dramatique Poetry of the Last Age*, in *Sidney: The Critical Heritage*, ed. Martin Garret (London: Routledge, 1996), p. 263.

40   *Comic Spenser*

as authors who played with words, Spenser was of the same camp: his works are full of double meanings, eye rhymes, and playfully divergent spellings; and, like Shakespeare, he uses puns in serious contexts. When, in a preamble to the portentous Elfin chronicles of *The Faerie Queene*, Book II, Spenser's narrator sagely observes that 'a mighty people *shortly* grew' (x.72.1; my italics), the joke at the expense of Elfin stature is not accidental, and nor is the description of Red Crosse heroically 'pricking' on the plain shortly before he is challenged by sexual desire (I.i.1).[29]

Wordplay was not an unselfconscious compulsion for Renaissance authors, though Johnson may have thought so. At a time when English was being expanded to compete with classical Latin, humanist wit thrived upon the period's heightened awareness of language. While linguistic command was considered to be a powerful civilising force, at the other end of the spectrum was pedantic display. Thus the serious pedagogical emphasis on copying, borrowing, and trained eloquence came with a negative flipside: pedantry, unintelligible inkhorn terms, and the sophistic use of persuasive argument.[30] The floodgates were opened for verbal wit, parody, and ironic allusion. Conspicuously 'low' productions such as Gascoigne's erotic chronicle *The Adventures of Master F. J.* (1573) and Nashe's picaresque novella *The Unfortunate Traveller* (1594) are imbued with classical awareness and with the very humanist values they seem to trample over. Like Rabelais before him, Nashe speaks the language of the orator, sonneteer, and brothel keeper in the space of one paragraph, peppering his speech with Latinate words, absurd neologisms, and rhetorical figures while describing grotesque scenes of crime and drunkenness.

As Nashe demonstrates, pedantry and pretension were easy targets for satire at a time when learning was held in the highest regard. *Love's Labour's Lost*, to take an obvious example, lampoons malapropisms, neologisms, and displays of classical learning, anticipating the farcical Dogberry of *Much Ado*. E. K.'s learned glosses on *The Shepheardes Calender* should be considered in the same cultural context. Though E. K. is not as obviously

---

29 The pun on 'pricking' is discussed in Chapter 3. For the Elfin joke see Kathryn Walls, 'Spenser and the "Medieval" Past', in *Spenser in the Moment*, ed. Paul J. Hecht and J. B. Lethbridge (Madison, NJ: Fairleigh Dickinson University Press, 2015), pp. 35–66 (p. 48 n. 51). Spenserian wordplay is an established area of critical interest; for an early study see Craig, 'The Secret Wit of Spenser's Language'. See also Hadfield, 'Spenser and Jokes', pp. 6–8; Maureen Quilligan, 'puns', in *SpE*, pp. 570–3.

30 See Sylvia Adamson, 'Literary Language', in *The Cambridge History of the English Language: 1476–1776*, ed. Roger Lass (Cambridge: Cambridge University Press, 1999), pp. 539–653.

Spenser and the comic Renaissance   41

ridiculous as Holofernes or Dogberry, his educated commentary is absurdly pedantic on numerous occasions.[31] To select a few examples, he diligently explains who Cupid is ('March', line 79); gives a detailed medical explanation for Achilles' vulnerable heel ('March', 97); translates 'Neighbour towne' as 'the Latine Vicina' ('Januarye', 50); and, more helpfully still, explains that 'A loorde was wont among the old Britons to signifie a Lorde' ('Julye', 33).

In company with Nashe and Shakespeare, Spenser shares his period's 'fascination with voice and its modulations' and is attuned to the ironic and absurd potential of discordant linguistic registers.[32] The 'base' style (line 44) of *Mother Hubberds Tale*, for example, is gate-crashed by epic when Jove sends Mercury to earth to sort things out ('streight with his azure wings he cleav'd / The liquid clowdes, and lucid firmament'; lines 1258–59), yet any assumption that a high style correlates with moral authority is undermined by the fact that Mercury is (like Spenser the satirical allegorist) as adept at disguise as the poem's rogues – suggesting that language, too, is a cloak or mask that can be donned and doffed with ease.[33]

Lucian and Apuleius

Testimony to the Renaissance taste for pastiche and learned parody was the popularity of two second-century authors: the Greek satirist Lucian of Samosata (*c.* 125–after 180) – whose 'fower volumes' were owned by Harvey and enviously eyed by Spenser – and the Latin prose writer Lucius Apuleius (*c.* 124–*c.* 170).[34] Both were Renaissance rediscoveries. These authors may be usefully considered together because both wrote colloquial and amusing prose and engaged irreverently with high-brow classical literary tradition. Lucian is best known for his satirical dialogues

---

31 As Cain observes, the scholarly apparatus of *The Shepheardes Calender* presents the poem as an 'instant classic', yet the pedantry of many of the glosses makes this a backhanded and ironic sort of promotion; *Shorter Poems*, pp. 6–9. E. K.'s silliness (besides other possible clues noted by Cain) is the strongest evidence for Spenser's involvement in fabricating the persona. For the critical debate see n. 18 above.

32 Anne Lake Prescott, 'Humour and Satire in the Renaissance', in *The Cambridge History of Literary Criticism: The Renaissance*, ed. Glyn Norton (Cambridge: Cambridge University Press, 1999), pp. 284–91 (pp. 290–1). See also William Keach, 'Verbal Borrowing in Elizabethan Poetry: Plagiarism or Parody?', *Centrum*, 4 (1976), 21–31.

33 I owe this point to William Oram, in *Shorter Poems*, pp. 327–33 (p. 333). On the theatricality of Spenser's epic voice see Chapter 2.

34 See Harvey's marginalia, p. 38 above.

42   *Comic Spenser*

and fantastical adventure stories. The latter include trips to the under-world, to heaven, to the moon, and to a fantasy island that turns social conventions on their head – all improbable destinations that variously reappear in *Orlando furioso, Gargantua and Pantagruel, Utopia,* and *Gulliver's Travels.* Direct allusion aside, any author adept at displaying erudition and debunking pretention simultaneously is in some sense 'Lucianic'.[35] Lucian's dialogues have two favourite themes: the vanity of philosophers and the domestic lives of the gods. *Dialogues of the Gods* comprises a series of burlesque vignettes in which the classical deities squabble and gossip amongst themselves (Zeus moans to Eros about his love problems; Hera, Athena, and Aphrodite sneer at each other while a rather tremulous Paris judges their beauty, and so on). All-too-human classical gods in *The Faerie Queene* are indebted to the *Iliad* and the *Metamorphoses* as well as to Lucian,[36] but some more overt instances of 'domestication' are distinctly Lucianic: for example, the passive-aggressive dialogue between Diana and Venus regarding the where-abouts of Cupid (III.vi.19–25), Proteus's blustering attempts to impress Florimell (not to mention the incongruous reference to his housemaid, Panope; viii.35–41), the depiction of a lovesick Mars shrieking with 'womanish teares' (xi.44.5), and Jove's sudden change of tone when, in the middle of castigating Mutability, he notices how attractive she is (VII.vi.31).

Apuleius's popularity was primarily based on his entertaining novel *Metamorphoses*, more commonly known as *The Golden Ass*, which tells the story of Lucius, a respectable citizen whose curiosity about witchcraft leads him to be transformed into an ass. In his bestial form Lucius undergoes a succession of trials as he changes hands from master

---

35 In the words of Diana Robin, the 'list of authors who translated or imitated Lucian chronologically spans and effectively epitomizes the Renaissance humanist canon'; 'Review of David Marsh, *Lucian and the Latins: Humor and Humanism in the Early Renaissance*', *RQ*, 53 (2000), 559–60 (p. 559). Lucian's split reputation as a legitimate classical model and as an irreverent joker is indicated by Erasmus's preface to *The Praise of Folly*, in which he warily predicts that zealous critics will 'clamour that I'm reviving Old Comedy or Lucian', but also, almost in the same breath, invokes him as an authorising precedent for his satire; Desiderius Erasmus, *'Praise of Folly' and Letter to Martin Dorp, 1515*, trans. Betty Radice, intro. and notes A. H. T. Levi (London: Penguin, 1971), p. 57; henceforth *Folly*.

36 Homer's comically fallible gods have attracted comment since classical times; see for example Longinus, *On Sublimity*, in *ALC*, pp. 470–1; and Plato, *The Republic*, trans. Tom Griffith, ed. G. R. F. Ferrari (Cambridge: Cambridge University Press, 2008 [2000]), pp. 71–80 (386a–391e). See also pp. 58–9 below. On the *Metamorphoses* see pp. 50–4.

Spenser and the comic Renaissance　　43

to master (masters who include thieves, runaways, slaves, a priest, a baker, and a farmer) before returning to human form with the help of the goddess Isis. William Adlington, Apuleius's Elizabethan translator, was quick to point out that Lucius's humiliating transformation and his religious conversion at the novel's end clearly suggest moral allegory, but Adlington also refers to the book as 'wanton' and as a compilation of 'joyous jests', situating *The Golden Ass* alongside jestbooks and other accepted light entertainment.[37] The novel is characterised by a swift-moving and digressive plot; sudden transitions into and out of pathos; a plethora of puns and wordplay; various caricatures drawn from the mercantile and peasant classes; and abundant references to eating, drinking, sex, deformity, money, and violence. Like Lucian (and, later, Nashe, Cervantes, and Rabelais), Apuleius combines colloquial diction and 'low' scenarios with learned and heroic allusions (losing sight of his unprepossessing form, Lucius compares his trials to those of Hercules and Odysseus).[38]

Bottom's transformation into an ass in *A Midsummer Night's Dream* is perhaps the most famous debt to Apuleius, although *Troilus and Cressida* also recalls Apuleius's habit of puncturing heroic mythology. Shakespeare's satirical characterisation of Ajax in that play certainly brings to mind Apuleius's allusion to the Greek hero's blundering massacre of a herd of livestock. (Cervantes adapted this same episode, as well as the story of Lucius's heroic defeat of three 'robbers' who turn out to be bloated wineskins).[39] The main narrative of *The Golden Ass* incorporates numerous inset stories, often fabulous or bawdy, overheard or recounted by Lucius during his humiliating adventure. Renaissance authors imitated a number of these. Boccaccio retold Apuleian tales of adultery in the *Decameron*, as did Boiardo in *Orlando innamorato* and Sidney in the first version of his *Arcadia*.[40] Spenser's best-known borrowing from Apulieus is his adaptation of the story of Cupid and Psyche (narrated in *GA*, Books IV–VI), which he freely adapts in 'The Legend of Chastity' (III.vi.49–51)

---

37 'To the Reader', in Apuleius, *The Golden Ass*, trans. W. Adlington (1566), rev. and intro. S. Gaselee (London: William Heinemann, 1965 [1915]), pp. xv–xviii.

38 E.g. II.32 (pp. 98–9), III.19 (pp. 128–9), IX.13 (pp. 420–1).

39 III.18–19 (pp. 126–9), II.32 (pp. 98–9), III.1–10 (pp. 100–17).

40 For details of Apuleius's revival and reception see Julia Haig Gaisser, *The Fortunes of Apuleius and the 'Golden Ass': A Study in Transmission and Reception* (Princeton: Princeton University Press, 2008), esp. Chapters 3, 4, and 7 (on Boccaccio see pp. 100–7 and on Boiardo see pp. 175–80). On Sidney see Robert H. F. Carver, *The Protean Ass: The 'Metamorphoses' of Apuleius from Antiquity to the Renaissance* (Oxford: Oxford University Press, 2007), pp. 366–72.

44 Comic Spenser

and in the mock-epic *Muiopotmos* (lines 113–44).[41] Another notable allusion is the Isis Church episode of 'The Legend of Justice' (V.vii.1–24), which is reminiscent of the Cult of Isis through which Lucius is redeemed in *GA*, Book XI. The mythological and occult emphases of these debts, apparently removed from the farce and humour so prominent elsewhere in *The Golden Ass*, have distracted attention from the question of Apuleius's broader comic influence upon *The Faerie Queene*. Yet Spenser evidently knew the novel well, and its narrative twists and turns, its grotesque caricatures, and its extravagant pathos were surely influential. *The Golden Ass* contains tales of adultery, a shape-shifting witch, and a temptress who transforms her lovers into animals – all narrative motifs well known to readers of *The Faerie Queene*. And the unchivalric intrusion of bandits, thieves, and merchants into 'The Legend of Courtesy' – which also features histrionic naked women and a rather ineffectual hero – certainly brings Apuleius's burlesque to mind. Specific echoes aside, however, there is a bigger picture to consider. For Renaissance readers such as William Adlington, *The Golden Ass* was, first and foremost, a moral allegory – one that forges a fundamental connection between spiritual growth and total humiliation. As such, it is a suggestive precursor for Spenser's treatment of Red Crosse's downfall in 'The Legend of Holiness', the comic nature of which is treated in Chapter 2 below.

Mock-encomium and mock-epic

A fashionable display of rhetorical skill in the Renaissance was the praise of something lowly or contemptible, the most famous (and most Lucianic) example being Erasmus's *Moriae encomium*, or *Praise of Folly* (published 1511, translated into English 1549). As Erasmus reminds his readers, the elevation of trivial subjects was an established literary exercise:

> those who are offended by frivolity and fun in a thesis may kindly consider that mine is not the first example of this; the same thing has often been done by famous authors in the past. Homer amused himself ages ago with his 'Battle of Frogs and Mice', Virgil with his Gnat and Garlic Salad, Ovid with his Nut.[42]

---

41 On allusions to Apuleius's story of Cupid and Psyche in Book II see Kathryn Walls, 'The "Cupid and Psyche" Fable of Apuleius and Guyon's Underworld Adventure in *The Faerie Queene* II.vii.3–viii.8', *SSt*, 26 (2011), 45–73.

42 *Folly*, p. 57. Erasmus's attributions to Homer, Virgil, and Ovid are now known to be incorrect. For detailed background on the mock-encomium, see Henry Knight Miller,

Spenser and the comic Renaissance

The studied frivolity of such works, ostensibly speaking from the margins of official culture yet with the stamp of classical approval, proved popular in the Renaissance. Spenser is, along with Harvey, Nashe, Harington, and Jonson, one of the better-known English authors to have experimented with 'praising the trivial'. This endeavour embraces both mock-encomium and mock-epic, but common denominators include several of the cornerstones of Renaissance humour already mentioned: a penchant for rhetorical parody and ventriloquism, a keen awareness of classical literary models, and the undercutting of heroic values.

First translated into Italian in 1469, the pseudo-Homeric *Batrachomyomachia* ('Battle of the Frogs and Mice') sends up epic conventions such as the *Iliad*'s precise inventory of battle wounds (instead we encounter various frog and mouse body parts impaled upon toothpick-sized weapons) and the interference of biased and bickering gods.[43] It is easy to see why this poem was frequently translated and reprinted during the sixteenth century; at a time when Homer was a benchmark for literary achievement, his reputation for playful self-parody must have been compelling. In other words, it helped to stake out a place for humour within the literary canon. The Roman poet Statius (*c.* 45–*c.* 96 AD) had observed the incursion of humorous poems into the serious poet's standard repertoire: 'nor is there any of the great poets who has not made prelude to his works in lighter vein'.[44] Echoing this idea in his *De arte poetica* (1527), the Italian humanist Marco Giralamo Vida (*c.* 1485–1566) recommended the pseudo-Virgilian *Culex* (the 'Gnat' referred to by Erasmus) as training ground for the prospective epic-poet.[45] As we know, Spenser ticked this box when he translated the *Culex* as *Virgils Gnat* early in his career.

Mock-epic was more than a prologue for Spenser, however. He was to return to the genre at least a decade later with *Muiopotmos*, published along with *Virgils Gnat* in his *Complaints* volume of 1591 shortly after the

---

'The Paradoxical Encomium with Special Reference to Its Vogue in England, 1600–1800', *MP*, 53 (1956), 145–78.

43 Homer was reputed to have written other 'fun poems' besides *Batrachomyomachia* and the *Margites*; see Homer, *Homeric Hymns, Homeric Apocrypha*, p. 224.

44 Publius Papinius Statius, *Statius, with an English Translation*, trans. J. H. Mozley, 2 vols (Cambridge, MA: Harvard University Press, 1967 [1928]), Vol. I, p. 3; cited by McCabe, 'Parody, Sympathy and Self', p. 8.

45 Gordon Braden, '*Complaints: Virgils Gnat*', in *SpE*, pp. 183–4 (p. 183); see Marco Girolamo Vida, *The 'De arte poetica' of Marco Girolamo Vida* (1517, 1527), trans. and ed. Ralph G. Williams (New York: Columbia University Press, 1976), Vol. I, pp. 459–65.

first instalment of *The Faerie Queene*. In both poems Spenser appears to delight in bringing the full weight of his rhetorical training to bear on the death of an insect hero. *Virgils Gnat*, following the *Culex*, tells the story of a gnat who stings a sleeping shepherd to warn him of a snake in the grass, and is rewarded for his good deed by a fatal swipe of the hand. The shepherd kills the snake and goes on his way, but later the ghost of the gnat appears to him in a dream ('With greislie countenaunce and visage grim', line 326), wailing at the injustice of his death and recounting the terrors of Hades. When the guilty shepherd wakes, he makes a tomb for the gnat and inscribes it in his memory. There is clearly something absurd about an insect pontificating from the underworld like Aeneas, and moreover being honoured with a tomb and epitaph, and this absurdity is compounded by the poem's high style. The narrator is full of praise for rural simplicity and contempt for ostentation, yet his speech (like the gnat's) is full of rhetorical extravagance and digressive mythological allusions – ironically overburdening the story's thin thread.

In contrast to *Virgils Gnat*, *Muiopotmos* is not a translation but an original composition. It is about a comically self-assured butterfly, Clarion, who is killed by a vindictive spider, Aragnoll. The poem is, in part, an origin myth: it draws on Ovid's story of the rivalry between Pallas and Arachne in order to explain why spiders have a grudge against butterflies. Opening with the ponderous announcement 'I sing of deadly dolorous debate', it is mock-epic in tone throughout but contains some especially amusing passages, such as the conversion of Clarion's insect anatomy into a formal 'arming of the hero'. The butterfly's head becomes a 'glistering Burganet', the tiny hairs on his back 'An hairie hide of some wilde beast', and his antennae 'two deadly weapons fixt … / Like two sharpe speares, his enemies to gore' (lines 65–88). These weapons are totally redundant, however. Once Clarion flies into the awaiting web, the 'griesly tyrant' Aragnoll rushes toward his prey 'Like a grimme Lyon' and the butterfly is easily overcome (433–40).[46]

It should be noted that *Virgils Gnat* and *Muiopotmos* have not always been met with amusement, or not first and foremost. This is because both poems hint at possible allegorical interpretations, and contain elements of pathos and moralising that (especially in view of their inclusion in the generally sober *Complaints* volume) can be difficult to gauge. As a result,

---

46 The commentary to *Muiopotmos* in the *Shorter Poems* notes two possible biblical allusions in the lion reference, although Spenser evidently also had Chaucer's mock-hero in mind; cf. 'The Nun's Priest's Tale', line 3179.

Spenser and the comic Renaissance 47

critics have tended to approach these poems as either purely lighthearted *or* purely serious. *Muiopotmos*, for example, has been characterised by different critics as 'the lightest and most delicious of Spenser's poems' and as a solemn allegory of the erring soul.[47] Others have read the poem as a political allegory, identifying the spider as Lord Burghley, for example.[48] *Virgils Gnat*, too, has been read as a veiled allusion to a personal incident – justifiably, because the poem's dedication to the earl of Leicester alludes to an injustice suffered by Spenser (the self-sacrificing gnat?) at the hands of his patron.

Burlesque may well have presented a safe cover for social or political critique.[49] It seems to me, however, that the key to appreciating these poems and their place in the comic milieu of the Renaissance is to approach their elements of levity and seriousness not as conflicting factions (as though humour were a superficial addition to real meaning, or moral allegory a burden upon amusement) but as inextricable complements. The *Praise of Folly* is the pre-eminent model here. Like Spenser's playful poems and like other self-consciously 'minor' productions of the period, Erasmus insists upon the triviality of his treatise when it is diplomatic to do so (anticipating fault-finding readers) and at other times acknowledges the seriousness of purpose that can underlie a jest. But the 'seriousness' of the *Praise of Folly* is not finally separable from its humour. Erasmus's satire forges a link between laughter and humility, targeting, for example, philosophers and churchmen who are too self-important to enjoy a joke or to laugh at themselves. But in this treatise, laughter at folly is compassionate as well as sardonic. Folly's 'praise' exposes the ubiquity of sin and vice, but it also satirises what might be called (relatively speaking) positive follies – infancy and old age; courtship, marriage, and sex; our need to be loved and praised; our inclination to laugh, for example. In a facetious yet profound account of the benefits she bestows, Folly (echoing

---

47 See William Nelson, *The Poetry of Edmund Spenser: A Study* (New York: Columbia University Press, 1963), p. 71, and Don Cameron Allen, *Image and Meaning* (Baltimore: Johns Hopkins University Press, 1968), Chapter 2, respectively.

48 On Burghley see Anne Kimball Tuell 'Note on Spenser's Clarion', *Modern Language Notes*, 36 (1921), 182–3. Tuell is inclined to see the allegory as lighthearted and exaggerated. For two readings that emphasise the poem's political pessimism, see Ayesha Ramachandran, 'Clarion in the Bower of Bliss: Poetry and Politics in Spenser's "Muiopotmos"', *SSt*, 20 (2005): 77–106; and Tom McFaul, 'The Butterfly, the Fart and the Dwarf: The Origins of the English Laureate Micro-Epic', *Connotations*, 17 (2007/8), 144–64.

49 *Virgils Gnat* is presented as a 'small Poeme' and 'jest' that no one should think too deeply about; yet the story itself (and the *Complaints* volume as a whole) insists that we disregard small things at our peril.

48   *Comic Spenser*

St Paul) associates herself with divine protection and forgiveness: 'the wise man receives no pardon'.[50]

The humour of Spenser's mock-epics is ambivalent and complex, too. As I have observed, the dedication of *Virgils Gnat* to the earl of Leicester alludes to a historical injustice seemingly experienced by Spenser, and pulls directly against the narrator's request that readers enjoy the tale without seeking hidden meaning. In other words, the poem appears to be making a point (under the cover of playful bucolic fable) about the complacency of the powerful and the vulnerability of gnats/poets, who sometimes get punished for doing a good turn. But humour is more than a 'cover'. Any point scored against Leicester is surely counterbalanced by the poem's ridiculously overcooked rhetoric, and by the fact that Spenser casts himself as a whining, self-important insect (we all know what mosquitos sound like).[51] If *Virgils Gnat* exposes injustice, I am suggesting, it equally makes fun of the melodrama and cliché of complaint, telescoping worldly grievances down to the scale of the insect world. In view of his poem's implied critique of a powerful patron, Spenser's self-representation as a gnat may well be diplomatic. But such self-effacing humour also achieves something quite profound in the context of the wider *Complaints* volume. If the diminution of the complainer turns complaint back on itself, so too (though in a more positive way) do the poem's hyper-literary qualities, its stylistic playfulness. In contrast to the 'depressed' style of some other complaints, this poem showcases pastoral, epic, elegiac, and comic literary voices – and in doing so announces Virgilian ambition, even in the midst of self-satire.

Similarly ambivalent, the humour of *Muiopotmos* is more directly comparable to the unheroic vision of the *Praise of Folly*. The poem's butterfly/web symbolism (familiar from emblem books of the period) indeed suggests an 'allegory of the erring soul', but humour plays an instructive rather than an incongruous role within this interpretation.[52] Most obviously, mock-epic satirises the protagonist's unwarranted confidence, as I shall argue it does in Book I of *The Faerie Queene*.[53] But, as I shall also argue of Book I, humour can equally imply the forgiving perspective that undergirds the *Praise of Folly* – the perspective according

---

50 *Folly*, p. 199. In Chaloner's translation, 'to Folie onely is geuin perdone and forgeuenesse of trespasses, wheras to wysedome not so muche as the least iote is remitted'; *Folie*, p. 119. Cf. I Corinthians 3:18–20.

51 Insects are powerful in the *Visions* poems, but here the effect is surely comic.

52 Cf. Judith Dundas, '"Muiopotmos": A World of Art', *Yearbook of English Studies*, 5 (1975), 30–8.

53 See Chapter 2.

Spenser and the comic Renaissance   49

to which sinfulness is, paradoxically, the positive foundation of our reliance upon God. In *Muiopotmos*, the butterfly's smallness, fragility, and fallibility play into the poem's moral warning about lurking spiders. But these same traits (and especially the conspicuous uselessness of the butterfly's heroic armour) are also key to the spiritual optimism that inheres in the poem's levity – a levity that encompasses the poem's 'tragic' (or, more accurately, mock-tragic) conclusion.[54]

Writing in 1910, T. W. Nadal declared *Muiopotmos* a failed mock-epic, Spenser's attempt at a genre he was temperamentally unsuited to, resulting in 'good poetry but little humour'.[55] Nadal seems to have taken all the pathos heaped upon the butterfly at face value – as the 'complaint' context invites us to do – or perhaps the combination of humour and seriousness implied a lack of clear authorial vision. If we entertain the idea that this combination is a carefully achieved balance, however, *Muiopotmos* and *Virgils Gnat* emerge as significant contributions to the Renaissance vogue for facetious literary exercises. Though they advertise their own frivolity, such works are more than mere exercises or prologues to weightier subjects; they touch the pulse of a profoundly unheroic temper in the literature of this period. As such they bear an illuminating relation to Spenser's 'real' epic, as I shall argue in the next chapter.

Ovid

Though immensely influential in the Middle Ages, there is nevertheless a sense in which Ovid was rediscovered in the Renaissance.

---

54 The narrator's formal summoning of the tragic muse to supply his 'lamentable cryes' is amusingly hyperbolic (lines 409–16). To interpret Clarion's death in Aragnoll's web as an allegory of unmitigated tragedy – the unregenerate soul succumbing to Satan and going to hell, for example, or, in the words of McFaul, 'the death of beauty and potential' ('The Butterfly', p. 152), is, in my view, to read against the grain of the poem's humour. If one considers that the Christian is ensnared by evil not once and finally but daily, then the Calvinist precept that God 'makes infirmity itself to be the cause of hope' provides a useful gloss on the poem's ambivalent handling of Clarion's downfall; see Calvin's commentary on Lamentations 3:21, in John Calvin, *Commentaries on the Book of the Prophet Jeremiah and the Lamentations*, trans. and ed. Revd John Owen, 5 vols (Edinburgh: Calvin Translation Society, 1850–5), Vol. V, pp. 405–7 (p. 407), accessible online via *Christian Classics Ethereal Library*, https://ccel.org/ccel/calvin/calcom21. iii.iv.xxiii.html (accessed May 2019). On the relation of *Muiopotmos* to mock-heroic humour in 'The Legend of Holiness' see further Chapter 2. On Christianity and mock-heroic see Michael Edwards, 'A Meaning for Mock-Heroic', *Yearbook of English Studies*, 15 (1985), 48–63.
55 T. W. Nadal, 'Spenser's *Muiopotmos* in Relation to Chaucer's *Sir Thopas* and *The Nun's Priest's Tale*, *PMLA*, 25 (1910), 640–56 (pp. 654–5).

50   *Comic Spenser*

Partly, this was a result of Arthur Golding's English translation of the *Metamorphoses* (published and republished from 1567 onward). But it is also because Renaissance authors increasingly broke away from the medieval tradition of interpreting the *Metamorphoses* allegorically. The allegorical approach remained influential, but the erotic, witty, and cynically pragmatic author of the *Ars amatoria* and *Amores* jostled with the Christianised, moralised Ovid. Preoccupied with the hypocrisies and vulnerabilities of lovers, Ovid's amatory works cast a thoroughly secular light on similar themes in the *Metamorphoses*. The latter provided a rich supply of stories about obsessive and ill-fated lovers, and intensified the vogue for narrative poems on amatory themes in the 1590s.

The dominant names here are, of course, Shakespeare and Marlowe, whose *Venus and Adonis* and *Hero and Leander* epitomise the playful and subversive spirit of the late Elizabethan epyllion. These are tragic poems, but they are also funny. While both contain elements of black humour and farce not found in Ovid's versions of the stories, the impulse to combine tragedy and humour is itself Ovidian. The *Metamorphoses* is characterised by sadness, violent punishments, and thwarted desires, even while it is full of irreverence and irony. It might be said that the poem's epic theme is not great deeds but great consequences, the cosmic repercussions of desire and egotism. Gods and mortals are equally fallible. Acts of piety can conceal a reptilian instinct for self-preservation and wish fulfilment, and the gods are often flattered or offended into intervening in human affairs. As E. J. Kenney observes, Ovid is rarely sententious about the flaws he is so good at anatomising:

> Ovid depicts a universe in which human beings, and more often than not the gods who are supposed to be in charge, are at the mercy of blind or arbitrary or cruel, and always irresistible, forces … [His] achievement in the *Metamorphoses* is to transmute what ought to be a profoundly depressing vision of existence into a cosmic comedy of manners.[56]

Desire is the great leveller in this 'comedy of manners'. As would-be lovers pursue their erotic prey, we witness their vulnerability and foolishness. Apollo ineffectually shouts 'I am the son of Jupiter' as Daphne runs away from him (I.496–530), and Jove disguises himself as the goddess of chastity to surprise the nymph Callisto with a kiss (II.414–52). Shakespeare's

---

56 Ovid, *Metamorphoses*, trans. A. D. Melville, intro. and notes E. J. Kenney (Oxford: Oxford University Press, 1987), pp. xviii–xix; henceforth *Met.*

Spenser and the comic Renaissance   51

comically human Venus may be unlike Ovid's goddess, but she is certainly reminiscent of audacious female lovers elsewhere in the Ovidian corpus. For example, another source for *Venus and Adonis*, the rape of Hermaphroditus, tells of the frenzied lust of Salmacis, who seizes her reluctant lover like a squid with 'whipping arms' (IV.355–88).[57] Even in the darkest of contexts, Ovid is a master of comic detail.

Like *Venus and Adonis*, *Hero and Leander* contains moments of exaggeration and irony not found in Ovid's version of the story (or in Marlowe's principal source, Musaeus's fifth-century retelling), but such elements are surely indebted to Ovid's dispassionate observations of erotic psychology in both the *Amores* and the *Metamorphoses*.[58] The idea of love as madness, and the ironic tug-of-war between idealising mythology and aggressive, self-interested desire (motifs encountered not only in Elizabethan epyllia, but also in prose romances and sonnet cycles of the period), can be traced in large part back to Ovid and to authors directly influenced by him, such as Petrarch, Chaucer, and Ariosto.

Spenser has been celebrated as an Ovidian poet, but his debt to Ovid's comic side has been neglected. Instead the focus has been on Spenser's philosophical and religious preoccupation with mutability, and his status as a poet in exile. These emphases are warranted, but the Ovidianism of *The Faerie Queene* has wrongly been placed in diametrical opposition to that of the late Elizabethan epyllion.[59] Spenser, like Shakespeare and Marlowe, was keenly responsive to Ovid's comic handling of amatory themes. As I shall argue in the central chapters of this study (Chapters 2, 3 and 4), desire is *the* comic subject of *The Faerie Queene*. Spenser joins Ovid and Lucian in humanising the pagan deities as part of his poetic

---

57 The rape of Hermaphroditus by Salmacis was later mined for comic potential in the epyllion *Salmacis and Hermaphroditus* (1602), attributed to Francis Beaumont; on the disputed authorship of this poem see William Keach, *Elizabethan Erotic Narratives: Irony and Pathos in the Ovidian Poetry of Shakespeare, Marlowe, and Their Contemporaries* (New Brunswick: Rutgers University Press, 1977), p. 190. The tragicomic aspects of *Venus and Adonis* may also have been influenced by another epyllion, Thomas Lodge's *Scillaes Metamorphosis* (1589). Based on Ovid's tale of Glaucus and Scylla, this poem is important because it is generally regarded as the first Elizabethan epyllion, but also because of its ambivalent tone. Lodge's heavy use of the conventions of love-complaint and wafer-thin moral have been taken at face value by some, and regarded as outright parody by others; see Keach, *Elizabethan Erotic Narratives*, pp. 36–51 (p. 38).

58 The most frequently translated version of the story of Hero and Leander in the sixteenth century was that of Musaeus, whom Marlowe identifies as his main source; see Keach, *Elizabethan Erotic Narratives*, pp. 85–8.

59 See for example Dympna Callaghan, 'Comedy and Epyllion in Post-Reformation England', *Shakespeare Survey*, 56 (2003), 27–38 (p. 30); Keach, *Elizabethan Erotic Narratives*, pp. 219–32; and Roma Gill, 'Marlowe, Christopher', in *SpE*, pp. 453–4.

52   *Comic Spenser*

machinery, depicting bickering and amorous gods – and a wily Cupid – as a means of reflecting on 'the way things are' in the human world. While professing to unite 'Fierce warres and faithfull loues' (Proem I, 1.9), moreover, Spenser generates considerable irony from the incompatibility of love and heroism, an awareness that plays out not only thematically in the quests of his fallible knights, but also structurally. Both Spenser and Ovid wilfully transgress Aristotle's ideal of unity of action to make amatory distraction a formal principle rather than an obstacle to be overcome (as it is in the *Aeneid*, for example).[60]

Another key aspect of Ovid's influence in the Renaissance relates to his handling of violence as a theme; and again, the characteristic sensibility of the *Metamorphoses* is distinctly unheroic, if not tragicomic. In the 'Battle of the Lapiths and Centaurs', for example, we hear of Theseus's foe 'vomit[ing] / Great gouts of blood with brains and wine from wound / And throat' and of the Lapith whose face is smashed beyond recognition: 'Both his eyes / Leapt out, cheek bones were shattered, nose forced back and wedged inside his mouth' (XII.223–56). Such scenes epitomise the emotional excess, arbitrary injustice, and bodily vulnerability that characterise so many of Ovid's stories. It is as though pain and horror are in some sense being matched with, or supplanted by, descriptive exuberance.[61] Even the tragic story of Niobe indulges in gratuitous gore. Black humour around violence and bodily vulnerability was to be pushed even further in the grotesque comic works of Rabelais, Nashe, and Cervantes, as it was in the Senecan revenge tragedies of the late sixteenth and early seventeenth centuries.

Ovid's influence in the latter contexts is palpable. But again, Spenser's Ovidianism has been felt to be of a different order, and he is not often mentioned in the same breath as these authors. Partly, this is understandable. *The Faerie Queene* is an eye-wateringly violent poem, but its fierce wars are allegorical. In other words, violence is not 'for its own sake' in the provocative way that it seems to be in the other works

---

60 See Syrithe Pugh, *Spenser and Ovid* (Aldershot: Ashgate, 2005), Chapter 2 (esp. pp. 42–5). Pugh foregrounds affinities between Spenser and Ovid in the area of sexual ethics. She acknowledges the disorderly influence of the libido but her focus is on the 'high ethical valuation of love and concern for the individual' that she finds to be characteristic of both the *Metamorphoses* and *The Faerie Queene*. As I shall argue, Spenser's comic handling of amorous themes affirms rather than negates this high valuation.

61 See David Hopkins, 'Dryden and Ovid's "Wit out of Season"', in *Ovid Renewed: Ovidian Influences on Literature and Art from the Middle Ages to the Twentieth Century*, ed. Charles Martindale (Cambridge: Cambridge University Press, 1988), pp. 167–90 (pp. 171–8).

Spenser and the comic Renaissance 53

I have just mentioned. Yet, as I shall argue in the next chapter, violence is frequently comic in *The Faerie Queene*, and Spenser can be seen to take his cue from Ovid in exploring the ironies of gratuitous gore. Most battles and bloody squirmishes in Spenser's epic are ostensibly about 'right versus wrong', but this moral clarity is characteristically undermined. Sometimes the moral point is to see just how similar right and wrong look when locking swords, or to reflect, as Ovid often does, on the indistinguishability of heroic action from crude animal aggression.[62] One further aspect of Ovid's comic influence that should be mentioned here relates to his authorial presence. Spenser's playful authorial personae (discussed in the Introduction) owe a significant debt to Ovid. In particular, the digressive narrative structure that *The Faerie Queene* shares with the *Metamorphoses* entails some characteristic ironies. On one hand, frequent segues between storylines can seem to supplant authorial prerogative with the principle of chance; on the other, they draw attention to the author's deft handling of multiplicitous materials. Spenser's authorial persona in *The Faerie Queene* plays upon both these impressions, sometimes disavowing control over his fiction (claiming incomplete information or feigning servitude to his sources, for example), and at other times teasing the reader (by abandoning a storyline at a critical or erotically charged moment) or implying that moral interpretation is a more straightforward matter than it really is. Sometimes the narrator will be overcome with emotion, sharing the plight of his characters or sharing their limitations. Chaucer and Ariosto use these devices too, but the primary model for such literary personae is Ovid.

For example, the *Amores* opens with a joke: the poet was about to write a heroic poem about war, when Cupid (laughing) stole a foot off his second line and turned the poem into elegiac verse about love. The poet has no choice but to write about love because love is in control of the poet. This kind of self-referential irony is also a feature of the *Metamorphoses*. On one hand, there is a tacit (this time self-flattering) analogy between cosmic and literary creativity: the gods manipulate mortals, and Ovid manipulates the gods. On the other hand, the authorial narrator recedes into the background as different characters tell stories (one of whom, ironically, is scathing about fame-seeking storytellers).[63] In other words,

---

62 On comic violence in *The Faerie Queene* (and ironies specific to allegorical violence), see Chapter 2.

63 In the story of Achelous and Hercules, Achelous asks his audience to believe him, claiming 'I seek no fame from fiction' (*Met* IX.30–65). On one hand, this claim is

54 *Comic Spenser*

Ovid is in creative control, even to the point of enjoying the pretence that he is *not* in control. Yet his jurisdiction as an author stops short of impinging on the reader's interpretative freedom. Beyond simple didactic lessons such as 'never underestimate a god's power!' and 'appearances can be deceptive!', the stories of the *Metamorphoses* are left to speak for themselves. One might well conclude that the poem's unheroic ethos entails (or, more accurately, arises out of) scepticism about moral certainties.

Of course, Spenser wrote in the shadow of the *Ovide moralisé* tradition, which allegorised the *Metamorphoses* in defiance of its open-endedness. Ironically, the desire to 'fix' meaning for didactic purposes drew attention to the Ovidian text's openness to interpretation – its adaptability to different readings. The tension between allegory's moral utility and its interpretative openness is generally regarded as a source of Protestant anxiety, but for Spenser it is precisely the 'gap' between sententious conclusions and conflicting interpretative possibilities that is morally productive. *The Faerie Queene* challenges the reader to look hard for meaning, and to question easy assumptions. Arguably, it is when Spenser's narrator is at his most naïve, prescriptive, or idealising that *The Faerie Queene* is most 'Ovidian' – which is to say, evasive and ironic.

Medieval humour

In the words of Helen Cooper, 'whenever you have a gap between what Classical writers were doing and what Renaissance writers do, it is almost always because of what happened in between.'[64] Humanists often wrote about their engagement with ancient civilisation in terms of a break with the medieval past, which they characterised as a time of ignorance before the arrival of learning. Nevertheless, the Middle Ages profoundly influenced the art, literature, and culture of the Renaissance. To some extent medieval influences were unconscious, but they were also there to be knowingly exploited, improved upon, and revered. Sidney's praise of

---

corroborated by the fact that his story (in which his shape-shifting antics fail him during a battle with Hercules) shows him in a comically unheroic light. Yet this dismissal of fiction from a fictional (and moreover fabulous) character reminds us of the fame-seeking author who is really pulling the strings.

64 Helen Cooper, *Shakespeare and the Middle Ages: An Inaugural Lecture Delivered at the University of Cambridge, April 2005* (Cambridge: Cambridge University Press, 2006), p. 11.

Spenser and the comic Renaissance 55

Chaucer (specifically, his *Troilus and Criseyde*) captures this paradoxical relationship of assumed superiority and indebtedness: 'truly I know not whether to marvel more, either that he in that misty time could see so clearly, or that we in this clear age go so stumblingly after him'.[65]

Quintessentially medieval genres such as chivalric romance, the religious lyric, and saints' lives presented early modern authors with material ripe for turning on its head in the light of new cultural values and religious convictions. But making fun of the excesses of errant knights and corrupt priests was a medieval prerogative, too, and later authors borrowed freely from comic medieval genres such as burlesque romance, ecclesiastical satire, beast fable, fabliau, and sermon exempla.[66] Medieval ecclesiastical satire was especially popular because it seemed to anticipate the position of the Reformers, and Chaucer and Langland were sometimes enlisted as proto-Protestants on these grounds.[67] Polemical works of the English Reformation, from John Bale's dramas attacking Roman Catholicism in the 1530s to *The Faerie Queene* in the 1590s, owe an obvious debt to the personification allegory of *Piers Plowman*, to Chaucer's portraits of hypocritical and greedy churchmen in the *Canterbury Tales*, and to the morality play tradition with its pantheon of profane and charismatic Vice figures.

Medieval literature was also known (which is to say, disapproved of as well as enjoyed) for its scatological and bawdy humour. Chaucer was the most revered English author of the period ('the fine young courtier', wrote Thomas Wilson, 'wil talke nothing but *Chaucer*'), but he was also looked down upon for his 'flat scurrilitie'.[68] The pleasure to be gained from Chaucer's irreverent sense of humour evidently vied with the moral value of his satirical portraits and the philosophical depth

---

65 *Defence*, p. 44.
66 On burlesque responses to the 'solemn piety of the saintly legends and devout tales' see George H. McKnight, *Middle English Humorous Tales in Verse* (New York: AMS Press, 1972 [1913]), p. xi.
67 Foxe famously referred to Chaucer as 'a right Wicleuian'; John Foxe, *The Unabridged Acts and Monuments Online* (Sheffield: Digital Humanities Institute, 2011), 1583 edn, Book 7, p. 863. Available from https://dhi.ac.uk/foxe/ (accessed May 2019); henceforth *Acts and Monuments*.
68 *Rhetorique*, p. 162. The phrase 'flat scurrilitie' is Harington's; 'A Preface', in *OF*, p. 12 (line 18). Stephanie Trigg rightly observes that Chaucer was loved in the Renaissance for his 'preeminence in romantic and courtly poetry', although her suggestion that his reputation for comedy and bawdy humour only became dominant in the eighteenth century finds plenty of contradiction in Brewer's *Critical Heritage*; Stephanie Trigg, 'Chaucer's Influence and Reception', in *The Yale Companion to Chaucer*, ed. Seth Lerer (New Haven: Yale University Press, 2006), pp. 297–323.

56 *Comic Spenser*

of his allegorical dream visions. Robert Greene disapprovingly notes Chaucer's popularity despite (or, more likely, because of) his 'broad' and 'homely' style. In *Greene's Vision*, a work of repentance for the author's own literary transgressions, Greene has Chaucer come back from the dead to point out that bawdy jokes never harmed his reputation: 'who hath bin more canonised for his workes, than Sir *Geffrey Chaucer*. What *Green?*'.[69]

As Esolen argues, the Elizabethan association of Chaucer with scurrility and irreverence bears implications for Spenser as a Chaucerian poet.[70] When Spenser refers to his master as the 'well of English vndefyled' (*FQ* IV.ii.32.8), he echoes a traditional compliment beginning most notably with Lydgate, who praised Chaucer for his 'gold dewe-dropis of rethorik so fyne'.[71] But both men neglect to mention those other Chaucerian words, 'arse', 'fart', and 'swyve'. As I have already observed, Spenser was evidently magnetised by this side of Chaucer. The Chaucerianism of *The Faerie Queene* ranges freely between both reputations, recalling the visionary, philosophical, and elegaic love poet as well as the caustically witty, earthy writer of 'mery tales'.[72]

Chaucer's notoriety as a humorist was founded not solely upon the *Canterbury Tales* but also on *Troilus and Criseyde*, which was regarded by some – largely on account of the character of Pandarus – as wanton and satirical.[73] *Troilus* is not a heroic poem primarily because it is about love rather than military deeds, but also because it mutes, and at times openly refutes, the whole notion of heroic dignity. Troilus's identity as a lover to a large extent facilitates this refutation: the world of the poem privileges the domestic sphere and individual psychology over the active world of the battlefield, and in doing so gives scope for unheroic humour.[74] This humour was subject to criticism, but, as I shall argue in Chapter 4, it influenced both Shakespeare and Spenser.

---

69 Brewer, *Critical Heritage*, p. 133.
70 Esolen, 'The Disingenuous Poet Laureate', p. 288.
71 Lydgate's phrase is from his *Troy Book*, excerpted in Brewer, *Critical Heritage*, p. 47. See also *FQ* VII.vii.9.3–4.
72 See Introduction.
73 See R. H. Bowers, 'Chaucer's *Troilus* as an Elizabethan "Wanton Book"', *NQ*, 7 (1960), 370–1. Notwithstanding his admiration for *Troilus and Criseyde*, Sidney spoke of the poem's 'great wants'; *Defence*, p. 44.
74 J. A. Burrow argues that these traits typify the literature of this period; *Ricardian Poetry: Chaucer, Gower, Langland and the 'Gawain' Poet* (London: Routledge & Kegan Paul, 1971), pp. 93–129 (pp. 99–100).

Spenser and the comic Renaissance

The inclusion of humorous and conspicuously low elements in serious contexts, the parodic treatment of revered subjects, the twilight between jest and earnest, and a grotesquely material imagination have come to be regarded as medieval trademarks. As we shall see, comic gestures and perspectives infiltrated romance, religious drama, sermons, and the margins of sacred texts. Such eccentricities were formally repudiated in the sixteenth century on the grounds of indecorum from a literary and aesthetic point of view and irreverence from a religious point of view, but such objections did not always make much difference to the *practice* of Renaissance authors, which was profoundly influenced by the medieval refusal to limit humour to designated genres.

It is telling that medieval and Renaissance literary works were, from the neoclassical perspective, similarly transgressive. Although Dryden was a great defender of Chaucer and numbered 'The Knight's Tale' among England's '*Epique*' poems, he criticised the medieval habit of mingling 'trivial Things with those of greater Moment'.[75] In the mid-seventeenth century, influential critics such as Thomas Hobbes underlined the obligation of epic to eschew humour: 'The delight of an *Epique* Poeme consisteth not in mirth, but admiration'.[76] As mentioned in the Introduction, Spenser was criticised in this period for his 'medieval' eccentricities. And he was not alone. Several generations after Dryden, Joseph Warton listed some of the greatest poets of the Italian Renaissance alongside Chaucer for their failure to distinguish comic from serious subject matter:

> On the revival of literature, the first writers seemed not to have observed any SELECTION in their thoughts and images. Dante, Petrarch, Boccace, and Ariosto make very sudden transitions from the sublime to the ridiculous. Chaucer, in his Temple of Mars, among many pathetic pictures, has brought in a strange line,
>
> The coke is scalded for all his long ladell.[77]

---

75 John Dryden, 'Preface' to *Fables Ancient and Modern* (1700), in Brewer, *Critical Heritage*, Vol. I, pp. 160–72 (p. 168). Dryden maintains, however, that Chaucer does not offend as much as Ovid, who 'would certainly have made *Arcite* witty on his Death-bed' (p. 163).

76 Thomas Hobbes, 'Hobbes's Answer to the Preface' (1650), in Davenant, *Gondibert*, ed. Gladish, pp. 45–55.

77 Joseph Warton, 'Essay on the Genius and Writings of Pope', in Brewer, *Critical Heritage*, pp. 212–14. The reference is to 'The Knight's Tale', where among the intimidating wall paintings in the temple of Mars is an image of 'The cook yscalded, for al his longe ladel' (line 2020).

58 *Comic Spenser*

An even more striking disregard for decorum (or, in Warton's phrase, 'selection') marred the Elizabethan and Jacobean tragi-comic drama. In the words of Joseph Addison,

> The Tragi-Comedy, which is the Product of the English Theatre, is one of the most monstrous Inventions that ever entered into a Poet's Thoughts. An Author might as well think of weaving the Adventures of Aeneas and Hudibras into one poem, as of writing such a motly Piece of Mirth and Sorrow.[78]

The term 'tragi-comedy' is now chiefly used to refer to the comic play that threatens to be, or partially is, tragic (*The Merchant of Venice, The Winter's Tale, Cymbeline, Pericles*). But many early modern tragedies are notable for their inclusion of comic scenes, too (*Hamlet, The Jew of Malta, Dr Faustus, Troilus and Cressida*).[79] Addison spoke for many of his contemporaries when he condemned such combinations of 'horror and humour' as 'monstrous'. Notwithstanding his own reservations, Johnson anticipated Romantic praise for such eclecticism. He refers to Shakespeare's practice of combining humour and seriousness as 'contrary to the rules of criticism', but also compliments him for 'exhibiting the real state of sublunary nature, which partakes of good and evil, joy and sorrow, mingled with endless variety of proportion and innumerable modes of combination'.[80]

Of course, the incorporation of humour in otherwise non-comic contexts was not restricted to the medieval period; classical authors could be similarly inclusive. But some neoclassical critics regarded the receptivity of the Elizabethans to this aspect of their classical sources as evidence that the age of Shakespeare had struggled to 'emerge from barbarity'.[81] Thus, where George Chapman's *Iliad* followed its Homeric source in being funny in places, Pope, in his later translation, was

---

78 *Spectator*, ed. G. Gregory Smith, 8 vols (London: J. M. Dent, 1897), Vol. I, p. 121; henceforth *Spectator*.
79 On the fluidity of generic boundaries in Elizabethan drama see Dillon, 'Elizabethan Comedy'; Lee Bliss, 'Pastiche, Burlesque, Tragicomedy', in *The Cambridge Companion to English Renaissance Drama*, ed. A. R. Braunmuller and Michael Hattaway, 2nd edn (Cambridge: Cambridge University Press, 2003), pp. 228–53 (p. 235); and Ros King, 'In Lieu of Democracy; or, How Not to Lose Your Head: Theatre and Authority in Renaissance England', in *Early Modern Tragicomedy*, ed. Subha Mukherji and Raphael Lyne (Cambridge: D. S. Brewer, 2007), pp. 84–100 (pp. 86, 91).
80 'Preface to Shakespeare', p. 66.
81 *Ibid.*, p. 81.

Spenser and the comic Renaissance 59

compelled to 'correct' his predecessors' lapses of decorum. In Jessica Wolfe's words, 'Chapman is far more comfortable with the persistently anti-heroic strains of Homeric epic than is his Augustan counterpart.'[82] For example, when Jove expresses reluctance to aid the Trojans in defiance of Juno's wishes, he appears in Chapman's translation as a hen-pecked husband:

> O, at this
> Juno will storme and all my powers inflame with contumelies.
> *Ever she wrangles, charging me in eare of all the Gods*
> That I am partiall still, that I adde the displeasing oddes
> Of my aide to the Ilians. Be gone then, lest she see.[83]

In an effort to elevate this passage, Pope replaces Chapman's 'Ever she wrangles' with 'Juno's fierce Alarms', and altogether omits Jove's wariness of being scolded in front of the other gods. Chapman's furtive 'Be gone then, lest she see' is replaced in Pope's translation with 'Go, lest the haughty Partner of my Sway / With jealous eyes thy close access survey.'[84] Pope similarly dignifies Homer's heroes: when Ajax's valour on the battlefield is compared to the stubbornness of a greedy ass trespassing on a crop, he replaces Chapman's 'dull mill ass' (XI.485) with 'Beast' (XI.682). And where Pope's beast 'Crops the tall Harvest' (XI.685), Chapman writes: 'simply he will eat … / not stirring till his panch be full' (XI.487–90), and so on.

As Wolfe demonstrates, Chapman was consciously receptive to Homer's satirical, unheroic, and humorous side. His annotations draw attention to this aspect of the original text, advertising his translation's fidelity to the 'sharpnes of wit in our Homer.'[85] Far from 'struggling to

---

82 Jessica Wolfe, 'Chapman's Ironic Homer', *College Literature*, 35 (2008), 151–86 (p. 170). On Chapman's attraction to Homer's sense of the admirable as well as foolish aspects of human nature, and his penchant for juxtaposing 'high and low' and 'jarringly different arenas of human experience', see in particular pp. 163, 175.
83 Homer, *Chapman's Homer: 'The Iliad', 'The Odyssey', and the Lesser Homerica*, trans. George Chapman, ed. Allardyce Nicoll, 2nd edn, 2 vols, Bollingen Series, 41 (Princeton: Princeton University Press, 1956), Vol. I, 500–4 (my italics). Further references are given next to quotations in the text.
84 Homer, *Iliad* I.672–7, in *The 'Iliad' of Homer*, trans. Alexander Pope, ed. Maynard Mack, 2 vols (London: Methuen, 1967), Vol. I. Further references are given next to quotations in the text. On Pope's apprehension of problematic comic elements in the *Iliad* see his annotations at II.255n and XVI.1032n.
85 Wolfe argues that Chapman wanted to bolster the authority of his translation by illuminating this aspect of Homer; 'Chapman's Ironic Homer', p. 159 (cf. Chapman's annotations to *Iliad* XXIII.489–581).

60   *Comic Spenser*

emerge' from the Middle Ages, Renaissance authors such as Chapman consciously play on the borderline between theoretical rules and actual freedoms and between mythic ideals and unheroic realities. As Ros King has shrewdly observed, tragicomedy 'developed in *full knowledge that it was contravening classical laws* of writing for the theatre'.[86] Ostensibly speaking from a more enlightened period in history, Addison deemed Renaissance tragicomedy 'monstrous'. But Sidney had already called it 'mongrel'.[87] Sidney could say this *and* write a pastoral romance that broke the rules: the *Old Arcadia*, not unlike the mongrel tragi-comedies Sidney describes, combines seriousness with farce and shows princes and clowns rubbing shoulders. And of course, the contention of this study as a whole is that Spenser's inclusion of humour within the frame of epic was self-conscious. Hobbes's assertion that epic poems are not supposed to be funny merely echoed sixteenth-century theory. As I shall argue below, neoclassical critics who passed judgement on *The Faerie Queene*'s 'medieval' aspects – its grotesque and fantastic romance tropes, its archaism, its inclusion of burlesque and fabliauesque humour, its romance digressiveness – were grappling not with naïve indecorum but with a sophisticated campaign to provoke and amuse.

Chivalry, romance, and humour

Love is one of the great comic subjects of the Renaissance, and, alongside Ovid, medieval romance was the richest source of erotic plots and tropes. Helen Cooper has emphasised the number of medieval romances in circulation during the sixteenth century, and the extent to which 'Renaissance comedies are imbued with romance elements'.[88] In medieval romance (as in the *Metamorphoses*), *eros* is often an anarchic influence: the high idealism of the chivalric code typically creates tensions between moral duty and self-interest, between secular and spiritual heroism, and between courtesy and desire. In *Le Morte d'Arthur*, Lancelot 'meddles' with his opponents on the battlefield but he also 'meddles' with the king's wife.[89] Of course, such tensions can be explored without

---

86 King, 'In Lieu of Democracy', p. 86 (my italics).
87 *Defence*, p. 46. For Addison see p. 58 above.
88 Cooper, *Shakespeare and the Middle Ages*, p. 24.
89 Compare Thomas Malory, *Le Morte d'Arthur* X.1–2 ('none of you all meddyll with this knight') and XIX.11–12 ('in no wyse he wolde meddyll with the queen'), in *The Works of Sir Thomas Malory*, ed. Eugène Vinaver, 2nd edn, 3 vols (Oxford: Clarendon Press, 1973 [1967]); henceforth *Works of Malory*. I am grateful to Helen Cooper for this observation.

Spenser and the comic Renaissance   61

humour, and can have tragic consequences. But the hallmarks of medieval romance – nostalgia, hyperbole, marvel, erotic interest – are fertile grounds for humour and irony. Accordingly, the genre is susceptible to lampoons such as 'The Tale of Sir Thopas', *Don Quixote*, and *The Knight of the Burning Pestle*.[90]

Significantly, however, 'real' medieval romances were capable of making fun of their own excesses through internal self-parody – as many critics have observed.[91] But the distinction between convention and pastiche is not always clearly demarcated as it is in lampoon. Whereas the description of Sir Thopas's physical excellence is obviously silly ('Whit was his face as payndemayn / His lippes rede as rose'; lines 725–6), hyperbole in less explicitly facetious contexts is liable to involve an *element* of absurdity. Likewise, romance conventions such as mistaken identity and coincidence can be extremely far-fetched without actually tipping over into lampoon. This more nuanced and ambiguous relationship between chivalric romance and humour was to influence Renaissance treatments of erotic and heroic themes in a range of contexts beyond explicit satire. Sidney's handling of romance tropes in the *Old Arcadia*, for example, continually borders on pastiche and farce. A dominant theme of this pastoral romance is artifice, and, in turn, its language and its handling of romance tropes are deliberately, and at times comically, contrived. The work is full of scenarios of mistaken identity and gender confusion, hyperbolic descriptions of feminine beauty and masculine prowess, gratuitous depictions of violence, and clashes between altruistic and erotic motivations.[92] Spenser generates humour from all of these tropes, too, as I shall demonstrate in Chapters 2, 3, and 4.

---

90 Romance formulae are also parodied in 'The Miller's Tale', 'The Merchant's Tale', and 'The Nun's Priest's Tale'.

91 On humour in medieval romance see, for example, Helen Cooper, *The English Romance in Time: Transforming Motifs from Geoffrey of Monmouth to the Death of Shakespeare* (Oxford: Oxford University Press, 2004), pp. 19–21; Sarah Kay, 'Courts, Clerks, and Courtly Love', in *The Cambridge Companion to Medieval Romance*, ed. Roberta L. Krueger (Cambridge: Cambridge University Press, 2000), pp. 81–96 (esp. pp. 87–92); *Arthurian Literature XIX: Comedy in Arthurian Literature*, ed. Keith Busby and Roger Dalrymple (Cambridge: D. S. Brewer, 2003); Judith Weiss, '"The Courteous Warrior": Epic, Romance and Comedy in *Boeve de Haumtone*', in *Boundaries in Medieval Romance*, ed. Neil Cartlidge (Cambridge: D. S. Brewer, 2008), pp. 149–60; Raymond Cormier, 'Humour in the *Roman d'Eneas*', *Florilegium*, 7 (1985), 129–44; and Wim Tigges, 'Romance and Parody', in *Companion to Middle English Romance*, ed. Henk Aertsen and Alasdair A. MacDonald (Amsterdam: VU University Press, 1990), pp. 129–51.

92 In these respects, Sidney was influenced by medieval romance (for example, the *Amadis de Gaule*) as well as classical and Renaissance European models (such as Heliodorus's

62 *Comic Spenser*

In contrast to the classical pastoral world of Sidney's *Arcadia*, however, Spenser's fairyland draws specifically on Arthurian romance, and (like *Orlando furioso*) embraces the fabulous and magical aspects of the chivalric romance tradition. Alongside the supernatural machinery of classical epic (gods and goddesses, the underworld, and so on), *The Faerie Queene* accommodates medieval fairies, giants, dragons, dwarfs, witches, and magicians. As I have argued (and as this study will continue to demonstrate), Spenser orchestrated this clash of high-brow and low-brow worlds. The 'Letter to Raleigh' insists on the ideal compatibility of Arthurian romance and classical epic; and indeed, Arthur was the legendary ancestor of the Tudor line (LR, line 12). Spenser was working with established tropes because the language of political loyalty in the Elizabethan court borrowed freely from medieval romance.[93] At the same time, however, Arthurian romance was considered by many to be laughably nostalgic, and fairies the stuff of village superstition – not epic poetry. E. K. is the mouthpiece of conservatism when he dismisses the 'Authors of King Arthure' as 'fine fablers and lowd lyers'.[94] As I shall argue in chapters to come, the resemblance of Prince Arthur to the fairy-queen-enamoured Sir Thopas at several significant junctures in his quest testifies to Spenser's exploitation of romance's equivocal reputation.

At the risk of stating the obvious, my point is that the naïve, fairytale components of fairy queens and fire-breathing dragons did not gradually become apparent as literary tastes changed (as neoclassical critics implied); these things were considered silly and even objectionable in Spenser's own time.[95] And surely an element of ironic complicity in the audience's suspension of disbelief has always been intrinsic to the way

---

An *Aethiopian History* and Ariosto's *Orlando furioso*); see Sir Philip Sidney, *The Old Arcadia*, ed. and intro. Katherine Duncan-Jones (Oxford: Oxford University Press, 1999), pp. x–xiii.

93 See Roy Strong, *The Cult of Elizabeth: Elizabethan Portraiture and Pageantry* (London: Thames and Hudson, 1977). Puttenham defended Arthurian romance and fabulous subject matter as legitimate 'historical' material, adaptable by poets for moral purposes; *ECE*, pp. 42–4.

94 Edmund Spenser, *The Shepheardes Calender*, in *Shorter Poems*, pp. 3–215: 'Aprill' (gloss to line 120), p. 82; hereafter *SC*.

95 On neoclassical criticism see Introduction. As Harvey's 'Hobgoblin' jibe (see p. 18 above) suggests, Elizabethan authors both mocked and enjoyed chivalric romance for the same reasons that later readers did: it is full of fantasy, marvel, and gratuitous love interests. Chivalric romance was also associated with England's Catholic past. Nashe spoke of 'the fantasticall dreames of those exiled Abbie-lubbers, from whose idle fantasticall pens proceeded those worne out impressions of the feyned no where

Spenser and the comic Renaissance   63

romance tropes horrify, engage, and please. Speaking of the 'grimly comic' episode of the St Michael's Mount giant in Malory's *Le Morte d'Arthur*, Donald L. Hoffman describes the humour attaching to mythic monsters (and grossly fabulous depictions in medieval romance more generally) as the carnivalesque 'comedy of the forbidden'. Hoffman links this sort of humour to catharsis, or the 'sacral comedy of cleansing and purification'.[96] This interpretation is certainly resonant for the dragon-slaying episode that concludes 'The Legend of Holiness' – an episode whose naïve and grotesque comedy is usually overlooked or defensively excused.[97]

The main way of 'excusing' Spenser's use of medieval romance motifs has been to call attention to his moral allegory. The humour of Spenser's commitment to an unfashionable genre has been acknowledged from precisely this point of view. Several critics, observing that Spenser's engagement with chivalric romance verges on pastiche and burlesque, conclude that this pervasive sense of irony stems from his sophisticated appropriation of an overtly popular genre. In the words of William Nelson, *The Faerie Queene* is 'a poem of the High Renaissance deliberately dressed in an outworn fashion'. Likewise, A. D. Nuttall has called it 'a romance made paper-thin, made evidently unreal'.[98] Writing three decades apart, both critics agree that the comic irony of Spenser's 'mock-gothic' narrative has moral utility: its deliberate naïveté (monsters, marvels, maidens) discourages our investment in the poem's fictional surfaces, prompting us to seek its deeper meaning. Nuttall cites Spenser's Protestant anxiety about visual art, and Nelson emphasises the humanist need for moral utility to prevail over (or through) delightful fictions. Thus Spenser was compelled to advertise the façade of his narrative by engaging a 'silly'

---

acts, of Arthur of the rounde table, Arthur of little Brittaine, sir Tristram, Hewon of Burdeaux, the Squire of low degree, the foure sons of Amon, with infinite others'; Thomas Nashe, *Anatomie of Absurditie* (London, 1589), in *The Works of Thomas Nashe*, ed. Ronald B. McKerrow (Oxford: Basil Blackwell, 1958), p. 11, cited by Nelson, *Fact or Fiction*, p. 75. The classic diatribe against chivalric romance is that of Roger Ascham, who summarised *Le Morte d'Arthur* as 'open manslaughter, and bold bawdrye'; *The Scholemaster* (Menston: Scolar Press, 1967 [1570]), p. 27. On the equivocal reputation of chivalric romance in the Renaissance (especially Arthurian) see Matthew Woodcock, *Fairy in 'The Faerie Queene': Renaissance Elf-Fashioning and Elizabethan Myth-Making* (Aldershot: Ashgate, 2004), pp. 88–91.

96 Donald L. Hoffman, 'Malory and the English Comic Tradition', in Busby and Dalrymple, *Comedy in Arthurian Literature*, pp. 177–88 (p. 178). On comic monsters see Bakhtin, *Rabelais and His World*, p. 91.

97 See further Chapter 2.

98 Nelson, *Fact or Fiction*, p. 79; Nuttall, 'Spenser and Elizabethan Alienation', pp. 214–15.

64   *Comic Spenser*

genre and signalling its limitations with 'burlesque, hyperbole, bathos, and patent illogic'.[99]

Undeniably, Spenser establishes an ironic tension between his chivalric fiction and its allegorical undercurrents. But Nuttall's argument that this was driven by anxiety is open to challenge. So too is Nelson's assumption that humour attaching to Spenser's provocative popularisation of his epic poem operates in the service of undercutting those same popular elements. A counterargument is that Spenser exploited the licence that allegory lends to the childish and fantastic imagination in order to poke fun at the 'High Renaissance' and its mythic ideals. In doing so, he ironised the secular romance tradition, but he was also responding to (and surely inspired by) the current of humour and self-parody already present within it.

For example, Spenser's allegory explores several ironic analogies popularised by the chivalric romance tradition. One of these is between martial endeavour and sexual passion – an age-old association with multiple roots (Cupid's arrows, the military metaphor of the Song of Solomon, the phallic symbolism of the sword, the horse as an emblem of passion, and so on). Although not exclusive to medieval romance (both Ovid and Apuleius use this analogy in bawdy contexts) it was certainly reinforced by the chivalric tradition with its ideal of 'service to ladies'. The association of heroic action and sexual desire could be subtle (as it is when Malory repeats the verb 'meddle') or heavy-handed (as it is when the chaste but hopeful Sir Thopas gallops around on his horse as a form of erotic substitution).[100] As well as being potentially analogous in a bawdy sense, the relationship between heroic action and romantic love was also, of course, one of legitimate association – as Spenser signals when he announces his subject as 'Fierce warres and faithfull loues' (Proem I, 1.9). However, as we shall see in Chapters 3 and 4, the relationship between loving and fighting in *The Faerie Queene* – as in medieval chivalric romance – is always tense, often ironic, and on significant occasions overtly comic. Moreover, Spenser (following Ariosto, who is notably inclined to capitalise on the bawdy possibilities of chivalric

---

99 Nuttall, 'Spenser and Elizabethan Alienation', p. 212; Nelson, *Fact or Fiction*, Chapter 3, pp. 56–72 and, for the quotation, p. 77.

100 See 'Sir Thopas', lines 772–7. While the horse is a traditional symbol of passion, interestingly Aristotle proposes a physiological link between horseriding and desire; *Problemata*, trans. E. S. Forster (Oxford: Clarendon Press, 1927), IV.877 b.15, retrieved from *Internet Archive*, https://archive.org/stream/worksofaristotle07arisuoft/ worksofaristotle07arisuoft_djvu.txt (accessed May 2019).

Spenser and the comic Renaissance 65

action) may be seen to exploit the phallic associations of the sword, the erotic metaphor of battle, and the horse as a figure for unruly passion.[101] Another ironic medieval romance analogy is the figuration of romantic love as religious devotion, a well-known courtly-love trope used, for example, by Chrétien de Troyes in his portrayal of Lancelot's adulterous affair with Guinevere.[102] Spenser (in the equally well-established tradition of biblical and medieval religious allegory) inverts this analogy in 'The Legend of Holiness' by figuring a spiritual quest in terms of romantic loyalties. However, as I argue in Chapter 3, Spenser generates sustained, acute irony from the customary tension in secular romance between moral duty and sexual desire in order to remind us, often very wittily, that holiness *actually involves the body*.

The high-mindedness of the courtly 'religion of love' tradition inevitably provoked comic and ironic responses both in the Middle Ages and in the Renaissance. Guillaume de Lorris establishes such a religion in the first half of *Le Roman de la rose* only for Jean de Meun to travesty it in his continuation of the poem, where the mysterious 'rose' sought by the dreamer plainly represents female genitalia. If Spenser's Garden of Adonis offers a serious rewriting of de Meun's irreverent 'religion', the rose of Belphoebe's chastity (III.v.51) is entirely in tune with the comic tension between sublimation and reductive literalism in the final pages of the *Roman*, as I argue in Chapter 5. Cervantes, on the other hand, recognised that the sublimation of desire is funniest not when it is undercut by physical realities but when it is taken at its word. One of Don Quixote's many failures to imitate the knights errant of medieval romance is that – notwithstanding the strong carnal impulses of his horse – he is (like Chaucer's Thopas) a genuinely chaste hero.

The overt, debunking satire of *Don Quixote* is often regarded as chivalric romance's death knell – the pastiching of an old and worn-out genre from a more sophisticated vantage point. And the Protestant moral allegory of *The Faerie Queene* would seem to offer a diametrically opposite strategy for overhauling an obsolete genre. In fact, both Cervantes and Spenser were at least partly inspired by medieval traditions of parody.[103] Subversive recontextualisations of romance formulae in Renaissance

---

101 See pp. 96–7, 118–20, 131–3 below.
102 On this tradition, see Kay, 'Courts, Clerks, and Courtly Love', pp. 81–2.
103 As L. A. Murillo points out, if Cervantes was sending up a somewhat absurd literary form, he was also inspired by the time-honoured proximity of romance and humour; 'Don Quixote as Renaissance Epic', in *Cervantes and the Renaissance*, ed. Michael D. McGaha (Easton, PA: Juan de la Cuesta, 1980), pp. 51–70 (p. 54).

66 *Comic Spenser*

literature may announce a break with the past, but they can equally testify to a keen responsiveness to ironies embedded within the medieval romance tradition.

Christianity and humour

Despite the attractive idea of a 'Merry England' unburdened by post-Reformation notions of propriety, it was during the Middle Ages that 'Christ never laughed' was proverbial. As a late-fourteenth-century Wycliffite sermon reminds us: 'of Cristis lawthyng [laughing] we reden never in Holy Writt, but of his myche penaunse, teris, and schedynge of blod'.[104] By contrast, laughter looked too much like worldly enjoyment and irreverence. This view finds support among the Church Fathers: St Basil, among others, asserted that laughter could never be appropriate in a fallen world. Against such a background, it is not surprising that Christ's warning about the abuse of worldly position, 'Wo be to you that now laugh; for ye shal wayle and weepe' (Luke 6:25), came to be interpreted literally as an injunction against laughter.[105]

This having been said, the association of medieval England with mirth and games has some grounding in fact – as vocal hostility toward laughter during this period testifies. In *Rabelais and His World*, Bakhtin describes the medieval world in terms of a division between 'official' and 'folk' culture: temporarily inverting the god-fearing, prohibitive, and hierarchical worldview of Church and State was the democratic, fearless, and irreverent laughter of the marketplace and carnival. Critics since Bakhtin have challenged this dichotomy, arguing that these

---

104 Anon., 'A Sermon against Miracle-Plays', in *Reliquiæ antiquæ: Scraps from Ancient Manuscripts*, ed. Thomas Wright and James Orchard Halliwell, 2 vols (London: William Pickering, 1841), Vol. I, pp. 42–57 (p. 43).

105 'The Christian ... ought not to laugh nor even to suffer laugh makers'; St Basil of Caesarea, 'On the Perfection of the Life of Solitaries', in *St Basil: Letters and Selected Works* (1895), trans. Blomfield Jackson, Vol. VIII of *Nicene and Post-Nicene Fathers*, second series, 14 vols, ed. Philip Schaff and Henry Wace (Buffalo, NY: Chistian Literature, 1886–1900). Revised and edited for New Advent by Kevin Knight, http://newadvent.org/fathers/3202022.htm (accessed May 2019). On the Church Fathers see M. A. Screech and Ruth Calder, 'Some Renaissance Attitudes to Laughter', in *Humanism in France*, ed. A. H. T. Levi (Manchester: Manchester University Press, 1970), pp. 216–28; and Terry Lindvall, 'Toward a Divine Comedy: A Plagiarized History, Theology and Physiology of Christian Faith and Laughter', *Lamp-Post of the Southern California C. S. Lewis Society*, 27 (2003), 12–31. For a literal interpretation of Luke see Anthony Munday, *A Second and Third Blast of Retrait from Plaies and Theatres* (New York: Garland, 1973 [1580]), pp. 11–12.

Spenser and the comic Renaissance 67

two worlds were in fact inseparable. In the words of Aron Gurevich, 'carnival elements were not cordoned off but latent in official culture'.[106] And indeed, speaking from the margins of the Church, the Wycliffite preacher spoke out against laughter because humour was a recognised feature of religious drama. In his view, the plays and pageants that were performed as part of the Church's seasonal rituals were all about impious *entertainment.*

Of course, many medieval religious plays were not funny (the Wycliffite sermon is equally outspoken about the impiety of weeping at such spectacles), but many, even on the most sacred of themes, incorporated 'japing'.[107] Today, we are perhaps most familiar with the 'savage farce' of Vice figures in medieval morality plays – charismatic personifications of evil who tempt the unguarded to do wicked things. This form of black humour continued after the Reformation, via Machiavellian stage villains such as Richard III (who compares himself to a medieval Vice figure) or smooth-tongued holy men such as Spenser's Archimago, whose austere hermitage is actually a hotbed of temptations.[108]

Other examples of humour in medieval religious drama are more disorientating for a modern audience, and more distinctively 'medieval'. For example, 'savage farce' of another kind infiltrates the York Play of the Crucifixion when blaspheming soldiers torment Christ. As David Bevington observes, the play devolves into 'gruesomely humorous attention to detail' as the executioners become absorbed in the mechanical details of erecting Christ on the cross.[109] A more overt and sustained combination of farcical humour and high religious seriousness may be found in the *Second Shepherds' Play*. This play features three very English shepherds (who complain about the weather and their wives) and, intriguingly, dramatises a grotesque parody of the Gospel Nativity story (in which sheep-stealers hide a lamb in a cradle) before moving on to a serious and moving treatment of the true miracle.

Humour in such contexts appears to have fulfilled several functions. As V. A. Kolve emphasises, when sinful characters laughed at and mocked Christ, the audience's appalled fascination at such wickedness was supposed to be morally rousing. This was certainly the rationale for

---

106 Gurevich, *Medieval Popular Culture*, p. 180.
107 Anon., 'A Sermon against Miracle-Plays', p. 51.
108 The phrase 'savage farce' is used by Verna A. Foster, *The Name and Nature of Tragicomedy* (Aldershot: Ashgate, 2004), p. 40. On the neglected comic function of Archimago, see further Chapter 2.
109 David Bevington, ed., *Medieval Drama* (Boston, MA: Houghton Mifflin, 1975), p. 569.

68 *Comic Spenser*

plays featuring comically wicked Vice figures: the audience laughed at them, not with them.[110] Moreover, such laughter did not just reprove evil, it could render it (temporarily at least) unthreatening and powerless.[111] Relevant, too, is Maynard Mack's observation about plays that combine religious mystery and domestic farce. Such incongruity, says Mack, seems 'calculated to impress us with the gap between the everyday world and its God'.[112] An illustration of this point may be found in the Wakefield Noah play.[113] Depicted as a belligerent harridan, Noah's wife is not wicked but she is unbelieving. The domestic caricature attaching to her character creates a lightning rod for the audience's own scepticism. Speaking of the *Second Shepherds' Play*, Mack further proposes that humour can widen the gap between the profane and the sacred in order to collapse it – by reminding us that the miracle of Christ's birth saved ordinary, fallible men.[114] Noah's wife is a social caricature drawn from the world of the play's medieval audience, and there is a place for her on the ark.

Another key function of humour – one that was explicitly acknowledged in the Middle Ages – was pleasure. While some (like the Wycliffite preacher) felt pleasure to be fundamentally impious, others defended it. Perhaps the most important defence of mirth (here meaning entertainment generally as well as laughter) in the Middle Ages is the fifteenth-century dialogue *Dives and Pauper*, in which the poor man Pauper argues that mirth is one of God's consoling gifts to man, and should not be shunned:

> pleyys & dauncis þat arn don principaly for deuocioun & honest merthe [to teche men to loue God þe more] … arn leful … þe reste & þe merthe & þe ese & þe welfare þat God hat ordeynyd in þe halyday is tokene of endeles reste, ioye & merthe & welfare in heuene.[115]

---

110 Kolve, *The Play Called Corpus Christi*, pp. 137–9. The argument that the audience is drawn to virtue by dramatisations of vice is refuted in 'A Sermon against Miracle-Plays', suggesting that it was a common defence.

111 Kolve, *The Play Called Corpus Christi*, pp. 141–2. See also Bakhtin, *Rabelais and His World*, p. 91.

112 Maynard Mack, 'The *Second Shepherds' Play*: A Reconsideration', *PMLA*, 93 (1978), 78–85 (p. 78). Kolve makes the same point; *The Play Called Corpus Christi*, p. 139.

113 Bevington, *Medieval Drama*, pp. 290–307.

114 Mack, 'The *Second Shepherds' Play*', p. 82.

115 *Dives and Pauper*, ed. Priscilla Heath Barnum, 3 vols, EETS, o.s. 275, 280, 323 (London: Oxford University Press, 1976–2004), Vol. I, pp. 293, 295 (Precept III, Chapter 17). For a discussion of this chapter see Kolve, *The Play Called Corpus Christi*, pp. 132–3.

Spenser and the comic Renaissance 69

Thomas More was to reiterate this argument in his *Dialogue of Comfort against Tribulation*. Addressing the argument that Christ never laughed, one interlocutor claims that to make up for it there will be a 'mery laughing hervest for euer' in heaven.[116]

Whether or not humour had any place in religious contexts, and moreover whether or not it had a place in Christian society more generally, became pressing questions after the Reformation. Partly, this was because Protestant England was divorcing itself from the traditions of the past, especially those associated with religious festivity and the visual representation of sacred subjects. Polemicists accused the medieval Church of allowing irreligious fun and games into its precincts: of praising fasting and self-denial while enjoying riotous feast days, of privileging holiday festivities over the preaching of scripture, and of staging entertaining plays in the name of religion.[117] The representation of Christ on the stage was condemned as heretical and idolatrous – to say nothing of humour in such contexts. In the words of Calvin, 'assoone as wee haue opened our mouthes for to speake of GOD, no merrie conceite or iest ought to enter in our matter'.[118]

But humour was also on the Reformers' minds because even as it was being driven out of some contexts, it was thriving in others. The Reformation led to a surge in theological satire, for example. The corrective energy of medieval morality plays was in some sense rerouted into the anti-Catholic polemical dramas of John Bale, and into prose tracts satirising the alleged abuses and hypocrisies of the Roman Church. Archimago formally belongs to this camp. Therefore, the traditional defence of humour as a moral instrument continued to be useful. Having acknowledged the old objection that Christ wept but never laughed, the Puritan theologian William Perkins (1558–1602) concluded that only two kinds of jesting should be acceptable to Christians: the moderate and harmless kind (Perkins does not elaborate, but presumably he excludes cruelty and profanity) and the kind used by the Prophets 'when they iested against wicked persons, yet so, as withall they sharply reprooved their sinnes'. Similarly, Calvin acknowledged a legitimate role for humour

116 Thomas More, *A Dialogue of Comfort against Tribulation*, ed. Louis L. Martz and Frank Manley (1976), Vol. XII of *The Yale Edition of the Complete Works of St Thomas More*, 15 vols (New Haven: Yale University Press, 1963–97), p. 42 (Book I, Chapter 13).
117 See for example Phillip Stubbes, *Anatomie of Abuses* (1583), ed. Frederick J. Furnivall (Vaduz: Kraus Reprint, 1965 [1877–9]), pp. 136–54 (Chapters 10–15).
118 John Calvin, 'John Calvyn unto the Readers', in Pierre Viret, *The Christian Disputations*, trans. John Brooke (London: Thomas East, 1579), sig. A5v.

70 *Comic Spenser*

in theological contexts, praising the French theologian Pierre Viret's use of 'merrie jestes' as a moral scourge.[119]

Early modern secular authors defended themselves with a version of the same argument. Faced with the success of public theatres and the growing book trade, moralists claimed that entertaining fictions directly opposed the interests and values of a Christian society. People who gawped and laughed at stage plays, for example, were pleasure-seeking, ill-mannered, and mocking – and, in big groups, dangerous. Authors were put on the defensive: the 'wantonest Poets of all', observed Webbe in his *Discourse of English Poetrie* (1586), 'in their most lacivious workes ... sought rather by that meanes to withdraw mens mindes ... from such foule vices than to allure them to imbrace such beastly follies as they detected'.[120] We should laugh *at*, not *with*, vice. A favourite analogy was the bee gathering honey from weeds: such was the reader or playgoer who could extract morality from dramatisations of vice and from seeming 'trifles'.[121]

Secular authors also defended the pleasure of amusement and cited its benefits, somewhat as *Dives and Pauper* had done. In his *Traité dv ris* (a treatise primarily concerned with the physiology of laughter), Joubert echoed the medieval argument that such pleasures are divinely ordained:

> Et d'autant qu'il convenoit à l homme d'etre animal sociable, politic & gracieus, asin que l'vn vequit & conversat avec ques l'autre plaisammant & beninemant, Dieu luy ha ordonné le Ris, pour recreacion parmy ses deportemans.

> (And since it is fitting for man to be a sociable, civil, and gracious animal, such that one might live and converse pleasantly and benignly with another, God has ordained, among man's enjoyments, laughter for his recreation in order to conveniently loosen the reins of his mind).[122]

---

119 Perkins, *A Direction for the Governement of the Tongve According to Gods Word*, in *The Workes of That Famovs and VVorthie Minister of Christ, in the Vniversitie of Cambridge, M. W. Perkins*, 3 vols (London, 1608–37), Vol. I, pp. 439–51 (p. 447); cited (from a later edition) by Fudge, 'Learning to Laugh', pp. 287–8. Calvin, 'John Calvyn unto the Readers', sig. A5v. On humour and the Reformation see further Keith Thomas, 'The Place of Laughter in Tudor and Stuart England', *TLS*, 21 (1977), 77–81.

120 *ECE*, Vol. I, p. 251.

121 See, for example, 'The Printer to the Reader', in George Gascoigne, *A Hundreth Sundrie Flowres*, ed. G. W. Pigman III (Oxford: Clarendon Press, 2000). This dual concern with laughter's frivolity on the one hand and its moral uses on the other can be found in the prefatory material of almost any Renaissance work that sets out to amuse.

122 *Traité*, p. 232 (see also p. 235) (Book III, Chapter 1); *Treatise*, pp. 94–5. Richard Mulcaster discusses the health benefits of laughter (and even recommends tickling children) in his treatise *Positions wherein those primitiue circvmstances be examined, which are necessarie for the training vp of children, either for skill in their booke, or*

Spenser and the comic Renaissance   71

Laughter may have been associated with disorderly behavior, but melancholy arguably posed the greater threat to Christian society. The spiritual danger of despair was particularly topical in the sixteenth century, and never far from the subject of faith. In *The Faerie Queene*, Red Crosse's spiritual sickness (anticipated by his 'solemn sadness' at the outset of his journey) is confirmed by his meeting with Despair at I.ix.35–54.[123] Simultaneously inflated and burdened by his sense of responsibility for virtuous action in the world, Red Crosse cannot, to quote Joubert, 'loosen the reins of his mind'. Indeed, he first appears to us in a vivid tableau of psychological conflict, 'pricking' and 'curb[ing]' his horse (i.1). As I argue in the following chapter, it is up to us as readers to laugh at him and repair the imbalance of his worldview – to place his heroic achievements in the context of human sinfulness, and his despair at sin in the context of the festivity and mirth of Canto xii.

The basic arguments for and against humour that I have reiterated were common to the Middle Ages and the Renaissance. Both Calvin's uneasiness about the impieties of laughter and his defence of moral satire, for example, have medieval precedents. But after the Reformation, these arguments were used in changed circumstances, often with a view to firmly distinguishing the present from the past. Although many Reformers were satirists, it is generally understood that Protestantism inaugurated a more self-consciously sober culture of devotion. The diminution of the medieval festive calendar and the habitual pairing of words such as 'gravity' and 'profit' in prefaces, sermons, and devotional literature of the sixteenth century reflected an increased emphasis on Christian piety as self-evidently non-comic terrain. Going a step further, the Puritan clergyman Richard Greenham asserted that 'The fear of the LORD is the beginning of wisdom … when a man is most merrie, he is nearest danger … The way to godlie mirth, is to feele godlie sorrow.'[124] The spiritual benefits of laughter were still acknowledged, but, tellingly, in secular, medical, and literary contexts rather than in works of theological orthodoxy such as *Dives and Pauper*.

---

    health in their bodie (London: Thomas Chard, 1581), Chapter 14, p. 64. See also Thomas Deloney's conventional defence of mirth, p. 13 above.

123 See Adam Potkay, 'Spenser, Donne, and the Theology of Joy', *SEL*, 46 (2006), 43–66.

124 'Of joy and sorrow', in *The workes of the reuerend and faithfull seruant of Iesus Christ M. Richard Greenham, minister and preacher of the Word of God* (London, 1601), p. 348; I am indebted for this quotation to Fudge, 'Learning to Laugh', p. 287.

72   *Comic Spenser*

Unheroic humanity

So far I have outlined some basic points pertaining to Christianity and humour, points that illustrate areas of common ground as well as a growing ideological gulf: by the mid-sixteenth century, the *Second Shepherd's Play* was part of a different world. In this section, however, we move away from the official story – the one recorded in polemical works and apologetic prefaces – to consider a more interesting (and difficult to calibrate) phenomenon: the profound influence upon the Renaissance of a medieval *sense of human folly*. The latter is inextricable from the religiosity of both periods, though by no means restricted to theological or devotional contexts. It is pervasive. As a number of historians and literary critics have shown us, the art and literature of the Middle Ages are characteristically adept at bringing the sacred and the profane into a single frame of reference, and of conveying a sense of humanity's smallness in the cosmos.[125] This inclusive and levelling perspective frequently found comic expression, preventing heroic works from being entirely heroic, tragic works from being entirely tragic, and sacred subjects from being entirely solemn. In 'The Knight's Tale', Theseus responds to the cousins' tragic rivalry with the rhetorical question, 'who may been a fool, but if he love?' (line 1799).[126] *Troilus and Criseyde* poses this same question on an epic scale, making Troilus's extreme emotions of agony and ecstasy the basis for tragedy as well as bedroom comedy. Neoclassical critics, as I have mentioned, saw this sort of descent from epic dignity as a failing; they wanted the (undeniably great) Chaucer to be more lofty and serious. But medieval humour was serious. Famously, *Troilus and Criseyde's* tragic end is followed by a transcendent vision: Troilus's spirit ascends to the eighth sphere and laughs at the 'litel spot of erthe' and all its vain concerns (V.1814–24). This moment amounts to a consoling if austere renunciation of the world and is, as Derek Brewer has argued, not comic so much as comedic.[127] Yet 'putting worldly affairs into perspective' and

---

125 See, for example, Kolve, *The Play Called Corpus Christi*; Erich Auerbach, *Mimesis: The Representation of Reality in Western Literature*, trans. Willard R. Trask (Princeton: Princeton University Press, 1991 [1953]), p. 154; Gurevich, *Medieval Popular Culture*, Chapter 6; and Michael Camille, *Image on the Edge: The Margins of Medieval Art* (London: Reaktion, 1992). This section is especially indebted to Burrow, *Ricardian Poetry*, Chapter 3.

126 See Burrow, *Ricardian Poetry*, p. 99.

127 Derek Brewer, 'Comedy and Tragedy in *Troilus and Criseyde*', in *The European Tragedy of Troilus*, ed. Piero Boitani (Oxford: Clarendon Press, 1989), pp. 95–109 (pp. 106–7).

Spenser and the comic Renaissance   73

denying tragedy is arguably what the comedy of Pandarus's bawdy go-between role had achieved in the foregoing poem.[128]

The point that Christianity embraces bathos has been well made. 'Christianity', writes Erich Auerbach, 'created an entirely new kind of sublimity, in which the everyday and the low were included, not excluded, so that, in style as in content, it directly connected the lowest with the highest'.[129] Auerbach calls the inclusion of the everyday and the low (which is to say, colloquial descriptions of familiar, domestic, and material details) 'creatural realism'. Even in otherwise elevated contexts, creatural realism 'actually savors crass effects'.[130] For Auerbach, this aesthetic finds its most profound reference point in the moment in which the divine became flesh: 'Christ's Incarnation and Passion ... realize and combine *sublimitas* and *humilitas* in overwhelming measure.'[131]

In order to appreciate how this dualist view could be comically fruitful, it is important to note that the connection of the 'lowest with the highest' can be approached from opposing perspectives. In many comic scenarios, 'the low' is defined in stark contrast to 'the high', but in Christian theology the high *redeems* the low, and inverts normative hierarchies. Christ descended to the level of fallen man, taking on his frailties and suffering humiliation at his hands, but at the same time he dignified humanity in its humblest guise, being born a carpenter's son and associating with the poor and outcast. It is specifically this second relation of high and low that is implicit in Christ's revelation to 'babes' instead of the 'wise and vnderstanding' (Luke 10:21), in his comparison of the Kingdom of God to a mustard seed (Matthew 13:31), and in his privileging of the meek (Matthew 5:5).[132]

Christian humour can tap into lowness as a 'thing to be mocked' *or* a 'thing redeemed', and at its richest it does both. Comic grotesquerie, for example, can point up man's utter unworthiness as a recipient of divine mercy, as in the medieval mystery play that shows Christ being scourged and taunted by rogues, or any moral caricature that foregrounds human

---

128 The humour of *Troilus and Criseyde* and its influence on Spenser are discussed in Chapter 4.

129 Auerbach, *Mimesis*, p. 154.

130 *Ibid.*, 247. Bakhtin's 'material bodily principle' refers to a related phenomenon, although he gives a secular interpretation; *Rabelais and His World*, p. 18.

131 Auerbach, *Mimesis*, p. 151. Gurevich similarly speaks of a 'dualist view of the world in which heaven and earth stood face to face' and of the influence of this view on medieval art and literature; *Medieval Popular Culture*, p. 183 (see also p. 181, on the Incarnation).

132 These reversals are enshrined in the Magnificat (Luke 1:51–3).

74 *Comic Spenser*

corruptibility and sinfulness. But a comic perspective can equally invoke the rehabilitative and hierarchically inversive nature of that mercy, as in moral allegory that narrates the humiliating inadequacies of a Christian Everyman (denying him a heroic role yet not condemning him either), or in the use of colloquial, 'creatural' diction to meditate on the state of one's soul.

Piers Plowman exemplifies both the satiric and rehabilitative dimensions of Christian humour. What one modern translator of Langland describes as 'the absurdity of the human situation in the face of eternity's uncompromising demands' is manifest in the almost clownish narrator and, more negatively, in the drunken, idiotic, and flatulent moral caricatures he encounters. But it is also grounds for a more affirmative kind of incongruity.[133] Allusions to divine mercy, heaven, and the end of time happily coexist with an abundance of earthy domestic detail (horse-biscuits, steak and onions, dung-carts, sowing and threshing), idiomatic speech, and proverbial wisdom. While there is a risk here of projecting a modern apprehension of ironic incongruity onto a notional medieval audience, at times the comic dimension is undeniable. In the acerbic words of the allegorical figure 'Holy Church', 'unless you love men truly, and give to the poor, generously sharing the goods God has given you, you shall have no more merit from your Masses and Hours than old Molly from her maidenhead, that no man wants.'[134] The dogma here is serious – good deeds must have substance to them, and virginity (the highest fruit on the tree of charity) is no great virtue if you cannot lose it. But the combination of informality and alliteration, and the sense that we all know poor Molly, are undeniably humorous.

Medieval Christian bathos profoundly influenced the character of Renaissance humour. An outstanding illustration of this point is the *Praise of Folly*, already discussed in this chapter as an exemplar of classical mock-encomium. And indeed, Erasmus self-consciously blended

---

133 William Langland, *Piers the Ploughman*, trans. and intro. J. F. Goodridge (Harmondsworth: Penguin, 1966), p. 12.

134 *Ibid.*, 36–7 (Book I, 'The Teaching of Holy Church'). I cite Goodridge's modern translation here to capture the full idiomatic effect. Robert Crowley's edition reads: 'You haue no more merit, in masse nor in houres / Than Malkin of her maydenhead, that no man desireth'; William Langland, *The vision of Pierce Plowman, nowe the seconde time imprinted*, ed. Robert Crowley (London: R. Grafton, 1550), Passus I, sigs. B3r–B4v; henceforth *Pierce Plowman*. This example of humour in *Piers Plowman* is also noted by Burrow, *Ricardian Poetry*, p. 111. On the potential challenges of gauging humour in medieval texts, see Auerbach, *Mimesis*, p. 72; and Gurevich, *Medieval Popular Culture*, pp. 183–4.

Spenser and the comic Renaissance　　　75

classical and Christian traditions of bathos. In his 'Letter to Martin Dorp', Erasmus underlines analogous paradoxes in these traditions when he describes Christ as 'a sort of Silenus'.[135] According to classical myth, Silenus was the tutor of Dionysus, and (like Socrates) he concealed his wisdom beneath a rough and even grotesque physical exterior. Erasmus had argued elsewhere that both the Incarnated Christ and Holy Scripture (which is written in a plain style, and teaches with simple parables) are like Silenus because both likewise conceal 'divinity under a lowly and almost ludicrous external appearance'.[136] It is precisely this sort of ironic disjunction that Erasmus sets out to epitomise in the *Praise of Folly*. He does so by having Folly praise herself, thereby exalting (in the most backhanded way) something widely accepted as undesirable, but also by insisting, in his defensive paratextual material, on the triviality of the exercise itself. The treatise is a kind of Silenus, too, disavowing its seriousness by uttering profound spiritual truths in comic and colloquial form. Erasmus simultaneously aligns humour with triviality, disarming his critics in advance, *and* implicitly affirms the medieval argument that mirth is one of God's consoling gifts to man, and can have real moral substance. For Erasmus, as for More (who, as I mentioned earlier, joked on the scaffold), openness to amusement could reflect not only temperate goodwill, but also humility and faith.[137] The *Praise of Folly* is an unusually clear example of 'medieval Christian humour' inflecting classical humanism: it is an overtly comic text whose fusion of two traditions is underlined for the reader. As such, it offers an illuminating point of comparison for Renaissance texts that display similar crosscurrents but are less self-advertising in their debts.

The Faerie Queene is a case in point. In Spenser's case, the rhetorical, generic, and cultural 'height' of national epic enabled bathos to a unique

---

135 *Folly*, p. 235. This analogy is also explored in Erasmus's *Sileni Alcibiadis*, as noted by Levi in *Folly*, p. 67 n. 8.

136 Desiderius Erasmus, *Enchiridion militis christiani*, trans. Charles Fantazzi, in *Collected Works of Erasmus*, Vol. LXVI: *Spiritualia*, ed. John W. O'Malley (Toronto: University of Toronto Press, 1988), pp. 1–127 (pp. 67–8).

137 For Christian humanists such as Erasmus and More, 'Aristotle's ideal of the urbanely jesting gentleman formed part of the bedrock of Christian ethics'; see M. A. Screech, *Laughter at the Foot of the Cross* (London: Penguin, 1997), p. 4. The point comes across clearly in Erasmus's Preface to *Folly*. The idea that a sense of humour could bespeak spiritual health was voiced a century later by John Donne, who praised 'loving facetiousnesse' and *'holy cheerfulnesse'* as 'one of the best *evidences* of a *good conscience'*; John Donne, 'Funeral Sermon on Magdalen Herbert, Lady Danvers, 1627', in *Donne's Sermons: Selected Passages*, ed. Logan Pearsall Smith (Oxford: Clarendon Press, 1959 [1919]), p. 37.

76 *Comic Spenser*

degree. Readers have always struggled to reconcile *The Faerie Queene*'s Virgilian ambitions and nationalistic mythology with its grotesque moral caricatures, rustic diction, low-brow literary affiliations, and tonal inconsistencies. This study contends that such disjunctions can only be fully understood in the light of Spenser's Christian heritage. They are not, as some early commentators assumed, a legacy of medieval artistic naïveté, but part of the same sophisticated and playful campaign to pitch worldly pretension against humankind's essential lowliness that readers have always appreciated in Erasmus.

It would of course be misleading to assert that all clashes of high and low cultural references in Renaissance literature (or for that matter medieval literature) must be grounded in Christianity. When Nashe, like Erasmus and Rabelais before him, uses the ornamental rhetoric of the humanist schoolroom to describe the body's 'comic-grotesque vulnerabilities', he would seem, if anything, to travesty the medieval conjunction of *sublimitas/ humilitas* discussed by Auerbach, and to be more influenced by Lucian and Apuleius than by Langland or Chaucer.[138] Renaissance tragicomedy, too, may be said thoroughly to secularise Christian humour. Ros King distinguishes between, on the one hand, the 'V-shape' tragicomedy, which enacts a passage from fall to redemption and lends itself to Christian analogy, and, on the other, the 'much darker beast' we encounter in the Elizabethan mixed-genre form. The latter, says King, seems to 'take delight in a complex, even contradictory, sense of good and evil'.[139]

Yet the tradition of Christian humour I am describing is deep-seated, and arguably many overtly secular texts can usefully be considered within it. That is, when noble protagonists interact with fools and Vice figures in Renaissance tragi-comedies we may recognise a medieval 'object lesson in clownish human imperfection' without necessarily finding a coherent Christian worldview reflected by the plays overall. Just so, we can connect the comic gravediggers of *Hamlet* to the medieval *contemptus mundi* tradition, and we may understand the peculiar fusion of moral satire and comic tolerance in Jonson's *Bartholomew Fair* as a legacy of medieval creatural realism while appreciating the play as a secular and distinctly post-Reformation production.[140]

---

138 See David Kaula, 'The Low Style in Nashe's *The Unfortunate Traveller*', *SEL*, 6 (1966), 43–57.
139 King, 'In Lieu of Democracy', p. 100.
140 On the 'medieval' comedy of *Hamlet*'s gravediggers, see Willard Farnham, 'The Medieval Comic Spirit in the English Renaissance', in *Joseph Quincy Adams Memorial*

Spenser and the comic Renaissance 77

I began this section on 'Medieval humour' by distinguishing between classical influences upon the Renaissance and medieval ones. Qualifying this division, I went on to acknowledge that some aspects of classical culture seemed to appeal to Renaissance authors because of their compatibility with native tradition. This was apparent to neoclassical authors who wanted to distinguish themselves from past ages by purifying their classical sources; but a number of modern critics have come to the same conclusion. That is, they have concluded that some classical authors were popular in the Renaissance because they were in some sense recognisably 'medieval'.[141] This idea is of course implicit in the above claim that Christian humanists such as Erasmus approached classical models through the lens of medieval attitudes to humour. But less likely candidates may be considered in the same light. For example, we might think of Nashe's debts to the bathetic humour and rhetorical games of Lucian and Apuleius, and of Chapman's receptiveness to Homer's unheroic gods and heroes, as being mediated through their medieval Christian heritage (and especially its strong tradition of moral satire) rather than in competition or conflict with it. Classical literature, too, abundantly exemplifies a double vision of the world where the sublime and ridiculous meet, and many Renaissance authors, with one foot, so to speak, in the Middle Ages, seem to have responded readily and instinctively to this quality, accentuating it and revelling in its capacity to unsettle and provoke.

Conclusions

While classical humanism and the Reformation together increased formal dialogue about humour during the Renaissance, it is evident that theories about how humour works (as encountered in literary prefaces, treatises, and polemical contexts, for example) cannot be relied upon accurately to reflect comic practices in this period.[142] Doubts about the morality and cultural value of amusement are everywhere in evidence,

---

Studies, ed. James G. McManaway *et al.* (Washington, D.C.: Folger Shakespeare Library, 1948), pp. 429–37 (pp. 435–6).

141 See for example Bakhtin, *Rabelais and His World*, pp. 97–8; and Auerbach, *Mimesis*, pp. 278–80. Auerbach regards Socrates as a figure whose 'personality and style … seemed to give classical authority to the mixture of genres which was a legacy of the Middle Ages'.

142 As Prescott observes, early modern comic theory 'lagged behind the imaginative complexity of actual practice'; 'Humour and Satire in the Renaissance', p. 284.

78 *Comic Spenser*

yet conventional defences of laughter as a weapon against vice and apologies for frivolous subject matter frequently preface works that challenge the assumptions that make such apologies necessary. Thus, to invoke once more the *Praise of Folly*, Erasmus uses his preface to endorse the conventional correlation between gravity and profit by describing his mock-encomium as a harmless diversion from meaningful pursuits, yet the treatise that follows deftly undermines the commonplace equation of humour and inconsequentiality. Joubert felt compelled to dismiss laughter as 'vne liesse vaine & follatre' ('an empty and foolish joyousness'), yet, as we have seen, he also argues that it is a gift from God and a profoundly humane trait.[143]

For Bakhtin, these contradictory ways of thinking about laughter eventually distinguished one cultural epoch from another:

> The Renaissance conception of laughter can be roughly described as follows: Laughter has a deep philosophical meaning, it is one of the essential forms of the truth concerning the world as a whole, concerning history and man; it is a peculiar point of view relative to the world; the world is seen anew, no less (and perhaps more) profoundly than when seen from the serious standpoint. Therefore, laughter is just as admissible in great literature, posing universal problems, as seriousness. Certain essential aspects of the world are accessible only to laughter. The attitude toward laughter of the seventeenth century and of the years that followed can be characterized thus. Laughter is not a universal, philosophical form. It can refer only to individual and individually typical phenomena of social life. That which is important and essential cannot be comical. Neither can history and persons representing it – kings, generals, heroes – be shown in a comic aspect. The sphere of the comic is narrow and specific (private and social vices); the essential truth about the world and about man cannot be told in the language of laughter. Therefore, the place of laughter in literature belongs only to low genres, showing the life of private individuals and the inferior social levels. Laughter is a light amusement or a form of salutary social punishment of corrupt and low persons.[144]

To an extent, this is an articulate description of the polarities between which humour operates in any period. Both paradigms are certainly in evidence during the Renaissance, sometimes on a single page: the assumption that 'that which is important and essential cannot be comical'

---

143 *Traité*, p. 235 (Book III, Chapter 1), p. 87 (Book I, Chapter 14); *Treatise*, pp. 95, 44.
144 Bakhtin, *Rabelais and His World*, pp. 66–7.

Spenser and the comic Renaissance

– an idea with classical and medieval antecedents – can be traced through arguments for and against laughter alike. On the other hand, as we have seen, conservative defences of humour that corroborate this view of things should not be taken at face value, for in practice Renaissance literature abundantly testifies to the claim that 'certain essential aspects of the world are accessible only to laughter'.

While in need of qualification, Bakhtin's narrative of a historical shift in how laughter was thought about is, however, illuminating – as the contradictions I am describing partly testify. The influence of medieval traditions of humour, which emphasise human fallibility in sharply satirical as well as profoundly democratic ways, was still strong in the sixteenth century; yet the 'neoclassical' desire to uphold heroic possibility (to purify and redignify classical epic, to limit humour to specific genres, and to use satire and mock-heroic to safeguard rather than to challenge heroic values) was also established in theory, if less so in practice. I began this chapter by invoking Renaissance *gravitas* – the self-conscious idealisation of non-comic seriousness that characterises the rhetoric of nationalism, literary criticism, and religious piety. I proposed that it was precisely the period's insistent theoretical benchmarks of decorum that fuelled its comic exposure of those benchmarks as unattainable, undesirable, or hypocritical. In other words, a defining feature of the 'comic Renaissance' was the productive tension between the two paradigms described above, and moreover the self-consciousness with which these tensions were negotiated. My essential claim is that this self-consciousness was especially acute and comically productive for the author of an epic, nationalistic, Protestant poem. It is the task of the following chapters to bear out this claim.

2

Humour and heroism

If comedy, in all its changing shapes, has one overriding preoccupation, it is this: that we resemble beasts more closely than we resemble gods, and that we make great fools of ourselves the moment we forget it.

Howard Jacobson, *Seriously Funny*

Coupled with serious myths were comic and abusive ones; coupled with heroes were their parodies and doublets.

Mikhail Bakhtin, *Rabelais and His World*[1]

'The Legend of Holiness' teaches us that piety does not demand a dour face: the story begins with fasting and ends with feasting. Yet many of us are influenced more than we know by Red Crosse's sad solemnity as he sets out on his quest (I.i.2.8), which at first glance fits so well with our expectations of both 'epic' and 'holiness'. I want to suggest that this instinctive privileging of gravity over levity as we approach Book I – all the more powerful where it is subconscious – fundamentally affects the way we read, inhibiting our appreciation of the humour with which Spenser eviscerates Red Crosse's heroic pretensions. Few readers, for example, have found much to laugh at in the poem's first canto, partly thanks to the narrator's earnest commentary, and partly because of the evident moral importance of the hero's first battle: his decapitation of the serpentine monster 'Errour'. I will argue, however, that the moral seriousness of

---

1 Howard Jacobson, *Seriously Funny: From the Ridiculous to the Sublime* (London: Penguin, 1997), p. 1; Bakhtin, *Rabelais and His World*, p. 6.

Humour and heroism 81

the episode is attested rather than contradicted by its comic absurdity – which is everywhere in evidence once we are willing to see it. The victory over Errour emerges as a parody of heroic action that is absolutely crucial (thematically, tonally, allegorically) to our understanding of Book I.

On one level, 'humour and heroism' is the subject of this study as a whole. As each chapter illustrates, Spenser insistently destabilises his poem's idealised postures. The specific focus of the present chapter is the conflict between secular heroism, which traditionally celebrates individual accomplishment and physical action, and its Protestant equivalent, which involves total reliance on God and the conquest of the ego. As Book I demonstrates, the path to Christian heroism is not glorious but humiliating. It is, of course, well acknowledged that the rhetoric of heroism is suspect in a Christian context, but the degree to which Spenser plays upon and problematises the tension between secular and spiritual heroism (models that are ostensibly reconciled through allegory, yet, it becomes clear, thoroughly confused in the mind of the book's hero) deserves closer attention.[2] To this end, I will consider Spenser's comic handling of three conventions associated with epic poetry: the exemplary qualities of the hero, the superiority of epic over pastoral, and violence.

A premise of this chapter is that humour is instrumental in exposing Red Crosse's spiritual pride. But this is not the whole story: humour has another serious role to play in the context of holiness. The root of Red Crosse's pride and fragile faith *is* his sad solemnity; in the language of the Reformers, he suffers from the burden of self-reliance, where he ought to be comforted by reliance on God. Humour in Book I provides an antidote to this egotism by satirising its effects, but also by providing a lightness – what might be called profound comic relief – that affirms the redemptive context of the knight's errancy. The imperfectly concealed clownishness behind Red Crosse's assumed heroic identity, I propose, testifies to his innate sinfulness but also to God's forgiveness.

---

2 On Spenser's subversion of martial heroism through Christian allegory see, for example, Kenneth Borris, 'Spenser's Heroic Allegory and the Politics of Ennobled Virtue, in *Allegory and Epic in English Renaissance Literature: Heroic Form in Sidney, Spenser, and Milton* (Cambridge: Cambridge University Press, 2000), pp. 164–80. While Borris acknowledges the tension between heroic models, his emphasis on the reconciliation of epic celebration and Christian values, though valid, deflects our attention from irony and satire (see p. 177).

82   *Comic Spenser*

Mock-heroism

The Faerie Queene opens with a heroic portrait:

> A Gentle Knight was pricking on the plaine,
> Ycladd in mightie armes and siluer shielde,
> Wherein old dints of deepe woundes did remaine,
> The cruell markes of many' a bloody fielde;
> Yet armes till that time did he neuer wield:
> His angry steede did chide his foming bitt,
> As much disdaining to the curbe to yield:
> Full iolly knight he seemd, and faire did sitt,
> As one for knightly giusts and fierce encounters fitt.
>
> (I.i.1)

The ensuing catalogue of chivalric traits and accoutrements conveys the eagerness of a knight newly possessed of his heroic identity as well as the eagerness of a poet in command of a new instrument: the 'trumpet sterne' of epic. Notwithstanding the humility of the self-professedly 'dull' poet of Proem I (2.9), at the beginning of the opening canto our narrator is evidently in full command of the weapons at his disposal: he begins *in medias res*, his hero's armour is fraught with symbolism, and his diction and syntax proclaim epic ambition. Craig A. Berry and Donald Cheney are among those critics who observe a parallel between the poet and his hero at this point in the narrative: each has taken on a task in the service of a great queen. Responding to the 'plethora of superlatives' in the description of Red Crosse, Cheney discerns gentle self-satire on Spenser's behalf: poet and protagonist alike, both of whom have risen above their humble backgrounds to seek preferment at court, are 'burning rubber' to earn their monarch's praise.[3]

An analogy between hero and poet would have been half expected by Spenser's first readers: a commonplace classical idea was that in order to write about heroic deeds and great civilisations a poet must himself be heroically minded and politically wise. 'The poet', wrote Longinus, 'is accustomed to enter into the greatness of his heroes'.[4] The joint motivation for praise noted by Berry and Cheney was another traditional point of connection between poet and hero, as was their promotion of national interests: Du Bellay looked back approvingly to a time when the monarch 'desiroit plus le renaitre d'Homere, que le gaing d'une grosse battaille'

---

3 Cheney, 'Spenser's Parody', p. 3; Berry, 'Borrowed Armor/Free Grace', pp. 142–51.
4 Longinus, *On Sublimity*, p. 470.

Humour and heroism 83

('desired the rebirth of Homer rather than the gaining of a great battle').[5] And Spenser's narrator himself reminds us that 'mightie Conquerours / And Poets sage' share the crown of laurel (I.i.9.1–2).

As Berry observes, Red Crosse's rusticity or 'clownishness' prior to becoming one of Gloriana's knights (which we learn about in the 'Letter to Raleigh' and at I.x.65–6) mirrors Spenser's Virgilian graduation from the 'lowly Shephards weeds' of pastoral to the 'trumpets sterne' of epic (Proem I 1.1–4).[6] In *The Shepheardes Calender*, clownishness is explicitly associated with pastoral poetry when Piers advises Cuddie to cast off his old identity and become an epic poet:

> Abandon then the base and viler clowne,
> Lyft up thy selfe out of the lowly dust:
> And sing of bloody Mars, of wars, of guists.
>
> ('October', lines 37–9)

In both poems, Berry notes, 'Spenser emphasizes that the rustic persona is a mask that can be abandoned.'[7] However, as Cheney observes, the analogy between Spenser's poetic persona and the hero Red Crosse is not one of straightforward mutual endorsement. The praise heaped upon Gloriana in the context of Red Crosse's suspect ambition to win 'earthly' grace (I.i.3.5) casts an ironic light on the similarly effusive tone of Proem I ('O Goddesse heauenly bright …'; 4.1).[8] This revised analogy, according to which the poet shares his protagonist's limitations and weaknesses – a device familiar from both Chaucer and Ariosto – invites a far more ironic and sceptical approach to the rhetoric of heroic aspiration in Book I.[9]

---

5 Joachim Du Bellay, *La Deffence et illustration de la langue françoyse*, ed. Jean-Charles Monferran, Textes littéraires français, 543 (Genève: Droz, 2001), p. 142; *Defence and Illustration of the French Language*, trans. Gladys M. Turquet (London: J. M. Dent, 1939), p. 78.

6 Berry, 'Borrowed Armor/Free Grace', pp. 142–3. Correspondingly, Spenser's alter ego Colin Clout is the 'Shepeheards boye' who is destined for poetic fame (*SC*, 'Januarye', line 1; 'October', line 88). (While, officially speaking, Red Crosse's background is not pastoral but georgic, Spenser's narrator also describes himself as a ploughman at III. xii.47).

7 Berry, 'Borrowed Armor/Free Grace', p. 140.

8 Cheney, 'Spenser's Parody', pp. 3–4.

9 For example, the fictive Chaucer who narrates 'Thopas' is laughably inept and the narrator of *Orlando furioso* claims to be maddened by love (and is evidently as distractable as his protagonists). See *Of* I.ii and II.i, for example, and Patricia Parker, *Inescapable Romance: Studies in the Poetics of a Mode* (Princeton: Princeton University Press, 1979), pp. 25–9.

84   *Comic Spenser*

After all, Red Crosse's sense of promotion is a dangerous delusion. In *The Shepheardes Calender*, Cuddie's clownishness corresponds to his identity as a shepherd who sings rustic songs, but, in the context of 'The Legend of Holiness', Red Crosse's humble beginnings represent mankind's unworthiness before God. While Cuddie's naïveté and cynicism – not to mention his silly name – makes Piers's grand ambitions for him seem unlikely, Red Crosse's clownishness is indelible in another sense. Beneath the armour of Christ's saving act, Red Crosse is a boy without inherent nobility or strength. As the unfolding crisis of Book I makes clear, however, Red Crosse himself is persuaded that his rusticity can be 'abandoned' and that, moreover, he deserves the armour gifted to him – an error of perception that guarantees his clownishness will continue to show itself. As we shall see, the knight's attempt to 'proue his puissance in battell braue' (I.i.3.7) turns him into a parodic hero. Like Braggadochio (that other knight who has not earned his armour), Red Crosse is a clown in the dual sense of low-born and laughable.[10]

'Clown' is glossed by A. C. Hamilton according to one of its primary meanings in the sixteenth century, 'a countryman, rustic, or peasant' (*OED*, *n.*, 1.); but the still current sense, 'a fool or jester … a buffoon' (*OED*, *n.*, 3.), is even older. In *The Shepheardes Calender* rusticity often proves to be funny, especially when paired with adolescent inexperience in matters of love. Colin uses the terms 'clownish' and 'foolish' interchangeably to describe his admirer Hobbinol ('Januarye', lines 57–9), and the relevance of both these meanings for Red Crosse can indeed be inferred from 'Letter to Raleigh':

> In the beginning of the feast, there presented him selfe a tall clownishe younge man, who falling before the Queen of Faries desired a boone (as the manner then was) which during that feast she might not refuse: which was that hee might haue the atchieuement of any aduenture, which during that feaste should happen, that being graunted, he rested him on the floore, vnfitte through his rusticity for a better place. [*a fair lady arrives and explains her plight, requesting the help of a knight*] Presently that clownish person vpstarting, desired that aduenture: whereat the Queene much wondering, and the Lady much gainesaying, yet he earnestly importuned his desire. (LR, lines 53–63)

---

10 A parallel between Red Crosse and Braggadochio is noted by Huston, 'The Function of the Mock Hero', pp. 212–13.

Humour and heroism 85

Tall, young, inexperienced, and conspicuously out of place in a royal court, Red Crosse presents a figure at once humble and laughable. If this scenario were acted on stage, the cue 'the Lady much gainesaying' could not help but provoke laughter; she is essentially imploring, 'anyone but him!'.[11]

This aspect of Red Crosse, and his subsequent fallibility as a questing knight, ironises the latent analogy between hero and poet, displacing what initially appears to be a dynamic of mutual endorsement with something far more ambivalent and provocative. Given that their quests to fulfil a heroic vocation are suggestively analogous, Red Crosse's naïveté and pretension give scope for authorial self-satire, although – to add an obvious but important point – the author in question is not Spenser but rather a fictional persona created by him. Spenser's narrator often slips into grandiose rhetoric and inflated heroic terms, using idealising descriptions and expressing admiration for characters in their weakest moments.[12] When he calls Red Crosse a 'Champion stout' (I.i.11.7) and announces 'nothing did he dread, but euer was ydrad' (i.2.9) we might recall similarly ponderous lines in *Virgils Gnat* and *Muiopotmos*. As discussed in Chapter 1, these two poems make fun of amplifying rhetoric by applying it to less than heroic subjects.[13] Though a 'real' epic, *The Faerie Queene* does the same thing. We will continue to see that at critical moments Spenser uses a conspicuously elevated register to indicate that Red Crosse is something of a Clarion, a little too proud of his imposing

---

11 There is a possible analogue for this humiliation in Malory's 'Tale of Sir Gareth', in which Lynette refuses Gareth the 'kychyn knave'; *Works of Malory*, I.22 (p. 297). The comic aspects of Gareth and Lynette's alliance are discussed by Hoffman, 'Malory and the English Comic Tradition', pp. 179–83.

12 On the unreliability of Spenser's narrator see Jerome S. Dees, 'narrator of *The Faerie Queene*', in *SpE*, pp. 498–500; and Kathryn Walls, *God's Only Daughter: Spenser's Una as the Invisible Church* (Manchester: Manchester University Press, 2013), p. 6 n. 21. See also my Introduction.

13 The irony of mock-epic is double-edged: if a high style accentuates the slightness of the subject, so too does the slight subject expose the potential absurdity of a high style. While Martin Scriblerus's often-quoted assertion that 'it is a common and foolish mistake, that a ludicrous parody of a grave and celebrated passage is a ridicule of that passage' makes an important point about satirical intent, there is a sense in which parodying a grave passage unavoidably undermines (if not ridicules) it; on this tension in neoclassical mock-epic, see H. A. Mason, *To Homer through Pope: An Introduction to Homer's 'Iliad' and Pope's Translation* (London: Chatto & Windus, 1972), p. 143; and Ulrich Broich, *The Eighteenth-Century Mock-Heroic Poem*, trans. David Henry Wilson (Cambridge: Cambridge University Press, 1990), p. 26. For the annotation see Alexander Pope, *The Dunciad*, ed. James Sutherland, in *Poems of Alexander Pope*, Vol. V (London: Methuen, 1953), p. 316 (II.405n).

86   *Comic Spenser*

armor when really he is a 'fraile, feeble, fleshly wight' (ix.53.1) – a description pointedly echoed in *Muiopotmos* (line 226).[14]

I am suggesting that the narrator is at once complicit with Red Crosse's ambitions and, as the proud, praise-seeking possessor of a new trumpet, to some degree identifiable with them.[15] What is being made fun of is not poetic ambition – *The Faerie Queene* is nothing if not ambitious – but rather the epic poem's trenchant secular associations: namely, political panegyric, the poet's aspiration for personal advancement, the glorification of warfare, and the celebration of human achievement. Trompart, whose task it is to 'blow the bellowes' to Braggadochio's vanity (II.iii.9.9), parodies the 'trumpet sterne' taken up by Spenser's narrator insofar as this symbolises the poet's epic duty to confer glory on those who do not necessarily deserve it.[16] Braggadochio, in turn, caricatures the quest for social advancement, and, more specifically, for courtly favour (iii.5) – a caricature that implicates Spenser himself. McCabe astutely notes that the 'masked Mock-knight' (as Braggadochio is called at IV.iv.13.4) is, like the masked/masquing muse of Proem I (1.1), associated with disguise and performance, and finds this verbal echo to be consistent with the 'strongly ludic element in Spenser's various authorial *personae*'.[17] Again, this is not to deny that Spenser wished to advance himself and be recognised (and remunerated) for his considerable achievement. Rather it is to acknowledge the sense of humour and theatrical distance with which he pursued these aims.[18]

Much of the humour of Book I, and the incisiveness of its moments of mock-heroic parody, hinge upon the fallibility and egotism of Red Crosse. Though universally recognised as central to Book I, this fallibility

---

14 On this line see further p. 100. *Muiopotmos* may have been written in the same year that the first instalment of *The Faerie Queene* was published; see Judith Dundas, 'Complaints: Muiopotmos; or, The Fate of the Butterfly', in *SpE*, pp. 186–7.

15 In Esolen's words, the climactic line of I.i.2 is 'so bad that only a great poet could get away with it'; 'Highways and Byways', p. 1. While the narrator at times ostentatiously embodies the role of epic poet, he is also self-deprecating in equal measure; see McCabe, 'Parody, Sympathy and Self', p. 10. On humility as an alternative form of theatrical naïveté, see Introduction.

16 See *OED*, s.v. 'trump', $v.^1$, 1: 'to blow or sound a trumpet', and $v.^2$: 'to deceive, cheat'.

17 McCabe, 'Parody, Sympathy and Self', p. 10.

18 To take McCabe's insight a step further, it is tempting to speculate about Spenser's mysteriously unnamed muse. The poet's description of his epic voice as a 'golden clarion' in *Tears of the Muses* led the early-twentieth-century critic Anne Kimball Tuell to surmise that Clarion, the diminutive hero of *Muiopotmos*, represents Spenser's epic muse; Tuell, 'Note on Spenser's Clarion', pp. 182–3. If the mock-hero of the minor poem is Spenser's epic muse, then the epic muse of *The Faerie Queene* may, as McCabe implies, be in part mock-heroic.

Humour and heroism 87

nevertheless tends to be underestimated by readers, especially at the outset of his quest. This is partly because Red Crosse's defeat of Errour in Canto i is generally thought to be a legitimate, if partial or provisional, victory over something evil.[19] According to this interpretation, things start to go badly for Red Crosse when he meets Archimago and is fooled into abandoning his lady – a lady who, interpreted as 'Truth', had previously acted as moral guide and guarantor for her companion's actions.

I take a different view of Canto i, and propose that Red Crosse's victory over Errour is an absurd and comically grotesque parody of heroic action. According to this view, Red Crosse's vanity and self-absorption are in evidence from the very beginning of his quest, and his victory over Errour only deepens his misguided sense of self-reliance.[20] Here I am indebted to the revisionary thesis of Kathryn Walls concerning Una's initial fallibility. According to this argument (which I discuss further in Chapter 3), the lady of Canto i shares Red Crosse's 'chronically fallible' perspective, and it is only after their separation at I.ii.6–7 that she represents the True or 'invisible' Church.[21]

It is generally understood that the youthful knight's lack of caution in the Wandering Wood, vividly symbolised when he finds himself 'wrapt in Errours endlesse traine', is corrected when he follows his lady's advice to 'add faith vnto to your force, and be not faint' (I.i.19.3) and defeats the monster. Notwithstanding the near-unanimous citation of the lady's words as exemplary Protestantism and as decisive to the moral resolution of the episode, Walls points out that the command to 'add faith' has a secular resonance that changes its meaning entirely:

19 See John M. Steadman, 'Error', in *SpE*, pp. 252–3.
20 Of course, the observation that Red Crosse's fallibility is in evidence from the beginning of Book I is hardly new: the very first stanza reports his 'angry steede['s]' disdain for authority (worrying for any rider, but particularly bad news for an allegorical one). Yet while the paradoxes and ambiguities of the opening portrait have been well noted, it is worth emphasising the hints of egotism beneath – or rather epitomised by – the knight's solemn demeanour (i.2.8). Red Crosse's heroic appearance is generally linked to the armour of God described in Ephesians 6, but a more pressing implication is that it bespeaks a novice's aspiration to show off his faith. The portrait's striking dissimilarity to the humble image of the unarmed Christ 'prickynge' into Jerusalem on an ass in *Piers Plowman* is telling; Langland, *Pierce Plowman*, ed. Crowley, XVIII.10–14. See Walls, *God's Only Daughter*, p. 192.
21 Specifically, Walls argues that in Canto i, Una (who, significantly, has not yet been named as such) embodies the community of the elect prior to regeneration in Christ. While Red Crosse may be considered a member of this community, he represents the trials of an erring individual in the present moment, whereas Una represents the wider Christian Church and its progress over time; Walls, *God's Only Daughter*, pp. 13–14.

88 *Comic Spenser*

> As explained in the *OED*, 'to add faith to [something]' was once an idiomatic expression for 'to give credence to [it], to believe in [it]'. Faith in the context of this definition is quite distinct from religious faith, faith (that is) in God ... Una has been urging Red Cross merely 'to believe in' his own 'force' (probably meaning no more than 'strength', after all) – which is tantamount to believing 'in himself'.[22]

This interpretation makes sense of the otherwise very puzzling fact that Red Crosse's subsequent victory over Errour bears no positive relation to his moral state – in fact, inaugurates his downfall. Having won his first battle, Red Crosse will almost immediately encounter hypocrisy and, very soon afterward, abandon his lady and form an alliance with Duessa. Even in the immediate aftermath of his victory over Errour he is twice shown casting about for new adventures like a generic romance hero, forgetful of his pledge to rescue his lady's imprisoned mother and father: 'So forward on his way (with God to frend) / He passed forth, and *new aduenture sought*' (I.i.28.7–8; my italics).

Once we recognise that Red Crosse's first victory merely affirms the erring Christian's capacity to self-validate, we can appreciate its reductive absurdity (not to worry folks, it was messy, but Error is dead – and in the first canto!), and the bigheadedness of the knight's earnest pronouncement: 'Vertue giues her selfe light, through darkenesse for to wade' (I.i.12.9).[23] On second glance, moreover, the casual parenthesis of '(with God to frend)' looks complacent indeed, as though Red Crosse is enjoying a sense of matey equality with his creator. From this more cynical angle we might well find amusement in the appellation 'valiant Elfe' (i.17.1), a conjunction that is mock-heroic not only from the point of view that elves are traditionally small, but also, more pressingly, because (as we will later find out) Red Crosse's elfin or 'changeling' identity refers specifically to his fallen nature.[24] It is *this* crucial point, not Errour's evil, that is reflected in the physical grossness and farcical indignity of the

---

22 *Ibid.*, 23.

23 As Cheney and others have noted, in view of the 'vertue gives herself light' claim, the description of the illumination provided by Red Crosse's brilliant armour as 'glooming ... like a shade' is damning. Cheney is alert to irony in Canto i, especially in connection with Spenser's subtle handling of Red Crosse's persistent naïveté, though he joins the majority of critics in maintaining that the knight's first victory has moral validity, albeit limited; Donald Cheney, *Spenser's Image of Nature* (New Haven: Yale University Press, 1966), pp. 25–7.

24 This becomes evident at I.x.65–6; see p. 94 below. For another Spenserian elf joke see *FQ* II.x.72.1 (on which see p. 40 above). On elves as diminutive see *OED*, s.v. 'elf', *n.*, 1.

Humour and heroism   89

episode – which, in Berger's words, amounts to 'indiscriminate ingestion, inefficient digestion, regurgitation as a form of combat' – and in the fact that Red Crosse breaks the chivalric code (in spectacular fashion) by attacking a female who is trying to retreat.[25] Traditionally, such discordant details have been regarded as corollaries of allegory: it makes sense, for example, that Red Crosse should force the monster against her will to fight him because error will always try to hide in obscurity away from the light of righteousness. But from the less flattering point of view that Red Crosse is *inciting* error – poking a proverbial sleeping dog – the unchivalric and indecent aspect of his battle with her is far from incidental. It is this perspective that renders the narrator's admiration mock-heroic, and the lady's praise of her knight's 'great glory' jarringly out of place (i.27.6).[26]

A moment of acute irony following the defeat of Errour further betrays Red Crosse's misunderstanding of what it means to be a Christian hero. Upon asking Archimago if he knows of any adventures to be had, the hermit refers to a 'straunge man' who is, paradoxically, 'homebredd' (I.i.31.2–3). This paradox, of course, holds a mirror up to Red Crosse himself. He hypocritically believes that evil is 'strange' – which is to say, 'out there' in the world. The real import of the word is that Red Crosse is as yet a stranger to himself: his focus is not on self-knowledge but on outward action. Asked how to find this 'wicked wight (i.31.7)', Archimago is uncharacteristically truthful: 'thorough great distresse' (i.32.3). Stretching the irony of this dialogue as far as it will go, one might say that Red Crosse issues a death threat against himself in the language of impeccable chivalric cliché: 'to all knighthood it is foule disgrace, / That such a cursed creature liues so long a space' (i.31.8–9).

Of course, Red Crosse's sinfulness leads to spiritual despair and he will indeed be tempted to kill himself, which is hardly cause for amusement. Yet (especially in light of the fact that it is Despair, not Red Crosse, who finally attempts suicide) this does not mean that his journey to despair is unrelieved by humour. Even the dark charisma of Despair himself – with his greasy locks, raw-bone cheeks, staring eyes, and collection of

---

25 Harry Berger, Jr, 'Sexual and Religious Politics in Book I of Spenser's *Faerie Queene*', *ELR*, 34 (2004), 201–42 (p. 207). Two critics amused by the circumstance that 'the valiant Elfe' is utterly overwhelmed by the smell of vomit are Anthony M. Esolen, 'Irony and the Pseudo-Physical in *The Faerie Queene*', *SSt*, 8 (1987), 61–78 (p. 61); and Gilbert, 'Spenserian Comedy', p. 101.

26 See Walls, *God's Only Daughter*, pp. 32–3. For further interpretation of the Errour episode as unheroic, see my discussion of its sexual imagery in Chapter 3.

90 *Comic Spenser*

nooses and rusty knives – captures the playfulness of Spenserian morality even (or perhaps especially) at moments of spiritual danger. As this study maintains, humour is not at odds with seriousness; moreover, sobriety is not the same as spiritual vigilance. As I proposed at the outset of this chapter, Red Crosse's sad solemnity is a kind of spiritual blindness, to be remedied in part by the reader's capacity to recognise the truth of Despair's assessment of Red Crosse – 'foolish man' (I.ix.38.2) – and yet smile at it.

An invitation to smile is latent in Red Crosse's very identity as St George – an identification that we should not be too quick to invest with Protestant dignity. As some critics have pointed out, the saint's burlesque potential was well established in the sixteenth century. While it is true that St George's potency as patron saint of England was, after the Reformation, channelled into his revised status as emblem of the Tudor dynasty, his enduring associations with Catholic superstition and hagiography and with 'the buffoonery of village ... plays' made him a 'figure composed of deep cultural contradictions'.[27] The court of Edward VI went to some lengths to dissociate the Order of the Garter from its traditional patron, and John Foxe describes the young king, surrounded by his advisors, laughing at the childishness of the dragon-slaying myth. A similar note of derision marks Bishop John Hooper's description of St George as a knight 'with a long spear upon a jolly hackney, that gave the dragon his death-wound, as the painters say, in the throat'.[28] While St George obviously survived as a prominent political and religious symbol in the late sixteenth century, Beatrice Groves has recently noted that the very patriotism that made the dragon slayer a fixture on tavern signs effectively accelerated his simultaneous demise into a popular, decidedly unheroic figure.[29]

27 Mary Ellen Lamb, 'The Red Crosse Knight, St George, and the Appropriation of Popular Culture', *SSt*, 18 (2003), 185–208 (p. 185). In a passage judiciously omitted from Chaloner's translation, Folly asserts that the superstitious 'piously deck out [St George's] horse with trappings and amulets and practically worship it'; *Folly*, p. 126 (for the corresponding passage in Chaloner's translation, see *Folie*, p. 56).
28 According to Foxe, at thirteen Edward impressed his advisors with his contempt for the medieval icon. Upon asking 'what saincte is S. George, that we here so honour hym?' and being briefed on the dragon-slaying story in the *Legenda aurea*, the young king, for a while unable to speak for laughing, said 'I pray you my Lorde, and what did he with his sworde the while?'; *Acts and Monuments*, Book 9, p. 1419. John Hooper, *Early Writings of Hooper*, ed. Samuel Carr, Parker Society Publications, 20 (Cambridge: Cambridge University Press, 1843), p. 320; cited by Margaret Aston, *England's Iconoclasts*, Vol. I: *Laws against Images* (Oxford: Clarendon Press, 1988), p. 437.
29 Beatrice Groves, 'The Redcrosse Knight and "The George"', *SSt*, 25 (2010), 371–6. On the saint's parochial and farcical associations see also Jennifer C. Vaught, 'The Mummers' Play *St George and the Fiery Dragon* and Book I of Spenser's *Faerie Queene*',

Humour and heroism   91

The saint's divided associations as a figure at once transcendent and farcical must have played into Spenser's hands.[30] While Red Crosse is destined to become a saint in the Protestant sense of the word, for the majority of Book I he is a Catholic St George, a would-be hero for whom worth is measured by deeds. When the narrator distinguishes between Archimago disguised as Red Crosse and the 'true *Saint George*' (I.ii.12.2), this is the distinction at issue. Archimago is an imposter – St Paul's 'old man' (as he is called at iii.38.7), here identifiable with Catholic sainthood.[31] While the narrator emphasises the difference between Red Crosse and Archimago, we need to remember that the knight's redemption is achieved at the end of the story, and that this is the only sense in which the true saint is 'far away' (ii.12.2) when Archimago impersonates him.[32] Far from being elsewhere in fairyland, Red Crosse – a mere impersonator of sainthood – *is* Archimago.

The comedy of Archimago's character is sometimes noted in passing, especially in relation to his shape-shifting antics: 'Now like a foxe, now like a dragon fell, / That of himselfe he ofte for feare would quake, / And oft would flie away' (I.ii.10.6–8).[33] There is a point here about the way hypocrisy inhibits self-recognition (the correlation between his own sinfulness and the 'dragon fell' really is a point of non-recognition for Red Crosse), and about the connection between hypocrisy and cowardice; but we also see that hypocrisy, as a form of folly, can be laughable in its creative duplicities.[34] Yet the really fundamental allegorical point is that this sinful, laughable figure is not a 'bad man' bent on sabotaging poor Red Crosse but rather a lively projection of the knight's own psyche. This irony often slips out of sight in criticism of Book I. No doubt it is precisely

---

LATCH, 3 (2010), 85–106; Richard F. Hardin, 'Spenser's Aesculapius Episode and the English Mummers' Play', *SSt*, 15 (2001), 251–3; and Nelson, *The Poetry of Edmund Spenser*, p. 150.

30 See Hardin, 'Spenser's Aesculapius Episode', p. 252.

31 Ephesians 4:22. Cf. I.x.65.6–9n. On Catholic versus Protestant sainthood see John King, 'Spenser's Religion', in *The Cambridge Companion to Spenser*, ed. Andrew Hadfield (Cambridge: Cambridge University Press, 2001), pp. 200–16 (p. 209).

32 When hypocrisy assumes the guise of the hero, we find confirmation that our hero is, for now, a hypocrite; see McCabe, 'Parody, Sympathy and Self', p. 12; and Hadfield, 'Spenser and Religion – Yet Again', *SEL*, 51 (2011), 21–46 (pp. 33–4).

33 As Quilligan notes, 'the Magician was a legitimate mask in and of itself in the *commedia dell'arte*, and one Archimago distinctly and comically wears'; Maureen Quilligan, 'The Comedy of Female Authority in *The Faerie Queene*', *ELR*, 17 (1987), 151–71 (p. 159). Quilligan here refers to Archimago's interaction with Trompart and Braggadochio in Book II, on which see pp. 186–8 below.

34 On the comedy of the dragon's representation in Canto xi, see pp. 106–11 below.

92   *Comic Spenser*

because Archimago is, narratively speaking, such a compelling dramatic figure that his allegorical relation to Red Crosse, and his function as a comic foil to the knight's serious self-conception, can be overlooked. Indeed, it is often implied that Archimago naughtily caricatures the *real* knight introduced to us in Stanza 1, when in fact the description of Archimago masquerading as St George merely underlines the mock-heroic content of the original portrait in a series of pointed echoes:

> In mighty armes he was yclad anon:
> And siluer shield, vpon his coward brest
> A bloody crosse, and on his crauen crest
> A bounch of heares discolourd diuersly:
> Full iolly knight he seemde, and wel addrest,
> And when he sate vppon his courser free,
> *Saint George* himselfe ye would haue deemed him to be.
>
> (I.ii.11.3–9)

One wonders if the multi-coloured plume is something that Red Crosse, for all his solemnity, has been wearing all along; whatever the case, it nicely captures the vanity of an impostor 'dressing up' as a hero.[35]

The suggestive analogy between Red Crosse and Braggadochio noted above is rendered explicit in the figure of Archimago; when Una sees him, we are told: 'A knight her mett in mighty armes embost, / Yet knight was not for all his bragging bost' (I.iii.24.4–5). In a mock-heroic moment worthy of the braggart (whose cowardice is a source of comedy in Book II), Archimago revises his plan to pursue Una when he notices, with horror, that she is travelling with a lion. Trying quickly to hide, he 'turned wyde / Vnto an hil' but – confirming that hills are poor hiding places – Una rides to greet him, effusive with relief (iii.26.4–5). This is a worrying moment in which we see a trusting Una being deceived by a villain who has already proved how dangerous he can be. Yet the humour of the episode focuses us on Archimago's vulnerability rather hers, reminding us that although hypocrisy is spiritually corrupting, it is also deeply foolish.[36] When Una lavishes praise on this mock-knight there is both pathos and tension – we

---

35 As Hamilton notes, Arthur's headgear is described in exactly the same terms at I.vii.32.2. While the latter context is not satirical, the lavish description of Arthur's armour does strike a comic note (*his* plume 'Did shake, and seemd to daunce for iollity, / Like to an Almond tree ymounted hye'; 32.4–5). On the dragon's 'haughty crest' (I.xi.15.5) and its relation to Archimago see n. 81 below. On the comedy of the allegorist's revelry in physical details, see Esolen, 'Irony and the Pseudo-Physical'.

36 And, when faced with an allegorical lion, suddenly low on resources. On the identity of the lion as Christ, see Walls, *God's Only Daughter*, pp. 48–56.

Humour and heroism 93

feel the extent of her faithful love for Red Crosse – but there is also comic incongruity. In particular, 'welcome now my light, and shining lampe of blis' (iii.27.9) is surely an example of Spenser over-egging the custard to emphasise how undeserving the object of this praise really is.[37] There is something funny, too, in the way that Archimago gains Una's trust with 'lovely words', smoothly playing the part of chivalric protector, yet cannot help but nervously enquire, as they ride forth in an awkward threesome, 'what the Lyon ment' (iii.32.8).[38]

Archimago is soon after wounded by Sansloy, who lets him go when he discovers his true identity. Sansloy's subsequent abduction of Una and slaying of the lion is suggestive in historical and political terms, as the numerous interpretations of this episode attest.[39] But concurrent with the historical allegory is the story of the present-day erring Christian whose sinfulness continues to obstruct his relationship with Una. It is on this level that Archimago (rather than embodying hypocrisy in purely abstract or historical terms) presents an aspect of our hero writ large. Archimago 'disappears' from the story at this point, but not because his backfired plan has put him out of action for the time being. He disappears because, allegorically speaking, the hypocrisy he represents lives on in Red Crosse – whose chronicle of vanity and humiliation we must return our attention to.

Pastoral interruption

no god or hero you bring on the stage, if he was seen not long ago in royal gold and purple, must lower his language and move into a humble cottage; nor, on the other hand, must his efforts to get off the ground lead him to try to grasp clouds and void.

Horace, *The Art of Poetry*[40]

As well as being signposted with mock-heroic exaggeration or inappropriate praise, moments of heightened pride and self-reliance in Book

---

37 On Una's misapprehension see *ibid.*, pp. 97–100.
38 Berger calls this 'the canto's most hilarious moment'; 'Sexual and Religious Politics', p. 225. 'Ment' can be interpreted as 'intends' and/or 'stands for'; see Walls, *God's Only Daughter*, p. 55 n. 47. Either interpretation is amusing in view of Archimago's cowardice, but if we infer the latter meaning this becomes an oddly self-referential moment in which Archimago seems to acknowledge that he is in an allegory – albeit playing the part of an inept reader.
39 Walls, *God's Only Daughter*, pp. 1–3 n. 6.
40 *ALC*, p. 285.

94   *Comic Spenser*

I are often punctured by rustic images, analogies, and words. Such interruptions, as I am calling them, are ironically timed reminders of the humble origins that Red Crosse is trying to disavow, and they heighten the burlesque aspect of the ostensibly heroic contexts in which they appear.[41]

As is often noted, Red Crosse's humble beginnings are recalled by the very name of St George, which derives from the Greek words for earth and labour. According to legend, the saint himself was a nobleman and warrior, with the earthy associations of his name signifying his humility before God and his metaphorical status as tiller of the flesh or the soul.[42] Red Crosse, too, is noble by birth, but his association with the earth is rendered literal (albeit in an allegorical context) in that he is revealed to be a foundling: a baby taken from his royal parents by a fairy and left in a furrow, later to be discovered and brought up by a ploughman (I.x.65–6). Rather than signifying his humility, Red Crosse's association with the earth testifies to his fallen nature, his 'true nobility' being the innocence forfeited by Adam and Eve. Notably, the positive association between earthiness and humility comes to the fore when Red Crosse attains the status of 'true *Saint George*'; at this point, I argue below, pastoral and georgic allusions take on an intensely positive or 'noble' significance in recognition of the innocence restored to mankind by Christ. But for the majority of Red Crosse's quest, allusions to rusticity are barbed – and at times funny – reminders of the lowliness (which is to say, sinfulness) our hero is so intent upon denying.[43]

At the height of his heroic self-conception, when Red Crosse feels insulted by the lukewarm hospitality at the House of Pride, we are told that he estranges himself from Lucifera's crowd of spectators, 'Whose fellowship seemd far vnfitt for warlike swaine' (I.iv.37.9).[44] That one cannot be both warlike and a swain is made clear when the narrator says of Braggadochio 'Yet knight he was not, but a boastfull swaine' (III.viii.11.6). 'Swaine' has lower-class connotations, but in particular it is associated with

---

41 Cheney, *Spenser's Image of Nature* is the seminal work on pastoral in Book I. Though our approaches differ and are at times opposed (see for example n. 23 above), the fundamental common ground is that, like Cheney, I read pastoral motifs as ironic reminders of Red Crosse's earthy origins, which are expressive both of his sinful, fallen nature and, finally, of the humility that is synonymous with true Christian heroism.

42 For the name's etymology and associated interpretations see Hugh MacLachlan, 'George, St', in *SpE*, pp. 329–30 (p. 329).

43 *Riders Dictionarie* (Oxford, 1612) supplies 'georgice' as a synonym for 'barbarously'; see Jones, *The Triumph of the English Language*, p. 8.

44 On the comedy of Red Crosse's arrogance at this point, see further p. 185 below.

Humour and heroism 95

farmhands (*OED*, *n.*, 4: 'a shepherd; a countryman, rustic') and country lovers (5: 'a wooer, sweetheart, esp. in pastoral poetry').[45] Modern readers easily miss the sly incongruity of the phrase with its insinuation that Red Crosse is a rustic playing at being both a knight *and* a lover. This moment of irony retrospectively casts light on the much-debated pastoral simile of Canto i, in which Red Crosse's battle with Errour is interrupted by a rural vision reminiscent of *Virgils Gnat*:

> As gentle Shepheard in sweete euentide,
> When ruddy *Phebus* gins to welke in west,
> High on an hill, his flocke to vewen wide,
> Markes which doe byte their hasty supper best,
> A cloud of combrous gnattes doe him molest,
> All striuing to infixe their feeble stinges,
> That from their noyance he no where can rest,
> But with his clownish hands their tender wings,
> He brusheth oft, and oft doth mar their murmurings.
>
> (I.i.23)

Red Crosse's representation as a shepherd watching over his flock like the good shepherd of the Gospels (John 10:11) would seem to confirm the righteousness of his cause, allowing us to interpret the comparison of Errour's brood to gnats as an affirmation of their powerlessness over him. From an alternative perspective, the gnat analogy conspicuously contrasts the heroism of Red Crosse's battle, reimaging his zeal as something petty. A similar moment of 'epic-puncturing' occurs in *Orlando furioso*, when Ruggiero's battle with a giant sea-monster is compared to a dog being pestered by a fly.[46] Quite possibly, heroism is being not only punctured in the Spenserian context, but also redefined: error ought to be 'brushed off' rather than violently attacked. Perhaps, too, there is a suggestion that the shepherd who is preoccupied with gnats is in danger of losing sight of his flock. From these alternative, unflattering perspectives, the bathos of the rustic analogy is telling, and offers an ironically timed reminder

---

45 'Swain' could also simply mean a youth, but with connotations of low status (see *OED*, *n.*, 1–3). Archimago calls Red Crosse 'vnhappy Swaine' at I.ii.4.6 (see Hamilton's note). The appellation is used positively ('courageous swayne') of Timias as Arthur's serving man (I.viii.13.6), perhaps because Timias's ambitions and social status are not in conflict. See also I.vi.21.6. Chaucer's Sir Thopas is a 'doghty swayn' (line 725), though humour also attaches to the adjective (in view of the knight's effeminacy).

46 *Of* X. See Daniel Javitch, 'The Advertising of Fictionality in *Orlando furioso*', in *Ariosto Today: Contemporary Perspectives*, ed. Donald Beecher *et al.* (Toronto: University of Toronto Press, 2003), pp. 106–25 (p. 117).

96 *Comic Spenser*

of Red Crosse's origins ('with his *clownish* hands their tender wings / He brusheth oft'; my italics). At the same time, the bucolic scene of rural beauty and the image of a 'gentle Shepherd' bathed in the light of 'ruddy *Phebus*' contrasts our bloodthirsty knight choked with the stink of vomit so jarringly that Spenser is surely enjoying himself at Red Crosse's expense (I.i.22–3).[47] This is not to trivialise the danger that Red Crosse faces, for the 'real monster' – his own misled sense of personal autonomy – will of course show its destructive power in the series of misadventures that follow (in 'The Legend of Holiness', as in *Virgils Gnat*, the shepherd who kills insects lives to regret his carelessness).

Shortly after the battle with Errour, the question of whether Red Crosse is a shepherd or a lost sheep is settled definitively. His second battle is with Sansfoy, and again the description of their encounter is interrupted by a discordant pastoral simile:

> As when two rams stird with ambitious pride,
> Fight for the rule of the rich fleeced flocke,
> Their horned fronts so fierce on either side,
> Doe meete, that with the terror of the shocke
> Astonied both, stand sencelesse as a blocke,
> Forgetfull of the hanging victory:
> So stood these twaine, vnmoued as a rocke,
> Both staring fierce, and holding idely,
> The broken reliques of their former cruelty.
>
> (I.ii.16)

At first glance, this simile is less obtrusive than the preceding one in that it is dressed in the high register of epic: 'ambitious', 'rule', 'terror', 'fierce', and so on. But it is also funnier as a result. First there is the absurd image of two stupefied sheep, senseless as blocks, attempting to maintain a threatening aspect by 'staring fierce' at each other. Second is the fact that in farmyard terms, a fight for 'rule' is a fight to impregnate a female.[48] Having secured this right, Red Crosse departs with Duessa as his prize

47 On Pope's alertness to the burlesque qualities of the gnat analogy, see Michelle O'Callaghan, 'Spenser's Literary Influence', in *Oxford Handbook of ES*, pp. 664–83 (p. 671). This satirical perspective contrasts the approach of Rufus Wood, for whom the sudden transition affirms the revelatory power of metaphor; *Metaphor and Belief in 'The Faerie Queene'* (Basingstoke: Macmillan, 1997), pp. 28–41.

48 *OED*, s.v. 'astonished', *ppl. a.*, 1: 'bereft of sensation; stunned, benumbed'; 2: 'bereft of one's wits; stupefied'. The comedy of this moment has been mentioned by a number of critics, including Frances McNeely Leonard, *Laughter in the Courts of Love: Comedy in Allegory from Chaucer to Spenser* (Oklahoma: Pilgrim, 1981), p. 141. I owe the point

Humour and heroism 97

and takes Sansfoy's shield for good measure – a visual reminder that, as in the battle with Errour, victory here amounts to a moral defeat.

Playing the part of vulnerable damsel, Duessa proceeds to bolster Red Crosse's growing ego, appealing to his 'mighty wil' and 'powre', crying for mercy and calling herself a 'silly Dame' and 'thrall' – a submissive performance that 'much emmoue[s] his stout heroicke heart' (I.ii.21–2). Red Crosse (whose 'quicke eies' are all the while roving over his new lady's face; ii.26.6) responds with exaggerated courtesy and begins to spout chivalric clichés ('Faire Lady hart of flint would rew / The vndeserued woes and sorrowes, which ye shew', etc; ii.26.8–9). As Hamilton observes of the especially inane remark 'Better new friend then an old foe is said' (ii.27.4), 'evidently this proverb is the knight's own, its triteness befitting a rustic ready to offer himself as a friend, i.e. "lover".'[49]

Red Crosse's clownishness (in both senses of the word) is further exhibited when he and his new lady find an attractive resting place among trees, and he sets about weaving her a garland (I.ii.30.5–7).[50] But, as the suddenly reliable narrator warns, this is no place of pastoral innocence:

> The fearefull Shepheard often there aghast
> Vnder them neuer sat, ne wont there sound
> His mery oaten pipe, but shund th'vnlucky ground.
>
> (I.ii.28.7–9)

This is the province of postlapsarian Eden, complete with men and women hiding among and entrapped by trees, where rusticity equates not to humility or innate wisdom but to sinfulness – the earth here providing the 'tiller' St George with a crude means of concealing Fradubio's bleeding bough (and, implicitly, forestalling recognition of his own part in Christ's suffering). This instance of pastoral interruption is ominous, but, like

---

about sexual competition to John W. Shroeder, 'Spenser's Erotic Drama: The Orgoglio Episode', *ELH*, 29 (1962), 140–59 (p. 143). On the specifically sexual comedy of Red Crosse's errancy, see Chapter 3 below. Ariosto also uses the ram analogy (though with less elaboration) in the context of a ludicrous battle scene; *OF* I.63.1–2. Behind Ariosto is the influence of Ovid: in *Met* IX, for example, Achelous compares his battle with Hercules to bulls colliding 'in contest for the sleekest cow / Of all the countryside' (lines 30–65) – before transforming into a savage bull himself (66–98).

49 *FQ* I.ii.27.4n. See also Cheney, *Spenser's Image of Nature*, pp. 35–6.

50 This recalls Red Crosse's erotic dream of Una 'with Yuie girlond crownd' (I.i.48.9). Speaking of the latter image, Cheney rightly observes that '[t]he image of the pastoral garland will be repeated throughout the Book as a mocking reminder of an erotic motive which lies hidden beneath the conscious level of the quest – a motive which is accommodated only at the end when Una is crowned … at the time of her betrothal to Red Crosse'; Cheney, *Spenser's Image of Nature*, p. 31.

98   *Comic Spenser*

other such moments, it incisively satirises Red Crosse's moral state. The sound of Fradubio's laments emanating from a tree literally petrifies Red Crosse, making his limbs freeze and his hair stand on end (I.ii.31.8).[51] This tree-like paralysis underlines his likeness to Fradubio – the latter's story of seduction by a witch is, after all, Red Crosse's own – as well as his incapacity to recognise it. Recalling the ram analogy of ii.16, Red Crosse is said to be 'Astond' (ii.31.8), suggesting – as though his very brain has turned arboreal – not just 'dismayed' but also 'stupefied'.[52]

Pastoral, as these examples illustrate, is an instrument of bathos in Book I; it undercuts the knight's pretension and betrays his limitations. Interestingly, Stanley Fish attributes a similar function to images drawn from the natural world in *Paradise Lost*. The famous simile comparing Satan's host to a swarm of bees, for example, impresses us with the sheer multitude of fallen angels, but it also has the effect of belittling their domain and power.[53] Fish observes that the angels' heroic stature is likewise undermined, though to different effect. For example, the heavenly host is compared to a wheat field waving in the breeze, watched over anxiously by a ploughman lest the wind should scatter the ripe grain before it is harvested (*Paradise Lost* IV.977–85). Where John Peter finds this to be 'an inappropriately debilitating simile' that effectively turns the angelic forces into 'a group of minstrels armed with toy spears – men, as it were, of straw', Fish regards such bathos as appropriate. As he argues, if we radically redefine heroism in a Christian context as the renunciation rather than accrual of personal power, we will understand how it is that straw men may prove powerful, and how – as Adam himself learns – 'things deem'd weak' may subvert 'worldly strong' (XII.567–8).[54]

---

51 While the similar encounter between Aeneas and Polydorus in the third book of the *Aeneid* lends this example of pastoral interruption notable pedigree, Ariosto's parody of the same Virgilian episode (in which the tree pragmatically acknowledges the limitations of his audience – 'Such knowledge as I have I've gladly shared, / Although I doubt if it will much avail you'; *OF* VI.53.1–2) ironically mediates the epic allusion. These same echoes are interpreted differently by Vaught, 'Spenser's Dialogic Voice in Book I of *The Faerie Queene*', *SEL* 41 (2001), 71–89.

52 *OED*, s.v. 'astonished', *a.*, 2, 3. Dull paralysis is also associated with despair (I.ix.24.4, 35.7).

53 The comparison of heroes to bees derives from a passage in Virgil's fourth Georgic that is itself mock-epic in comparing bees to heroes; Stanley Fish, *Surprised by Sin: The Reader in 'Paradise Lost'* (Basingstoke: Macmillan, 1997), pp. 162–80 (on the bee simile see p. 8 n. 1, and pp. 167–8). For the simile itself see John Milton, *Paradise Lost*, ed. Christopher Ricks (London: Penguin, 1989), I.767–76. On Satan as a mock-hero see also McCabe, 'Parody, Sympathy and Self', pp. 7–8.

54 Fish, *Surprised by Sin*, pp. 173–5. For Peter's remark (which Fish cites) see John Peter, *A Critique of 'Paradise Lost'* (New York: Columbia University Press, 1960), pp. 24–5. Terry

Humour and heroism 99

While, as these examples illustrate, bathos can operate independently of humour, Fish does find cause for amusement in Milton's ambivalence toward heroism, and in doing so adds to a thread of criticism dating back to at least the eighteenth century. Readers from Addison onward have found Milton's dramatisation of heaven to be in some respects farcical, the battle between the angelic and demonic forces even being marked by a 'String of Puns, and those very indifferent ones'.[55] Pope pondered whether Milton had picked up the bad habit of including 'ludicrous descriptions' in epic from Homer, though, I would suggest, we might equally speculate about the possibility of a Spenserian influence.[56] One such Homeric description (which anticipates both Ruggiero's fly-like valor and Red Crosse's gnats) occurs when Minerva is said to reward Menelaus by

> breathing in his breast the courage of a flie
> Which loves to bite so and doth beare man's bloud so much good will
> That still (though beaten from a man) she flies upon him still.[57]

It is precisely this kind of sly incongruity that Fish is concerned to draw our attention to in *Paradise Lost*. Although Fish concedes that Milton's humour 'is never side-splitting', he proposes that there is 'more than a smile' behind the strategy of splicing together ostentatious epic formulae and lowly analogies – sometimes in such a way as to make the angels look slightly absurd in their role as heavenly shadow-boxers, fulfilling duties God has no need of.[58]

Humour plays a more marked and persistent role in *The Faerie Queene* than it does in *Paradise Lost*, though the strategic clash of heroic and anticlimactic elements discussed by Fish is directly comparable to the effect of pastoral interruption in Book I. We may compare Red Crosse's impotence, as fallen man, to that of the angelic *and* the satanic forces.

Richard similarly finds that Milton 'counterpointed great and small in order to urge a Christian morality'; ' "Meaner Themes": Mock-Heroic and Providentialism in Cowper's Poetry', *SEL*, 34 (1994), 617–34.

55 *Spectator*, Vol. IV, p. 108. On puns see Fish, *Surprised by Sin*, p. 179; and on contemporary responses to Milton's heaven see pp. 173–5, 179.

56 Homer, *The 'Iliad' of Homer*, ed. Mack, II.255n. Of course, Spenser himself may well have been influenced by Homer's use of unheroic and bathetic similes, as was, no doubt, Ariosto. On the Homeric simile see Wolfe, 'Chapman's Ironic Homer', pp. 170–2; and pp. 58–9 above.

57 Homer, *Iliad*, trans. Chapman, XVII.489; cf. Wolfe, 'Chapman's Ironic Homer', pp. 165, 170.

58 Fish, *Surprised by Sin*, pp. 173–9. 'Shadow-boxing' is Fish's phrase (p. 170).

100 *Comic Spenser*

In a Christian and, moreover, Protestant context, entire reliance on God is essentially positive. When Red Crosse attempts to contradict this reliance, therefore, pastoral allusions accentuate his folly and remind us of his fallen status. But it is ultimately the positive meaning of the knight's lowliness that prevails in Book I.

This positive dimension has been implied all along by the serio-comic nature of Red Crosse's failings, for what makes these laughable rather than tragic is the promise of salvation. When Una reasserts Red Crosse's true unheroic identity during his seduction by Despair, there is a sense in which she is drawing out the seeds of sympathy implicit in the earlier satirical portrayals of the 'warlike swaine' (I.iv.37.9), reasserting the intersection of these same conflicting identities (hero and rustic) but in a positive light. She calls him away from Despair: 'Come, come away, fraile, feeble, fleshly wight' (ix.53.1). The parallel appeal at the end of the same stanza, 'Arise, Sir knight arise, and leaue this cursed place', deliberately contrasts with the first, for between the assertion of his lowliness ('fleshly wight') and the confirmation of his nobility ('Sir knight') is, in the form of a rhetorical question, a bridge between these two identities: 'In heauenly mercies hast thou not a part?' (53.4). The allusion to God's mercy allows both sides of Red Crosse to coexist without contradiction and, this time, without satirical intent.

It is in this light that we should interpret the amusingly homely description of Eden's inhabitants after Red Crosse's defeat of the dragon. Among 'the folke' (I.xii.12.1) who come running in the wake of the knight's victory are 'the fry of children yong' (I.xii.7.1), 'the raskall many ... / Heaped together in rude rablement' (9.1–2), 'a foolehardy chyld' (11.1), and 'gossibs' (11.4). All these people 'flocked ... him rownd about' (12.1), reversing Canto i's image of Red Crosse being molested by gnat-like baby Errours. The knight's clownish bungling of that first fight is overwritten in Canto xii by the positive meaning of clownishness: innocence, artlessness, and – especially in the emphasis on fry, babes, and foolish children – the childlike simplicity honoured by Christ in the Gospels: 'Suffer the litle children to come vnto me, and forbid them not: for of such is the kingdome of God' (Mark 10:14).[59] The image of a village child boldly approaching the dead dragon to its mother's horror may reflect Red Crosse's new understanding of what he is beneath the armour of God: a child touching the claws of a beast

---

59 See also I Corinthians 1:21–3 and 4:10 on being a fool for Christ's sake. On the 'foolishness' of Christ himself see Erasmus's 'Letter to Martin Dorp', *Folly*, pp. 211–52 (p. 233).

Humour and heroism 101

that has already been defeated (xii.11.1–3).[60] This realisation *is* holiness. Contrasting his laughable dissimilarity to Christ in Canto i, Red Crosse's triumphant entry into Eden as the folk lay down their clothes before him is indeed Christ-like: 'a great multitude spred their garments in the way: and other cut downe branches from the trees, and strawed them in the way' (Matthew 21:8).

As mentioned in my Introduction, John Upton, the eighteenth-century editor of *The Faerie Queene*, described the moment in which the villagers come forth to prod and marvel at the beast's dead body as a 'mixture of the dreadful with the comic, the serious and the ridiculous'.[61] The essentially comic nature of the battle and its aftermath (which we will come to in a moment) reconfigures pastoral bathos, hitherto satirical, as comedic. The crowning of Una with a 'girland greene' (I.xii.8.6) in a manner 'twixt earnest and twixt game' (8.7) recalls Red Crosse's former garland-making for Duessa (ii.30.5–7), and reminds us that both gestures are at once comic and serious. When Red Crosse venerates Duessa he is ridiculous (seriously sinful, yet childishly stupid, judged, yet forgiven); when Una is crowned by the children of the kingdom of God, it is evidence of reverence but also of play. The scene of celebration recalls us to the province of the pastoral world in its idyllic, recreative mode. The Edenic world of merry folk, gaiety, singing contests, games, and musical instruments (the 'mery oaten pipe' of ii.28.9) pointedly contrasts the sad demeanour of the freshly invested and self-consciously heroic knight in Canto i as well as the 'sterne' sound of epic (Proem I, 1.4).

In contrast to the theme of 'bloody Mars' that Piers advocates as the highest possible vocation, the coming of the Messiah promises a return to the land, the prophesied time when swords and spears will be turned into mattocks and scythes (Micah 4:3).[62] Thus where the renunciation of pastoral was associated with affected gravity, its return at I.xii is marked

60 On the Christian vs chivalric connotations of 'child' see Borris, *Allegory and Epic*, p. 178. Red Crosse becomes notably child-like in the House of Holiness, where he is placed in the 'schoolehous' of Fidelia to be taught by her (I.x.18), and where Mercy takes him by the hand 'As carefull Nourse her child from falling oft does reare' (x.35.9).
61 *Var* III, p. 306.
62 On the trumpet as an instrument of fallen, as opposed to glorious, mankind see I.x.60–2 and Proem V, 9.5. Richard Helgerson detects ironic equivocation in the poet's description of his epic undertaking as 'a farre unfitter taske' (Proem I, 1.3), raising the possibility that epic is unfit for a pastoral poet and not the other way around; 'poet, role of the', in *SpE*, pp. 549–51 (p. 550). This is one implication of Book VI, where irony is generated not by pastoral interruption into the elevated world of epic so much as by chivalric interruption into the idyllic world of shepherds and, as it turns out, visionary poets. If Red Crosse is a mock-knight, Calidore – a champion of courtesy prone to poking his nose where it is not welcome – is a mock-shepherd. A courtly outsider, he poses with a shepherd's

102 *Comic Spenser*

by levity. The great rejoicing at the defeat of the dragon is compared to the mirth of a 'solemne feast' (xii.4.6–8), and not one but two such feasts follow Red Crosse's victory (xii.14–15, 40). 'Solemn' here has an association with joy that pointedly revises its melancholy connotations in Canto i.[63] In contrast to the showily sparse entertainment at Archimago's house ('rest is their feast'; i.35.3), the populace of the liberated city feast upon 'meates and drinkes of euery kinde' until 'Their feruent appetites they quenched had' (xii.15.1–2). By Canto xii we have achieved piety without the self-congratulation, seriousness without the dour face.

And yet, while bathos has been reconfigured as comedic and Red Crosse now resembles Christ, he is, because human, still very much vulnerable to comic exposure.[64] Proving this point, acute dramatic irony attends the moment in which Una's father asks his prospective son-in-law to tell-all about his quest. This request for the hero's story is impeccable epic convention, but in this case, of course, that story does not involve brave deeds but rather deep disgrace. Glossing over the details of what amounts to a forced public confession, the narrator reports that Red Crosse 'with vtt'rance graue, and count'nance sad, / From poynt to poynt … / Discourst his voyage long' (I.xii.15.7–9). Yet his audience's tearful lamentations about their hero's suffering at the hands of 'luck', 'fortune', and 'fate' (xii.16) seem very suspicious – as it turns out, rightly so, because when a breathless Archimago arrives with a letter from Duessa a few stanzas later, we see that hypocrisy is exposing Red Crosse once again. It is clear that the victorious knight has said nothing about the part of Duessa in his quest. Allegorically, this makes sense if the letter punningly symbolises the 'letter of the law'. That is, the letter appropriately fixates upon Red Crosse's wrongdoing, leaving his salvation out of the picture, just as Red Crosse's victory over the dragon had allowed him to leave behind his former wrongdoing. Yet, in narrative terms, the revelation that Red Crosse's long tale of misfortune had entirely omitted any mention of his affair is richly ironic.[65] The sudden arrival of the letter (which is to say,

crook to gain the favours of Pastorella (who has proved unimpressed by chivalric display; VI.ix.36), and in the process stumbles upon and ruins the ephemeral and transcendent beauty conjured by Colin's rustic piping (VI.x.18), a vision of poetic achievement utterly at odds with the ambitious renunciation of pastoral in Proem I.

63 *OED*, s.v. 'solemn', *a.*, 6: 'of a serious, grave, or earnest character'; 7(b): 'gloomy, dark, sombre'; but also 1(a): 'having a religious character; sacred'.

64 On 'imperfections in the redeemed' see Walls, *God's Only Daughter*, pp. 56–8; and Hadfield, 'Spenser and Religion' on Calvinist theology, pp. 24–5.

65 Numerous critics have responded to this point. Suttie, 'Edmund Spenser's Political Pragmatism', argues that such flattering versions of events have an ethical justification

Humour and heroism   103

the sudden reminder of our certain condemnation by the law) ensures that Red Crosse is embarrassed just as he is being most honoured. Having said this, the letter's magnanimous reception in the court of Una's parents reminds us that although the redeemed may still be proud, it is the prerogative of generous fathers to forgive.

Comic violence

> There was in Spenser ... an incontinence of the descriptive faculty.
>
> R. W. Church, *Spenser*[66]

Homer established the graphic description of combat – detailed to the point of specifying which organs and limbs are on the receiving end of whose spear – as a convention of epic poetry that, notwithstanding its focus on the body at the crudest level, became an instantly recognisable signifier of the highest category of literature. Yet, as an expression of man's lowest self (irrational, uncontrolled, inhumane), violence is also the archetypal unheroic theme. Mock-heroic works typically revel in this tension; *Don Quixote*, for example, confronts us with an unrelenting stream of beatings and thrashings that pit the high idealism of chivalric romance against the grotesque realism of the picaresque novella.[67]

As we have seen, Spenser, too, is keenly attuned to the proximity of valor and grotesquerie, and the fact that wounding and bloodletting

in that dwelling on sinfulness 'is not conducive to salvation'; pp. 71–6 (p. 73). While Red Crosse's omissions (and Una's father's clemency in the face of Duessa's accusations) are indeed suggestive of the way salvation rewrites the story of our sinfulness (see also Caelia's words at I.x.17), there is nevertheless considerable irony in the fact that Red Crosse is caught being generous to himself. It is surely appropriate that the knight's fallible and vulnerable humanity is strikingly evident even as his faults are being 'overlooked'. After his embarrassment by the entry of Archimago (who, we must constantly recall, is a figure of the Christian's own hypocrisy), Red Crosse's stumbling depiction of himself as a victim of Duessa's evil (see especially the passive construction at I.xii.32.1) before being rescued from the impossible task of justifying his claim to Una's hand (at xii.33.1) reminds us that salvation from the Protestant point of view is unmerited. For a provocative reading of Red Crosse's self-exculpation as indicative of a narcissistic, scapegoating impulse interrogated by Book I as a whole, see Harry Berger, Jr, 'Displacing Autophobia in *Faerie Queene* I: Ethics, Gender, and Oppositional Reading in the Spenserian Text', *ELR*, 28 (1998), 163–82 (pp. 170–2).

66 Church, *Spenser*, p. 177.

67 See Adrienne Martin, 'Humor and Violence in Cervantes', in *The Cambridge Companion to Cervantes* (Cambridge: Cambridge University Press, 2002), pp. 160–85 (p. 177). On the connection between Spenser's parodic treatment of epic values and his experiences in Ireland, see McCabe, 'Ireland: Policy, Poetics and Parody', in *The Cambridge Companion*

104   *Comic Spenser*

are (for the most part) tropes rather than literally at issue only deepens their potential for irony. First, this is because allegorical battles parody real ones: the narrator's scrupulous commentary on the order of blows, quantity of bloodshed, and this or that feat of strength or bravery are part of a game we are complicit in playing.[68] At times the level of detail demanded by the narrative would seem to exceed the allegorical point, creating an amusing imbalance between violence as moral trope and violence as spectacle. Conversely, there is irony in the crude physicality of violence as compared to the complexity of spiritual and psychological issues – which is to say, there are times where the allegorical point would seem to exceed the narrative terms available. Combat is a versatile metaphor for conflicts and trials of every kind, but its terms are not subtle. When Red Crosse hacks off the dragon's tail at the fifth joint 'but the stump him lefte' (I.xi.39.9), the tension between crude violence and spiritual allegory is acute – and funny.[69]

Of course, Red Crosse's battle with the dragon is distinguished from his prior violent encounters, in that the moral opposition at issue is genuine: for once this really is a fight with a 'goody' and a 'baddy'. For the majority of Book I, violence offers a metaphor not for spiritual resilience but for reductive and fixed habits of mind – for psychological crises where self-validating aggression is ultimately self-destructive. In such cases the semblance of heroic action is especially ironic. All the while insisting on the righteousness of Red Crosse's cause, Spenser typically exploits the way opponents mirror each other as they exchange blows by introducing ambiguous pronouns and dubious analogies ('As when two rams …'; I.ii.16.1) into the mix, loosening our grip on the moral distinction supposedly at issue. The fact that each of Red Crosse's victories

    to Spenser, ed. Andrew Hadfield (Cambridge: Cambridge University Press, 2001), pp. 60–78 (p. 69). On the black comedy of Ovidian violence see pp. pp. 52–3 above.

68 It is also a game Spenser appears to enjoy; *Piers Plowman* and *The Pilgrim's Progress*, which engage pilgrimage rather than battle as a dominant metaphor for spiritual education, are restrained by comparison. For example, when Christian gives Apollyon a mortal wound, we are told that his foe 'spread forth his dragon's wings, and sped him away, that Christian saw him no more'); John Bunyan, *The Pilgrim's Progress*, ed. Roger Sharrock (London: Penguin, 1987), p. 54. On the lush descriptions of Spenser's dragon fight, see below.

69 On the pleasures of this tension, see Esolen, 'Irony and the Pseudo-Physical'. For a more ambivalent response to the 'gratuitous' and 'incongruous' aspects of Spenser's battle scenes see Michael West, 'Spenser's Art of War: Chivalric Allegory, Military Technology, and the Elizabethan Mock-Heroic Sensibility', *RQ*, 41 (1988), 654–704 (pp. 684–6). West proposes that we need to bring more of a sense of humour to our readings of Spenser, though at times his analysis makes it unclear whether we are supposed to laugh with him or at him.

Humour and heroism 105

(over Errour, Sansfoy, and Sansjoy) merely signals his fuller identification with his enemy makes the narrator's reassuring commentaries ('So th'one for wrong, the other striues for right'; v.8.1, 9.1) comically naïve.

In their irony and ambivalence, Spenser's battles parody not only the heroic tradition but also traditions of Christian allegory grounded in moral dichotomies. Consider Faith's battle against Worship-of-the-Old-Gods in Prudentius's *Psychomachia*:

> illa hostile caput phalerataque tempora vittis altior insurgens labefactat, et ora cruore de pecudum satiata solo adplicat et pede calcat elisos in morte oculos, animamque malignam fracta intercepti commercia gutturis artant, difficilemque obitum suspiria longa fatigant.

> (but she, rising higher, smites her foe's head down, with its fillet-decked brows, lays in the dust that mouth that was sated with the blood of beasts, and tramples the eyes under foot, squeezing them out in death. The throat is choked and the scant breath confined by the stopping of its passage, and long gasps make a hard and agonising death).[70]

We are obliged to turn a blind eye to the black comedy of such gratuitous violence in the latter context, but not so in *The Faerie Queene*. When Red Crosse chokes Errour and makes her vomit (I.i.20), or cleaves Sansfoy's head in two and forces him to kiss 'his mother earth' (ii.19.6), grotesquerie ostensibly points up the grossness of evil and the exertion required to repress it as it does in the *Psychomachia*, but what it *actually* conveys is the gruesomeness, and inherent violence, of dogmatic and self-affirming morality.

Red Crosse's battle with Sansjoy renders violence absurd not only by insisting on an illusory moral opposition but also by juxtaposing the festive trappings of chivalric tournament (court entertainers, wine, a royal canopy, trumpets, gaping spectators) with the grim bloodthirstiness of Red Crosse as he wields his instrument of 'wrath and heauinesse' (I.v.6.5). Like the jarring 'gentle Shepheard' analogy of I.i.23, the gorgeous description of Phoebus rising above the horizon like a happy bridegroom 'dauncing forth, shaking his deawie hayre' (v.2.4) is a comically incongruous point of contrast for our insomniac knight as he rises from his bed to enter the lists with Joylessness personified.[71] Implicitly, Spenser's narrator is one of the cunning chroniclers

---

70 Prudentius, 'Psychomachia' (lines 30–5), in *Prudentius, with an English Translation*, ed. and trans. H. J. Thomson, 2 vols (Cambridge, MA: Harvard University Press, 1949), Vol. I, pp. 280–1.

71 For a non-comic reading of the analogy between Red Crosse and Phoebus see *FQ* v.2.1–5n.

106   *Comic Spenser*

who can turn futile conflict into something to celebrate, describing bloody
hacking and grovelling in the dust as 'glorie excellent' (v.1.4) and 'gay
cheualree' (v.16.5) for the benefit of restless readers wishing to hear about
'warres for Ladies doen by many a Lord' (v.3.9).

Yet comic irony is not reserved only for those battles that epitomise Red
Crosse's spiritual malaise. Arthur's righteous defeat of the giant Orgoglio
(viii.6–25) is funny, as is, significantly, the victorious culmination of Book
I: the dragon fight (xi.4–55). Both these battles bear comparison to the
Psychomachia in that grotesquerie facilitates a meditation on the repugnant
character of evil, yet both are also marked by notable moments of humour
and mock-heroic irony. As I will argue in Chapter 3, the evil represented
by Orgoglio is treated humorously in Canto vii, where he appears as Red
Crosse's phallic nemesis. There is black comedy, too, in his systematic
dismemberment by Arthur: where Red Crosse severs the dragon's tail at the
fifth joint, Arthur chops off Orgoglio's left arm (viii.10.6) and half his right leg
(viii.22.4) followed by his head, at which point, in a dreamlike development,
the giant deflates before our eyes (viii.24).[72] However insubstantial the
enemy turns out to be, there is plenty of Ovidian gore in the meantime;
when Arthur splits one of the heads of Duessa's beast down the middle he is
left wading ankle-deep in blood:

> His monstrous scalpe downe to his teeth it tore,
> And that misformed shape misshaped more:
> A sea of blood gusht from the gaping wownd,
> That her gay garments stayned with filthy gore,
> And ouerflowed all the field arownd;
> That ouer shoes in blood he waded on the grownd.
>
> (I.viii.16.4–9)[73]

An equally lurid description occurs when Red Crosse spears the dragon
under the left wing:

---

72 Acts of dismemberment are liable to play uncomfortably on the boundary of the
shocking and the comic, as may be seen in works as diverse as the *Metamorphoses*,
Beowulf, *Fergus*, and *Titus Andronicus*, for example. See further E. L. Risden, 'Heroic
Humor in Beowulf', in *Humour in Anglo-Saxon Literature*, ed. Jonathan Wilcox
(Cambridge: D. S. Brewer, 2000), pp. 71–8 (esp. 76–7).

73 'Over shoes' (minus the blood) was proverbial; see M. P. Tilley, *A Dictionary of the
Proverbs in England in the Sixteenth and Seventeenth Centuries* (Ann Arbor: University
of Michigan Press 1950), p. 601 (S379, S380). The dominant sense is 'having gone this
far, keep wading'. See for example William Shakespeare, *A Midsummer Night's Dream*
3.2.48. All references to Shakespeare are to *The Riverside Shakespeare*, ed. Herschel
Baker *et al.*, 2nd edn (New York: Houghton Mifflin, 1997).

Humour and heroism

> The steely head stuck fast still in his flesh,
> Till with his cruell clawes he snatcht the wood,
> And quite a sunder broke. Forth flowed fresh
> A gushing riuer of blacke gory blood,
> That drowned all the land, whereon he stood;
> The streame thereof would driue a water-mill.
>
> (I.xi.22.1–6)

One might object that what I am calling 'Ovidian' hyperbole has a distinctly non-comic biblical precedent in, for example, Revelation 14:19–20:

> And the Angel thrust in his sharpe sickle on the earth, and cut downe the vines of the vineyard of the earth, and cast them into that great wine presse of the wrath of God. And the wine presse was troden without the citie, and *blood came out of the wine presse, vnto the horse bridles*. [my italics]

Spenserian gore is, after all, biblical – the copious black gore that issues from both the dragon's side and from Orgoglio's dismembered body ('like fresh water streame from riuen rocke'; I.viii.10.9) pointedly contrasts Christ's purifying blood. Nevertheless, I would argue that Spenser's use of the Christian tradition of bold and affective imagery in Book I deliberately courts absurdity.[74] His moral seriousness is not undermined by this current of humour but invigorated by it; as Thomas Wilson remarked, 'the occasion of laughter, and the meane that maketh us mery is the fondnes, the filthines, the deformitie, and all such evill behaviour, as we see to be in other'.[75] But even more to the point is Hamilton's description of the 'superb extravagance' of Spenser's imagery as a kind of victorious exuberance (xi.22.4–6n). Terror and humour pull in opposite directions, demanding that we be afraid and insisting that we need not. These battles are, as it were, comically apocalyptic.[76]

Once we are attuned to it, the conjunction of terror and humour is everywhere in evidence. The vision of gallons of dragon blood propelling a watermill is alarming yet wryly provincial – as evocative of rural

---

74 See also p. 190 below.
75 *Rhetorique*, pp. 135–6.
76 On the 'joco-serious' and exuberant aspects of the dragon fight as affirming Christ's victory over death, see James Nohrnberg, *The Analogy of 'The Faerie Queene'* (Princeton: Princeton University Press, 1976), pp. 196–7; and, more tentatively, J. B. Lethbridge, 'The Poetry of *The Faerie Queene*', in *Spenser in the Moment*, ed. Paul J. Hecht and J. B. Lethbridge (Madison, NJ: Fairleigh Dickinson University Press, 2015), pp. 169–216 (p. 180).

108 *Comic Spenser*

industry as of Satan.[77] Similarly, Arthur's truncation of Orgoglio's arm provokes an enraged roar which sounds like

> An heard of Bulles, whom kindly rage doth sting,
> Doe for the milky mothers want complaine,
> And fill the fieldes with troublous bellowing
>
> (I.viii.11.6–8)

An intimidating enough sound, no doubt, but the bathos of the comparison (accentuated by 'complaine') displaces terror with amused pity.[78] Repeated suggestions that the air through which the dragon flies and the weapons that quiver in his scaly flesh are themselves terrified ('The clowdes before him fledd for terror great' (I.xi.10.8); 'the stiffe beame quaked, as affrayd' (xi.20.5), and so forth) likewise supposedly augment horror but actually – because such personification is essentially playful – undermine it. Even the narrator's insistence on the enormity of the dragon is paradoxical in this way. When he admires the terribleness of the dragon or seems to linger with delectation over its hideousness (which he finds 'wondrous'; xi.13.1), and when we picture the dragon sunning himself on 'a great hill, himself like great hill' (xi.4.6) or throwing fire from 'his large nosethril' (xi.22.9), the effect is fantastic and naïve.[79]

Not surprisingly, the dragon fight has troubled readers who sense a disconnection between Christian eschatology and childish romance fictions. But far from being something we need to tolerate or defend, such naïveté is theologically crucial. Allusions to infancy and childhood are significant in the final cantos of Book I, reflecting the special status of the child in God's kingdom, and it seems appropriate that the reader

---

77 The humour of the watermill reference is noted in passing by David Norbrook, *Poetry and Politics in the English Renaissance*, rev. edn (Oxford: Oxford University Press, 2002), p. 100.

78 Here we may see Spenser's kinship with the humour of medieval religious drama, a function of which was to affirm God's power and to make evil look foolish and impotent – to make one feel small in the cosmic scheme of things but also to domesticate and embarrass apocalyptic threats; see Chapter 1, and Kolve, *The Play Called Corpus Christi*, pp. 124–44.

79 The same naïveté or storybook quality may be felt when we are told, in Canto i, of Red Crosse's enemy, 'a Dragon horrible and stearne' (I.i.3.9). Vaught, '*St George and the Fiery Dragon*', discusses the comic aspects of the dragon at some length, arguing persuasively for the influence of a Mummers' play of the period. However, Vaught's emphasis on the patriotism of Spenser's popular allusion leads her to conclude, as I do not, that the comic dimension of the battle bolsters Red Crosse's 'heroic stature' (pp. 98–9).

Humour and heroism 109

should at this point feel like a child listening to a story.[80] To feel this way is to sense the promise of a happy ending even (or especially) in the midst of powerlessness or danger. In the context of 'The Legend of Holiness', this promise is theologically profound, and it should be noted that humour – or more precisely latent humour – is its primary vehicle. The externalisation of evil as a physical thing that can be seen and defeated is no longer indicative of the literal-minded, demonising mentality that gave rise to Errour (which was funny in a different way), but rather expressive of the finite nature of evil.[81] However enormous, it is surely reassuring that that the dragon can actually be measured. After the dragon's defeat, the image of 'bold' villagers coming forth to 'proue how many acres he did spred of land' (I.xii.11.8–9) may be a wry dig at theological nit-picking, but it is also comically affirmative.

Having said this about humour and empowerment, there is an even more pressing theological point to be made here about humour and limitation. The element of naïveté and childishness speaks directly to this connection, too. The episode's storybook quality, and its occasional moments of disarming bathos, remind us that, however climactic and affirming Red Crosse's victory over his enemy may be, this is only a 'mock' battle. When the narrator asserts that the Well of Life into which the knight plunges excels 'th'English *Bath* and eke the german *Spau'* (I.xi.30.7), we are playfully reminded of the immeasurable difference between poetical anticipations of salvation and the thing itself. The naïveté of what Carol Kaske has called Red Crosse's 'folksy dragon fight' reminds us of the same thing.[82] This is an artistic rendering of the internal victory of faith that happens within the Elect, which is itself a reflection of the victory of Christ's sacrifice and a foreshadowing of the victory promised in Revelation. The culmination of Red Crosse's quest is, as

---

80 See pp. 100–1 above, as well as *FQ* I.x.16 for an implicit reference to Red Crosse as a newborn baby.
81 Yet of course we are still tempted to see the dragon as fundamentally 'other' to Red Crosse (and, in those moments where the dragon gets the better of him, we may suspect that our hero is struggling with the same temptation). Subtle echoes remind us that the threat posed by the dragon has been integral to Red Crosse's flawed humanity all along: the dragon's 'haughty crest' (I.xi.15.5) reminds us of Archimago impersonating Red Crosse (ii.11.5) shortly after shape-shifting into a dragon (ii.10.6). See Vaught, '*St George and the Fiery Dragon*', on the etymological link between the 'furlongs' of the dragon's tail (xi.11.7) and the furrow in which Red Crosse was discovered as a baby (pp. 98–9).
82 Carol Kaske, 'Review of Harold W. Weatherby, *Mirrors of Celestial Grace: Patristic Theology in Spenser's Allegory'*, *SN*, 26 (1995), 15–19 (p. 16).

110   *Comic Spenser*

Contemplation asserts, an '*earthly* conquest' (x.60.7; my italics).[83] Comic naïveté is as appropriate here as victorious exuberance: this is a shadow of a shadow of the heroism that Christians celebrate. Where Spenserian bathos places evil within limits, it also implies the limitlessness of good. In Esolen's words, 'there is often a bright humor, not despair at the impossibility of the task, in Spenser's channeling of the inexhaustible ideal into what seems physical'.[84]

I am suggesting, then, that Protestant amusement at the naïveté of the dragon-slaying story (which contributes to the satirical aspect of Red Crosse's identification with St George for the majority of Book I) does not cease during the final victorious battle so much as become instrumental in another way. Yet there is consistency in the humour too, because while Red Crosse is now the 'true *Saint George*', the comic negation of his personal heroism continues. Such moments pull us in two directions because Red Crosse is the flawed vessel of Christ's immeasurable goodness: he is weak but he is strong. Thus the visual comedy of the dragon plucking up knight and horse (reminiscent of the Eagle plucking up Geffrey in *The House of Fame*) and soaring over the fields with them like a hawk with a fowl (I.xi.18–19) reminds us of the knight's human vulnerability and fallibility, and, by the same token (especially when the dragon is forced to drop his thrashing bundle), of the generosity of grace. While such moments might well be described as burlesque, there is a clear retreat from the mock-heroic language of Red Crosse's prior battles. Moving away from his prior zeal, the narrator explicitly tunes the pitch of the battle lower than epic, asking his muse to 'lett downe that haughtie string' (xi.7.7) and lay aside the 'furious fitt' associated with martial deeds and trumpets (xi.7.1).[85]

---

83 I owe this point to Suttie, 'Edmund Spenser's Political Pragmatism', p. 70.

84 Esolen, 'Irony and the Pseudo-Physical', p. 68 (spoken in relation to the defeat of Munera). On irony and representations of Christian faith see Wayne Booth, *A Rhetoric of Irony* (Chicago: University of Chicago Press, 1974), p. 269, cited by Esolen, 'Irony and the Pseudo-Physical', p. 76 n. 4.

85 Though, as the comparison of Red Crosse to Hercules suggests (I.xi.27), at times the narrator cannot help himself. See Cheney, *Spenser's Image of Nature* on the deprecatory invocation as befitting a battle that is 'personal and ahistorical'; p. 73. For a comparable approach to the narrator's renunciation of epic height, see Wilson-Okamura, *Spenser's International Style*, Chapter 6 (esp. pp. 193ff.); and p. 29 above. Wilson-Okamura proposes that Spenser, had he lived, would have risen to a true high style to write about war in a second instalment of the poem. While my antiheroic reading of Red Crosse's battle concerns violence as a metaphor in the context of an allegory of holiness, and not the real heroic deeds Wilson-Okamura projects as the likely focus of Spenser's unwritten instalment, it seems to me that the scepticism toward personal heroism fostered in this foundational allegorical context holds unavoidable implications for any treatment of military glory, as well as for the high style associated with its celebration.

Humour and heroism 111

Where the burlesque (as I have argued, Catholic) St George was heaped with flattering titles in his most ignominious moments ('Sir', 'liege', 'stout', 'valient', 'Heroicke', 'Champion', 'mighty', 'noble', 'glorious', 'prowest', etc), the true saint of Canto xi is repeatedly referred to simply as the 'knight' (xi.5.1, 9.9, 16.1, 20.2, 25.1) and the 'man' (xi.7.9, 16.9, 17.1, 18.9, 41.1). His heroic strength lies, paradoxically, in his repeated defeat (xi.29, 46). As one critic has put it, the birth of a saint would seem to be the death of a hero.[86] Red Crosse kills the dragon, and heroism with it.

---

86 West, 'Spenser's Art of War', pp. 693–4. As Kathryn Walls has pointed out to me, when Una does praise Red Crosse using heroic terms, the heroism in question belongs first and foremost to God: 'Then God she praysd, and thankt her faithfull knight, / That had atchieude so great a conquest by his [i.e. God's] might' (I.xi.55.8–9).

3

Spenser's bawdy; or, Red Crosse's problem with desire

Supposing truth to be a woman – what? is the suspicion not well founded that all philosophers, when they have been dogmatists, have had little understanding of women? that the gruesome earnestness, the clumsy importunity with which they have hitherto been in the habit of approaching truth have been inept and improper means for winning a wench?

Friedrich Nietzsche, *Beyond Good and Evil*[1]

Vnto the pure are all things pure, but vnto them that are defiled, and vnbeleeuing, is nothing pure, but euen their mindes and consciences are defiled.

Titus 1:15

In 'The Miller's Tale', Nicholas is a resourceful philanderer – a Paridell – whose blatant sexuality and cunning are there to be censured, admired, and laughed at. Rather than looking like a fool himself, he is (for most of the story at least) good at making fools out of others. Absolon, however, is a much funnier stereotype. He has a delicate constitution and is squeamish about bodies, yet is also magnetically attracted to the most wayward wench in town. In what follows I contend that Red Crosse is a bit of an Absolon: a prude at the mercy of his libido.

Chapter 2 considered the comic exposure of Red Crosse's spiritual pride in detail, but the connection between this pride and what I am calling his 'problem with desire' demands a chapter of its own. Some will object that 'The Legend of Holiness' only superficially concerns romantic

---

1 Friedrich Nietzsche, *Beyond Good and Evil*, trans. R. J. Hollingdale (London: Penguin, 2003), p. 31.

Spenser's bawdy   113

themes: Red Crosse looks like a foolish lover, but his foolishness is our collective fallen nature, and he is seduced by falsehood, not a woman. Yet, rather than leaving sexual ethics at the door, we need to recognise the extent to which they go right to the heart of Red Crosse's spiritual errancy. This is not the same as 'reading literally', however. The sexual satire of Book I is teasingly veiled. Contradicting the dominant (and implicitly prohibitive) biblical metaphor of whoredom that governs Red Crosse's seduction by Duessa, Book I employs bawdy wordplay, innuendo, and counterintuitive irony to subvert the idea that holiness is a disembodied and poker-faced virtue, fundamentally at odds with our earthly needs and appetites.

Bodily holiness

The fact that Book I is not *really* about the romantic relationships of knights and ladies has made it a standout example of Spenser overgoing Ariosto, as well as the foundation upon which his 'sage and serious' reputation has most assuredly been built. Holiness, the unspoken argument goes, is not about bodies but 'higher things', spiritual matters; for Spenser's thoughts on romantic love, we must turn to the legends of temperance, chastity, and friendship.

From another perspective, however, spiritual and earthly loves are not mutually exclusive or even fully distinguishable preoccupations for Spenser. As I shall argue further in Chapter 4, sexuality places a magnifying glass on the intersection of sin and redemption in Christian life. Prelapsarian according to both St Augustine and the Elizabethan marriage service, sexual union is divinely ordained; yet desire also epitomises the rebelliousness of the flesh and is considered proof of our fallen state.[2] That fallen state is linked to desire, but it is also – perhaps most compellingly – evident in sexual shame. After eating from the Tree of Knowledge, Adam and Eve did not fall into a lascivious embrace but covered their nakedness with fig leaves, foolishly thinking they had something to hide from God. Spenser's Garden of Adonis, a place where 'Franckly each Paramor his leman knowes' (III.vi.41.7), reverses this

2 St Augustine of Hippo, *The City of God against the Pagans*, ed. R. W. Dyson (Cambridge: Cambridge University Press, 1998), pp. 620–7 (XIV.21–4); see also p. 142 below. According to the Elizabethan marriage service, matrimony was 'instituted of God in paradise in the time of man's innocency'; 'The Form of Solemnization of Matrimony', in *The Book of Common Prayer 1559: The Elizabethan Prayer Book*, ed. John E. Booty (Charlottesville: University of Virginia Press, 2005), pp. 290–9 (p. 290).

114   *Comic Spenser*

guilty inhibition, reinstating the simplicity of God's injunction to 'increase and multiply' (vi.34.6). Similarly, *Epithalamion* celebrates sexual love as generative and thus as the very foundation of the Church. The point to emphasise here is the positivity of Spenser's response to sexuality as something that is, however vulnerable to worldly perversion, potentially restorative or whole-making, and in this sense not merely compatible with holiness (derived from Old English *hál*, 'free from injury, whole, hale') but central to it.

An opposite connotation of holiness, touched upon above, connects wholeness not with earthly unions but with apartness from human affairs, and especially bodies. Erasmus, whose *Encomium matrimonii* appeared in two English translations and nine separate editions over the course of the sixteenth century, articulates the connection between this understanding of holiness and the Catholic esteem for celibacy:

> What is a thing of more equite, then to rendre that [i.e. life] to the posterite whiche we our selfes receyued of oure auncestrye? What acte on the contrarye syde is done with les consideration, than under the zele of *holynes* to flee yt, as *unholy* & ungodly, which god the well and father of all *holynes* wolde haue counted most *holy*?[3]

In the course of his book-long reflection upon what it means to be holy, it makes sense that Spenser should confront his subject's strong historical kinship with ideals of bodily, and in particular sexual, self-denial. To an extent, this point has been done justice. Most notably, Spenser's Protestant esteem for marriage, and the relevance of this esteem for the allegory of Book I, are now generally acknowledged. The best work in this area does more than take Red Crosse's story of erotic misadventure at face value. In very different ways, Janet Adelman, Syrithe Pugh, Harry Berger, Richard Levin, and Judith H. Anderson all find sexual morality implicated at detailed subtextual levels, and not just 'on the surface' of the narrative.[4] Adelman, Pugh, and Berger argue further that the narrative

---

3 My italics; Desiderius Erasmus, *A ryght frutefull epystle, deuysed by the moste excellent clerke Erasmns [sic], in laude and prayse of matrymony*, trans. Richard Taverner (London: Robert Redman, 1536), p. 8.

4 Janet Adelman, 'Revaluing the Body in *The Faerie Queene* I', Hugh Maclean Memorial Lecture, *SR*, 36 (2005): 15–25; Pugh, *Spenser and Ovid*, Chapter 2, esp. pp. 58–66; Berger, 'Sexual and Religious Politics'; Richard Levin, 'The Legende of the Redcrosse Knight and Una; or, Of the Love of a Good Woman', *SEL*, 31 (1991): 1–24; Judith H. Anderson, '"A Gentle Knight was pricking on the plaine": The Chaucerian Connection', *ELR*, 15 (1985), 166–74.

Spenser's bawdy   115

offers a misleading guide to Spenser's sexual ethics. Both Adelman and Berger interrogate the intensely negative images of female sexuality in Canto i. In Adelman's view, these images reflect Red Crosse's own fears and prejudices prior to his spiritual and bodily rehabilitation in Canto xii; relatedly, Berger argues that Spenser's personification of virtue and vice in sexualised terms ironises rather than endorses the misogynistic use of the female figure as a trope. Pugh (in contrast to Adelman's more straightforward interpretation of his subsequent disinhibition with Duessa) interprets Red Crosse's affair as anti-erotic, associating Duessa with the empire in whose name Aeneas had to abandon his love for Dido.[5]

These readings offer valuable challenges to those who would approach allegory as a language of essential or synechdochal correspondences, in the manner of the Puritan Henry Smith: 'In the Reuelation, Antichrist is described by a woman, & in *Zacharie*, sinne is called a woman, which sheweth, that women haue many faultes.'[6] Spenserian allegory, we know, demands more of the reader than this. The relationship between form and meaning in *The Faerie Queene* can be mimetic (sometimes ironically, reductively so), but it can also be deliberately ambiguous and even counterintuitive.[7]

The remainder of this chapter builds upon Adelman's argument that bodily shame, not lust, is the primary target of Spenser's satire in Book I, as well as on Pugh's contention that Red Crosse's promiscuity with Duessa is (in good Duessan fashion) the opposite of what it seems to be.[8] Existing interpretations of Spenser's sexual ethics are almost always guided by the literal story: Red Crosse's unrestrained sensuality with Duessa constitutes a serious distraction from his quest, but desire finds a positive outlet

---

5 According to Pugh's argument, Duessa, who is often associated with Dido (and by extension with sexual distraction as a threat to civilisation), should be aligned with the seductiveness of imperial power – the very thing that love must be sacrificed for; *Spenser and Ovid*, p. 64. Pugh makes a strong case for Spenser's ironic treatment of the Stoic repression of desire elsewhere in *FQ*; see Syrithe Pugh, 'Acrasia and Bondage: Guyon's Perversion of the Ovidian Erotic in Book II of *The Faerie Queene*', in *Edmund Spenser: New and Renewed Directions*, ed. J. B. Lethbridge (Madison, NJ: Fairleigh Dickinson University Press, 2006), pp. 153–94.

6 Henry Smith, *A preparatiue to mariage* (London: Thomas Man, 1591), p. 21.

7 On the difference between mimetic and emblematic allegorical traditions, see Walls, *God's Only Daughter*, pp. 2–3.

8 While Adelman interprets the cause of Red Crosse's waywardness as bodily shame, not desire per se, she nevertheless joins most other critics in interpreting that waywardness as tending toward promiscuity: Red Crosse's 'self-disgust … drives him toward the shame of coupling with [Duessa], as though he is forced to enact the most debased version of bodily desire that he can imagine in order to make himself as disgusting as he already feels'; Adelman, 'Revaluing the Body', p. 22.

116   *Comic Spenser*

when he is betrothed to Una. So far as it goes, this reading is sound, for there is little doubt that Spenser deemed infidelity and lust to be at odds with a life of holiness or that he had a high regard for marriage. However, in order to understand the true direction and ingenuity of Spenser's satire we must resist the temptation to read Red Crosse's promiscuity literally.

'A Gentle Knight was pricking on the plaine'

Our expectations of a book combining holiness and heroism are deftly punctured by *The Faerie Queene*'s very first line. Anderson notes that in the poetry of both Chaucer and Spenser *prick* (in the sense of 'spur') often plays on the margins of bawdy innuendo. 'The Tale of Sir Thopas', for example, suggestively associates the hero's 'prikyng' of his horse with his 'love-longynge' and his 'corage' (another potential pun).[9] *The Faerie Queene* provides numerous comparable examples of lustful knights – from Sansfoy to Arthur – pricking and being pricked in their pursuit of various women, although the most direct and provocative echo of Red Crosse's entry into the poem occurs when Paridell (an adulterer who 'lusted after all, that him did moue') is sighted 'pricking on the playne' (III.viii.44.7). An early snigger at Spenser's opening line is recorded in *The Return from Parnassus* (*c.* 1600), in which the would-be poet Ingenioso writes: 'A gentle pen rides prickinge on the plaine, / This paper plaine, to resalute my loue' – to which his patron Gullio replies, 'thou haste a very lecherous witt'.[10]

Arguing for the intentionality of this wit in *The Faerie Queene*, Andrew Hadfield asks, 'after all, what is the Red-Cross Knight's problem? It is his prick'.[11] Hadfield's inference is, on one level, undeniable. A tension between desire and control hovers over the first stanza, in which the knight is described as 'jolly' (meaning gallant but also possibly amorous) and is, moreover, spurring *and* reining in his horse.[12] This tension is played out explicitly in the cantos that follow: while Red Crosse rejects the advances of the lascivious sprite in Archimago's house (i.51–3), he soon falls into the arms of Duessa. Nevertheless, elaboration on the poem's opening

---

9 Anderson, 'A Gentle Knight', pp. 167–9; cf. 'Sir Thopas', lines 754–80 and p. 119 n.19 below.

10 *FQ* IV.i.1181–3; anon., *The Three Parnassus Plays (1598–1601)*, ed. J. B. Leishman (London: Ivor Nicholson & Watson, 1949). I am grateful to Helen Cooper for this allusion.

11 Hadfield, 'Spenser and Jokes', p. 9; see also Hadfield, 'Spenser and Religion', p. 33.

12 See *OED*, *a.*, II.5(a), III.7. The connotations of 'jolly' are similarly noted by Anderson, 'A Gentle Knight', p. 168.

Spenser's bawdy 117

line is warranted, not only to substantiate a pun that some readers have dismissed as fanciful, but also because it establishes, right from the start, Spenser's strategy of supplementing the erotic narrative with wordplay and symbolism.[13] For, far from being exceptional, 'pricking' inaugurates an ironic sexual subtext that extends throughout Book I.[14]

On the face of it, Red Crosse's first heroic test, his battle with Errour at the heart of the Wandering Wood, has nothing at all do to with sex. Yet the language and symbolism of the episode insist that it does. The storm that prompts the couple to take shelter in the wood is described as Jove making love to – or possibly raping – the earth:

> And angry *Ioue* an hideous storme of raine
> Did poure into his Lemans lap so fast,
> That euerie wight to shrowd it did constrain,
> And this faire couple eke to shroud themselues were fain.
>
> (I.i.6.6–9)

In view of this metaphorically eroticised landscape, the situation of Red Crosse and his lady as they seek refuge in a forest recalls the beginning of the love affair between Dido and Aeneas, and, even more strikingly (given the association between rain and divine anger), of the sexual awareness that made Adam and Eve hide from God.[15] We are reminded of the erotic consequences of the Fall and of the punishment of the Flood, God's outpouring of anger at man's evil 'imaginations' (Genesis 3:8, 6:5).

Errour, the serpent-monster that lurks at the wood's centre, intensifies this biblical echo, recalling as she does the iconographical tradition whereby Eve and the serpent are conflated. The labyrinthine wood 'Breedes dreadfull doubts' (I.i.12.4), while Errour literalises the connection between the procreative body and doubt by making fertility

---

13 For resistance to pricking as a bawdy pun in Spenser see Larry D. Benson, 'The "Queynte" Punnings of Chaucer's Critics', *SAC*, 1 (1984): 23–47 (p. 27); and for an alternative reading of 'pricking' see Chris Butler, ' "Pricking" and Ambiguity at the Start of *The Faerie Queene*', *NQ*, 253 (2008): 159–61.

14 My delineation of this subtext in Canto i runs closely parallel to Adelman's, in that it concentrates on the circumstance of the couple's entry into the Wandering Wood and on the negatively charged images of female sexuality and fecundity that follow.

15 Jove's action of pouring and the earth's identity as his 'leman' recall the god's sexual exploits in classical mythology, as well as the creation myth in which the sky impregnates the earth as told in Hesiod's *Theogeny* and Virgil's *Georgics*; see *FQ* I.i.6.6–7n. The parallel with Dido and Aeneas is well noted, e.g. Cheney, *Spenser's Image of Nature*, pp. 23–4; and Adelman, 'Revaluing the Body', p. 19.

118   *Comic Spenser*

look dangerous and disgusting.[16] She suckles 'A thousand yong ones' with her 'poisnous dugs' (i.15.5–6), and her mouth doubles as a birth canal through which her babies, who can access the 'hellish sinke' of her stomach/womb at will, are repeatedly reborn (i.22.5). Yet, for all her repulsiveness, Red Crosse is compulsively drawn to her lair – in Adelman's words, a 'suspiciously anatomical "darksome hole"' at the heart of the forest:[17]

> But full of fire and greedy hardiment,
> The youthfull knight could not for ought be staide,
> But forth vnto the darksom hole he went
>
> (I.i.14.1–3)

Ambushed without warning, the serpent defensively swallows her babies and rushes out 'effraide', whereupon she tries to retreat but is prevented by Red Crosse, who leaps upon her with his 'trenchand blade' (I.i.15–17). She then coils herself around the knight, nearly killing him, but he manages to strangle her until she lets go and vomits (i.19). As Adelman notes, Errour is a descendant of Hesiod's Echidna, and her strategy of entwining and strangling bears comparison to pseudo-scientific accounts of vipers dating back to Herodotus. Passed on through a long line of natural historians and religious allegorists, these accounts typically focus on vipers' unusual (or, for didactic purposes, depraved) mating ritual. In Pliny the Elder's account, the snakes 'mate by embracing, intertwined so closely with each other that it might be thought there was one snake with two heads'.[18] The inference that Red Crosse is effectively copulating with Errour as 'her wrethed sterne … / All suddenly about his body wound' (i.18.5–7) is surely funny in view of his heroic intentions (the unconvincing nature of which I discussed in Chapter 2). Moreover, the inference is backed up by

---

16 See Adelman, 'Revaluing the Body', p. 17. The topos of the labyrinth or maze is traditionally associated with the confusions of love and with the female body. Chaucer underscores the latter analogy with a pun on the 'queynte weyes' of the labyrinth; see Carolyn Dinshaw, *Chaucer's Sexual Poetics* (Madison: University of Wisconsin Press, 1989), pp. 78–9. In his prefatory Epistle to *The Shepheardes Calender*, E. K. reports that the author 'had long wandred in the common Labyrinth of Love'; *Shorter Poems*, p. 19 (line 171).

17 Adelman, 'Revaluing the Body', p. 18. Northrop Frye, too, reads Errour's cave in this way; *Northrop Frye's Notebooks on Renaissance Literature*, ed. Michael Dolzani, Collected Works of Northrop Frye, 20 (Toronto: University of Toronto Press, 2006), p. 11.

18 Adelman, 'Revaluing the Body', pp. 19–20; for the quotation see J. D. Pheifer, 'Errour and Echidna in *The Faerie Queene*: A Study in Literary Tradition', in *Literature and Learning in Medieval and Renaissance England*, ed. John Scattergood (Dublin: Irish Academic Press, 1984), pp. 127–74 (p. 137). See also Steadman, 'Error', in *SpE*, pp. 252–3.

Spenser's bawdy 119

heavy-handed double entendre in the stanzas that follow. The comparison of Errour's vomit to the waters of the Nile presents a cluster of words not merely suggestive but explicit: 'swell', 'pride', 'fertile slime', 'ouerflow', 'breed', 'seed' (i.21.1–8). The conjunction 'swell'/'pride' is followed up in the next stanza by Red Crosse's distinctly postcoital 'shrink[ing]' 'corage' (i.22.4).[19] Finally, the knight's labours are 'fruitfull': in response to her opponent's flagging energy, Errour 'pour[s] forth out of her hellish sinke / Her fruitfull cursed spawne of serpents small' (i.22.5–6).

Of course, the subtext I am detailing runs directly counter to the main current of the story, according to which Red Crosse is not copulating with Errour but bravely combating the threat she represents. Notwithstanding our inclination as readers of romance to take the couple's attachment for granted, there is no explicit indication that the knight is in love with his lady or motivated by a desire to win or marry her.[20] And most importantly, when Red Crosse is soon after tempted in Archimago's house he rejects the sexual advances of his lady's false double with horror and dismay (I.i.53–4).

What, then, are all the sexual puns and hints of the Errour episode telling us? If we trust the dialectic between virginity and promiscuity that governs the wider narrative of Book I and accept that sexuality metaphorically represents sinfulness, and suggestively implicates sexuality itself as sinful, then the subtext I have been detailing suggests that (as I have already argued in Chapter 2) there is something very misleading about the knight's triumph over Errour. The irony here is considerable, but limited to a didactic and cautionary message: 'Red Crosse is struggling to vanquish his sinfulness, and this failure will soon become explicit in his relationship with Duessa.' However, the twist on this interpretation proposed by Adelman, that *Red Crosse's* values govern the representation of evil in Canto i, yields a richer and more morally complex irony – one, moreover, that makes sense of the disconnection

19 Sheila Delany's work on Chaucerian bawdy is governed by the premise that 'a word is known by the company it keeps'; 'The Logic of Obscenity in Chaucer's *Legend of Good Women*', *Florilegium*, 7 (1985): 189–205 (p. 191). 'Pride' could mean 'sexual desire' or 'sexual organ' (*OED*, n.³); see also Eric Partridge, *Shakespeare's Bawdy*, 3rd edn (London: Routledge, 1990 [1968]), p. 167. All these senses are present elsewhere in *FQ*, as when Spenser describes the amorous assault upon Leda by that 'proud Bird': 'Shee slept, yet twixt her eielids closely spyde, / How towards her he rusht, and smiled at his pryde' (III.xi.32.8). 'Corage' could refer to the 'heart as the seat of feeling' (*OED*, s.v. 'courage', n., 1.) but could also mean 'sexual vigour and inclination; lust' (n., 3(e)). For other Spenserian examples of the latter sense see II.xii.68.9 and III.viii.23.4.
20 See Levin, 'The Legende of the Redcrosse Knight', pp. 3–4.

120   *Comic Spenser*

between the knight's triumph and his subsequent moral state.[21] If we surmise that Red Crosse's fear of sexuality as something dangerous and sinful is what makes Errour so insistently sexual, then the fact that he is irresistibly drawn to her lair becomes a matter of amusement rather than simple anxiety for the reader. Not only does his attack propagate a whole brood of Errours, his very antagonism toward female sexuality reveals – as it were, consummates – his desire for it.

Red Crosse as celibate St George

If the conventional topoi of chivalric romance (horses, swords, forests, caves, monsters) are susceptible to bawdy analogy, it is the genre's traditional concern with the altruistic protection of women that makes such analogies so irresistible and so ironic. Theoretically at least, Christian appropriations of the genre for religious allegory and hagiography provide exceptions to this rule. Stories that dissociate chivalric deeds and romantic interests (either by directing the hero's quest away from the conventional goal of romantic fulfilment or by allegorically interpreting the love object as spiritual) highlight the less pure motivations of knights at the secular end of the spectrum – Chaucer's Thopas or Ariosto's Rinaldo, for example. One of the best-known Christian romance works of this kind is, of course, the St George legend.

In Jacobus de Voragine's telling, St George enjoins the rescued virgin to use her girdle to lead the defeated dragon into the city, an act vividly symbolising chastity's triumph over bestial appetite. In his foreword to the legend, Voragine emphasises St George's freedom from (or successful repression of) sexual desire with the help of some creative etymology: 'George is derived from *gerar*, holy, and *gyon*, sand, therefore, holy sand; for he was like the sand, heavy with the weight of his virtues, small by humility, and *dry of the lusts of the flesh*.'[22] St George's commitment to celibacy is confirmed when he does not, as romance heroes traditionally do, marry the rescued princess. This is also spelt out in an alternative version of the legend, Mantuan's *Georgius*. In this version (here in Alexander Barclay's late-fifteenth-century translation), the king offers his daughter's hand only to be met with pious refusal:

---

21 On the victory over Errour as a measure of the knight's capacity to self-validate, see pp. 87–9 above.

22 Jacobus de Voragine, *The Golden Legend*, trans. William Granger Ryan, 2 vols (Princeton: Princeton University Press, 1993), Vol. I, p. 238 (my italics).

Touchynge your doughter/ fayre and of tender age
your londe/ and cyte/ none shall remayne with me
My mynde disposyd/ is *nat to maryage*
But from all lust/ to kepe my body fre.[23]

As we saw in Chapter 2, it is this archetype of medieval piety who was so irresistibly burlesqued in the sixteenth century.[24] Red Crosse's intention to be just such a champion of celibacy is signalled not only by his iconic resemblance to St George, by the insistent sexual symbolism of Errour, and by the repeated indications that he believes in his own capacity for virtuous action (see Chapter 2), but also by his very introduction as *'Patrone of true Holinesse'*. As Northrop Frye observes, ' "patron" is a crack at the R. C. [Roman Catholic] saint cult'.[25]

Spenser's vision of sainthood, in striking contrast to the celibate model, exalts the marriage bed as the foundation of the Church. The prayer at the close of *Epithalamion*, which redefines merit and sainthood in Protestant terms, encapsulates this revised theology:

> Poure out your blessing on us plenteously,
> And happy influence upon us raine,
> That we may raise a large posterity,
> Which from the earth, which they may long possesse,
> With lasting happinesse,
> Up to your haughty pallaces may mount,
> And for the guerdon of theyr glorious merit
> May heavenly tabernacles there inherit,
> Of blessed Saints for to increase the count.
>
> (*Shorter Poems*, lines 415–23)

Red Crosse, we may recall, experiences god's fertile rain not as a blessing but as a sign of wrath: an angry downpour that one must escape (I.i.6.5–9). The other half of the story – the fact that Jove is enamoured of his 'Leman' and fertilises rather than destroys her with his downpour – is sidelined by Canto i's atmosphere of subtle menace. Red Crosse evades

---

23 Alexander Barclay, *The Lyfe of St George*, ed. William Nelson, EETS, o.s. 230 (London: Oxford University Press, 1955), p. 54 (lines 1198–204; my italics). This translation was first published in 1515; on Spenser's knowledge of it see *Var* I, pp. 385–6.

24 See Groves, 'The Redcrosse Knight', esp. p. 374, where she notes the saint's association with both celibacy and bawdy jokes.

25 Frye, *Notebooks*, p. 34. By 'crack' Frye implies a momentary irony registering the changed significance of sainthood in Protestant allegory. Contrastingly, I argue that the joke of Red Crosse's 'Catholic' sainthood is persistent in Book I; see Chapter 2.

122 — Comic Spenser

God's perceived wrath partly by appropriating it as his own: in attacking Errour he is attacking female sexuality and the desire it awakens in him. He is St George battling the flesh, not in the abstract (lust, greed, idolatry, envy) but quite literally (the physical, sexual body). In illustration of the Pauline dictum 'unto the pure all things are pure', Errour's physical grossness does not symbolise her intrinsic evil but rather the evil Red Crosse sees in her.

The sexual subtext of the Errour episode bubbles to the surface of the narrative when, shortly after leaving the Wandering Wood, the couple accept Archimago's invitation to stay with him. Outwardly, Archimago (which is to say, Red Crosse's own hypocrisy) epitomises the idea that holiness demands self-denial.[26] His house, where no entertainment is looked for and where 'Rest is their feast' (I.i.35.3) parodies the idea that 'being spiritual' is essentially a pleasureless, abstemious, and solemn affair – a cliché whose alliance with hypocritical hot air is comically underlined when the hermitage turns out to be a hotbed of fantasies and bed-swapping antics. This conjunction of showy sobriety and erotic turmoil is, of course, a projection of Red Crosse's own psyche.[27]

Under Archimago's roof the knight is subjected to erotic dreams, to a sexual proposition, and to a vision of his lady in bed with a squire. Notably, lust and guilt are suggestively conflated during this episode. When Red Crosse wakes from his dream, we are told: 'In this great passion of vnwonted lust, / *Or wonted feare of doing ought amis* / He starteth vp' (I.i.49.1–3; my italics). Later in the night, after thinking he has seen his lady with the squire, he is said to be anguished by his 'guilty sight' (ii.6.2). It would seem that the episode is not concerned with Red Crosse's rejection of evil (in which case we would expect his staunch resistance to have a positive consequence) but about his *perception* of evil.

The narrative at this point demands allegorical interpretation, but sexuality, I am arguing, is morally at issue as well metaphorically resonant. The crisis at Archimago's house bears out, and retrospectively casts light on, the subtextual implications of the Errour episode concerning sexual shame. The point here is not to offer a boldly one-dimensional reading of Red Crosse's spiritual errancy ('it is all about sex!'), but to acknowledge just how complex and revealing sexuality is as a theme. It is not a

---

26 On Red Crosse and Archimago see Chapter 2.

27 Consider the punning description of the house as a 'hidden cell' (I.i.30.6); *OED*, s.v. 'cell', n., II.7(a): 'any of the (imaginary) cavities or compartments in the brain thought to be the seats of particular mental faculties, or to serve as pigeonholes for the storage of knowledge' (a sense first recorded in the fourteenth century).

Spenser's bawdy 123

superficial 'vehicle' for talking about something else, but a touchstone for thinking about the very condition of embodiment. One's attitude to sexuality implicates a whole host of issues that any definition of holiness must navigate: appetite, pleasure, procreation, and romantic love, but also, more broadly, ideas about sin, guilt, virtue, and self-control. If this reasoning leads us full-circle back to sexuality as a metaphor, it does so by acknowledging, rather than repressing, its literal relevance.

It is tempting, though very misleading, to imagine that one's relationship with the Church, Book I's central preoccupation, is somehow on a different plain from the personal, practical, and daily concerns just referred to (indeed, this is Red Crosse's mistaken assumption). In fact one's relationship with the Church is indistinguishable from thoughts about, and responses to, the condition of embodiment – which is to say, it is indistinguishable from one's relationship with oneself.

The unnamed lady

Before we consider Red Crosse's alliance with Duessa, the identity of his original lady (generally referred to as Una, though not initially named as such) and her allegorical relation to Archimago's sprite need to be addressed. For if Errour represents a subjective conception of sin, we cannot take it for granted that the monster's symbolic opposite, the lady, is objectively good.

Few critics have entertained the possibility of the lady's fallibility, and most readings of Book I in fact depend upon her positive signification. As mentioned in Chapter 2, a notable exception is Kathryn Walls's argument that Una is not imperfect so much as 'chronically fallible' prior to her dislocation from Red Crosse near the beginning of Canto ii. Walls contends that prior to this point, the pair (notwithstanding the narrator's flattering assessments of both) are equally fallible: in particular, their entry into and disorientation within the Wandering Wood, Una's suspect injunction to Red Crosse to 'Add faith vnto your force' and subsequent flattery of his victory over Errour, and their shared inability to recognise Archimago as a threat, establish their moral equivalence.[28] A key point underpinning Walls's argument is that the Church is not an abstraction (i.e. 'Truth') but *people*: as such, its story – while destined to conclude in perfect unity with Christ – necessarily encompasses the human fallibility and weakness that are the condition of redemption. For Walls, the Church's perfection is indeed represented

---

28 Walls, *God's Only Daughter*, Chapter 1; on 'Add faith' see pp. 87–8 above.

124 *Comic Spenser*

(or rather anticipated) by Una, but only once her story diverges from that of Red Crosse at I.ii.7.

It is remarkable that the transformation from fallibility to perfection noted by Walls – striking once it has been pointed out – has for so long gone unnoticed.[29] Not least, it explains why the lady remains unnamed until she is distinguished from her false double at I.i.45.9, and is not identified as Truth until the argument to Canto ii – this being the moment in which we learn of Red Crosse's dislocation from her:

> *The guilefull great Enchaunter parts*
> *The Redcrosse Knight from Truth:*
> *Into whose stead faire falshood steps,*
> *And workes him woefull ruth.*

Prior to this point, on one level the lady represents *Red Crosse*'s truth.[30]

Subjective perceptions are, in a sense, self-validating. Protestant Reformers were preoccupied with the problem, both because it supported their denunciation of rival sects and because it necessitated faith in the revealed nature of their own truth. Bishop John Hooper, while acknowledging that the human mind can be guided by grace, articulated the dangers therein:

> The mind of man, when it is not illuminated with the Spirit of God, nor governed by the scripture, it imagineth and feigneth God to be like unto the imagination and conceit of his mind, and not as the scripture teacheth. When this vanity or fond imagination is conceived in the mind, there followeth a further success of the ill. He purposeth to express by some figure or image God in the same form and similitude that his imagination hath first printed in his mind; so that the mind conceiveth the idol, and afterward the hand worketh and representeth the same unto the senses.[31]

---

29 Walls notes a few exceptions; *God's Only Daughter*, pp. 19–20.

30 This point diverges from, though does not exactly contradict, Walls's argument that in Canto i Una represents the fallibility of the Church. Although our arguments follow very different paths, Andrew King recognises the mediating role of Red Crosse's flawed perspective, calling the chivalric romance world of Book I 'a naive, puerile landscape that we are seeing through his eyes, scripted as it is by his mindset'; Andrew King, 'Spenser, Chaucer, and Medieval Romance', in *The Oxford Handbook of Edmund Spenser*, ed. Richard A. McCabe (Oxford: Oxford University Press, 2010), pp. 553–72 (p. 565).

31 Hooper, *Early Writings*, p. 318, cited by Aston, *Laws against Images*, pp. 436–7. Hooper is talking about making and honouring images, but, as Aston observes, 'the "idols" of the Reformation, like the word "image" itself, moved from a predominantly physical to a largely mental connotation' (pp. 459–65).

Proving how seductive and true-seeming these idols can be, Red Crosse's Truth convinces us, too.[32] Her fallibility is indeed striking in the light of Walls's argument, although such a reading is nevertheless undertaken against the grain of the narrative, which affirms the lady's goodness and beauty. As she appears in Canto i, the lady represents the 'imagination and conceit' of Red Crosse's mind – a false idol – but, seen through his eyes, her virtue seems to be indisputable.

Inclined to accept the lady as Spenser's – as opposed to Red Crosse's – imaginative representation of perfection, critics have been reluctant to subject her to critical scrutiny. But if we do so, we might question not only her presence inside the Wandering Wood and her inability to recognise Archimago for what he is, but also her resemblance, in her wimple, black stole, and mournful aspect, to a nun:

> A louely Ladie rode him faire beside,
> Vpon a lowly Asse more white then snow,
> Yet she much whiter, but the same did hide
> Vnder a vele, that wimpled was full low,
> And ouer all a blacke stole shee did throw,
> As one that inly mournd: so was she sad,
> And heauie sate vpon her palfrey slow.
>
> (I.i.4.1–7)

The few critics who have discussed this resemblance do not necessarily find it to be problematic. According to C. S. Lewis's influential argument, Spenser deliberately reappropriates rejected forms of piety through allegory, prompting the reader to actively interpret – and so rehabilitate – 'Catholic' images. In a similar vein, Frye says of Una: 'note that she's dressed as a nun, an allegory the R. C. Ch. [Roman Catholic Church] takes literally'.[33] In the view of both Lewis and Frye, to assume that Red Crosse's lady endorses Catholicism because she looks like a nun, or that the House of Holiness does likewise because it resembles a convent, is wrongly to ascribe to the poet our own overly literal – as it were Catholic – impulses. As Lewis points out, all the aspects of the lady's appearance that identify her as a nun are consonant with Protestant theology if we interpret them emblematically. This is true, and Lewis is right to free Spenser from the

---

32 My argument bears comparison with Fish's seminal thesis that the ideal reader of *Paradise Lost* will be made by Milton to 'realize his inability to read the poem with any confidence in his own perception'; *Surprised by Sin*, p. 3.

33 Lewis, *The Allegory of Love*, pp. 322–3; Frye, *Notebooks*, p. 10. Other critics who note Una's resemblance to a nun are Walls, *God's Only Daughter*, p. 36 n. 61; and, as cited by Walls, Hadfield, 'Spenser and Religion', p. 32.

126 *Comic Spenser*

charge of inadvertent Catholicism.[34] But in doing so, he frees Red Crosse of the same charge.

Traditionally, 'false-Una', summoned by Archimago to tempt Red Crosse, has assured us (if we needed assuring) of the original lady's authenticity. The sprite embodies a false account of what the true lady's nature is really like – in terms of the allegory, she represents a slanderous account of the Church by an unbelieving outsider. Yet Red Crosse – who is that unbeliever, because the hypocrisy at issue is his own – does not 'suddenly' misapprehend truth. The sprite's act of impersonation does indeed contrast Una's authenticity, but equally, in terms of Red Crosse's spiritual development, it affirms a misapprehension that has been latent since Stanza 1. This point becomes easier to appreciate if one considers that Red Crosse's values are consistent: the figure of the loose woman or whore embodies the belief that sexuality is sinful just as compellingly as does the figure of the nun-like virgin. Again, I am not here suggesting that Red Crosse's attitude to sexuality is exclusively at issue, but rather acknowledging that this attitude epitomises, and compellingly articulates, a religiosity informed by bodily shame on the one hand and a belief in meritorious self-control on the other.

Archimago's seductress, then, is not an impostor at all, or at least not a new one. Insofar as the subjective truth she stands for has not changed, neither, in allegorical terms, has the lady. And indeed, there is even a certain consistency in her identity at the narrative level, if we credit John Foxe's polemical depiction of outwardly chaste nuns with riotous sex lives behind closed doors.[35] Spenser's irony, however (in contrast to the majority of Protestant polemic against Catholic vows of celibacy) is directed not at human weakness in failing to live up to a high ideal, but at the questionable human desire for heroic control in the first place.

'I that do seeme not I, *Duessa* ame'

From Canto ii onward, it would seem that Red Crosse breaks free of his guilty self-rule and, running to the opposite extreme, becomes sexually

---

34 The lady's beauty may be said to represent the integrity of the True or invisible Church, her virginity affirms her status as bride, her concealing garments signify the temporal inaccessibility of Truth, her sadness is for the state of innocence forfeited by her parents Adam and Eve, and her status as an only child is resonant of 'one Lord, one Faith, one Baptisme' (Ephesians 4:5). Nevertheless, her virginity, her black stole, and her sadness may also be interpreted literally as traits associated with Catholic penitentialism. Archimago is celibate, sad, and dressed in black also.

35 See for example *Acts and Monuments*, Book 2, p. 152.

Spenser's bawdy 127

liberated in the worst possible way. Readers tend to accept this sudden change of heart as a downward spiral into sin. According to Adelman's psychological reading, Red Crosse's about-turn dramatises the counterproductive nature of repression. According to the traditional view, inconsistencies at the narrative level (as when Red Crosse spurs his steed while keeping pace with his plodding lady) remind us that we are, after all, reading allegory. If we consider that misconceiving truth is the same as believing falsehood, then it follows that (however contradictory this may seem in narrative terms) alienation from truth in Archimago's house should segue quite naturally into an alliance with falsehood thereafter.

Yet the narrative inconsistency in question is striking. Red Crosse, troubled by guilt and fear, rejects a seductive Duessa-figure in Archimago's house yet, immediately afterward, is happy to dally with Duessa herself under the midday sun, making a garland for her and kissing her (I.ii.29–45). While the points just mentioned have some validity, I would like to suggest a very different explanation for this perplexing narrative sequence.

Specifically, I propose that an abrupt change does indeed take place when the knight's departure from Una – as she may now be called – is confirmed at I.ii.6.9, but this change is to the reader's circumstances, not Red Crosse's. The appearance of a crisis is not misleading, for the knight's spiritual health is in a critical state. Yet his situation and his loyalties remain the same. The act of galloping away from Una represents the recognition-failure or denial that characterises his relationship with Truth from the beginning. What is new is the revelation of this distance in terms of the narrative, an indication that the perspective available to the reader, hitherto mediated by the protagonist's subjectivity, is now 'objective'. In the moment we cease to share Red Crosse's perspective, we begin to judge his decisions critically.

Duessa, I am contending, is the same false lady we have been speaking of all along. Trusting the tacit equation sex = sin, we instinctively feel that Red Crosse is right to resist the false lady's blandishments in Archimago's house. Yet, resisting the sprite is not the same as resisting falsehood; counterintuitively, such resistance (which is to say, his misapprehension of Una) allegorises Red Crosse's ongoing seduction in this respect. Duessa makes this seduction apparent at the narrative level. Far from signalling a newly unrestrained sensuality in consequence of his earlier repressive tendencies, as Adelman and others have argued, Duessa's seductiveness is the seductiveness of penitence.

Spenser is being boldly ironic at this point in the allegory. Yet the representation of bodily shame as seduction is not exactly out of left field.

128   *Comic Spenser*

We are familiar with the idea that, allegorically speaking, Red Crosse's affair with Duessa describes not a sexual relationship but an idolatrous one: the idolatry of false worship, and more specifically, of faith in deeds. Yet in view of this cornerstone of interpretation, it has been insufficiently noted that for many Reformers, the Catholic idealisation of celibacy epitomised the idolatrous mindset. The rule of celibacy for priests was among the most controversial legacies of the rejected doctrine of merit, while the alleged sexual transgressions of those unable to abide by their vows were deemed outward expressions of an inwardly carnal faith.[36] The proposition that Red Crosse's idolatry – his affair with Duessa – in part represents a commitment to celibacy is not, in this light, entirely paradoxical.

It may be objected that such challenging allegory runs counter to Spenser's aims as a teacher and Christian moralist. But (to risk stating the obvious) the value of *The Faerie Queene* hardly lies in the transparency of its moral messages; few readers would deny that Spenser challenges and even deliberately misleads his readers at times.[37] This of course may be politically expedient (there were obvious reasons not to satirise vocational celibacy openly during the reign of Elizabeth), but counterintuitive play also has a theological grounding. As Fish observes, obscurity and riddling have been a part of Christian pedagogy since Christ's parables; overhasty or overconfident interpreters are supposed to be tripped up.[38] Perhaps allegory's best Christian thesis statement is Folly's warning about the deceptiveness of appearances: 'if ye take prudence after the rate, as whan it resteth in iudgement and discourse of thynges, herken ye (I praie you) howe farre they are wyde therof, who dooe make it their chiefest possession'. Asserting her dominion, Folly claims that 'all humaine thynges' are double and misleading.[39] Duessa, of course, is doubleness

---

36 Calvin was especially vocal on this issue. He devotes a whole chapter of the *Institutes* to 'The Miserable Entanglements Caused by Vowing Rashly', and awards 'the first place of insane audacity' to vows of celibacy. Those who make such vows, he asserts, are 'forgetful of their infirmity'; John Calvin, *Institutes of the Christian Religion*, trans. Henry Beveridge, 2 vols (Edinburgh: T. & T. Clarke, 1863), Vol. II, pp. 472–90 (pp. 474–5). See also Heinrich Bullinger, *The christen state of matrimonye*, trans. Miles Coverdale (Amsterdam: Theatrum Orbis Terrarum, 1974 [1541]), Chapter 12 ('they crye out that chaistite is an holy thinge. And yet are they become more vayne then vanite itself').

37 As the 'Letter to Raleigh' implies, it is possible to benefit from the poem's 'general intention or meaning' (in this case, Duessa's evil, which is patently obvious) while bypassing or even misunderstanding 'particular purposes or by-accidents therein occasioned' (lines 6–7).

38 Fish, *Surprised by Sin*, p. 21.

39 *Folie*, p. 37.

itself: 'I that do seeme not I, *Duessa* ame' (I.v.26.6). An old hag who looks like a beautiful young woman can also be asceticism made to look sensuous, celibacy dressed up as a whore.[40]

Duessa's grief for her dead fiancé is reminiscent of the mournful lady of Canto i, only now from a perspective that allows us to see that sadness as a seductive façade. Recalling the Protestant accusation that the rival Church was carnally focused on death as opposed to spiritually focused on the Resurrection, Duessa refers to herself as a 'widow' (I.ii.24.8; xii.27.1) in mourning for her prince's vanished 'corse' (ii.24.6), the whereabouts of which is ostensibly her sole concern.[41] In her tinsel and scarlet and palfrey tricked out with bells, however, Duessa unmistakeably displaces nun-like austerity with the aesthetic of Catholic worship in its sumptuous guise. While this first and foremost suggests 'barbaric and papal splendour' and the Whore of Babylon (Revelation 17:4), there may also be a satirical allusion here to the Cult of the Virgin.[42] Beautiful, ideally proportioned, and sometimes lavishly adorned, depictions of the Madonna and other saintly virgins sought to express inward virtue through outward beauty.[43] Red Crosse, in other words, is not alone in courting the celibate ideal in the form of something outwardly sensual; in fact, this irony is at the very root of Catholic worship. Authors besides Spenser, moreover, have found humour in this circumstance. *The Name of the Rose*, Umberto Eco's novel set in a fourteenth-century Benedictine monastery, shows how Mary's beauty could pose a problem for celibate devotees. Standing before a statue of the Virgin, the senior clergyman advises the troubled protagonist:

> 'There is she in whom femininity is sublimated. This is why you may call her beautiful, like the beloved of the Song of Songs ... the body's grace is a sign of the beauties of heaven, and this is why the sculptor has portrayed her with all the graces that should adorn a woman' ... I blushed violently, feeling myself stirred as if by an inner fire. Ubertino ... promptly added,

---

40 This binary is particular appropriate from the point of view that, as Berger, 'Sexual and Religious Politics' argues, the virgin and the whore in Book I are two sides of the same misogynistic coin. It is an added irony that in judging Red Crosse for his promiscuity with a witch, we enter more deeply into his fear of women.

41 See for example Hugh Latimer, *Sermons of Latimer*, ed. George Elwes Corrie, Parker Society Publications, 27 (Cambridge: Cambridge University Press, 1844), p. 479.

42 The quotation is from Douglas Brooks-Davies, 'Una', in *SpE*, p. 705.

43 See Eamon Duffy, *The Stripping of the Altars: Traditional Religion in England c. 1400–c. 1580* (New Haven: Yale University Press, 1992), p. 114.

130   *Comic Spenser*

'But you must learn to distinguish the fire of supernatural love from the raving of the senses. It is difficult even for the saints.'[44]

Byron's Don Juan is similarly affected, if considerably less troubled:

> For woman's face was never formed in vain
> For Juan, so that even when he prayed
> He turned from grisly saints and martyrs hairy
> To the sweet portraits of the Virgin Mary.[45]

The full comic potential of the Virgin's attractiveness is brought out brilliantly in *Don Quixote* when the eponymous hero mistakes a statue of the Madonna for a damsel in distress, and the entourage of self-flagellating penitents carrying her for a band of rapists.[46]

Spenser's eroticisation of penitentialism is similarly pushed to the point of comic absurdity. Depicted as 'getting into bed' with the false Church, Red Crosse looks most like a lover when he is most eagerly distancing himself from this identity. More ironically still, this portrayal points to the allegedly counterproductive nature of vows of celibacy. Many polemicists besides Foxe claimed that such vows, by cutting off the lawful outlet of marriage, drove people sex-mad. It was assumed that even if celibate clergy refrained from engaging concubines their thoughts would be sinful (the true place where adultery takes place is the heart, according to Matthew 5:28). As when Red Crosse's attack on female sexuality in Canto i began to resemble rape, in other words, the representation of his commitment to celibacy as a sexual liaison betrays a desire he has no control over – indeed, only exacerbates by fighting.

The consummation scene between Red Crosse and Duessa (I.vii.4–7) is worth revisiting in this light. Taking refuge from the 'boyling heat' (4.3) among trees, the couple 'bathe in pleasaunce' (4.2) by a fountain's side, which Red Crosse then lies down next to and drinks from. The fountain, whose waters are enchanted, causes Red Crosse to experience a loss of 'manly force' and to become feeble, cold, and faint (vii.6.4–8).

---

44 Umberto Eco, *The Name of the Rose* (London: Minerva, 1992), p. 230.
45 Lord [George Gordon] Byron, *Don Juan*, ed. T. G. Steffan *et al.* (London: Penguin, 1982), p. 139 (II.149.5–8). A similar tension between inaccessibility and attractiveness attended the pagan Diana (famous for being spotted with her clothes off) and, of course, was positively appropriated and exploited by Elizabeth I.
46 Miguel de Cervantes, *The History of Don Quixote of the Mancha*, trans. Thomas Shelton, 2 vols (London: Navarre Society, 1923 [1612–20]), Vol. I, pp. 537–9 (in other editions, Vol. I, Chapter 52).

Spenser's bawdy 131

The scene as a whole is erotically suggestive, with references to pleasure, heat, water, melting, torpor, and pouring out. Yet there is also, as John W. Shroeder pointed out in the 1960s, a detailed correspondence between the episode's descriptive details and Aristotle's account of what happens in the male body during and immediately after intercourse. As Shroeder points out, the knight's perseverance after drinking from the fountain is admirable: he continues to make 'goodly court' to his lady even after turning chill and faint and losing 'corage' (vii.6.7–7.1).[47] As though the point had not been sufficiently made, Spenser cannot resist adding a chivalric joke at Red Crosse's expense: 'scarsely could he weeld his bootlesse single blade' (vii.11.9).

The latter observation follows the entry of the phallic, club-wielding giant Orgoglio (Italian for 'pride'), whose assault on Red Crosse's potency pushes the episode into the realm of broad comedy. In addition to cataloguing the close parallels between Orgoglio's association with wind, earth, and slime and Aristotle's physiology of erection and ejaculation, Shroeder makes the point that giants in *The Faerie Queene* and elsewhere are often emblematic of unruly sexuality (Lust, Argante, and Ollyphant, for example). As in Canto i, wordplay and symbolism reinforce this subtext. The familiar allusions to 'pride' and 'courage' and the suggestive metaphors of pool/fountain, verdant glade, and good foraging are joined by references to hollow wombs, hidden caves, hell-pits, darksome dens and deep dungeons on the one hand, and to clubs, swords, towers, and cannon-shot on the other. The symbolism of the episode begins to seem, like Hitchcock's train speeding though a tunnel, absurdly transparent.[48]

If our focus is, as it should be, on the topography of the unruly human body, Orgoglio's threatening advance is reduced to a moment of adolescent embarrassment. The phallic giant

> gan aduaunce
> With huge force and insupportable mayne,
> And towardes him with dreadfull fury praunce
>
> (I.vii.11.1–3)

---

47 Shroeder, 'Spenser's Erotic Drama', p. 145 (on 'corage' see p. 119 n. 19 above). According to Aristotle, semen is formed most plentifully in hot and moist conditions, and requires heat to liquefy. At the same time, excessive heat causes enervation in men. This enervation is markedly increased by ejaculation, which, causing a sudden loss of nourishment and moisture, makes the male 'languid and cold'; Aristotle, *Problemata*, IV.876–80.

48 Shroeder, 'Spenser's Erotic Drama', pp. 155–6 puts his finger on the word for this: 'funny'. The following is a list of suggestive words and phrases from I.vii.6–18: 'lying downe

132   *Comic Spenser*

The comedy of Orgoglio's dreadful prancing is matched only by his reception of Arthur after he has retired with Duessa as his prize. As Shroeder notes, being caught in the act by a third party is a stock comic motif, but the description of Orgoglio 'rushing forth from inner bowre, / With staring countenance sterne' (I.viii.5.6–7) pushes the scenario to the next level of farcical – if not pornographic – indignity.

Shroeder, who teases out more detailed innuendo than I have here, is alert to the humour of the episode, but his reading does not seek to revise the standard one of Red Crosse's imputed lustfulness as a straightforward metaphor for idolatry, 'pride' in the sexual sense being a punning reference to the term's spiritual equivalent.[49] Lust is condemned in a highly satirical manner, that is, but in the service of a larger point that has little to do with sexual conduct. Yet there is a countercurrent in the episode that Shroeder's reading does not account for. First, this consummation scene hints not at intercourse so much as masturbation. Recalling the biblical story of Onan, who spilt his seed on the ground to avoid begetting offspring (Genesis 38:9), Red Crosse is said to be 'Pourd out in loosnesse on the grassy grownd, / Both carelesse of his health, and of his fame' (I.vii.7.2–3). Further, there are repeated references to Red Crosse being emasculated: he is frail, feeble, and faint; his manly forces are failing; his weapons are unready and he can hardly wield his sword; he is 'dismayde' (11.6) by Orgoglio's stature; and so on. In my view, the episode's connections with Ovid's story of Salmacis and Hermaphroditus help us to make sense of these details.

As told in the *Metamorphoses* IV, Salmacis is a sensual, idle nymph who lusts after the youth Hermaphroditus. After her advances are rejected, she pounces on him as he bathes in her pool, entwining her body with his and calling on the gods to keep them united. Her wish granted, the pair blend into one and become half man, half woman. Hermaphroditus then prays to his mother and father to grant his wish that whoever bathes in the fountain should be likewise unmanned. Clearly, the enervating fountain from which Red Crosse drinks is reminiscent of this Ovidian pool, and the

---

vpon', 'manly forces', 'corage', 'melt', 'feuer fit', 'Pourd out', 'loosnesse', 'looser', 'vnready weapon', 'monstrous', 'sturdie', 'horrible and hye', 'groned vnder him', 'tallnesse', 'stature', 'hight', 'tallest', 'seed', 'hollow womb', 'secretly inspyre', 'fild her hidden caues', 'conceiu'd', 'wombes', 'expyre', 'earthly slyme', 'fild', 'growen great', 'delight', 'huge', 'strooke so maynly', 'stony towre', 'deepest', 'ramd', 'Conceiueth', 'heaued vp', 'vanquisht', 'possessed', 'hastie forse', 'deep', 'ybredd', 'filthy', 'darksom', 'filth', 'breed', 'wondrous length'.

49 See Edmund Spenser, *The Faerie Queene: Book I*, ed. and intro. Carol Kaske (Indianapolis: Hackett, 2006), p. xxii.

Spenser's bawdy 133

resemblance is supported by the narrator's backstory about the lazy nymph who 'Satt downe to rest in the middest of the race', provoking Diana into making her waters dull and enfeebling (I.vii.4–5). The obvious connection lies in the culpability of a nymph and the effect of the enchanted waters, but there is a further connection in the circumstance that Salmacis, too, avoids Diana's chase (*Met* IV.285–319). Insofar as this Ovidian analogue is discussed at all, critics understandably draw an analogy between the sensual idleness of Salmacis, the lazy nymph in Spenser's story, and Red Crosse himself, who is likewise resting 'in the middest of the race' (vii.5.4). In my view, however, we need to associate Red Crosse not with Salmacis but with Hermaphroditus, the beautiful youth who 'knew not what love was' (*Met* IV. 320–54). In the *Metamorphoses*, Salmacis's passion is actually rewarded, while Hermaphroditus's refusal of sex is punished when he is tricked into forfeiting his masculinity. And it is Hermaphroditus who is ultimately responsible for the emasculating quality of the waters. The part of Ovid's story omitted by Spenser, conspicuous by its absence, is surely relevant given the additional hints that Red Crosse's desire is repressive, masturbatory, and emasculating.

While the comedy of the episode is assured either way, I am suggesting that a more complex and ironic humour attends Orgoglio's aggression if we consider that Red Crosse, rather than simply being wilfully lustful, is at the mercy of his rebellious body, and that, moreover, this state of conflict epitomises rather than 'stands in for' his spiritual errancy. The subsidence of that bodily rebellion is indicated by the entry of the 'wofull Dwarfe' following Orgoglio's retreat – surely a sexual joke.[50] Here humour embarrasses and satirises, but it also possesses the affirmative function that I have been attributing to Spenserian humour throughout this study. Far from being paradoxical or inappropriate, the invitation to laugh at a moment of moral crisis and high pathos assures us that Red Crosse is saved. The image of the dwarf lugging his fallen master's armour – tragically described as 'The ruefull moniments of heauinesse' (I.vii.19.8) can afford to be funny, even as it intimates Red Crosse's diminutive stature

---

50 While the point hardly needs elaboration, it is interesting that the folklorist Bruno Bettelheim interprets dwarfs as symbolic of sexual dormancy; *The Uses of Enchantment: The Meaning and Importance of Fairy Tales* (London: Thames and Hudson, 1976), pp. 210–11. Exemplifying what I have called the 'first wave' of humour criticism (see Introduction, n. 4), Bernard W. Bell emphasises the comic aspect of the dwarf's role in Book I, but does not interpret his findings as such; 'The Comic Realism of Una's Dwarf', *Massachusetts Studies in English*, 1 (1968), 111–18.

134   *Comic Spenser*

behind Christ's protecting armour, because that armour ensures that the knight's story is not, finally, a tragic one.

As well as attributing a different tenor of humour to the Orgoglio episode than that discovered by Shroeder, my identification of Red Crosse's desire as repressive looks beyond sexual misconduct as a surface metaphor that, in Kaske's phrase, is 'literal and ancillary' to the episode's moral meaning.[51] Sexual ethics, I have been arguing, are not tangential but central to Spenser's anatomy of idolatry. Indeed, it would be extraordinary if moral pride did not directly implicate one's attitude to embodiment – the fundamental condition of being human. It makes sense that the man 'that boasts of fleshly might' (I.x.1.1) should express his moral pride through attempted mastery of his own body, and through the overconfident and reductive identification of sin as bodily in the first place. Yet, as I have been at pains to emphasise, sexuality does not lose its metaphorical depth if we attribute to it literal significance. For the marriage poet whose conception of holiness incorporates bodily health and sexual desire, the idolatrous mindset (and all the pride, self-reliance, and literal-mindedness that this implies) is epitomised by, not restricted to, bodily shame.

My claim that shame and not disinhibition is the chief symptom of Red Crosse's spiritual errancy not only in Canto i but right up until his rehabilitation in the House of Holiness demands an active and ironically attuned approach to allegory – the kind of sceptical interrogation of Duessa's appearance that Red Crosse himself avoids with disastrous results. Such a reading looks beyond the simplistic equation of lust and idolatry to support a more fundamentally positive view of Spenser's sexual ethics. Red Crosse's relationship with Duessa does more than parody the uninhibited sensuality of the Garden of Adonis; it utterly reverses everything that the garden represents. The ostensible sensuality of their relationship is in fact sterile and repressive, 'masturbatory' in the sense of wilfully self-reliant and in the sense – by no means ancillary to Spenserian holiness – that Red Crosse cannot yet give himself over to a loving relationship.[52]

---

51 Spenser, *The Faerie Queene: Book I*, ed. Kaske, p. xxiii. The relevance of sex even as a metaphor is hardly mentioned in Hamilton's lengthy annotations to the episode, and not at all in Kaske's much briefer notes. Hamilton allows that the description of Red Crosse 'pourd out' suggests that he is 'sexually expended and exhausted' (I.vii.7.2n), though he makes no further mention of the episode's sexual content.

52 While the allegory necessarily makes the latter point indirectly, Arthur seems almost to create a breach in the surface of the story when he compares Red Crosse's downfall to his own past pride and naïveté in scorning love (I.ix.10–12). Yielding to Duessa is

Spenser's bawdy 135

It is appropriate, therefore, that Red Crosse's rehabilitation begins with positive images of procreation in the House of Holiness. As Adelman observes, it is here that Errour's 'thousand yong ones' (I.i.15.5) and the repulsiveness of the reproductive body are reinterpreted positively as the 'multitude of babes' that cluster about Charissa's breasts (x.31.1).[53] The implication that Red Crosse himself has been reborn – that he is the 'one sonne more' whom Charissa has recently brought into the world – is reinforced by a verbal parallel: 'By this *Charissa*, late in child-bed *brought* / Was woxen strong, and left her fruitfull nest; / To her fayre *Vna brought* this vnacquainted guest' (x.29.7–9; my italics on 'brought'). That Red Crosse's spiritual rebirth entails the banishment of his former prudishness may even be indicated by a punning allusion, in 'vnacquainted', to *vna's quaint*. While few readers would be prepared to recognise a bawdy pun in this context, it is worth noting a carefully timed instance of sexual humour during Red Crosse's fight with the dragon – which is to say, on the very brink of Satan's defeat. Having retired for the night in a state of wakeful anxiety over the wellbeing of her wounded knight, Una rises on the third day to see the battle's end. The gorgeous description of daybreak clearly anticipates Red Crosse's defeat of the dragon. Not only is it joyous and affirming, it is also funny – and bawdily so:

> The ioyous day gan early to appeare,
>   And fayre *Aurora* from the deawy bed
>   Of aged *Tithone* gan her selfe to reare,
>   With rosy cheekes, for shame as blushing red;
>   Her golden locks for hast were loosely shed
>   About her eares, when *Vna* her did marke
>   Clymbe to her charet, all with flowers spred,
>   From heuen high to chace the chearelesse darke;
> With mery note her lowd salutes the mounting larke.
>
> (I.xi.51)[54]

Like the song of the lark, this description of the dawn in a state of post-coital disarray displaces cheerlessness with merriment, using humour and (notwithstanding Aurora's red cheeks) unabashed sensuality to signal the coming victory. It also anticipates what can only be described

---

not, as Hamilton states, tantamount to being bound by beauty (I.ix.12.1–2n); rather, to quote Arthur, it is boasting 'in beauties chaine *not* to be bownd' (ix.11.7; my italics).
53 Adelman, 'Revaluing the Body', p. 24.
54 The humour of this description is noted by Gilbert, 'Spenserian Comedy', p. 101.

136 *Comic Spenser*

as the consummation scene between Red Crosse and Una: 'Her ioyous presence and sweet company / In full content he there did long enioy / ... swimming in that sea of blisfull ioy' (I.xii.41.1–5). As has been well noted, technically Red Crosse and Una are not married but betrothed, in recognition of the fact that the Christian community must await the fulfilment promised in Revelation (xii.40.4–5n). The marked resemblance of their betrothal rite to a wedding, and their evident pleasure in each other prior to Red Crosse's forced departure would, then, appear to be an apocalyptic foreshadowing – though, I would argue, one that not only appropriates sex and marriage as metaphors, but also celebrates them on their own terms.[55]

---

55 The relationship between temporal marriage and Christian eschatology allows betrothal (in the eschatological sense) and marriage (in the earthly sense) to function as allegories for each other, which may, as Walls notes, explain the ambiguity of the ceremony between Una and Red Crosse, which is formally a betrothal but looks very much like a marriage, complete with epithalamium and apparent consummation (*God's Only Daughter*, pp. 15–16). (Though note the divergent perspective of Hadfield, 'Spenser and Religion', pp. 29–37, who, recognising the importance of marriage to Spenser, takes a dim view of what he takes to be the couple's unconsummated union; on the latter see also Levin, 'The Legende of the Redcrosse Knight', pp. 20–2.) Earthly marriage ritually affirms a couple's joint betrothal to God, and in this sense symbolically foreshadows the Marriage of the Lamb; more than symbolically, though, it is also the means by which the Christian community – which is to say, God's spouse – is created and sustained.

4

Laughing at love: *The Faerie Queene* III–IV

not Venus hir selfe (what euer Lucretius writeth) will denie, but that hir might in engendrure remaigneth voyde, and of small effect, without thaccesse of mine ayde.

Erasmus, *The Praise of Folie*, p. 15

majesty and love go ill together.

Ovid, *Metamorphoses* II.846–7

That being in love dignifies man and turns his mind to virtue is a familiar Renaissance claim. More incisive, however, is Folly's assertion that sex may be counted upon to turn even the most distinguished pillar of society into a helpless fool. The first claim is typically Spenserian, but in this chapter I argue that the tension between virtue and folly in matters of love is even more so. Willye's motto (or 'Embleme') at the end of the March eclogue of *The Shepheardes Calender* makes this point succinctly: '*To be wise and eke to love, / Is graunted scarce to God above*' ('March', lines 119–20). In part, it is love's distance from rationality and utility that allows it to be a vehicle for transcendent causes on one hand and laughed at as the archetypal human folly on the other. These contrary associations reflect a collision of abstract ideals and physical realities: love is at once a high theme – something battles are fought for and that evokes noble emotions – and, ineradicably, a low theme – something bodily and irrational.[1]

---

1 A similar paradox is sketched by Oram, 'Human Limitation', pp. 36–7. As indicated where relevant, the findings of this chapter cross paths at several points with Oram's essay.

138   *Comic Spenser*

Early modern theorists of the epic poem recognised that heroic virtue and affairs of the heart are irreconcilable, or reconcilable only insofar as civic duty is shown to overthrow passion, as in the *Aeneid* or *Gerusalemme liberata*, or insofar as love is forced into the background of male affairs, as in the *Iliad*.[2] This hostility to romantic distraction was influenced by the Aristotelian ideal of unified and linear narrative development as well as a reaction against medieval authors who privileged erotic plot lines over the 'matter of Mars', without, moreover, seeking to idealise love. To explore love's irrationality during the Renaissance was to open oneself up to a certain amount of criticism. As Tasso disdainfully remarked, 'non meritano lode alcuna coloro che hanno descritti gli abbracciamenti amorosi in quella guisa che l'Ariosto descrisse quell di Ruggiero con Alcina o di Ricciardetto con Fiordispina' ('they merit no praise at all ... who have described amorous embraces in the fashion of Ariosto depicting Ruggiero with Alcina, or Ricciardetto with Fiordispina').[3] Lord Burghley similarly censured Spenser for his love poetry. In a thinly veiled retort, Spenser's narrator feigns respect for the statesman who is too busy and too serious to indulge the frivolity of 'louers deare debate' (mock-heroically praising 'The rugged forhead that with graue foresight / Welds kingdomes causes') while pointing out that such men know little of the subject they censure (Proem IV, 1–2).

Ariosto, of course, more than hints at a clash between heroism and romance. His knights generally want something from the damsels they rescue and are unafraid to show it. And when it constitutes more than sexual opportunism, love is revealed to be a chaotic, destabilising force, notable for inciting violence rather than valour. The eponymous hero Orlando is driven mad by love, whereupon (instead of taking to his bed like Troilus) he goes on the warpath in a state of psychosis. In singing of 'Fierce warres and faithfull loues' (Proem I, 1.9), Spenser has traditionally been accredited with reforming Ariosto through moral allegory and a Protestant emphasis on marriage, freeing romance from triviality and reforming its adulterous themes in the process.[4] While these arguments

---

2 See Bernard Weinberg, *A History of Literary Criticism in the Italian Renaissance*, 2 vols (Chicago: University of Chicago Press, 1961), Vol. II, Chapters 19 and 20.

3 *Discorsi*, p. 500; *Discourses*, pp. 11–12.

4 See for example Craig A. Berry, '"Sundrie Doubts": Vulnerable Understanding and Dubious Origins in Spenser's Continuation of "The Squire's Tale"', in *Refiguring Chaucer in the Renaissance*, ed. Theresa M. Krier (Gainesville: University Press of Florida, 1998), pp. 106–27 (esp. pp. 120–1); Lawrence F. Rhu, 'Romancing Eliza: The Political Decorum of Ariostan Imitation in *The Faerie Queene*', *Renaissance Papers* (1993), 31–9; Peter DeSa Wiggens, 'Spenser's Use of Ariosto: Imitation and Allusion in Book I of *The Faerie Queene*', *RQ*, 44 (1991), 257–79.

Laughing at love: Books III–IV   139

are valid, Spenser nevertheless shares Ariosto's attentiveness to the less than ideal connections between sexuality and violence, as well as his wry awareness of the large dose of self-interestedness that even faithful love requires if it is to get off the ground.[5] Spenserian morality involves getting to the root of human hypocrisies, not cauterising humour. While the narrator of *The Faerie Queene* characteristically asserts black-and-white oppositions between love and lust and between nobility and baseness, such assertions do not play out in the murkier plots of the stories they refer to. Spenser's heroic lovers are typically both dignified and comically vulnerable, in love and in lust. Love is that 'Most sacred fyre [...] Whence spring all noble deeds' (III.iii.1.1–9) but has a habit of finding its victims 'vnawares at disauantage' and can be counted upon to 'pluck downe' the 'prouder vaunt' (I.ix.11.4, ix.12.3–4). Desire 'stirredst vp th'Heroes high intents' (III.iii.2.8) but is also a troubling imperative for 'liuing clay' (III.iv.26.3) and 'weake mankind' (IV.xi.5.4) – a force that makes Mars himself 'shreek, / With womanish teares, and with vnwarlike smarts' (III.xi.44.5–6).

Focusing on Books III and IV, this chapter examines *The Faerie Queene*'s representations of romantic love in detail. My purpose is to draw attention to the ways in which Spenser draws out the comedy of love by blurring the distinctions between love and lust, noble suffering and self-indulgence, altruism and self-interest. If there is cynicism in this amusement, it tends to be directed at the notional ideals themselves, and at the conventions of chivalric romance, rather than at the human imperfections they expose.[6] Spenserian humour often emanates from the lightest touches of realism, of human character closely and sympathetically observed, and his depictions of lovers in particular draw this talent out. 'Character' and 'personality' are sometimes regarded as inappropriate terms in Spenser criticism, as though their use implies a disregard for allegory. From another point of view, a narrative and its allegorical suggestions can (and should) be mutually revealing. As this chapter contends, the psychological complexity that Spenser achieves at the level of the narrative, where we may accept that characters have social

---

5 For critical recognition of Spenser's affinity to Ariosto, see n. 16 below.
6 Such irony is well recognised in the *Amoretti*; see Louis L. Martz, 'The *Amoretti*: "Most Goodly Temperature"', in *Form and Convention in the Poetry of Edmund Spenser*, ed. William Nelson (New York: Columbia University Press, 1961), pp. 146–68; Elizabeth Bieman, '"Sometimes I … mask in myrth lyke to a Comedy": Spenser's *Amoretti*', *SSt*, 4 (1984), 131–41; and Donna Gibbs, *Spenser's 'Amoretti': A Critical Study* (Aldershot: Scholar Press, 1990).

140   *Comic Spenser*

interactions and think and feel things, warrants detailed and appreciative analysis on its own terms.

Laughing at love

Instances of smiling and laughing in *The Faerie Queene* are habitually linked to the subject of love. Sometimes a propensity to laugh indicates licentiousness, as in the case of the 'grenning' satyrs (I.vi.11.7); the wanton Phaedria with her storehouse of 'merry tales' (II.vi.6.4); or, more threateningly, the monster Lust with his 'grenning laughter' (IV.vii.24.9). Laughter can be cynical, as when Sir Satyrane and the Squire of Dames are amused by female inconstancy (III.vii.57.5, 58.5, ix.6.6; IV.v.18–19). But it can also mark a more congenial kind of wry knowledge. Artegall smiles inwardly at Britomart's blushing response to Glauce's bawdy insinuations (IV.vi.32.8), and Leda (depicted on Busirane's tapestry) smiles at Jove's amorous approach in the form of a swan (III.xi.32.8–9). Laughing and smiling are also what the gods are said to do when sympathetic to lovers. As Arthur says of the day he fell in love with Gloriana, 'The fields, the floods, the heauens with one consent / Did seeme to laugh on me, and fauour mine intent' (I.ix.12.8–9).[7] But, as Laurel L. Hendrix has pointed out, it can be difficult to distinguish between divine affirmation and divine amusement: are the gods laughing at human affairs? Arthur's resemblance to Sir Thopas at this moment suggests they may be.[8] Venus is certainly amused when, in her hunt for the fugitive Cupid, she hears the love-complaints of the many people her son has wounded: 'She sweetly heard complaine, both how and what / Her sonne had to them doen; yet she did smile thereat' (III.vi.15.8–9). Like Chaucer's 'Venus ful of myrthe' (*Troilus and Criseyde* III.715), Spenser's Venus is the 'Mother of laughter, and welspring of blisse' (IV.x.47.8), suggesting that being in love makes people joyous, but also that lovers are the playthings of an amused goddess. Gower's Venus in *Confessio Amantis* is comparable to Spenser's in that her amusement at human frailty appears to blend scorn and sympathy. Amans narrates:

---

7 Similarly interpreted as a sign of favour, Venus laughs at Scudamour (IV.x.56.4), as Hamilton notes (I.ix.12.8–9n).

8 Arthur's sense of divine favour immediately precedes his Thopas-like dream of the 'Queene of Faries', on which see further pp. 174–5 below. Hendrix surveys classical and Renaissance authorities on laughter, arguing that Venus's ostensibly 'amiable' laughter at Scudamour as he takes Amoret from her temple (IV.x.56.4) marks a crisis point in the poem; Laurel Hendrix, ' "Mother of laughter, and welspring of blisse": Spenser's Venus and the Poetics of Mirth', *ELR*, 23 (1993), 113–33.

Laughing at love: Books III–IV 141

Venus behield me than and lowh,
And axeth, as it were in game,
What love was.[9]

One is reminded of Geffrey in *The House of Fame*, who in his quest to learn about love seems to be the butt of a joke whose punchline is always on the brink of being told.

Cupid possesses a number of different personae in *The Faerie Queene*, but predominantly he represents a more blackly comic view of human affairs than does his mother. He is 'the God of loue' (III.vi.26.1) but also that 'dreaded impe' (Proem I, 3.1), the master of ceremonies at Busirane's castle who takes off his blindfold to survey the damage he has caused, clapping his wings 'on hye', much as Hellenore, under Cupid's influence, gleefully applauds her husband's ruin (III.x.12.9, xii.23.7). The craftier and crueller Cupid's triumphs, the more amused he is: we hear that he 'Did smyle full smoothly' at Britomart's initial ignorance of her own lovesick state (ii.26.9), and 'close did smyle' at Paridell's adulterous seduction of Hellenore (x.5.7). As this echo suggests, love can be a great leveller. Britomart may be the founder of a great dynasty and Paridell may be a cheating scoundrel, but Cupid smiles at them both.

Love makes Jove himself laugh in *The Faerie Queene*. When he is said to have 'laught on *Venus* from his souerayne see' at the birth of Belphoebe (III.vi.2.7), Richard J. Berleth finds confirmation of Jove's dominance over Venus as well as an affirmation of 'perfect harmony and friendship between planets'.[10] This may be, but Jove's laughter may also suggest a wry, satyr-like carnality. Despite the narrator's polite insistence that Belphoebe's conception was virginal (and occurred as 'reason teacheth'; III.vi.8.3), the passage narrating her mother's impregnation by the sun is one of the most erotically charged in the whole poem.[11] And perhaps, too, Jove is laughing *at* Venus because the birth of Belphoebe – archetype of virginal chastity – is hardly good news for her (Venus and Diana will shortly squabble; III.vi.20–5).

---

9 John Gower, *Confessio Amantis*, ed. Russell A. Peck (Toronto: University of Toronto Press, 1997 [1980]), p. 484 (VIII.2870); quoted by Burrow, *Ricardian Poetry*, p. 105. Burrow observes that Venus's playful superiority over mortals, familiar from classical literature, is especially evident in medieval love allegory.

10 Richard J. Berleth, 'Heavens Favourable and Free: Belphoebe's Nativity in *The Faerie Queene*', *ELH*, 40 (1973), 479–500 (p. 488); see *FQ* III.vi.2.7n.

11 The congeniality of Jove is elsewhere linked to passion. Erasmus's Folly asserts: 'Iupiter, *father of the Goddes, and kynge of kynges, who with his onely becke, can shake all heauen, must laie downe his threforked thunder, and also his grimme countiaunce* … in

142   *Comic Spenser*

Cupid's nasty side, Venus's amused superiority, and the topos of divine congeniality each capture something different about what it feels like to be in love, and together suggest that laughter bears an ambivalent relation to desire: romantic love is conducive to laughter and vice versa, but it is also potentially laughable. This is what William Hazlitt meant when he identified love as 'half of the business and gaiety of comedy'.[12] While comedies that end in marriage seem to insist, along with the lover in Spenser's Temple of Venus, that love is 'the root of all that ioyous is' and of all 'that merry is and glad' (IV.x.47.3–6), they reliably tap into desire as a reservoir of collective weakness and amusing social mishap.

While classical gods laugh at love in *The Faerie Queene*, the combination of judgement and clemency in that laughter has Christian resonance. Sexual love bears witness to both sin and redemption: it offers compelling proof of our fallibility and appetitive weakness ('those ioyes that weake mankind entyse'; IV.xi.5.4) but is also divinely ordained, and one of the highest expressions of Christian charity ('love is the lesson that the Lord us taught'; *Amoretti* LXVIII). Even St Augustine, for whom the libido was the single most compelling expression of our fallen nature, regarded sexual love as prelapsarian in origin.[13] Admittedly there are few laughs in *The City of God*, but it is possible to see how this paradoxical view of romantic love might generate comic tension in the hands of a poet whose lovers are both admirable and fallible. If humour tends to accentuate the fallible side of the bargain, it can also cast the deceptions and vulnerabilities of the human ego in a sympathetic light, allowing them a part in our higher destinies.

Guyon and Arthur

Fresh from his achievements as hero of temperance, Guyon is made to look slightly silly when Britomart easily knocks him out of his saddle at the beginning of Book III. The comedy of the man-beaten-by-a-woman-in-disguise

---

    case he woulde dooe the thing, that he always practiseth (whiche is) *to gette children*'; *Folie*, p. 14.

12   William Hazlitt, 'On Wit and Humour', in *Lectures on the English Comic Writers* (London: Taylor and Hessey, 1819), pp. 1–53 (p. 21).

13   In contrast to Jerome, who argued that sexuality followed original sin (and that God's injunction to Adam and Eve to increase and multiply was meant spiritually), Augustine maintained that marriage and the imperative to procreate preceded sin; see St Jerome, 'The Virgin's Profession', in *Select Letters of St Jerome*, trans. F. A. Wright (London: Heinemann, 1933), pp. 89–97; and Augustine, *City of God*, pp. 620–7 (XIV.22–4).

Laughing at love: Books III–IV

143

scenario is generally acknowledged, but the subtle undermining of Guyon's masculine dignity (built up by the narrator in Stanzas 3–5) is worth pausing over. The narrator's admiration for his skilful manner of falling off his horse illustrates how heroic praise in *The Faerie Queene* can be backhanded:

> But *Guyon* selfe, ere well he was aware,
> Nigh a speares length behind his crouper fell,
> Yet *in his fall so well him selfe he bare,*
> That mischieuous mischaunce his life and limbs did spare.
>
> (III.i.6.6–9; second italics mine)

Knowing how to fall from a horse may be an important skill for knights, but the ironic nature of this praise is confirmed when Arthur and the Palmer continue to cushion the blow to Guyon's ego.[14] Although a good craftsman never blames his tools, Arthur

> laid the blame, not to his carriage,
> But to his starting steed, that swaru'd asyde,
> And to the ill purueyaunce of his page,
> That had his furnitures not firmely tyde
>
> (III.i.11.5–8)

In this way Arthur pacifies his friend and convinces him to reconcile with Britomart rather than try his luck in battle a second time. The analogous episode in *Orlando furioso*, in which Bradamante knocks Sacripante from his horse, has Angelica (whom we know to be deceitful and manipulative) utter similarly soothing words to her red-faced knight (*OF* I.67). Another equally loaded Ariostan echo follows: 'O goodly vsage of those antique tymes, / In which the sword was seruaunt vnto right' (III.i.13.1–2). As a number of critics have noted, a very similar apostrophe ('Oh gran bontà de' cavallieri antiqui!') occurs at an acutely unheroic moment in *Orlando furioso* – namely, at the point in which Ferraù and Rinaldo agree to put off trying to kill each other in order to chase Angelica on the same horse.[15] Andrew Sanders voices the traditional view that Spenser either missed Ariosto's irony or sought to reform it: 'The very stateliness of [Spenser's] lament for the decline of chivalric virtue in the first canto of Book III, though closely modelled on a stanza of Ariosto's, completely lacks the ironic twist

---

14 Cheney rightly observes that temperance may be encouraged by a little 'diplomatic duplicity'; 'Spenser's Parody', p. 9.
15 *Of,* I.xxii.1. Harington translates: 'O auncient knights of true and noble hart' (*OF,* 1.22.1).

144   *Comic Spenser*

of the original.'[16] This, however, is to take Spenser's earnest narrator at face value. In fact the only difference between the poets' facetious apostrophes is that the context of Spenser's praise is less jarring and morally dark than Ariosto's (whose knights are engaged in sexual pursuit).

Allegorically, Britomart's easy defeat of Guyon implies that the self-restraint sought by the latter in Book II is an inadequate response to desire, which instead needs to be channelled into marriage; but we may equally conclude from Britomart's aggression and from Guyon's shamefaced ineffectuality that Spenserian chastity permits, or even necessitates, some bold intemperance. Whatever Spenser's narrator may say about the perfection of antique heroes, between the lines we are being told to prepare for some very human motives and actions.

Notably, Spenser does approach the darker irony of Ariosto at one critical point, and it is Arthur, magnificence personified, who bears its brunt. Soon after Guyon's embarrassing defeat and his reconciliation with the disguised Britomart, the party seek adventures together. After a long and fruitless search the knights find themselves in a wild forest where suddenly (presumably to their relief) a beautiful lady with golden locks gallops past, along with a 'griesly foster' in hot pursuit (III.i.14–17). It becomes clear that Guyon and Arthur, who gaze after the lady before chasing after her (the antagonist being left to Arthur's page), are motivated by desire.[17] Britomart's story intervenes for several cantos, but when we next hear of these 'two gret champions' we are told that they are pursuing Florimell much as a hunter chases a hare (iv.46.1–5) or a falcon preys on a dove (iv.49.4–9). We are reminded of Ariosto's tendency to conflate the roles of rescuer and rapist – identities that are, after all, hard to distinguish when we see a knight on horseback pursuing a lady.[18] Florimell is both damsel in distress and 'goodly pray' (iv.46.9), and Arthur is as threatening from her perspective as was the 'griesly Foster' who had been chasing her in the first place: 'she no lesse the knight feard, then that villein rude' (iv.50.9). The narrator assures us that Florimell is needlessly fearful, and indeed Arthur is no rapist. Yet the confusion over his motives (and the

---

16 Andrew Sanders, *The Short Oxford History of English Literature*, 3rd edn (Oxford: Oxford University Press, 2004), p. 132. See also *FQ* III.i.13n. Sanders echoes the classic statement of R. E. N. Dodge, who in the late nineteenth century declared that Spenser read Ariosto 'in the light of his own serene idealism'; 'Spenser's Imitations from Ariosto', *PMLA*, 12 (1897), 151–204 (p. 172). The assumption that Spenser's Christian allegorisation of Ariostan romance involved missing or ignoring the Italian's humour is commonly encountered, although notable exceptions are Gilbert, 'Spenserian Comedy', pp. 97–9; Silberman, 'Spenser and Ariosto'; and Cheney, 'Spenser's Parody'.

17 This ironic echo of *Orlando furioso* is noted by Cheney, 'Spenser's Parody', p. 10.

18 See Silberman, 'Spenser and Ariosto', p. 26.

Laughing at love: Books III–IV   145

probability that Florimell would manage quite well if only men would stop chasing her) underlines an irony familiar to readers of chivalric romance: the alignment of heroic deeds for 'Ladies sake' (v.11.9) and self-interest.[19] As the boar imprisoned beneath the mount of the Garden of Adonis reminds us, an aggressive drive underlies the entire reproductive world. This can be disturbing (the besieged Florimell is gifted trapped animals from another suitor; vii.17.6–7), but it can also be funny. Like Apollo in his pursuit of Daphne, Arthur calls out to Florimell as he gallops full-tilt and 'oft let fall / Many meeke wordes' (iv.48.9).[20]

At this point, however, Arthur more closely resembles Sir Thopas than Apollo. Like Chaucer's mock-knight, Arthur is at the mercy of his own confused impulses as well as the reader's superior perspective on them. The resemblance is first established in Book I, when Arthur tells Una about his dream of the 'Queene of Faries', the search for whom has become his life's quest (I.ix.12–15). When he loses sight of Florimell at nightfall and is forced to give up the chase, the resemblance once again becomes pointed (III.iv.53–4). Like Sir Thopas, Arthur lets his 'steed' 'forage' and lies down on the grass in a fit of love melancholy (III.iv.53.6–9; 'Sir Thopas', lines 772–83).[21] In Chaucer's lampoon, the hero (who appears to have enjoyed a deep sleep between stanzas) cries:

> 'O Seinte Marie, benedicite!
> What eyleth this love at me
> To bynde me so soore?
> Me dremed al this nyght, pardee,
> An elf-queene shal my lemman be
> And slepe under my goore.
>
> 'An elf-queen wol I love, ywis,
> For in this world no womman is
> Worthy to be my make
>   In towne;
> Alle othere wommen I forsake,
> And to an elf-queene I me take
> By dale and eek by downe!'

(784–96)

---

19 See also I.v.12.5 and I.vii.14.6, for example.
20 *Met* I.496–530.
21 Arthur heroically makes the 'cold earth ... his couch' and 'the hard steele his pillow' (III.iv.53.9). As Hamilton notes, the parallels with 'Sir Thopas' at this point (including a shared misuse of 'forage') are discussed by Anderson, 'The "couert vele": Chaucer, Spenser, and Venus', *ELR*, 24 (1994), 638–59.

146 *Comic Spenser*

The vacuity and vanity of Sir Thopas's outburst anticipates similar traits in Arthur's love complaint. There are differences, of course (Arthur does not sleep, he has a lot more to say, and his tone is less optimistic), but there are comparable elements of absurdity. Even in the narrator's secondhand account, Arthur's adolescent petulance rings through pitch-perfect:

> disdaine
> Of his hard hap did vexe his noble brest,
> And thousand fancies bett his ydle brayne
> With their light wings, the sights of semblants vaine:
> *Oft did he wish, that Lady faire mote bee*
> *His faery Queene, for whom he did complaine:*
> *Or that his Faery Queene were such, as shee:*
> And euer hasty Night he blamed bitterlie.
>
> (III.iv.54.2–9; my italics)

A comparison with Bottom's Pyramus would be taking it too far, perhaps, but Arthur sounds a bit like Colin Clout when he breaks his pipe because Rosalind laughs at his songs (*SC*, 'Januarye'). There is also a telling analogue in Sacripante's lament for Angelica in *Orlando furioso*, which Ariosto's narrator derisively passes over:

> Mentre costui così s'affligge e duole,
> e fa degli occhi suoi tepida fonte,
> e dice queste e molte altre parole,
> che non mi par bisogno esser raccconte.
>
> Sacripante lies there sorrowing,
> Making a fountain of his streaming eyes,
> Saying first one and then another thing
> I see no reason to immortalize.[22]

The silliness of Arthur's predicament and his self-pitying rhetoric are worth emphasising, because his apostrophe to Night is often read without irony, and has been used to place Spenser within the serious tradition of medieval complaint.[23] To an extent this is understandable: when Arthur describes night's

---

22 *Of* I.xlviii.1–4; *OF* I.48.1–4. Thomas P. Roche, Jr comments that although Angelica's flight is a clear source for Florimell, the latter's adventures 'owe little to Ariosto'; 'Florimell', in *SpE*, pp. 309–10 (p. 309). But this is a good example of the subtlety with which Spenser taps into the humour of *Orlando furioso*.
23 See *FQ* III.iv.55–60n; and Mark David Rasmussen, '*Complaints* and *Daphnaida* (1591)', in *Oxford Handbook of ES*, pp. 218–36 (p. 232). Others argue that Arthur's state of

Laughing at love: Books III–IV 147

persecution of the heavy-hearted (III.iv.57) and affirms God's blessings on the 'children of day' (iv.59.5), the sentiment is moving. Clearly, however, we are not expected to take this outpouring from an 'ydle brayne' (iv.54.4) quite seriously. Rejecting the idea that sleep might be gentle or restorative (iv.54.1, 56.9) or that dreams may be visionary (as they have been in the past; 57.6), Arthur berates the darkness that is keeping him from Florimell: 'Night thou foule Mother of annoyaunce sad, / Sister of heauie death, and nourse of woe' (iv.55.1–2). His tone is reminiscent of *Virgils Gnat*, in which the insect-protagonist melodramatically rehearses his 'intollerable cares' (line 632). Six fulsome stanzas later, Arthur commands the sun to banish night to hell in a notably petulant manner: 'Chace her away, from whence she came, to hell. / *She, she it is*, that hath me done despight' (iv.60.6–7; my italics). When the sun does come up, it reveals a grumpy and 'lumpish' Prince, who, in a final echo of 'Sir Thopas', 'clombe vnto his steed' (61.6–7).[24]

What, then, should we make of this burlesque treatment of *The Faerie Queene*'s most exalted hero? Critics have gone to a lot of trouble to explain why Spenser made Chaucer's 'Sir Thopas' pivotal to his poem's epic design, and to the character of Arthur in particular. While such efforts have yielded valid insights into Spenser's creative and strategic appropriations of Chaucer, the strong tendency has been to show how Spenser defuses and redirects the comic energy of his source.[25] By contrast, I join Anderson and McCabe in arguing that the rift 'Sir Thopas' opens up in *The Faerie*

frustration is morally suspect, but find no humour in the circumstance; see for example Sheila T. Cavanagh, *Wanton Eyes and Chaste Desires: Female Sexuality in 'The Faerie Queene'* (Bloomington and Indianapolis: Indiana University Press, 1994), p. 24.

24 Hamilton (III.iv.61.6n) notes the humour of this ungainly verb. Cf. 'Sir Thopas', line 797 (and editor's note).

25 J. W. Bennett proposes that *The Faerie Queene* underwent a major generic shift at some point in the composition process, from a comic to a serious poem – the 'Sir Thopas' allusions being traces of an earlier draft; *The Evolution of 'The Faerie Queene'* (New York: Burt Franklin, 1960), pp. 1–23 (esp. pp. 15, 18, 22–3). Other critics assume that Spenser either missed the joke of 'Sir Thopas' or sought to reform it. J. A. Burrow proposes that Spenser ignored the joke in order to draw seriously on Sir Thopas's association with chastity; ' "Sir Thopas" in the Sixteenth Century', in *Middle English Studies Presented to Norman Davis*, ed. Douglas Gray and E. G. Stanley (Oxford: Clarendon Press, 1983), pp. 69–91 (p. 87). See also Anne Higgins, 'Spenser Reading Chaucer: Another Look at the *Faerie Queene* Allusions', *JEGP*, 89 (1990), 17–36 (pp. 24–7); and, to a lesser extent, Quilligan, 'The Comedy of Female Authority', p. 165. Andrew King has argued that Spenser was engaged in rehabilitating the native tradition that 'Thopas' burlesques as part of a nationalistic, Protestant programme to resurrect England's medieval inheritance; '*The Faerie Queene' and Middle English Romance: The Matter of Just Memory* (Oxford: Clarendon Press, 2000), pp. 9–11. Elsewhere King points out that Spenser's apparent obliviousness to the humour of 'Sir Thopas' is itself

148   *Comic Spenser*

Queene between epic and burlesque, earnest and game, does not need to be resolved. To mend the rift is to miss the essential point that 'in matters of the heart the sublime and the ridiculous must meet'.[26] This is not, however, to lose sight of the fact that Arthur's love-longing is allegorical. His quest is, officially speaking, an aspiration for glory, not a hunt for a woman. But Arthur is distracted from his vow to Gloriana by the sight of Florimell, which is to say, beauty.[27] When the narrator tells us that 'Oft did he wish, that Lady faire mote bee / His faery Queene … / Or that his Faery Queene were such, as shee' (III.iv.54.6–8), we are reminded that glory and beauty, in their most exalted Spenserian definitions, do actually coalesce in a Christian-Platonic ideal. But we are also reminded that both glory and beauty refer to worldly things that have a habit of rerouting aspirational energies away from that ideal. As the allusions to Sir Thopas are surely intended to intimate, Arthur's quest is a very human one.[28]

This point continues to be underlined in Book IV, when Arthur finds consolation in the appearance of two damsels in distress, Amoret and Ameylia. They explain that they have been rescued from a lustful monster 'by Virgins hond' (IV.viii.21.6). Inwardly wondering if this might be *his* virgin (whether the fairy queen or Florimell is unclear, although it is hard to imagine Florimell rescuing anyone), Arthur 'oft of them did earnestly inquire, / Where was her won, and how he mote her find' (viii.22.3–4). When he realises neither damsel can tell him what he wants to know, he promptly puts them on his horse – 'No seruice lothsome to a gentle kind', as the narrator observes (viii.22.7). The narrator proceeds to moralise that only a 'rash witted wight' would imagine that Arthur is gratified by having two ladies on his horse in any sense other than a purely altruistic one (viii.29.1–5). In case we miss the heavy-handedness of this assurance, another nostalgic appeal to

> something of a Chaucerian irony; 'Spenser, Chaucer, and Medieval Romance', p. 561. Berry, too, sees Chaucerian irony as instrumental (though not especially comically productive) in *The Faerie Queene*: he argues that Spenser drew upon Chaucer's ironic handling of poetic authority in 'Sir Thopas' to negotiate anxieties about his own reception; 'Borrowed Armor/Free Grace', pp. 152–66.

26 McCabe, 'Parody, Sympathy and Self', pp. 12–13. On Arthur's comic side see further Anderson, 'A Gentle Knight', pp. 171–2; and Judith H. Anderson, 'Arthur, Argante, and the Ideal Vision: An Exercise in Speculation and Parody', in *The Passing of Arthur: New Essays in Arthurian Tradition*, ed. Christopher Baswell and William Sharpe (New York: Garland, 1988), pp. 193–206.

27 On Florimell as beauty, see Roche, 'Florimell', in *SpE*, pp. 309–10; and pp. 162–4 below.

28 On the implications of this irony for Queen Elizabeth as Gloriana, see p. 174 below.

Laughing at love: Books III–IV 149

bygone virtue follows: 'But antique age yet in the infancie / Of time, did liue then like an innocent / In simple truth and blamelesse chastitie' (viii.30.1–3). Not only does this contradict everything we know to be true about Spenser's fictional world, which possesses all the moral grey areas that life does, but it is also at odds with the fact that the party spend the night in Slander's house (viii.23–4). Although slander is by definition untrue, we may nevertheless conclude that the scenario of two women and one man turns heads not only among the poem's corrupt modern readership but also among the inhabitants of Fairyland.

Troilus and Criseyde as comic model

As the very human responses of both Guyon and Arthur to unexpected failure (and, in the case of the two damsels, unexpected consolations) demonstrate, Spenser's close observations of human nature can be very amusing. The purpose of such humour is not cynically to undermine romantic love but rather to acknowledge that desire is liable to expose our foibles and frailties at the least convenient moments. Spenser's willing exploration of this fact, not only through slightly naïve characters such as Willye in the pastoral world of *The Shepheardes Calender* but also through the heroes of *The Faerie Queene*, bears comparison with, and may well have been influenced by, *Troilus and Criseyde*.[29]

The comic side of Chaucer's great poem is often commented upon. Derek Brewer has argued that the character of Pandarus soaks up all of the poem's humour like a sponge, enabling Troilus to be a serious and ultimately tragic character. In part this is true: much of *Troilus and Criseyde*'s comic irony is generated by Pandarus's manipulative and verbose speeches and is reserved for the poem's audience alone.[30] But Troilus, though not a humorous character, does not always escape comic treatment.

---

29 Critical discussions of Spenser's use of *Troilus* tend to focus on metre, language, and specific allusions, whereas my discussion here draws attention to generalised tonal and thematic similarities. On the relation of the Spenserian stanza to Chaucer's rhyme royal see William Blisset, 'stanza, Spenserian', in *SpE*, pp. 671–3.

30 Pandarus rather unscrupulously warns his niece that her rejection of Troilus would kill both Troilus and him (*Troilus and Criseyde* II.319–25). Having said this, not all of Pandarus's humour is reserved for the reader; Criseyde often engages her uncle in witty repartee, and on several occasions is said to laugh so hard 'That she for laughter wende for to dye' (II.1169, 1108).

150   *Comic Spenser*

In the instant Troilus falls in love, he is compared, in his prior mockery of lovers, to a wayward (and well-fed) horse:

> As proude Bayard gynneth for to skippe
> Out of the weye, so pryketh hym his corn,
> Til he a lasshe have of the longe whippe –
> Than thynketh he, 'Though I praunce al byforn
> First in the trays, ful fat and newe shorn,
> Yet am I but an hors, and horses lawe
> I moot endure, and with my feres drawe'
>
> (I.218–24)

The narrator's next comment clinches the bathos of this simile: 'So ferde it by this fierse and proude knyght' (I.225). Attempting to rouse Troilus from his lovesick stupor, Pandarus later shouts at his friend much as the eagle squawks at Geffrey in *The House of Fame*:

> 'What! Slombrestow as in a litargie?
> Or artow lik an asse to the harpe,
> That hereth sown whan men the strynges plye,
> But in his mynde of that no melodie
> May sinken hym to gladen, for that he
> So dul ys of his bestialite?'
>
> (I.730–5)

In striking contrast, Pandarus paints his friend in an overtly flattering light when talking to Criseyde. He tells her that he has overheard Troilus's impassioned soliloquy in one of the court gardens, adding that this confession of love took place after a jousting session and discussion of military tactics with Pandarus himself. As well as implying closer intimacy with affairs of state and of the heart than he actually enjoys, Pandarus fabricates a scene that corresponds to what we might expect of a heroic lover. In fact we know that Troilus is refusing to get out of bed, and, in contrast to the kind of confessional speech Pandarus might wish for, is being frustratingly evasive. On the page it is possible to overlook, but if Pandarus's self-flattering lies were relocated to the stage before a credulous Criseyde and a knowing audience, the dramatic irony of the episode would be impossible to ignore. Shakespeare, of course, *did* transfer the story to the stage, and his accentuation of Troilus's bedridden ineffectuality and reliance on an aggressive go-between suggests that he was alert to Chaucer's unheroic humour.

Laughing at love: Books III–IV 151

Notably, Chaucer's narrator shares something of Pandarus's artful unreliability. On the occasion of the lovers' meeting at Pandarus's house on a stormy night (allowing Pandarus to insist that his niece stay over), the narrator delivers a mock-heroic apostrophe when the expected storm materialises ('O Fortune, executrice of wyerdes, / O influences of thise hevenes hye!'; III.617–18) as though fate, not Pandarus, were orchestrating the event. As in *The Faerie Queene*, moments of high rhetoric, especially when voiced by an enthusiastic narrator, invite our amused scepticism.

It goes without saying that *Troilus* is a serious and tragic story about love. Its humour, rather than being inappropriate or incongruous as some have suggested, is at home in this context and capable of enriching it. When Troilus, after death, sees how small the world is he laughs inwardly at his companions' grief for him and, implicitly, at his own former suffering for love (V.1814–25). His laughter disavows life's dramas as vanity, and indeed the narrator concludes by invoking Christian truth and advising his readers to think on higher things (V.1835–69). The message is austere yet consoling. As I suggested in Chapter 1, the humorous perspective we bring to Troilus's extreme emotions of agony and ecstasy as a lover throughout the poem in fact anticipates this final transcendent vision. In both cases, laughter (however inward and muted) marks a sense of human smallness in the cosmos, and places high drama in the levelling context of folly.

And yet, there is an important difference between the poem's comic aspects and its final renunciatory vision. Humour in the poem is characteristically directed toward *enabling* rather than belittling sexual desire, and, in this sense, offers quite a different kind of consolation. The dominant effect is to moderate life's tragic potential with empathetic rather than judgemental laughter. Even its most tense dramatic moments are brought down to earth by domestic detail and by humour, as when Pandarus disingenuously tells Criseyde that Troilus has braved the storm and clambered up 'a goter, by a pryve wente' to reach her (III.787). This is J. A. Burrow's Ricardian world of 'humorous awareness and acceptance of things as they are', in which 'the folly of amorous concerns' is subject to grave and sententious *and* comic treatment.[31] The poem's final transcendent perspective reminds us that romantic love is merely an earthly thing; comedy reminds us that earthly things tolerate modesty and the language of high idealism for only so long.

---

31 Burrow, *Ricardian Poetry*, p. 114.

152 *Comic Spenser*

Spenser shares Chaucer's willingness to show us serious characters in a comic light, his knack for empathetic satire in matters of the heart, and his use of a narrator whose pronouncements need to be taken with a grain of salt. For all her bravery, furthermore, Britomart shares Troilus's need for an audacious alter ego to convert idealistic love-longing to pragmatic action.

Britomart and Glauce

Her easy defeat of Guyon early in Book III corroborates our impression that Britomart is a peerless exemplar of chastity, although what this means is not immediately clear. What is chastity, and in what sense might one exceed others in exemplifying it? If we take the terms with which the narrator praises Britomart in Canto i at face value, we might assume that chastity is primarily a virtue of self-restraint or disengagement – or, more specifically, of not pursuing ladies. While Arthur and Guyon are unchastely chasing Florimell, the narrator reports:

> faire *Britomart*, whose constant mind,
> Would not so lightly follow beauties chace,
> Ne reckt of Ladies Loue, did stay behynd
>
> (III.i.19.1–3)

But this is the familiar voice of Spenser's naïve narrator, ever eager to flatter and to moralise. As Cheney observes, Britomart 'Ne reckt of Ladies Loue' for no other reason than that she is female and has set her sights on an embodiment of *masculine* beauty.[32] The supposition that Britomart is more temperate than her counterparts is, as I have suggested, negated at the outset when she charges at Guyon without provocation. For many this action, and her easy victory over him, confirm the superiority of chastity to temperance in the context of Book III; an alternative slant is that temperance (the stoical kind at least) must be cast aside if Britomart's quest is to be successful. The distinction is subtle, but the second formulation is decidedly less heroic than the first. That Britomart should begin her search for Artegall by overthrowing the knight of temperance is certainly suggestive given the lengths to which she must go to attain her goal. As Erasmus's Folly would agree, temperance is not simply an inadequate response to love; it is a positive hindrance. Folly declares that even

---

32 Cheney, 'Spenser's Parody', p. 10.

Laughing at love: Books III–IV   153

the Stoic, if he is to be a lover, will at some point have to 'caste awaie those his yronlike lessons, and precepts of doctrine' and 'haue recourse vnto [me]'.[33] The lover must be prepared to become, from a rational standpoint, absurd. Our initial impression that Britomart as paragon of chastity will expose others' flaws is, in sum, wrong.

In his *Arte of English Poesie*, Puttenham lists 'the old nurse & the yong damsell' as stock characters of the comic theatre, and Spenser's version of this time-honoured partnership does not disappoint.[34] The comic appeal of Britomart's nurse, Glauce, is widely recognised; along with Braggadochio, it was her character that sparked interest in Spenserian humour in the early twentieth century.[35] The perspective of Guyon and Arthur mediates our first impression of the pair, so we share their assumption that the approaching knight and squire are male:

> They spide a knight, that towards pricked fayre,
> And him beside an aged Squire there rode,
> That seemd to couch vnder his shield three-square,
> As if that age badd him that burden spare,
> And yield it those, that stouter could it wield
>
> (III.i.4.2–6)

If we initially assume that Glauce is a venerable figure like Guyon's Palmer, hindsight twists the above description into something more along the lines of Sancho Panza – another makeshift squire to a self-appointed knight. The humour of Glauce's representation deserves our serious attention; all too often the words 'comic relief' spell the end of the subject. In fact, we should ask why Glauce provides this comic foil for Britomart's high purpose in seeking her royal mate.

While Britomart has been placed on a pedestal by some critics, her alliance with someone who knows the 'old game' reminds us that, as well as being the wellspring of a glorious race of kings, she is also a young girl with a crush (a 'silly Mayd'; III.ii.27.7). Moreover, she is embroiled in scenes straight out of the world of fabliau.[36] She is drawn into a bed-swapping fiasco in Malecasta's castle after her effort not to be noticed (by eating dinner in full armor with only her visor up) proves

---

33 *Folie*, p. 14.
34 Puttenham, *ECE*, Vol. II, p. 34 (also p. 33).
35 See Introduction, n. 4.
36 On Britomart's exemplary status see, for example, Cavanagh, *Wanton Eyes*, pp. 25–6; and A. C. Hamilton, 'General Introduction', in *FQ*, pp. 1–20 (p. 10).

154   *Comic Spenser*

counterproductive (i.42–62). Equally misled by Britomart's masculine appearance after being liberated by her from Busirane's castle, Amoret is thrown into a state of anxiety when her rescuer, in an effort to 'hide her fained sex the better', feigns sexual motivation ('to her she purpos made / Of loue, and otherwhiles of lustfulnesse'; IV.i.7.3–8). Earlier on, Britomart had ingloriously battled Paridell for his place in a 'swyne' shed out of the rain, and was present for that knight's Ovidian seduction of Hellenore (III.ix.11–17; 27–52).

Countering such farcical moments, Britomart's grief-stricken apostrophe to the ocean at III.iv.8–10 would seem to offer a prime example of Spenserian seriousness. Yet, on second reading, it sounds suspiciously like Arthur's self-indulgent complaint to Night. In part, Britomart's melodramatic side is aided and abetted by Glauce, who is an expert on the 'tyranny of loue' in young girls' hearts and not a little partial to drama (ii.40.9). Yet the nurse is also the pragmatist whose task it is to snap Britomart out of moments of stasis and lofty abstraction. Thus Britomart's torrid words ('Huge sea of sorrow, and tempestuous griefe, / Wherein my feeble barke is tossed long'; iv.8.1–2) are met, perhaps to the relief of some readers, with a 'sharpe repriefe' from Glauce (iv.11.4). Britomart does possess something of Glauce's expediency when it suits her, however: the nurse's dishonest dealings with Merlin, which he quashes by 'brusting forth in laughter' at her nerve (iii.19.2), recall the string of lies with which Britomart manipulates Red Crosse into talking about Artegall (ii.5–16).

Hamilton has complained that Britomart, more than any other character in *The Faerie Queene*, attracts readings 'as though she were no more than a dramatic and human character'.[37] I would contend that while her story is complexly allegorical, as are her encounters with Malecasta and Busirane for example, interest in her 'personality' should not automatically be considered misplaced, reductive, or in conflict with allegorical interpretation. Love is nothing if not dramatic and human, and surely it is this that gives depth to the national and dynastic allegory, not the other way around. After all, national destiny for the Elizabethans actually hinged on a female's willingness to find a mate – an irony not lost on readers of Book III. Britomart may be representative of other things, but her story loses meaning if she is not also a young woman in love.[38]

---

37 See Hamilton's introduction to Book III in his first edition of *The Faerie Queene* (London: Longman, 1995 [1977]), pp. 299–303 (p. 301).
38 On the comic productivity of the relationship between a narrative and its allegorical suggestions see Leonard, *Laughter in the Courts of Love*, p. 11. Among those critics of *The Faerie Queene* who place character and allegory at odds are J. B. Lethbridge and

Laughing at love: Books III–IV   155

It is fitting that Glauce in particular should make such an appealing dramatic character, given that it is she who asserts that love is not abstract but tangible; as she reminds Britomart, the object of her affections is 'No shadow, but a body' (III.ii.45.7). Glauce is allegorically suggestive, too, of course. Her name has been etymologically linked to the Greek words for 'owl' and 'grey' (ii.30.2n) and, by association, to wisdom, although these connotations are somewhat elevated. In fact she seems to embody a rather low-brow part of the female lover's psyche: pragmatism and cunning in matters of sex and marriage, with a dose of superstition and melodrama thrown in. She is the descendant of earthy nurse-figures in classical literature (most notably the pseudo-Virgilian *Ciris*) and of *La Vieille* ('Old Woman') in *Le Roman de la rose*.[39] As the enabler and guide of the lover's search, 'Glauce' also suggests 'glance' – Britomart's passing vision of Artegall in her father's magic mirror (*OED*, v., 5) – as well as its cognate meaning (alternatively spelt 'glace'), 'to slip, to fail in giving a direct blow ... to glide, pass easily through' (*OED*, s.v. 'glace', v., 2). The latter meaning suggests the passage of Cupid's dart 'shot / So slyly, that she did not feele the wound' (ii.26.7–8).[40] The two meanings coincide when Britomart is wounded by Gardante, 'looking', in Malecasta's castle (the blow is glancing here too: 'yet was the wound not deepe, / But lightly rased her soft silken skin'; i.65.6–7).

Yet we can still appreciate the psychological realism of Glauce's interactions with Britomart, in which their respective characters are sketched with a real lightness of touch. The narrative flashback in which Britomart confesses her lovesickness to Glauce (at III.ii.30–47) is a case in point. Their night-time conversation is laced with subtle humour. Once the full story is known, Glauce – evidently a connoisseur of Ovidian tales about perverse sexual appetites – is relieved to learn that her charge has fallen for an eligible man rather than for a bull or her own father

---

Susanne Lindgren Wofford. Lethbridge argues that 'dramatistic readings' bark up the wrong tree, and present a red herring for the allegorical reader Spenser's poetry truly speaks to; 'The Poetry of *The Faerie Queene*', pp. 169–216. By contrast, Wofford argues that Spenser consciously dramatises – and genders – the tension between dramatic and allegorical interpretative approaches, aligning attempts to reduce character to an allegorical scheme with male hegemony; Susan Lindgren Wofford, 'Gendering Allegory: Spenser's Bold Reader and the Emergence of Character in *The Faerie Queene* III', *Criticism*, 30 (1988), 1–21.

39 Hamilton notes Spenser's imitation of *Ciris*; ii.30–51n. See Sandra S. Clark, 'Glauce', in *SpE*, p. 333 for other analogues.

40 Merlin uses 'glaunce' twice in conversation with Britomart; III.iii.24.2, 24.5.

156   *Comic Spenser*

(ii.40–2).[41] As it contributes to the nurse stereotype, Glauce's familiarity with classical stories of sexual deviance is amusing in its own right. But with the benefit of hindsight we see that lurid possibilities are playing on her mind from the beginning of the conversation, before Britomart has even admitted to being in love. Glauce's taste in literature has, in other words, led her to form a conclusion in advance, and all her questions subsequently tend in one direction. She refers to Britomart's malaise as 'vncouth', 'euill' (ii.30.7), and 'wicked' (32.4), and expresses the hope that she has fallen in love with someone worthy not only of her lineage but of her 'race' – the implication being that she fears the love object may be non-human, never mind non-royal (33.4). In a comedy of cross-purposes, everything Britomart says, strung out over three stanzas for maximum suspense, seems to confirm Glauce's preconceptions: 'mine is not … like other wownd […] for no no vsuall fire, no vsuall rage / Yt is, O Nourse […] Nor Prince, nor pere […] Nor man … nor other liuing wight' (ii.36–8). When the object of Britomart's desire is finally revealed to be human, male, a non-relative, and even aristocratic, Glauce is effusive in her relief, lingering with evident delectation, now that the danger has passed, over the numerous perverse desires that Britomart *might* have fallen victim to.[42]

The subtle comedy of Glauce's portrayal extends to her concern over what King Ryence would think if he knew of his daughter's state – an anxiety that pragmatically turns to thoughts of her own job security. Before determining to help Britomart find Artegall, Glauce tries to reverse her charge's lovesickness with prayers and eventually with a magical spell, 'for feare least blame / Of her miscarriage should in her be fond' (III. ii.52.7–8). As Hamilton notes, the magic rite in question is based upon a similar episode in the *Ciris*, yet is exaggerated and vulgarised ('spit vpon my face, / Spitt thrise vpon me, thrise vpon me spitt') to the point that it sounds like a 'schoolboy's joke' (ii.50.7n). That Glauce's hopeless attempt

---

41   Spenser considerably extends a suggestion in the *Ciris*; see Virgil, *Virgil, with an English Transation*, trans. H. Rushton Fairclough, rev. edn, 2 vols (London: Heinemann, 1950 [1934]), Vol. II: *'Aeneid' VII–XII and the Minor Poems*, pp. 423–5 (*Ciris*, lines 220–49).

42   Glauce's attraction to sensational tales may contain something of Spenser himself: the incestuous desire of Myrrha is recalled repeatedly, and sometimes inexplicably, in Book III (Amoret, Florimell, and Britomart are each compared to her), and, between the sadomasochism of Busirane (and the exhaustive array of exploits depicted on his tapestry; III.xi.29–46), the onanism of the phallic monster 'Lust' (IV.vii.20.3–8), and the nymphomania of Argante (III.vii.47–50), *The Faerie Queene* has perhaps rightly been called 'the most extended and extensive meditation on sex in the history of European poetry'; Camille Paglia, 'sex', in *SpE*, pp. 638–41.

Laughing at love: Books III–IV   157

to cure Britomart is motivated in part by an instinct for self-preservation is underlined once more in the following canto. Glauce hates to see her charge suffering, but, even more than this, she fears 'fowle repriefe / And sore reproch' (iii.5.7–8) from Britomart's father.

Britomart, conversely, is so preoccupied with Artegall that she refrains from telling Glauce the cause of her distress for fear her nurse might die of suffering too ('Is not enough, that I alone doe dye, / But it must doubled bee with death of twaine?'; III.ii.35.3). Her inability to recognise the subjectivity of her suffering recalls King Lear's mad assumption that anyone in a state of torment must necessarily have three daughters. Yet this is the kind of adolescent self-absorption that Britomart needs to pursue her destiny with Artegall. If she looks into Merlin's prophetic mirror and initially sees her own reflection ('Her selfe awhile therein she vewd in vaine'), she sees the image of her lover not by looking beyond her reflection but by becoming more deeply self-absorbed: 'she gan againe / Her to bethinke of, that mote to her selfe pertaine' (ii.22.6–9).

Far from being about not chasing women, chastity in *The Faerie Queene* has more in common with the stubborn single-mindedness with which almost every living species, plant, and animal ensures its survival in the face of natural competition and the dictates of chance than with the conventional ideal of blushing and passive femininity. Britomart's unwavering resolve to seek Artegall has long been celebrated as her quintessential heroic attribute, but, as her alliance with Glauce reminds us, the single-mindedness of love is funny too. When Britomart puts Artegall on a pedestal and imagines him as ideal in all respects, she is forced to '[turn] her head aside' (V.vii.38.4) when she finally lays eyes on him and sees not a knight but a man in a dress spinning with a distaff. Hero-worship in *The Faerie Queene* is always suspect, and the subtle humour of her portrayal encourages us to take Britomart off her pedestal too, and to see her irrationality, egotism, and vulnerability as legitimate and deeply human aspects of her role as heroine of chastity.

Comic timing: Florimell and Satyrane

Cantos vii–viii and ix–x of Book III mirror each other significantly in juxtaposing idealised and debased treatments of a single theme. In Cantos vii–viii, the story of Florimell's besieged chastity sits cheek by jowl with the Squire of Dames's tale of female incontinence. In Cantos ix–x, Paridell's sleazy re-enactment of the adultery that sparked the Trojan war vies (even at the same dinner table) with Britomart's quest to renew the glories of her

158 *Comic Spenser*

Trojan ancestry. While these episodes are particularly striking and provocative examples of Spenserian humour (which some critics find to be out of keeping with the rest of the poem) the element of bathos they provide is familiar.[43] Much as pastoral interrupts epic in Book I, in Book III antifeminist satire interrupts pathos and fabliau interrupts romance. In the process, Spenser draws material from two well-known comic sources: the Squire of Dames's tale is lifted straight from *Orlando furioso*'s most notorious pages, and the story of Malbecco, Paridell, and Hellenore combines allusions to Ariosto's Canto XXXII and Chaucer's 'Merchant's Tale'.

The chief subjects of Cantos vii–viii are Florimell's ongoing harassment (she has been fleeing from a string of persecutors since we first met her in Canto i), Satyrane's encounter with the Squire of Dames, and the creation of Florimell's false double ('snowy' Florimell). Satyrane, an ambivalent figure who says all the right things but is ultimately more satyr than hero, spikes a pathos-laden story with an unsettling (if relieving) element of black humour. In Canto vii he arrives too late to rescue Florimell, who has escaped a monstrous hyena only to take refuge in the boat of a lecherous 'fisher old and pore' (III.vii.27.5). Satyrane arrives upon the scene to discover Florimell's 'embowelled' palfrey (29.1) being eaten by the hyena, and, nearby, her 'golden girdle' lying on the ground (31.8). Understandably concluding that the lady has been eaten, Satyrane later reports, 'dead, I surely doubt, thou maist aread / Henceforth for euer *Florimell* to bee' (viii.47.5–6). Given that Florimell is not only an innocent victim but also 'dearely loued' (vii.31.6), and 'in all / [Satyrane's] famous conquests highly magnifide' (31.6–7), it is somewhat surprising to find that in the period between his gruesome discovery of her palfrey in Canto vii and his report of the tragedy in Canto viii, 'the good Sir Satyrane' – meanwhile allowing the hyena to escape – may be found laughing at antifeminist jokes with the Squire of Dames.

Initially, Satyrane is distracted from thoughts of Florimell by a second crisis in which he plays a critical role: he is injured while saving the Squire of Dames from the lustful giantess Argante (III.vii.38–44). Commendable though Satyrane's actions appear to be, the unheroic comedy of his rough treatment (he is 'pluckt' (43.3) from his saddle and thrown across Argante's lap 'like to a carrion corse' (43.5) before being thrown aside) underscores the negative implication of his contact with a figure of monstrous lust. This ironic subtext is confirmed when he and the Squire, once safe, engage

---

43 See for example Hough, *Preface to 'The Faerie Queene'*, p. 169.

Laughing at love: Books III–IV 159

in banter about how easily women of all ranks may be seduced. The Squire tells Satyrane of the two antichivalric quests his lady has sent him on: the first to seduce as many women as possible in the space of a year, the second to find an equal number of chaste women to reject him. The task of proving his 'trusty true intent' (vii.55.8) through sexual disloyalty proved easy, but the Squire is now on a seemingly hopeless mission to find truly chaste women. After searching for three years, he has found only three who rejected his advances, one of whom was a 'common Courtisane' who wanted more money, and another of whom was a nun who suspected (rightly) that the Squire would not be discreet about their affair. Only the third is implied to be chaste. At this dismal account Satyrane laughs 'full hartely' (vii.58.5, 57.5) and mock-heroically compares the Squire's efforts to '*Alcides* labours' (vii.61.4). (The Squire will similarly provoke laughter among the Knights of Maidenhead when he jests at the ladies' failure to wear Florimell's girdle; IV.v.18–19.) Satyrane's laughter is in keeping with his amused response later in Book III to the Squire's report of the suspicious old miser Malbecco and his pretty young wife:

> Thereat Sir *Satyrane* gan smyle, and say;
> Extremely mad the man I surely deeme,
> That weenes with watch and hard restraynt to stay
> A womans will, which is disposd to go astray.
>
> (III.ix.6.6–9)

Of course, the lascivious and jovial nature of satyrs is proverbial, and will feature prominently in the extra-marital adventures of Malbecco's wife Hellenore. The theme is close to Satyrane's heart: like Hellenore, his own mother once strayed from her husband to 'serue her turne' with a satyr (I.vi.22). But even if we can expect little more from the offspring of a human and a satyr, Spenser would seem to be soliciting our attention with the blackly comic timing of Satyrane's amusement – especially as this is uncomfortably close to our own amusement as readers. Do not we, too, welcome the break from the high pathos of Florimell's travails, and laugh at the Squire's story?

Spenser accentuates his narrator's chivalric language at a dramatically critical moment. As Florimell is about to be raped by the fisherman, the narrator cries: 'O ye braue knights, that boast this Ladies loue, / Where be ye now' (III.viii.27.6–7).[44] As well as recalling the ironic timing of the last such apostrophe to chivalry ('O goodly usage'), this question – ostensibly

---

44 On the comic unreliability of the narrator at this point see Oram, 'Human Limitation', p. 47.

160 *Comic Spenser*

rhetorical – is unfortunately one that we can all too readily answer. The narrator continues:

> But if that thou, Sir *Satyran*, didst weete,
> Or thou, Sir *Peridure*, her sory state,
> How soone would yee assemble many a fleete,
> To fetch from sea, that ye at land lost late;
> Towres, citties, kingdomes ye would ruinate,
> In your auengement and dispiteous rage,
> Ne ought your burning fury mote abate;
> But if Sir *Calidore* could it presage,
> No liuing creature could his cruelty asswage.
>
> (III.viii.28)

Yet, at the end of the canto, when Paridell successfully persuades Satyrane not to give Florimell up as dead, all talk of fleets and fury is conspicuously absent. In view of the narrator's confidence, it is acutely ironic that the Squire should interrupt the pair's discussion of Florimell and suggest finding a bed for the night, addressing his companions 'Ye noble knights' (III.viii.51.1). The reference to nightfall and the need to gather strength is conventional, although in this case it sits ill with the fact that the party stays up talking (and flirting) until the 'heuenly lampes were halfendeale ybrent' (ix.53.5). Moreover, when the knights do get around to launching a campaign, they decide to host a tournament (beauty pageant?), where the prize of Florimell's girdle seems to have supplanted the lost lady herself (as we learn at IV.ii.25–7).

The juxtaposition of Florimell's besieged chastity with a comic story about female inconstancy and male incompetence is more complex and more rewarding than the narrator's straightforward moral reading allows, for what we are in fact being presented with are two equally silly stories – stories that are two sides of the same coin. In the manner of Boccaccio's *Decameron* – a collection of tales by turns idealising and demonising, pathetic and bawdy – or Petrarch's sonnets, which venerate and vilify their female subject, Cantos vii and viii seem to illustrate the dependence of one extreme image of women upon the other. Formally, the virgin is venerated and the whore is vilified, but in practice the opposite can be true: Florimell's chastity incites endless aggression, while Hellenore ('Helen-whore') ends up being quite literally adored (III.x.44).

Spenser seems to enjoy anatomising the hypocrisy that desire incites. In narrative terms, Satyrane's ordeal with Argante forces him to free the hyena that had persecuted Florimell; in *allegorical* terms, both the

Laughing at love: Books III–IV　　　161

Argante episode and the amusing conversation with the Squire that follows confirm Satyrane's own satyr-like carnality, thus implicating him in Florimell's ordeal at the hands of the old lecher. And yet, while Satyrane is shown in a compromising light, it is evident that his laughter at the Squire's antifeminist is not, as the narrator politely suggests it is, purely at his own expense (III.viii.44.1–3). If Satyrane's earthy irreverence is critiqued, it also justifiably places the high pathos of the earlier episode in an absurd light. Let us reconsider the narrator's apostrophe to Florimell's absent knights: 'Towres, citties, kingdomes ye would ruinate, / In your auengement and dispiteous rage' (viii.28.5–6). Such destruction over a sexual offence is being billed as desirable and right, but it is disproportionate to Florimell's need to be rescued from the unwanted attentions of an old man (which would not have been challenging had anyone been paying the right kind of attention). The heroic scenario longed for by Spenser's narrator is reminiscent of the Trojan War, but also of the burlesque heroics of *Orlando furioso*, in which a knight driven by thoughts of his lady may well wipe out a city or impale ten men on the point of his spear. The decadence of this sort of heroism is made clear later in Book III when, to impress Hellenore, Paridell speaks of Helen of Troy's great beauty and in the same breath eulogises the 'carcases of noble warrioures' who died in her name (ix.35.7). Satyrane's unchivalric behaviour, in other words, pokes fun at the ideal he is failing to live up to as much as it underlines the failure itself.

Key to the ideal being undermined is the female object of desire, here Florimell. Notably, her plight in the fisherman's boat is imbued with comic irony.[45] Consider Florimell's inadvertent use of sexual puns when she addresses the fisherman:

> But thou good man, sith far in sea we bee,
> 　And the great waters gin apace to swell,
> That now no more we can the mayn-land see,
> 　Haue care, I pray, to guide the cock-bote well
> 　　　　　　　　　　　　　　(III.viii.24.1–4)

At this the lecher 'did nought but fondly grin, / And saide, his boat the way could wisely tell' (24.6–7). There is considerable irony in the circumstance that Florimell, accustomed to viewing all men without exception as sexual predators, has failed to recognise the dangers of this stock comic

---

45　See Hadfield, 'Spenser and Jokes', pp. 7–9; and Oram, 'Human Limitation', p. 46.

162   *Comic Spenser*

figure – the old man who feels 'in his old corage new delight' (23.4). How should we as readers respond to our enjoyment of this irony, given that the threat is rape? Most obviously, the disarming use of humour confirms what we already inwardly know: that one way or another, the consequences of this crisis are not going to be tragic. Another function of Florimell's unwitting arousal of the fisherman is to distinguish her from her false double. 'False Florimell', created by the witch (to console her doltish son for the loss of the real lady; viii.5–9), is a consummate flirt and would never be this slow to read the signs of desire or so unattuned to the hidden meanings of words.

However, I would further propose that the humour of the episode can only be fully appreciated if we recognise that Florimell bears a nuanced rather than a starkly opposed relation to her false double.[46] Allegorically Florimell is 'beauty', but only beauty as it is perceived. Thus when the fisherman attempts to rape her, even though in terms of the narrative it is the real Florimell, we should understand that he is engaging a false version of what she stands for, because a true understanding of beauty could not incite rape. Whereas her false or 'snowy' double (who never suffers hardship) represents beauty specifically as it fools, abuses, and passively manipulates others, the so-called real Florimell at this point would seem to represent a different aspect of beauty: namely, its abuse and subjection by men. As Berger rightly observes, 'Florimell is no less a male invention than the False Florimell. Both equally project and reflect male desires, and their effects sometimes converge.'[47] Importantly, this determines not only how Florimell is treated but also how she is represented, and it is in this light that we need to consider the humour attending the pathos of that representation. Although very different in other respects, Florimell resembles her false double in that, as a possession that endlessly changes hands, she is deflected from her purpose – love – and in the process is turned into a caricature of herself.

Spenser's use of humour to underscore *false* Florimell's status as a caricature is unambiguous. In the story of her creation by the witch, the familiar literary joke of the mock-blazon is taken a step further in that the lady is literally constructed out of (as opposed to merely compared to) a series of far-flung components. The result is a feast of visual

---

46 The apparently concrete distance between 'true' and 'false' figures in Spenser's allegory can be misleading, as I argue of Una and her double (see Chapter 3).

47 Berger, 'Kidnapped Romance', pp. 220–1.

Laughing at love: Books III–IV   163

absurdity – what Bergson would call the comic spectacle of 'something mechanical encrusted on the living' – as we imagine 'two burning lampes ... set / In siluer sockets' stirring and rolling 'like to womens eyes' and framed with 'golden wyre' for hair (III.viii.7.1–5).[48] As well as making fun of Petrarchan excess (as the *Amoretti* often do), the material reproduction of Florimell's virginity would seem to point up reductive emphasis on chastity as a merely physical qualification – moreover using language familiar from serious panegyric of the Virgin Queen: the body is a mixture of congealed snow collected from a secret shady location and 'virgin wex that neuer yet was seald' (6.7). The witch then inspires these lifeless ingredients with an infernal spirit. Ironically for those who later court her, this spirit is masculine, perhaps in recognition of the fact that it is chiefly men who give life to, and perpetuate, a false ideal of feminine attractiveness (this may also explain why snowy Florimell is so good at reading men's minds).

The 'real' Florimell, I am arguing, also courts absurdity. Hough thought her so devoid of character as to call her a 'hapless object of desire' and 'the inevitable desirability of beauty, and its helplessness when unallied to any other qualities'.[49] Shrieking for help, Florimell is the archetypal damsel in distress – until, that is, her staunch resistance to the charms of her rescuer, Proteus, turns her into the cold lady of the Petrarchan sonnet tradition. Hadfield has drawn a comparison between the fisherman episode and the world of the Renaissance jestbook, wherein individuals rely on cunning and wit to satisfy their appetites and to survive.[50] Sexually naïve and reliant on supernatural intervention, Florimell is the extreme antithesis of the wily jestbook rogue she finds herself up against. Hadfield further suggests that the puns in her speech reveal her repressed desire: Florimell is ignoring her body and its appetites. When Proteus saves her from the fisherman only to try (albeit in a more restrained manner) his own luck with her, Hadfield proposes that she is 'punished for her lack of sexuality with a frozen kiss':

> Her vp betwixt his rugged hands he reard,
> And with his frory lips full softly kist,
> Whiles the cold ysickles from his rough beard,
> Dropped adowne vpon her yuory brest
>
> (III.viii.35.1–4)

48 Bergson, 'Laughter', in *Comedy*, p. 748.
49 Hough, *Preface to 'The Faerie Queene'*, p. 171.
50 Hadfield, 'Spenser and Jokes', pp. 7–9.

164 *Comic Spenser*

Hadfield is surely right that the world of *The Faerie Queene* is at this point overtly and comically masculine, and that Florimell fares badly as a result. But the target of the episode's humour is not Florimell's repressed sexuality, or not only, but also the fetishisation of chastity as something sexually alluring in itself. Angelo ponders this phenomenon when aroused by the novice nun Isabella in *Measure for Measure*: 'Can it be, / That modesty may more betray our sense / Than woman's lightness?' (II. ii.167–9). False Florimell knows that it certainly may, insisting, because she knows it is what men like to hear, that 'her honor...she more then life prefard' (III.viii.14.9). The real Florimell says this too, only she means it. But, as Hadfield observes, there comes a point when rigorous chastity *is* laughable. When in *Measure for Measure* Isabella is asked to forfeit her chastity to save the life of her brother Claudio, she nobly refuses, explaining: 'O, were it but my life, / I'd throw it down for your deliverance / As frankly as a pin' (i.103–5). At a recent performance I attended of this play, Claudio's understated reply, 'Thanks, dear Isabel' (i.105), prompted more laughter than all the comic scenes about brothels and whores put together. Isabella, like Florimell, is 'too cold' (II.ii.56). But rather than casting in his lot with the dog-eat-dog world of the jestbook in teasing Florimell's 'Benumbd' heart (III.viii.34.8), Spenser does something more critical and reflective. He satirises the ideal of chastity that serves to venerate women even as it polarises the majority of them as either lascivious or frigid. And indeed, at this point in the allegory of Book III, the two Florimells may be regarded as Petrarchan ciphers, each inciting both desire and vilification.

That we should refrain from reading Florimell's temporary fate in a spirit of high seriousness is further suggested by the figure of Proteus. Despite his imprisonment of Florimell, Proteus is a charismatic character, as the description of his icy beard and 'frory lips' (and of his attempts to win Florimell's favour by endlessly changing shape, a tactic that only scares her further) somehow conveys. The combination of fearsomeness with charm continues in the description of Proteus's oceanic dungeon. This is a hollow cave 'Vnder a mightie rock, gainst which doe raue / The roring billowes in their proud disdaine', where 'ne liuing wight was seene'. No living person except, that is, 'one old *Nymph*, hight *Panope* to keepe it cleane' (III.viii.37.2–9). Proteus is a bit of a bachelor; he is also, says the narrator, like a spaniel with a partridge (viii.33.3–6) – almost unintentionally cruel. Given that he will not keep beauty in thrall for long, we may employ Satyrane's cynical words to new, optimistic

Laughing at love: Books III–IV 165

purpose: 'Extremely mad the man I surely deeme, / That weenes with watch and hard restraynt to stay / A womans will' (ix.6.7–9).

The pathos of the episode more or less verges on the absurd throughout, but this becomes marked when the narrator refers to Florimell's near-rape by 'that old lechour' (III.viii.36.1) as 'Fit song of Angels caroled to bee' (viii.43.1). That the tone here is one of mawkish sentiment would seem to be confirmed at the end of the same stanza when the narrator (as Ariosto's narrator often does) professes reluctance to change storylines, and suggests that this amounts to a cruel abandonment.[51] The last of a string of men to treat Florimell roughly, the narrator laments: 'Yt yrkes me, leaue thee in this wofull state, / To tell of *Satyrane*, where I him left of late' (viii.43.8–9). The canto had opened with the narrator's equally ironic pretence that the outcome of Florimell's story was *not* entirely in his hands:

> sure I weene, the hardest hart of stone,
> Would hardly finde to aggrauate her griefe;
> For misery craues rather mercy, then repriefe.
>
> (III.viii.1.7–9)

As Dorothy Stephens comments: 'with wide-eyed innocence, Spenser's narrator deplores the fact that a maiden as genteel as Florimell has ended up in such a sea of troubles. The cause of those troubles is, of course, Spenser.'[52] In abandoning Florimell to follow the adventures of Satyrane and Squire, the narrator is once again exchanging high pathos for a bawdy story: this time that of Malbecco and Hellenore (III.ix–x). It might be said that we as readers are complicit with him (and, moreover, comparable to Satyrane in Canto vii) in allowing Florimell to be kept prisoner if this is the price of a titillating story about female concupiscence.

---

51 See for example *Of* VIII.lxvi–lxvii, or X.xxxiv.7–xxxv.1. With similar irony, both poets advertise their bawdy material by excessively apologising for it (*FQ* III.ix.1–2; *Of* XXVIII.i –iii). On Ariosto's use of disingenuous apology and feigned passivity as an ironic narrative device see Parker, *Inescapable Romance*, pp. 25–6; and Javitch, 'The Advertising of Fictionality', pp. 110–13.

52 Edmund Spenser, *'The Faerie Queene', Books III and IV*, ed. Dorothy Stephens (Indianapolis: Hackett, 2006), III.viii.1.6n. On the way such humour reminds us of the gap between Spenser the poet and the overtly male perspective of his narrator, see Wofford, 'Gendering Allegory', pp. 5–7.

166   *Comic Spenser*

Spenser's comic lovers in context

The comic side of love is everywhere in Renaissance literature. Comic plays and prose narratives revolve around lovers' mishaps and reconciliations, epyllia wittily present mythological erotic vignettes, and romance – as we have seen in this and previous chapters – turns the spotlight on conflict between altruism and self-interest. Non-comic genres such as the lover's complaint or sonnet cycle, moreover, created a language around romantic love that, in its self-conscious conventionality, was ripe for parody – sometimes within nominally serious works themselves. The absurd *Gullinge Sonnets* of John Davies (*c.* 1596) poke fun at the excesses and clichés of Elizabethan sonnet sequences, but so, somewhat more subtly, do Spenser's *Amoretti*, whose narrator is not above Arthuresque self-pity and indulgence. Indeed, the occasionally thin distinction between convention and cliché in the *Amoretti* is not accidental – it is psychologically pertinent. To express the feeling that 'no one else has ever felt like this before' with the help of formulae makes a serious and amusing point about the phenomenon of being in love.[53]

As the example of the *Amoretti* suggests, we are not always informed by clear generic cues which things are supposed to be amusing – we might, for example, have to appraise the narrator's tone with care and scepticism. Or to put it another way, what differentiates the humour discussed in this chapter from, say, comic plays; epyllia; or, at the far end of the spectrum, fabliaux, is its relative subtlety. Spenser's lovers are not overtly comic figures, and we are invited to invest in their quests. But at times we are also invited to enjoy comic distance. Spenser, in contrast to Dryden, who insisted that 'Passions are serious, and will admit no Playing', followed Chaucer and Ovid in making love an epic subject whilst keeping one eye firmly on its capacity to make us behave in foolish ways.

Yet while Chaucer and Ovid were routinely criticised by neoclassical poets for being too humorous in their treatment of love, Spenser was not. This historical disinclination to recognise Britomart's self-absorption or Arthur's petulance as funny – or even to recognise these traits at all – persists to the present day, and is not solely due to Spenser's lightness of

---

53 Davies wrote 'serious' sonnet sequences also. Sir John Davies, *The Gullinge Sonnets* (*c.* 1596), in *The Complete Poems of Sir John Davies*, ed. Revd Alexander B. Grosart, 2 vols (London: Chatto and Windus, 1876), Vol. II, pp. 55–62; etext (created by Anniina Jokinen) in *Luminarium Editions*, www.luminarium.org/editions/gullingsonnets.htm (accessed May 2019). On tongue-in-cheek Petrarchanism in the *Amoretti* see Martz, 'The *Amoretti*'.

Laughing at love: Books III–IV

touch. It is also a reflection of the expectations we bring to a poem whose main characters are presented as personifications of virtues. To an extent we are prepared to recognise moral flaws in Spenser's heroes – flaws they must overcome to demonstrate the virtue in question – but it is another thing to be amused by shortcomings that seem so innately human that they may never be 'overcome'. Far from obstructing or minimising the task of moral interpretation as might be assumed, being amused at such shortcomings allows us to recognise the characters' quests as our own – to absorb the important point (surely key to any moral valence their stories have for us) that they are not extraordinary heroes of a bygone golden age but exemplars of challenges that shape our lives every day.

Bringing heroics down to earth by prompting empathetic self-recognition is, I would argue, the chief purpose of Spenser's humour in these central books. The result is not a denigration of romantic love (as we have seen, a sharper irony is reserved for the fetishisation of virginity) so much as recognition that sexuality in some sense epitomises the contradictions of human experience. Desire can be (and is sometimes imperatively) selfish, aggressive, and irrationally consuming, yet it is also a catalyst for growing up, for experiencing vulnerability and imperfection, and for finding meaning outside oneself for the first time.

5

Parody and panegyric

Humour is not resigned; it is rebellious.

Sigmund Freud[1]

A singularly humourless encounter with *The Faerie Queene* is preserved in a copy of the 1611 folio, the margins of which record the response of an early Puritan reader of the poem. Adjacent to the invocation beginning 'O Goddesse heauenly bright' in Proem I (4.1), this reader indignantly scrawls: 'he prayeth to Queen Elizabeth to aid him after the manner of the heathens, who deified their emperors, and invocated their help. But if a man should ask how a creature can raise the thought and express it home, he could never answer.'[2] The same annotator takes issue with the crucifix on Red Crosse's breastplate, with the idea of fairy ('Fairies are devils, and therefore fairyland must be devil's land'), and with the apparent humility of Archimago ('this commendation of an hermetical life is naught').[3] The unintended comedy of this poker-faced approach to the text lies in the reader's refusal to recognise that panegyric, like the motifs of chivalric romance and the appearance of Catholic religiosity, is part of the theatrical and provocative game Spenser is inviting us to play. The accusation that he is heathenishly invoking the queen as a presiding goddess is, after all, accurate. Many readers are willing to add a pinch of salt (for we know that Spenser is not an idolater, but drawing upon

---

1 Freud, *Art and Literature*, p. 429.
2 Stephen Orgel, 'Spenser from the Gutters to the Margins: An Archeology of Reading', in *The Construction of Textual Identity in Medieval and Early Modern Literature*, ed. Indira Ghose and Denis Renevey, Swiss Papers in English Language and Literature, 22 (Tübingen: Narr, 2009), pp. 125–41 (p. 129).
3 *Ibid.*

Parody and panegyric 169

convention) and, at the same time, to take the panegyric more or less seriously – in other words, to credit Elizabeth I's status as the symbolic centre of a celebrated, nationalistic work of Protestant morality.[4] It takes a reader to accuse Spenser of actually being an idolater for us to see that our pinch of salt has perhaps not been sizeable enough, and that the idea of *praying* to the queen should not be taken even half seriously.

The Puritan reader had good reason to be touchy. Officially speaking, the divinity of Elizabeth I was more than a poetic fancy: as well as being a commonplace of Tudor panegyric, it was supported by belief in the sacredness of monarchy and the Sovereign's status as God's earthly representative. While this honour was at times invoked to humble the queen and remind her of her responsibilities as God's (fallible) servant, it also licensed her veneration as a sacred figure of incontestable authority.[5] While the diplomatic contexts in which such ideas were expressed were capable of carefully blurring the distinction between these two positions, the ambiguity between them was apparently more than merely rhetorical for the queen herself; in 1576 the Archbishop of Canterbury, Edmund Grindal, felt compelled to remind her that she was, like all Church members, 'a mortal creature'.[6]

Spenser, I argue in this chapter, takes it upon himself to remind Elizabeth of precisely the same thing. If Karl Marx was right to dub him Tudor England's 'arse-kissing poet', he failed to take into account the alternative orientation to the royal posterior represented when Red Crosse is expelled from the 'priuy Posterne' of Lucifera's House of Pride and finds himself in the company of a 'Donghill' of fallen courtiers (I.v.52.7, 53.8).[7] These two extremes, exalted panegyric and crude satire, are the

---

4 Classical goddesses were conventionally used to represent aspects of Elizabeth's virtue, and here 'divinity' is first and foremost a literary trope; cf. Helen Hackett, *Virgin Mother, Maiden Queen: Elizabeth I and the Cult of the Virgin Mary* (Basingstoke: Macmillan, 1995), p. 88. Another common way of reconciling Spenser's participation in the myth of the queen's divinity with Protestant condemnation of idolatry is to regard the radically idealised figure of Gloriana as an example for Elizabeth to emulate. And third, as I acknowledge above, the monarch's status as God's earthly representative lent considerable licence to Elizabethan panegyrists wishing to praise her in quasi-religious terms; see Hackett, *Virgin Mother*, pp. 142–3.

5 *Ibid.*, pp. 79–87, 96–105.

6 Claire Cross, *The Royal Supremacy in the Elizabethan Church* (London: Allen & Unwin, 1969), p. 63. On Elizabethan panegyric and the issue of idolatry see Hackett, *Virgin Mother*, pp. 78–87, 105.

7 The phrase used by Marx is 'der Elizabeths Arschkissende [*sic*] Poet *Spenser*'; Karl Marx, *The Ethnological Notebooks of Karl Marx*, ed. Lawrence Krader, 2nd edn (Assen: Van Gorcum, 1974), p. 305; cited in Anthony W. Riley *et al.*, 'Marx & Spenser', in *SpE*, pp. 457–8 (p. 457).

170   *Comic Spenser*

poles between which representations of Elizabeth I operate in *The Faerie Queene*. In McCabe's words, 'Spenser invites [Elizabeth] to view herself "in mirrours more then one" (3 Proem 5), and as she moves amongst them her image veers from the ideal to the grotesque.'[8] Duessa, Lucifera, Argante, false Florimell, and Radigund vie for our attention alongside positive figures of female power, and even these are not unequivocally positive. Britomart reminds us that Elizabeth was *not* searching for a mate to secure England's future, Belphoebe is prone to jealous rages, Mercilla displays womanish indecisiveness, and Gloriana is – absent. Spenser's flattering narrator asserts that even Zeuxis would quake at the prospect of capturing Elizabeth's perfections (Proem III, 2.3), but it may be significant that the master painter in question reputedly died laughing after painting an old woman who had demanded to be depicted as Aphrodite.[9] In the late nineteenth century, R. W. Church expressed disappointment that Spenser should have joined his contemporaries in flouting reality, making his queen all sweetness and beauty when in fact she was 'capricious, vain, ill-tempered, unjust, and in her old age, ugly'.[10] Yet Spenser is very capable of countering panegyric with negative caricature when he wishes to.

Spenser's attitude toward Elizabeth is, of course, among the most debated subjects in Spenser criticism. Far from being a matter to be settled, it is a shifting reference point for the poet's complex handling of a range of issues: patronage and the poetic vocation, gender, sex and marriage, the institutions of Reformed faith, policy in Ireland, the question of the royal succession, and the proper powers of the monarch, for example. Close attention to these and other subjects in recent decades has replaced *The Faerie Queene*'s old incarnation as a work of Tudor propaganda with a poem of satirical daring and political tightrope-walking. Many readers negotiate the poem's combinations of praise and apparent critique through the (in application hugely varied) thesis that Spenser saw faults in the Elizabethan regime but was a bottom-line political loyalist whose objective was to endorse, or at least influence, rather than 'subvert'.[11] Others, however, discover sharper criticism, the

---

8 Richard A. McCabe, *Spenser's Monstrous Regiment: Elizabethan Ireland and the Poetics of Difference* (Oxford: Oxford University Press, 2002), p. 8.
9 Mary Beard, 'Ha Ha: What Made the Greeks Laugh? The Funny, the Peculiar, and a Possible Ancestor of Monty Python's Parrot', *TLS* (February 2009), 3–5 (p. 5).
10 Church, *Spenser*, p. 179.
11 While Spenser is still sometimes regarded as an unequivocal spokesman for monarch and empire (for example, Kent R. Lehnhof, 'Incest and Empire in *The Faerie Queene*',

Parody and panegyric   171

kind that does not qualify *The Faerie Queene*'s official mythology so much as obliterate it. Here the shortfall between the poem's high praise and the reality of Elizabeth and her court is not constructive (in the Sidneyan Golden World sense of 'encouraging emulation') so much as darkly, at times pessimistically, ironic.[12]

In the late 1990s, Paul Suttie took issue with the revisionist portrayal of Spenser as a dissident poet whose attacks on authority may be gleaned 'between the lines'. He rejects, for example, the idea that Lucifera satirises Elizabeth I, arguing that our temptation to read subversion into the episode is itself an object of criticism and that we should resist such obvious bait. Conversely, Suttie regards Spenser's panegyric not as ironic or blind-eyed but as ideologically affirmative – 'sympathetic' to the fallen conditions in which we pursue high ideals.[13] While caution when gauging subversion in a poem as complex as *The Faerie Queene* is surely justified, I wish to argue that greater responsiveness to Spenser's sense of humour opens up the iconoclastic appeal of episodes such as the one centring on Lucifera without unduly narrowing our reading of the poem's politics. As Suttie rightly argues, a text's subversive potential, even (or especially) where it begs our attention, should not be automatically equated with the author's 'real meaning', let alone his personal opinion. But whereas Suttie makes this point to defuse particular instances of subversive potential in Book I of *The Faerie Queene*, I am suggesting

---

ELH, 73 (2006), 215–43), others affirm Spenser's loyalty to the Elizabethan regime while recognising varying degrees of critique; see, for example, Norbrook, *Poetry and Politics*, Chapter 5; Suttie, 'Edmund Spenser's Political Pragmatism'; Hackett, *Virgin Mother*, pp. 105–12, 139–44, 190–7; Esolen, 'The Disingenuous Poet Laureate'; and David Lee Miller, *The Poem's Two Bodies: The Poetics of the 1590 'Faerie Queene'* (Princeton: Princeton University Press, 1988). For a nuanced account of Spenser's engagement with Elizabethan politics, especially on the much-debated question of his absolutist-vs-republican sympathies, see David J. Baker, 'Spenser and Politics', in *Oxford Handbook of ES*, pp. 48–64.

12 See, for example, Louis Montrose, 'Spenser and the Elizabethan Political Imaginary', *ELH*, 69 (2002), 907–46; and McCabe, *Spenser's Monstrous Regiment*. The subject of Spenser's sexual politics (in particular, his attitude to Elizabeth's marital negotiations, to her cultic virginity, and to other issues relating to female regiment) has been especially productive of satirical/critical readings. See Judith H. Anderson, '"In liuing colours and right hew": The Queen of Spenser's Central Books', in *Poetic Traditions of the English Renaissance*, ed. Maynard Mack and George deForest Lord (New Haven: Yale University Press, 1982), pp. 47–66; Kimberly Anne Coles, '"Perfect hole": Elizabeth I, Spenser, and Chaste Productions', *ELR*, 32 (2002), 31–61; and Mary Villeponteaux, '"Not as women wonted be": Spenser's Amazon Queen', in *Dissing Elizabeth: Negative Representations of Gloriana*, ed. Julia M. Walker (Durham, NC: Duke University Press, 1998), pp. 209–25.

13 Suttie, 'Edmund Spenser's Political Pragmatism', pp. 73–6.

172 *Comic Spenser*

that the same observation might equally be called upon to substantiate that potential.[14]

Take, for example, the nymphomaniac Argante (the giantess born in the act of coitus with her twin brother), who kidnaps good-looking young men at every opportunity (III.vii.47–50). As Hamilton and others have observed, Argante's literary ancestry makes her a 'demonic Faerie Queene' figure.[15] To go a step further and identify her as a satirical image of Elizabeth is not to claim this as her sole function in the poem, nor to imply that she offers an accurate measure of Spenser's cynicism. If anything, Argante may be said to parody rather than endorse the kind of salacious rumours that circulated about Elizabeth's monstrous sexuality.[16] That is, we need not seriously credit this subversive image in order to recognise Argante's iconoclastic power in a poem allied to the (equally partisan and exaggerated) image of a quasi-divine Virgin Queen. Likewise, we need not regard Lucifera as a reflection of 'what Spenser really thought of Elizabeth' or as evidence of his Republican sympathies in order to read the House of Pride episode as genuinely subversive. Beyond its primary function as a satire on the sin of pride, it presents a dystopic image of monarchy – a grotesque magnification of the human failings Elizabeth's position made her uniquely susceptible to, and a vision of this susceptibility pushed to its logical conclusion without check, inhibition, or redemption. The episode is a parable and a warning to Elizabeth and to every reader. This warning is not 'eschew the folly of pride' (for belief in his own capacity for heroic virtue is what lands Red Crosse in Lucifera's court in the first place) so much as 'recognise that you are proud'. Politically, what is under attack here is the official mythology that Spenser himself has helped to create – which is to say, the idea that Elizabeth is more than human.

If we miss the humour of this attack, it seems to me, we also miss its point. *The Faerie Queene* is a hall of mirrors, but fiction itself is the fun fair – the sphere of play. Spenser's 'subversive agenda' is to speak freely,

---

14 In rejecting the dichotomous approach to Spenser's politics (according to which he is viewed either as an uncritical supporter of Elizabeth or as utterly disillusioned with monarchical rule), Suttie principally rebuts the latter position, arguing for Spenser's bottom-line loyalty to the Elizabethan regime. While I agree in most part with this rebuttal, my own reading allows far greater scope for satire within the bounds of 'support that is not uncritical'. Suttie is surely right that Spenser's idealisations have genuine positive valence and reflect his absolute distinction between good and evil, although it is the contention of this study that such idealisation and such moral absolutes cannot be applied to any human figure without irony.

15 See *FQ* III.vii.47.2n. On the connections between Elizabeth and Argante see further Anderson, 'Arthur, Argante, and the Ideal Vision'.

16 On which see Villeponteaux, 'Not as women wonted be', pp. 214–15.

Parody and panegyric 173

which is not to say openly or even truthfully but according to the rules of the game he is playing. As McCabe observes, superlative praise and bathos orbit the truth together: '[t]he creators of political and social "myths" are best placed to recognise their distance from reality, and unfounded eulogy inevitably promotes satire'.[17] Grotesque distortions are no trustworthier than flattering ones; rather, the two 'quit' each other in the Chaucerian sense. A comparable phenomenon may be witnessed in the *Amoretti*: the narrator alternately venerates and villainises his lady with equal degrees of playful posturing.[18]

Another consideration where the game of fiction is concerned is the paradoxical discretion of exaggerated and close-to-the-bone satire. Early modern authors were aware that in matters of political critique the injunction of Busirane's castle, '*Be bolde*' but '*not too bold*' (III.xi.54.3–8) does not always hold; at times it could be prudent to abandon half-measures and subtlety altogether and dare readers to cry offence.[19] In response to the accusation that *The Adventures of Master F. J.* transparently satirises certain prominent courtiers, Gascoigne incredulously replied that if that were his meaning, he would have gone to greater trouble to hide it: 'all the world might thinke me verie simple if I would call John, John, or Mary, Mary'.[20] As I argue below, Spenser's self-absorbed 'mayden Queene' (I.iv.8.5), close enough to Elizabeth that we are obliged dexterously to deny the resemblance, is a cunning double bluff.

My argument that we need to approach Spenser's images of Elizabeth with more humour than cynicism is not, of course, a blanket strategy for interpreting his poetry's political allegory – there is plenty of evidence that Spenser could be pointedly critical of Elizabeth and her court at times, and numerous critics have persuasively documented his growing disillusionment in the latter books of *The Faerie Queene*, especially concerning policy in Ireland, for example. Rather, I am suggesting that we need to be better attuned to the way humour plays a part in reasserting the queen's humanity against claims of her transcendent virtues: her otherworldly virginity and her claims to closer proximity to God than ordinary mortals. The usefulness of the term 'humour' here as opposed

---

17 McCabe, *Spenser's Monstrous Regiment*, p. 16.

18 See Martz, 'The *Amoretti*'.

19 As Erasmus asserts in his preface to *Folly*, 'anyone who protests that he is injured betrays his own guilty conscience' (p. 60; see also Erasmus's 'Letter to Martin Dorp', in *Folly*, p. 219). Harington similarly claimed that *Orlando furioso* is 'neither vicious nor profane but apt to breede the quite contrarie effects *if a great fault be not in the readers owne bad disposition*'; 'An Advertisement to the Reader', *OF*, p. 16 (my italics).

20 'To the reverende Divines', in Gascoigne, *Works of Gascoigne*, Vol. I, p. 7.

174   *Comic Spenser*

to 'satire' should be emphasised: throughout this study I have linked
Spenser's humour to a fundamentally unheroic understanding of human
nature, but this vision – closely allied to Christian humility – is distinctly
self-inclusive. While the term 'satire' is often taken to imply higher moral
ground, the panegyrist who questions the morality of flattery is engaged
in a game of self-subversion, too. As I shall argue, Spenser's acerbic and at
times very funny political satire never loses sight of the fact that the poet's
ambitions are inextricable from those of his queen.

Elizabeth as fairy queen

Gloriana's idealised, transcendental status in *The Faerie Queene* may
be read in the light of Folly's assertion that flattery, 'vnder coulour of
praise', 'teacheth, and admonissheth princes of theyr duities ... without
offendyng'.[21] The familiar premise here is that idealisation moves the sub-
ject to live up to expectations. Yet I agree with McCabe that Spenser's
idealisations also challenge us to think about the 'psychology of icon-
making'.[22] As I have argued in foregoing chapters, from a Christian point
of view pretensions to perfectibility are often more worthy of scrutiny
than the failures that belie them. It is fitting, therefore, that Arthur's recol-
lection of the fairy queen is subject to the vagaries of dream-like recollec-
tion, suggesting that she might be – as indeed strictly speaking she is – a
product of the imagination, an intoxicating vision without substance. As
a fount of glory, magnanimity, and justice, Gloriana may be allied with
divine grace, and her transcendent status and her absence from the text
read uncynically. But as a figure of Elizabeth I, this tactful recourse to
mystification becomes, like the genre of romance, another central irony
of *The Faerie Queene* – the 'perfect hole' (III.xii.38.9) that suggests integ-
rity but also absence. In Chapter 4, I argued that allusions to Sir Thopas's
adolescent dream of accessible female perfection humanised Arthur's
quest. Yet Gloriana's fleeting resemblance to the elf-queen who becomes
Thopas's 'lemman' and has the pleasure of sleeping under his gown ('Sir
Thopas', lines 787–9) demystifies her, too. As David Norbrook puts it, 'the
erotic physicality of [Arthur's] dream is difficult to reconcile with Platonic
transcendence' – suggesting, instead, a very earthly Virgin Queen.[23]

---

21 *Folie*, p. 62.
22 McCabe, *Spenser's Monstrous Regiment*, p. 8.
23 Norbrook, *Poetry and Politics*, p. 102. For a humorous reading of the clash between
   Spenser's 'Sir Thopas' allusions and his panegyrical agenda see Esolen, 'The

Parody and panegyric   175

'Sir Thopas' aside, the fairy queen was by no means a stable figure in the Middle Ages and Renaissance. Fairies were, and still are, regarded by many as childish and unsophisticated storytelling fodder, but they were also associated with superstition. Lewis observes: 'within the same island and the same century Spenser could compliment Elizabeth I by identifying her with the Faerie Queene and a woman could be burned at Edinburgh in 1576 for "repairing with" the fairies and the "Queen of Elfame".[24] The native folklore inherited by Spenser compounded this ambivalent association. In some cases the figure of the fairy queen possesses otherworldly beauty and virtue; in others (suggestively for our reading of Arthur's encounter) she appears as a sexually obliging mistress; and, in others still, she is an intimidating and unpredictable source of power. In the words of Helen Cooper, 'goodness, mercy, and due reward are not a necessary predicate of fairies … if there is a single defining quality of the fairy monarch, of either sex, it is not just sexuality but power: power that may well be exercised in the cause of justice, but which is primarily characterized by its arbitrariness'.[25] If the latter characteristic makes 'fairy' an appropriate vehicle for a temporal monarch, it also lends an acutely ironic dimension to that monarch's potential role as patron. For Gloriana, as her name partly suggests, is a conferrer of fame.[26] In the world of *The Faerie Queene*, she confers fame where it is deserved, but at least one episode of the poem implies that the real-life Gloriana was indeed characterised by fairy-like arbitrariness, and that, moreover, this could cause problems for financially stretched poets.

Elizabeth as goddess Fame

Although she is not a fairy, the female monarch at the centre of *The House of Fame*, Chaucer's complex allegory of worldly ambition and

---

Disingenuous Poet Laureate'. On the suggestive connection between Arthur's vision of the fairy queen and Red Crosse's vision of false Una, see Anderson, 'A Gentle Knight', p. 171.

24 C. S. Lewis, *The Discarded Image: An Introduction to Medieval and Renaissance Literature* (Cambridge: Cambridge University Press, 1970 [1967]), p. 124; cited by Woodcock, *Fairy in 'The Faerie Queene'*, p. 88. See further Cooper, *The English Romance*, pp. 173–87; Woodcock, *Fairy in 'The Faerie Queene'*, pp. 88–94; and Norbrook, *Poetry and Politics*, p. 102: 'the Fairy Queen of folklore was not a dignified and transcendent figure but a mischievous, black-faced trickster'.

25 Cooper, *The English Romance*, p. 178.

26 Also Christian glory (see p. 148 above).

176   *Comic Spenser*

limitation, is certainly a figure of arbitrary power. From her throne, the goddess Fame determines the fate of her suppliants with haughty complacence, randomly ordering her assistant Eolus to blow his golden trumpet of renown or his black trumpet of slander or, worst of all, to blow neither. The second canto of 'The Legend of Chastity', too, is preoccupied with questions relating to fame, truth, and slander and, though these have been little commented upon, it is not surprising to find a series of allusions to Chaucer's meditation on these themes. Through these allusions Spenser slyly invokes – and satirises – the mutual dependence of poets and monarchs when it comes to bestowing fame. Even as the narrator sermonises on truth and justice, between the lines we may see both Elizabeth and Spenser himself take the throne of Chaucer's capricious goddess.

Canto ii opens with a meditation on women's fame that reads like a thinly veiled commentary on poetry, replete with all the stock themes of early modern literary dedications. The narrator's praise of female warriors and their uncelebrated heroic deeds at III.ii.1–2 demonstrates one of poetry's greatest responsibilities – the bestowal of fame where fame is due – and implicitly identifies one of the poet's greatest fears: being neglected or maligned. Just as the reputation of female warriors is in the hands of poets, so too, we may infer, is the poet's reputation in the hands of those more powerful than he. In drawing a flattering parallel between Britomart and Elizabeth (the one a model of 'warlike puissance', the other of 'wisedom'; ii.3.1–3), the narrator would seem to gesture toward the queen as precisely the figure of fame-bestowing power he has in mind. She stands to benefit from his recognition of female virtue, he from reciprocal goodwill in the form of patronage and protection against 'foolish men' (ii.2.9). Strictly speaking, the narrator is concerned only with women warriors and the gender inequality he perceives, but the canto's wider preoccupation with issues of fame, art, and royal gifts suggestively broadens the relevance of his words.

Most obviously, the 'wondrous myrrhour' (III.ii.*Arg*.3) given to King Ryence by Merlin later in the canto recalls the narrator's own description of his work as 'this fayre mirrhour' (Proem II, 4.7) – and resembles it further in being a 'famous Present for a Prince' (III.ii.21.6). It is often noted that, in company with Archimago and Busirane, Merlin is a poet-figure on account of his status as image-maker or artificer. Correspondingly, the poet is something of a magician: as the narrator observes when Red Crosse defends Artegall to Britomart, 'pleasing wordes are like to Magick art' (III.ii.15.5). Further establishing an analogy between Merlin's magic

Parody and panegyric 177

mirror and *The Faerie Queene* itself is Spenser's use of 'to read' for 'to see' – one 'reades' the mirror (III.ii.20.1). Notably, Merlin's mirror is in the business not of pleasing those who gaze into it so much as warning them, revealing in its glass 'What euer foe had wrought, or frend had faynd' (ii.19.5) – suggesting that it is incisive social and political commentary, not flattery, that makes magicians (and poets) indispensable to the realm. If King Ryence stands to gain something from the mirror, so too does Merlin stand to gain something in return: the mirror, we are told, is a 'worthy worke of infinite reward' (ii.21.7).

This indirect petition for patronage on Spenser's part is reinforced by allusions to *The House of Fame*. These are especially prominent during Britomart's conversation with Red Crosse. Like Chaucer's Geffrey, Britomart seeks 'Tydings' about love as it applies to herself (III.ii.8.7; cf. *House of Fame*, lines 1884–9); also like Geffrey, she keeps getting distracted from this endeavour by conversations about fame. Dissembling her true purpose, Britomart tells Red Crosse of having left her native soil to 'seeke for praise and fame' (ii.7.9) because 'Fame blazed hath, that here in Faery lond / Doe many famous knightes and Ladies wonne' (ii.8.1–2). Her use of the word 'blazed' recalls Eolus's trumpet:

> This Eolus anon up sterte,
> And with his blake clarioun
> He *gan to blasen* out a soun
> As lowde as beloweth wynd in helle
> (*House of Fame*, lines 1800–3; my italics)

In *The House of Fame*, 'tydynges' – verbal utterances – are the lifeblood of fame, and notably this word is used not only by Britomart but also by the narrator: Merlin's mirror tells King Ryence of approaching enemies even before the 'tydings' of messengers can reach him (III.ii.21.5). While the emphasis in the latter context is on reliability and truth, 'tydynges' according to Chaucer's use of the word encompass all communicable human knowledge (from the written word and oral history to idle gossip), and as such may be true or false, or 'fals and soth compouned' (*House of Fame*, line 2108).[27] The string of lies Britomart tells to provoke Red Crosse into praising Artegall is evidently intended to call up the Chaucerian resonance of the word, for while she seeks the truth

---

27 Rumour, Geffrey reports, 'is the moder of tydynges' (line 1983). Fame is a variety of highly successful rumour, and knowledge comprises famous ideas – tidings as they evolve through the endless channels of individual subjectivity and agenda.

178 *Comic Spenser*

about her lover, she slanders him in the process. Britomart's lies cause her a pang of anxiety: 'The word gone out, she backe againe would call' (ii.9.1). In *The House of Fame*, words really do 'go out'; following an outward and upward trajectory, they rise through the atmosphere to Fame's palace and jostle at the windows to escape the house of rumour (lines 2084–7). In an example of Ariostan antifeminist humour, Britomart's dishonesty follows hard upon the narrator's effusive praise of women, proving that those favoured by fame are not always so kind in return. It is against the background of these literary echoes that Britomart's debt to Merlin's mirror – for it is to the mirror that she owes her knowledge of Artegall – and the narrator's insistence on the great value of the royal gift present a tacit invitation to Elizabeth to prove herself unlike Chaucer's goddess (and, for the moment, unlike Britomart) by giving freely where it is most deserved.

For a poet courting the favour of a queen with a reputation for parsimony, a glance at Chaucer's grotesque and comically fickle personification of fame (conveniently figured as a female monarch) must have been hard to resist. But Spenser – which is to say, his authorial persona – does not get off scot-free. *The House of Fame*, we may recall, reserves its sharpest satire not for the goddess but for her suppliants. Spenser's narrator's implicit identification with the latter, both in their abject and their impudent aspect, entails a characteristic element of self-satire. Such identification is, of course, another theatrical pose, a pose that on one hand entails a heavy-handed profession of humility ('But ah my rymes too rude and rugged arre, / When in so high an obiect they doe lyte'; III.ii.3.6–7) and, on the other accommodates a bold and barely concealed identification with the great Merlin shortly afterward. But further to the usual combination of self-abasement and self-promotion, Spenser's satire extends to the poet's role as liar.

Spenser as goddess Fame

As a metaphor for *The Faerie Queene*, Merlin's mirror makes a large claim for poetry – one apparently at odds with the sceptical spirit of *The House of Fame*. The mirror tells the truth (III.ii.19.1), is comprehensive in its scope (ii.19.2–3), is wondrously made (ii.18.8, 20.1), is deservedly famous (ii.18.8–9, 21.6–7), and merits reward (ii.21.7). In the hands of the monarch, further, it safeguards the realm (ii.21.8–9). These assertions have led William Blackburn to conclude that, as a poet figure, Merlin contrasts Archimago and Busirane in representing the poet's truth-telling

Parody and panegyric   179

capacities.[28] Merlin would also seem to contrast starkly with that other poet figure, Chaucer's Geffrey. Where the latter is confused, naïve, and self-deprecating, Merlin is enlightened, authoritative, and indispensable. Indeed, Merlin is comparable to the 'man of gret auctorite' Geffrey seeks but never finds (*House of Fame*, line 2158). This contrast might be deemed indicative of the gulf between medieval and Renaissance sensibilities, or even proof of Spenser's intention to 'overgo his literary father'.[29] But appearances are deceptive. Or to rephrase, they are not entirely deceptive, for Spenser really is making a large claim for poetry's worth. But on closer inspection it is not necessarily a claim that the poet of *The House of Fame* (or Archimago for that matter) would be bound to disclaim.

In fact, a distinctly Chaucerian caveat attends the episode's assertion of poetic authority, at least in the narrower senses in which authority implies truthfulness. The first clue in Canto ii that the narrator is unreliable lies in the clash between the narrator's effusive praise of women and Britomart's dishonesty about Artegall and her past. Another clue comes when the subsequent, 'true' version of Britomart's back-story is ushered in with the line 'As it in bookes hath written beene of old' (III.ii.18.3), an assertion of poetical truth in the still narrower sense of 'historically attested'. Spenser's narrator, like Ariosto's and Cervantes's, tends to reserve such avowals for his most gratuitously fictional narratives – here, a story about a magic mirror.[30] The narrator's authority is the poet's fib, for the mirror's pedigree in fact begins with *The Faerie Queene*.[31] If Merlin's glass contains a true and comprehensive image of the world, the glass itself is contained by a work of fiction – like *The House of Fame*, an unfinished one. Further, perhaps recalling fame's trumpets as they resonate 'thrugh the world' (*House of Fame*, lines 1674, 1724, 1770), the narrator reports that the virtues of the mirror 'through the wyde worlde soone were solemniz'd' (ii.18.9). Even as the narrator affirms the mirror's truthfulness, we are

28 William Blackburn, 'Spenser's Merlin', *Ren&R*, 4 (1980), 179–98 (p. 190).
29 On Spenser overgoing Chaucer, see for example Berry, 'Sundrie Doubts'.
30 In another such example, the narrator provides highly specific directions to Merlin's underground cave before earnestly warning readers against visiting there for fear of 'cruell Feendes' (III.iii.7–8).
31 As Blackburn notes, 'Merlin's magic glass is unlike anything attributed to the magician in the romances that have come down to us'; 'Spenser's Merlin', p. 185. With similar irony, Ariosto regularly calls upon his pseudo-authority 'Turpin': e.g. *Of* XXIII.lxii.1–2. On the comparable irony of 'Fama' in *Aeneid* IV, and Spenser's alertness to Virgil's sceptical treatment of putative authority, literary and political, see Syrithe Pugh, 'Reinventing the Wheel: Spenser's "Virgilian Career"', in *Spenser in the Moment*, ed. Paul J. Hecht and J. B. Lethbridge (Madison, NJ: Fairleigh Dickinson University Press, 2015), pp. 3–34 (pp. 19–26).

180 *Comic Spenser*

entering Chaucer's world of reverberations and Chinese whispers. This not only casts doubt on *The Faerie Queene*'s 'truthfulness', but, in a spirit of self-satire that we have encountered before, suggests that its virtues are liable to be exaggerated by rumours – not least those started by the poet himself.

The mirror was, of course, a common and highly unstable trope in the sixteenth century. In *The Steele Glas* (1576), Gascoigne uses the metaphor of the mirror to distinguish between two kinds of poetry: the steel glass reflects things as they are, showing 'all things in their degree', while the crystal glass 'shewes the thing, much better than it is'.[32] That other metaphor for poetic voice in *The Faerie Queene*, the trumpet, is no less ambiguous in its connotations, as *The House of Fame* amply demonstrates. Notwithstanding the conventional early modern argument that poets teach by example, holding up an ideal image for their patron or monarch to aspire to, at some point the admirable fictions of Sidney's Golden World inevitably give way to the boldfaced flattery of Chaucer's golden trumpet.

How does this apparently cynical view square with poetry's great worth? One answer lies in the mirror's timely warnings. The manner in which Britomart looks into the mirror is instructive: faced with her reflection, 'Her selfe awhile therein she vewd in vaine' (III.ii.22.6). But then she begins to concentrate, looking within and trying hard to think of what 'mote to her selfe pertaine' (ii.22.9). An incisive metaphor for textual interpretation, the mirror colludes with the perspective of the viewer, revealing that which 'to the looker appertayn[s]' (ii.19.4). In a slippery line that anticipates this acknowledgement of the interpreter's active and creative role, Spenser's narrator, ostensibly unfit for the task, invites Elizabeth to 'Thy selfe thy prayses tell' (ii.3.9) – an invitation whose tone may be earnest or tongue-in-cheek depending on the perspective of the reader. Reading with a self-critical eye, Elizabeth might well discern a hard lesson in *The Faerie Queene*; alternatively, she can, like Lucifera admiring herself in her 'mirrhour bright' (I.iv.10.6), rest content with the poet's 'arse-kissing' praise ('O Goddesse heauenly bright' etc.; Proem I, 4.1).[33]

In order to learn from the poem's timely warnings, Elizabeth would need to approach the poet's praise with scepticism. She would also need

---

32 Gascoigne, *Works of Gascoigne*, Vol. II, pp. 148–9.
33 In his 'Letter to Martin Dorp', Erasmus describes himself as the ideal reader of satire: 'if something is touched on and I see myself mirrored there, there's no reason ... for taking offence. If I'm wise I'll hide my feelings and not give myself away. If I'm honest I'll take warning'; *Folly*, p. 222.

Parody and panegyric 181

to learn to see herself not only in the mirror that shows things as they are, but also in the mirror that shows things worse than they are: the grotesque mirror of the fun fair. This mirror finds its counterpart in Chaucer's slanderous 'blake clarioun' but, in contrast to the trumpets of Revelation (or their echo in, for example, John Knox's *First Blast of the Trumpet against the Monstrous Regiment of Women* (1558)) it makes no claim to truth; rather it is an alternative lie. The kind of self-recognition required here would be such that Elizabeth would judiciously weigh such images against their idealised counterparts. In what sounds like a pragmatic acknowledgement of the poet's limited ability to bring about such careful reflection, the narrator speaks of the monarch's cautious consultation of the mirror as a thing of the past, reflecting somewhat wistfully: 'Happy this Realme, had it remayned euer since' (III.ii.21.9).

Far from undermining poetry's value, to destabilise or even deny poetic 'authority' can in fact be to make a large claim in its defence. By reducing all language-based communication to a mixture of truth and lies, *The House of Fame* dismantles the truth–fiction hierarchy that has historically devalued works of the imagination.[34] Chaucer shows how the very things that are matters of anxiety and trouble in life – the unreliability of language, the corrupted and partial nature of shared truths – are turned to account in fiction, the best examples of which are enriched rather than impoverished by endless mutation through imitation and interpretation. It is this, not the objective, historical truthfulness that Spenser's narrator claims to preserve, that makes *The Faerie Queene* a 'worthy worke of infinite reward' (III.ii.21.7) – one that, like *The House of Fame*, comically undermines figures of would-be authority (poets and monarchs alike) without any sacrifice of its own profundity or worth.

Elizabeth as Lucifera

The House of Pride (I.iv–v) is one of *The Faerie Queene*'s great satirical set pieces. Through Red Crosse's judging eyes, we see the puppet-like courtiers and their grotesque queen in all their vanity and arrogance, though the knight himself is no less ridiculous. As a parodic female monarch, Lucifera bears a family resemblance to goddess Fame, although, as an embodiment of pride, she is emphatically self-absorbed: her task is not to trouble herself with the fate of others but to think exclusively about

---

34 See Carol A. N. Martin, 'Authority and the Defense of Fiction: Renaissance Poetics and Chaucer's *House of Fame*', in Krier, *Refiguring Chaucer*, pp. 40–65 (p. 49).

182 *Comic Spenser*

her own glory. That Lucifera is a caricature of Elizabeth I is indisputable – the arguing point lies in the spirit of that caricature. The interpretation Spenser officially invites is necessarily that the relation is one of antithesis, and a number of critics (while recognising the potential irony of the portrait) accept this reading. But working against this interpretation is the circumstance that grounds for comparing the two queens are far more numerous and nuanced than one would expect of a straightforward *in bono et in malo* opposition. Their similarities are persistently invoked and, at times, daringly close to the bone.

Some points of comparison are admittedly subtle. For example, Lucifera's vanity about her parentage, and her willingness to ignore the truth in favour of a more flattering genealogy (I.iv.11), may invoke the illegitimacy charge hanging over Elizabeth. Equally suggestive is the narrator's comparison of Lucifera's rule to Phaethon's progress through the heavens as he presumes 'with weaker hand to rayne' (iv.9.4) – the conventional pun on rein/reign suggesting the 'weaker hand' of female regiment.

Other likenesses are harder to ignore, however. Lucifera is a 'mayden Queene' who believes herself to be 'pearelesse' (I.iv.11.3), an epithet that captures her sense of superiority, but also brings to mind the literal peerlessness of a monarch who will not dilute her power by marrying. Beyond this allusion to Elizabeth's core public identity, her virginity, the most obvious characteristic shared by the fictional and the historical queen is a taste for splendour and display. As Brooks-Davies remarks, 'it would not have taken a very astute courtly reader to notice a satiric equivalence between some of Lucifera's aspects and trappings and those of Elizabeth'.[35] It is, after all, our familiarity with Tudor portraiture that allows us readily to envisage Lucifera upon her throne:

> High aboue all a cloth of State was spred,
> And a rich throne, as bright as sunny day,
> On which there sate most braue embellished
> With royall robes and gorgeous array,
> A mayden Queene, that shone as *Titans* ray,
> In glistring gold, and perelesse pretious stone
>
> (I.iv.8.1–6)

Appropriately, the narrator's lavish twenty-three-stanza description of Lucifera's 'sage Counsellours', personifications of six of the seven deadly sins (Pride herself making up the number), is occasioned by a pageant

35 Douglas Brooks-Davies, 'Lucifera', in *SpE*, pp. 441–2 (p. 441).

Parody and panegyric

whose only purpose is display. In a moment of amusing anticlimax, the queen and her entourage return home after pausing in a nearby field to 'take the solace of the open aire' (I.iv.37.2). At this point, the general resemblance to royal spectacle gives way to more targeted satire. Joan Heiges Blythe rightly refers to the scene outside the House of Pride as 'ludicrous pomp', but Roy Strong's account of the St George's Day procession in 1576 suggests that such pomp was not far from reality:

> Elizabeth appeared arrayed in her Garter robes and wearing a diadem of pearl upon her head, the sword of state borne before her by the Earl of Hertford, her mantle supported by the Earl of Northumberland and Lord Russell, and her train carried by the Countess of Derby assisted by the Earl of Oxford. In this manner the Queen and her Knights descended into the Chapel to their stalls and, after a song had been sung by the choristers of the Chapel, the solemn procession was formed. At the head of it was the Sergeant of the Vestry, rod in hand, followed by choristers and then chaplains, vested in copes … Behind them came the heralds and then the Knights and finally the Queen. As the procession left the Hall and went out into the courtyard, Gentlemen Pensioners joined it, flanking the Queen at either side, and a sunshade of green taffeta was provided to shelter her from the sun.[36]

Surely such annual events were not far from Spenser's mind when he composed these lines in honour of Lucifera: 'The heapes of people thronging in the hall, / Doe ride each other, vpon her to gaze' (I.iv.16.7–8). The fact that St George himself is relegated to the sidelines of this spectacle, and Lucifera is portrayed with a 'deadfull Dragon' beneath her 'scornefull feete' (iv.10.4–5), may, moreover, recall the Catholic objection that the queen had appropriated a legitimate saint's day in the name of royal propaganda, Elizabeth herself being accredited with rescuing England from a reign of darkness. And it is perhaps fitting, in the light of Elizabeth's allegedly lukewarm Protestantism, that there is some uncertainty as to whether Lucifera is stamping the dragon underfoot or whether it is lying before her like a submissive pet.[37]

---

36 Joan Heiges Blythe, 'Spenser and the Seven Deadly Sins: Book I, Cantos IV and V', *ELH*, 39 (1972), 342–52 (p. 342); Strong, *The Cult of Elizabeth*, pp. 168–9. Strong draws on the official records of the Garter Feasts in the *Liber ceruleus* (British Library, Additional MS 36768); Additional MS 10110; and Elias Ashmole, *The Institution, Laws and Ceremonies of the Most Noble Order of the Garter* (London, 1672).

37 While St George and the dragon came to represent the Church Militant slaying the Papal Antichrist, this sat uncomfortably alongside what many Protestants regarded as the order's residual Catholicism; see Strong, *The Cult of Elizabeth*, pp. 176–8.

184   *Comic Spenser*

When Red Crosse kneels before Lucifera after his victory over Sansjoy, he is, in what looks like a parody of Garter investiture, effectively dubbed as one of her knights (I.v.16.1–2). But more obviously, perhaps, this act of submission parodies Elizabethan tiltyard etiquette, as Hamilton notes. The tilts, held annually to celebrate the queen's accession, were more than a game for those courtiers invited at their own immense cost to take part, and there may be a degree of irony in the narrator's description of the bloodthirsty scuffle between Red Crosse and Sansjoy (joylessness) as 'gay cheualree' (v.16.5).[38]

Like the St George's Day celebrations, the tilts quickly evolved in the direction of maximum spectacle. A comparison of the personified sins riding on different beasts (as described at I.iv.18–35) with Elizabeth's courtiers is hard to resist when one considers the fashion for tilters to make their entry before the queen mounted upon horses and wagons made up to look like exotic beasts such as lions, bears, and camels.[39] Turning Tudor propaganda against itself, Spenser would seem to push the fashion for medieval revival one critical step further, displacing the world of chivalric romance with the cast of a morality play. Reinterpretation of royalist chivalry as an allegory of pride may have been invited by the circumstance that Accession Day was dubbed a 'Holy Day' (on the strength of which the Puritan Robert Wright compared Elizabeth to classical subjects of idolatrous worship such as Romulus and Alexander, and was duly imprisoned).[40]

However critical, Spenser's pastiche of royal pomp does not, finally, claim the moral high ground. As Strong observes, the tilts were, among other things, an occasion for fun, and the romantic speeches and devices of the challengers were 'clearly meant to be funny'.[41] Something of this good humour arguably survives the travesty of I.iv. What is most funny about the scene outside the House of Pride is 'the stout Faery['s]' sense of superiority as he condemns the court's pomp and sycophancy (iv.15.6–9).[42] For *The Faerie Queene*, of course, is something of a chivalric pageant in honour of the queen, and is referred to as such (II.i.33.6; DS 8.6). In its vision of Elizabeth as Gloriana, moreover, the poem is also a House

---

38 On the irony of this description see p. 106 above.

39 Spenser's emblematic portraits bear comparison to the heraldic devices and mottoes worn by Elizabeth's tilters; see Strong, *The Cult of Elizabeth*, pp. 133, 137–8.

40 *Ibid.*, 125–6; and Hackett, *Virgin Mother*, p. 87.

41 Strong, *The Cult of Elizabeth*, p. 139.

42 Vaught, '*St George and the Fiery Dragon*' captures the worthiness of Red Crosse when she compares him to a 'Lenten killjoy during … carnivalesque festivities' (p. 93).

Parody and panegyric   185

of Pride: covered over with 'golden foile' (I.iv.4.4) in a travesty of Sidney's
Golden World, Lucifera's palace looks more splendid than it is, thereby
speaking 'the praises of the workmans witt' (iv.5.2). In a further allusion
to the work of the flattering artist (one that recalls Duessa's disrobing), the
palace's 'hinder partes, that few could spie, / Were ruinous and old, but
painted cunningly' (iv.5.8–9). But if the palace, like the mirror Lucifera
gazes into, alludes to *The Faerie Queene*'s public-relations campaign on
behalf of an ageing queen, surely the pride in question equally implicates
a poet seeking patronage and immortality. It is testimony to Spenser's
capacity for wry self-satire that Red Crosse condemns the 'glorie vaine'
from which he is excluded (iv.15.7, cf. 37.8–9), yet drops before the queen
'on lowly knee' (16.2) at the first available opportunity.[43]
     The contradictory erotic dimension of Lucifera's court also deserves
mention. The fictional queen is surrounded by effeminate courtiers who
'frounce their curled heare' and 'prancke their ruffes' (I.iv.14.7–9), while
many of her victims are male: the carcasses strewn outside her castle walls
are simply described as 'murdred men' (v.53.3) and, as though political
and sexual ruin are to be equated, the prisoners who cram her dungeons
have fallen 'from high Princes courtes, or Ladies bowres, / Where they
in ydle pomp, or wanton play, / Consumed had their goods' (v.51.6–8).
Nevertheless, there remains a manifest difference between Lucifera and
the witch of Book II who turns her sexually exhausted suitors into beasts.
Voyeurism at the House of Pride is aligned with narcissism rather than
eroticism: Lucifera's idea of 'sport' is not sexual dalliance but being seen
by as many people as possible. The effeminacy of her courtiers and her
punishment of dissolute lovers imply that her attitude to sexuality is,
if anything, prohibitive. Given that the prisoners of the House of Pride
are said to be victims 'of that proud Tyrannesse / Prouokt with *Wrath*,
and *Enuyes* false surmise' (v.46.6–7), the possibility emerges that their
captivity testifies not to their own pride but, reading more literally, to
the pride of an angry and envious monarch. This scenario is certainly
resonant from the point of view that some of Elizabeth's favourites really
did fall from 'Ladies bowres' into prison.[44] This subtext hardly incites

43 On the analogy between Red Crosse and Spenser see Chapter 2.
44 The queen's objection to the marriage of her courtiers and her bishops is well attested.
    As Matthew Parker wrote to Sir William Cecil on 12 April 1561, 'her Majesty continueth
    very evil affected to the state of matrimony in the clergy. And if [I] were not therein
    very stiff, her Majesty would utterly and openly condemn and forbid it'; Matthew
    Parker, *Correspondence of Parker*, ed. John Bruce and Thomas Thomason Perowne,
    Parker Society Publications, 33 (Cambridge: Cambridge University Press, 1853),

186 *Comic Spenser*

laughter, unless we recognise the 'Donghill' (v.53.8) of fallen courtiers as a grotesque and perhaps cathartic exaggeration of the situation. But negotiation of the same territory elsewhere in *The Faerie Queene* shows how humour can humanise (as opposed to dehumanise, as in the Lucifera cantos) a figure of intimidating, and sexually prohibitive, authority.

Elizabeth as Belphoebe

The themes raised in Spenser's allegory of pride – desire, wrath, and envy – find their fullest exploration in the figure of Belphoebe. It is no coincidence that she, like Gloriana, makes her first appearance in a mock-heroic context (II.iii.21). The episode in question begins with a comic interaction between the upstart Braggadochio and his vassal Trompart, who are being recruited by Archimago to sabotage Guyon's progress (iii.4–18). In a parody of the excesses of medieval chivalric romance familiar from *Orlando furioso*, Trompart and Braggadochio together supply not one but three formulaic explanations for the latter's lack of sword – the best being Braggadochio's vaunt, 'Is not enough fowre quarters of a man, / Withouten sword or shield, an hoste to quayle?' (iii.16.7–8). His subsequent contradictory claim that he would only deign to fight with the sword of the 'noblest knight on earth' (17.9) leads Archimago unexpectedly to call his bluff, promising him Arthur's sword. At this point the magician suddenly vanishes, causing Braggadochio and Trompart to flee into a nearby forest where even the sound of rustling leaves 'greatly them affeare[s]' (20.5).

It is into this farcical scene that Belphoebe steps forth, instigating a nine-stanza catalogue of her beauties that is also a celebrated blazon of Elizabeth I (II.iii.22–31).[45] Immediately following the blazon, Belphoebe enters into a dialogue with both Trompart and (once he has struggled out from under a bush) Braggadochio, who, fast regaining confidence, leaps upon her in a fit of 'filthy lust' (42.5). Maureen Quilligan has argued that the episode exemplifies the kind of humour Elizabeth enjoyed, and

---

p. 148. As Raleigh's imprisonment in 1592 following his secret marriage demonstrated, the boundary between political and sexual loyalty could on occasion become fragile indeed; see *FQ* IV.vii.8–9n. On the sexual politics of the Elizabethan court, see further Paul Johnson, *Elizabeth I: A Study in Intellect and Power* (London: Weidenfeld and Nicolson, 1974), pp. 112–15.

45 Hannah Betts, 'The Pornographic Blazon, 1588–1603', in *Dissing Elizabeth: Negative Representations of Gloriana*, ed. Julia M. Walker (Durham, NC: Duke University Press, 1998), pp. 153–84 (p. 160).

Parody and panegyric　　　187

that the comedy of Belphoebe's interaction with the cretinous pair would have pleased more than it offended. Theresa M. Krier similarly affirms that the comic aspect of Belphoebe's entry into the poem 'is a salute to Elizabeth's presence'.[46] This is perhaps partly true; the description of Braggadochio attempting to crawl out from the undergrowth in a heroic manner ('standing stoutly vp, his lofty crest / Did fiercely shake, and rowze'; iii.35.8–9) is among the funniest spectacles in the whole poem. Yet the degree to which the description of Belphoebe's physical beauty sits on a knife-edge between the playfully reverential and the offensive has been considerably downplayed.

The blazon is as rhetorically fulsome as it could possibly be, surpassing even those rare occasions when Britomart allows her hair to cascade from under her helmet, sending the narrator into raptures. Its progress, however, is not top to toe but (mimicking Braggadochio's lecherous perspective) up and down, with an abrupt half-line signalling the perilous transition from hem to ham (II.iii.26.9) – a polite *occupatio* and bawdy play on the 'no-thing' of Belphoebe's genitalia.[47] Such innuendo should prepare us for the blazon's rhetorical excess:

> And in her cheekes the vermeill red did shew
> Like roses in a bed of lillies shed,
> The which ambrosiall odours from them threw,
> And gazers sence with double pleasure fed,
> Hable to heale the sicke, and to reuiue the ded.
>
> (II.iii.22.5–9)

Reflecting the critical tendency to take this passage seriously, Hamilton observes that Belphoebe's complexion 'combines the powers of the well of life and the tree of life'.[48] But it is precisely these reference points that render the compliment absurd. Characteristically, Spenser cuts down the blasphemous effigy he has created. Interpreted as an example of Spenserian bawdy, Belphoebe's ability to perform resurrections with her

---

46　Quilligan, 'The Comedy of Female Authority', p. 156; Theresa M. Krier, *Gazing on Secret Sights: Spenser, Classical Imitation, and the Decorums of Vision* (Ithaca and London: Cornell University Press, 1990), pp. 70–9 (p. 75). Krier emphasises the comedy of the episode, though she firmly resists the idea that Belphoebe herself is being made fun of, arguing that Braggadochio's comic debasement if anything augments our sense of her majesty, while Trompart is not such a knave that we cannot take his Aeneas-like appreciation of her quasi-divine beauty seriously (pp. 77–8).

47　Cf. *Hamlet* 3.2.112–24.

48　*FQ* 22.5–9n. See also Krier, *Gazing on Secret Sights*, p. 73: '[Belphoebe's] kindling of felicity is of such potency as to bear thaumaturgic powers to those who gaze at her'.

188 *Comic Spenser*

beauty is funny indeed. 'Raising the dead' is a known bawdy joke in this period, although this example has, typically, been overlooked.[49]

Hannah Betts has shown how the conflation of sexual and political registers in the sphere of Elizabethan Petrarchan politics, according to which loyalty to the queen was figured as romantic courtship, fuelled pornographic satire as a vehicle for political critique and as a means of expressing disaffection with court culture more generally. As Betts acknowledges, Belphoebe's blazon registers the ease with which sexuality could become a transgressive metaphor, figuring not only political loyalty but also the naïve or frustrated ambitions of would-be courtiers such as Braggadochio, whose social pretentions are epitomised by his attempt to rape the object of his desire.[50] But the satire in Betts's view is directed at the upstart Braggadochio, and she distinguishes between Spenser's ironic handling of Elizabethan Petrarchanism and the politically subversive, more sexually explicit poetry written for and by Inns of Court and university men especially in the 1590s. However, Betts's incisive analysis of the manner in which the latter 'dismantled the panegyric blazon' is resonant not only for Shakespeare, Lodge, and Marlowe, but also for Spenser. Belphoebe's combination of sexual attractiveness and unavailability makes a fool of Braggadochio, but the follies of Braggadochio and Trompart in turn place the Petrarchan iconographic tradition surrounding Elizabeth in an absurd light.

Trompart's expostulation 'O Goddesse, (for such I take thee to bee)', and his respectful desire to know 'which of the Gods I shall thee name, / That vnto thee dew worship I may rightly frame' (II.iii.33.2–9) recalls Aeneas's famous meeting with Venus in disguise (*Aeneid*, Book I), but the exalted allusion is heavily ironic in the mouth of a character known for his 'knauery' (iii.9.6). Braggadochio, too, debases the currency of conventional panegyric when he addresses Belphoebe 'O fairest vnder skie' (iii.38.1), an irony accentuated by the virgin's apparent inability to recognise base flattery (iii.37.6–9).[51] If the satire is still relatively playful at this point, the critique of court life that gradually emerges is more incendiary.

---

49 See for example Betts, 'The Pornographic Blazon', p. 167. For 'resurrection' as a bawdy joke, see Boccaccio's tenth story on the third day; Giovanni Boccaccio, *The Decameron*, 2 vols (London: J. M. Dent, 1963 [1930]), Vol. I, pp. 220–5 (p. 222). In the tradition of Victorian propriety, the central part of Boccaccio's story is left untranslated.

50 Betts, 'The Pornographic Blazon', p. 161.

51 This may support the theory that Braggadochio and Trompart represent the duc d'Alençon and his agent Simier (see *FQ* II.iii.32–3n). For a contrasting perspective see Krier, *Gazing on Secret Sights*, pp. 70–9.

Parody and panegyric 189

In a conveniently timed fit of lust, Braggadochio pounces on Belphoebe just as she is about to condemn the vanity of 'Princes court' (II.iii.42.1). Spenser's polite narrator later makes amends for this insult with a faux-naïve address to 'faire ladies' who, he acknowledges, must be confused as to how Belphoebe could have possibly attained such perfection away from 'court and royall Citadell, / The great schoolmaistresse of all courtesy' (III.vi.1.5–6). But of course the damage is already done: Belphoebe's description of 'prowd estate' (II.iii.40.1) as the surest road to moral oblivion is as damning as Braggadochio's admiration for it.

Returning to the blazon in the light of these observations, the element of absurdity in the narrator's effusiveness is easier to appreciate. His battery of metaphors is conventional – ivory skin, lamp-bright eyes, teeth like pearls and lips like rubies, hair like golden wire, snowy breast, and so forth – but then it is precisely this conventionality that makes the line between praise and parody wafer-thin. Of course, the blazon 'formula' is what made its mockery so irresistible in the sixteenth century, though, as Bakhtin recognised, parody can be covert as well as blatant: 'any strict adherence to a genre begins to feel like a stylization, a stylization taken to the point of parody'.[52] In this broadest sense of the word, the 'parodic' element of Belphoebe's blazon is obvious, and may be considered part of the episode's playful compliment to Elizabeth. But if we take another look at the sexual bathos of 'reuiue the ded' (II.iii.22.9), the parody takes on a distinctly provocative edge, especially in view of the blazon's traditional association with the highest heights of Elizabethan panegyric. Once we have permitted ourselves to join Spenser in laying aside all reverence, we can acknowledge rather than repress the absurdity of the imagery that follows ('In her faire eyes two liuing lamps did flame / Kindled aboue at th'heuenly makers light'; 23.1–2 etc.).[53]

There is also humour in the blazon's architectural metaphor: Belphoebe's legs are 'Like two faire marble pillours … / Which doe the temple of the Gods support' (II.iii.28.1–2). On one hand, such imagery recalls the allegory of *Le Roman de la rose*, in which the lady is figured as a castle waiting to be besieged. In Belphoebe's case, however, the metaphors are mixed. The interweaving of sensuous, realistic descriptions of Belphoebe's

---

52 Mikhail Bakhtin, *The Dialogic Imagination: Four Essays*, trans. Caryl Emerson and Michael Holquist, ed. Michael Holquist (Austin: University of Texas Press, 1981), p. 6. On Spenser's parody of Petrarchan excess elsewhere in *FQ*, see p. 163 above.

53 Spenser may have been alert to the numerous instances in *Orlando furioso* where Ariosto's lavish praise of his patron and dedicatee Ippolito d'Este sits on a knife-edge between flattery and absurdity (see for example *Of* III.iii and III.lvi).

190   *Comic Spenser*

body and clothes on the one hand, and distancing architectural similes on the other, epitomises the paradox of desirability and unavailability so central to Elizabethan panegyric, but it also recalls the metaphorical range of the Song of Solomon. The power and mystery of the latter does not carry over into the blazon, however. In the biblical text, military and architectural similes convey awe in the body of the lover as well as a sense of being 'vanquished' by love. For the Christian reader of the Song, this effect oscillates between frank eroticism and the spiritual interpretation sanctioned by the Church – an unsettling dynamic not unlike the position claimed by Elizabeth's devotees, caught between desire and prohibition, a 'beautifull Lady' and a virginal 'Empresse' (LR, lines 35–6). However, in contrast to the erotic power of the Song, the description of Belphoebe's legs as temple pillars feels (and perhaps this is only appropriate) like a bucket of cold water.

The tension between sublimation and facetiousness underpinning Belphoebe's blazon is pushed to breaking point in Book III. Belphoebe's refusal to relieve Timias's love-longing instigates a meditation on the 'rose' of her chastity, the detailed description of which veers between metaphysical symbolism and the kind of gynaecological detail that Betts associates with 1590s pornographic satire. Chastity is a gift from God that resides in the heart, but it is also a diligently concealed body part, a 'daintie Rose' whose silken leaves must be protected – and here one could be forgiven for blushing – from heat and moisture (III.v.51.1). An obvious reference point here is, again, *Le Roman de la rose*, in which Guillaume de Lorris's comparatively periphrastic version of courtly love descends, in the hands of Jean de Meun, into a consummation scene in which Pilgrim pokes his staff into the shrine of the rose. Another reference point is the love of Medoro and Angelica in *Orlando furioso*, their story being the chief source for that of Belphoebe and Timias. Spenser's only substantial revision is to their happy ending, according to which the haughty Angelica falls in love with Medoro and 'la prima rosa / coglier lasciò' (allows him to 'take … That fragrant rose').[54] Our knowledge of these other roses as we read Spenser's tribute to Belphoebe's chastity complicates what appears to be straight-faced panegyric.[55] Aside from the tension between piety and bawdy in the description of the rose, there is uncertainty as to what differentiates Belphoebe from Angelica – greater

---

54 *Ibid.* XIX.xxxiii; *OF* 19.25.1–3.
55 For a related example of 'a bawdy undertext [intruding] into a carefully repressive discourse', see Oram, 'Human Limitation', p. 38 (and, for the quotation, p. 46).

Parody and panegyric 191

virtue or greater pride. These same tensions are brought out in a more explicitly comic context when Faunus laughs at Diana's 'some-what' (VII. vi.46.3) in the *Mutabilitie Cantos*, as I argue in the epilogue to this study (Diana, of course, being yet another figure of Elizabeth).

Immediately following the rose panegyric, we are told of Belphoebe's miraculous conception and birth. Berleth rightly notes that the story of Chrysogone's impregnation by the sun parodies the Christian mystery, and 'could easily offend'.[56] The offence lies in the blasphemy of the comparison, as well as in its glaring distance from the truth of Elizabeth's parentage. Berleth attempts to resolve this double irony by reading Belphoebe's immaculate conception as a metaphor for Elizabeth's providential election.[57] While the text certainly allows for such a reading, the comic incongruity of the implicit comparison with Christ remains – indeed, it is consistent with the equally absurd idea that Belphoebe's beauty should approximate the powers of the well and tree of life.

Spenser had broached the sensitive subject of Elizabeth's parentage once before. The famous eulogy to 'fayre Eliza' in *The Shepheardes Calender* bears comparison with Belphoebe's 'vnspotted' conception: 'shee is *Syrinx* daughter without spotte, / Which *Pan* the shepheards God of her begot' ('Aprill', lines 50–1). Whether 'without spotte' refers to Syrinx (Anne Boleyn) or to her daughter, the implication is that Elizabeth was not the product of adultery – although Henry VIII as Pan is comically appropriate. With similar irony, the narrator's sanitising insistence on the non-sexual nature of Belphoebe's conception vies with the unabashed description of sunbeams playing upon Chrysogone's naked body before they 'pierst into her wombe' (III.vi.7.7).[58]

If Belphoebe's virginity is powerless to undo the sensuality of her conception, neither does it preserve her from bouts of sexual jealousy.

---

56 Berleth, 'Heavens Favourable and Free', p. 481.
57 Note that even the 'judicial astrology' that for Berleth points to this election – namely Jove's laughter at Venus 'from his souerayne see' (III.vi.2.7) – may be read in an ironic light (see p. 141 above). Kaske interprets Spenser's use of religious language in connection with Belphoebe more straightforwardly as evidence of his high esteem for virginity; Carol Kaske, 'chastity', in *SpE*, p. 143.
58 As Quilligan notes, the narrator's appeal to spontaneous generation on the banks of the Nile as analogous to the virginal conception and birth of Belphoebe radically rewrites the distinctly negative Nile analogy of I.i.21; Maureen Quilligan, *Milton's Spenser: The Politics of Reading* (Ithaca and London: Cornell University Press, 1983), pp. 190–1. Where Quilligan argues that an earlier male vision is overwritten by a female perspective, I would suggest that two equally distorted visions of reproduction are placed in the balance: the one accentuating earthly 'slime', the other overtly sanitised.

192   *Comic Spenser*

In Book IV, Belphoebe spurns Timias after she sees him behaving affectionately toward Amoret (IV.vii.35–6). Such is his grief in exile that he becomes unrecognisable, and when Belphoebe later mistakes him for a stranger she asks, 'what heauens hard disgrace, / Or *wrath of cruell wight* on thee ywrake?' (viii.14.7–8; my italics). Timias has long been compared to Raleigh after his fall from favour (vii.36.8–9n), showing that Belphoebe's condemnation of the court in Book II is not the only instance in which she, as a figure of Elizabeth, becomes a mouthpiece for self-accusatory critique. But it seems to me that the story of Belphoebe's anger reaches beyond Elizabeth's relations with Raleigh to implicate her prohibitive stance on marriage more generally. One indication that this is so is Timias's resemblance to Orlando in his madness on one hand, and, as Hamilton notes, to an Anchorite or desert father on the other (vii.40.6n). He retreats from the world, grows his hair long, fasts, and takes a vow of silence. This juxtaposition of love melancholy and extreme penitentialism is surely suggestive given that, for some Protestants, Elizabeth's prejudices against marriage signalled a return to Catholicism.[59]

Most provocative of all, however, is Belphoebe's attack on the monster 'greedie lust' (IV.vii.*Arg*.1). The monster, with his 'wide deepe poke, downe hanging low' and his 'huge great nose … / Full dreadfully empurpled all with bloud' (vii.6.2–6) is, as Hamilton also notes, a grotesque personification of male genitalia. Thus it is with considerable comic irony that Belphoebe stops to gaze with fascination at his dead body: 'ouer him she there long gazing stood, / And oft admir'd his monstrous shape, and oft / His mighty limbs' (vii.32.6–8). This moment of victorious inspection has been treated as a moral tableau, 'the triumph of chastity over lust', and presumably it was on these grounds that Walter Crane selected it for illustration in the nineteenth century. But a more incisive and humanising caption for Crane's illustration – one, moreover, that might serve equally well for Spenser as he anatomises Elizabeth's faults – is the Freudian axiom 'disgust bears the impress of desire'.[60]

---

59 See for example Bullinger's complaints to Archbishop Grindal; Hastings Robinson, trans. and ed., *The Zurich Letters*, 2 vols, Parker Society Publications, 50–1 (Cambridge: Cambridge University Press, 1842–5), Vol. I, p. 358.

60 Peter Stallybrass and Allon White, *The Politics and Poetics of Transgression* (London: Methuen, 1986), p. 77.

Epilogue: Humour and allegory

Arthur Schopenhauer's theory of laughter seems almost to have allegory in mind: 'in every case, *laughter* results from nothing but the suddenly perceived incongruity between a concept and the real objects that had been thought through it in some relation; and laughter itself is just the expression of this incongruity'.[1] Not all allegory is funny, but its intrinsic irony – saying one thing and meaning another – helps to explain why it is fertile ground for humour. The foregoing chapters are all in some way concerned with the relationship between humour and allegory, and the connections that have been made warrant our full attention here. Allegory is fundamental to Spenser's comic achievement. As readers of *The Faerie Queene*, we are not simply asked to see through a story to its moral applications; we are asked to engage with a mode of representation whose secondariness, limitations, and pleasurability are philosophically and theologically suggestive. The survey of allegorical methods below will help us to understand *how* Spenser is funny but also, in the most far-reaching sense, *why* he is funny.

As well as thinking about ironic disjunctions (a Catholic monastery representing Protestant repentance, for example), we need to consider the larger incongruity at the heart of allegory: the distance between what it promises and what it delivers. Claims have traditionally been made for allegory's utility as an engaging didactic tool and for its visionary possibilities as a mode that points beyond itself. But equally, allegory is a problematic didactic tool because it multiplies interpretative possibilities

---

1 Arthur Schopenhauer, *The World as Will and Representation*, trans. E. F. J. Payne, 2 vols (New York: Dover, 1969), Vol. I, p. 59; cited by Freeman, 'Vision', p. 76. On the 'incongruity' theory of laughter see Introduction.

194   *Comic Spenser*

(in a more self-advertising way than other forms of linguistic expression), and its oblique methods of representation can be bathetic as well as visionary. That is, speaking indirectly can be profound but it can also be clumsy or limited. Even as it invites the reader to look beyond its narrative terms to a privileged secondary meaning, moreover, allegory is characterised by a peculiar wealth of distracting imaginative forms. In the words of Louise Gilbert Freeman, the allegorical image offers 'itself as a bridge to the truth at the same time that the visual pleasure it affords may supersede the desire to search for the unity, the idea, behind its surface'.[2] These inherent tensions are understandably regarded as sources of authorial and readerly anxiety, especially in the context of Protestant epic, yet they also spark interpretative nuance, irony, and humour.

Drawing on the foregoing chapters, this epilogue reflects on the many ways allegory can be comically productive. In conclusion, I shall turn to one of *The Faerie Queene*'s better-known comic episodes, the story of Faunus and Molanna (VII.vi.38–55). This episode, as a number of critics have noted, may be read as a meditation on the limits of temporal perception – something that allegory, in its accentuation of the breach between sign and meaning, is uniquely placed to facilitate. Getting to the ambivalent heart of Spenser's Christian humour, I propose that the faun's laughter foolishly betrays his limited vision, yet is also a wise response to it.

Allegory has a time-honoured association with caricature, visual absurdity, and postured naïveté. This is because narrative realism is not the allegorist's priority (witness Una 'vpon her palfrey slow' (I.i.4.7) keeping pace with Red Crosse's 'angry steede' (1.6), or Munera's 'golden hands and siluer feete'; V.ii.10.2), because of the usefulness of tangible and potentially grotesque things such as bodies and acts of violence as tropes, and because hackneyed conventions can be reinvigorated in a figurative context. But absurdity and naïveté are not only byproducts of allegory; they are also privileges of the mode. From one perspective the allegorist uses an entertaining story as a vehicle for an intellectual or didactic purpose; from another, he or she gratuitously manufactures an occasion for storytelling unlimited by the demands of realism or good taste.[3]

Gratuitousness can have moral implications, of course. For example, in 'The Legend of Holiness' falsehood is a foul woman disguised as a beautiful one. When Duessa is finally exposed in the light of day, Spenser's

---

2 Freeman, 'Vision', p. 75.
3 See Rosemond Tuve, *Allegorical Imagery: Some Medieval Books and Their Posterity* (Princeton: Princeton University Press, 1966), p. 391.

Epilogue: Humour and allegory   195

narrator lingers over her sagging breasts and rump for three stanzas, all
the while insisting that he is too modest to do so ('good manners biddeth
not be told'; I.viii.46.9, cf. 48.2). This grotesque blazon is more than a
simple meditation on the repugnance of evil, as it might have been in the
context of Prudentius's *Psychomachia*. It is ironically voyeuristic. To say
so, however, is not to share the view that 'if we insist that every shred of
Spenserian irony must have some point or other, we may miss the fun
Spenser has'.[4] Fun always has a point in *The Faerie Queene*. Where the
stripping of Duessa is concerned, the narrator's compulsion to describe
her body in detail makes an astute point: all things sinful fascinate us,
even when we see them for what they are. Yet, at the same time, we do
not see sin for what it is. Duessa and Archimago confront us not only
with the badness of the qualities they represent, but also with the magnetic
vitality of vice. They make us want to keep reading. Duessa is doubleness,
allegory itself, and our fascination in her surfaces bespeaks our seduction
by the visual sign. The point is not to castigate the reader or to encode
'anxiety' – or to express puritanical disgust at the body in the process. It is
to encourage humility through amused self-recognition at 'the way we are'.
    The body is one of allegory's most enduring and inexhaustible motifs, as
well as a universal comic theme. Spenser bestows bodies on abstract ideas
and represents bodies as inanimate things, sometimes playfully recalling
us to the task of interpretation; sometimes signposting absurdities of
perspective; and sometimes, as in the case of Duessa, exploiting the
body's unique hold on our attention. Allegory also gives considerable
licence: divesting the body of its corporeality, or the body part of its
usual context, can lend itself to polite distancing as well as (sometimes
simultaneously) to pornographic scrutiny. Such strategies permit the poet
to say things that might otherwise be difficult or impossible to articulate.
This is true of the House of Alma's *Port Esquiline*, of Venus's Mount at the
centre of the Garden of Adonis, of the rose of Belphoebe's chastity, and
of the crumbling 'hinder partes' (I.iv.5.8) of Lucifera's cunningly painted
House of Pride.
    In addition to the humour generated by bodily (and especially taboo)
subjects, the above examples illustrate the playfully congruous end of the
incongruity spectrum (where allegory is not obscure or counterintuitive,
but neatly analogical). Such humour need not be sexual or scatological;

---

4 Esolen, 'Irony and the Pseudo-Physical', p. 63. Though we disagree on this point, Esolen
  has done much to reconcile Spenserian humour with serious meaning – as my many
  debts to his essays indicate.

arguably the House of Alma's ivy mustachio and digestive cooking pots are no less amusing than its back door for dumping waste. But because humour thrives upon compromising bodily demands, it *is* often sexual in nature. In Chapter 5 I alluded to the crude symbolism of the rosebud and staff at the end of de Meun's continuation of *Le Roman de la rose*. De Meun is 'getting away with something', but there is also irony in our recognition that, for the allegorist, sex is difficult to represent in simpler or more tangible terms than it already involves. Allegory's traditional association with mysteries that cannot be accessed by direct illustration is, in effect, sent up: where we might expect the *Roman* to be at its most visionary, transitioning from worldly love to divine love for example, the shift is emphatically downward on the scale of representation, from abstract thoughts and feelings to a physical act.[5] As I argued in the previous chapter, the *Roman* provides an ironic analogue for the 'rose' of Belphoebe's chastity. Officially, the latter represents a transcendent virtue, but we cannot escape the inference that the virtue in question is a euphemism for a body part (one that is no less troubling for not being in use). Chastity's most reductive and superficial status as a bodily state is treated with different though comparable irony when Snowy Florimell is constructed out of lumps of snow and virgin wax.[6] In the latter case, familiar metaphors for virginity are rendered absurdly material but, in contrast to Belphoebe's rose, they are *de*anthropomorphised and rendered distinctly *un*erotic. Calculated deception is grotesque. However, men find it hard to tell the difference; chastity's alluring qualities from the male perspective are Belphoebe's problem, and Florimell's advantage.

Allegory's capacity to replicate the creativity and distortion of cognition – our compulsion to think analogically and materially – is a powerful comic tool. Visual absurdity can be instrumental in satirising prudish, narrow-minded, or otherwise fixated attitudes to the body. One of allegory's strengths is its capacity to mimic literal-mindedness: if allegory sometimes says one thing and means another, there is arguably even greater irony when it says what it means. Both Red Crosse and Belphoebe to a large extent blame the ills of the world on the opposite sex's genitalia, and their prejudices manifest themselves with comic, outsized literality.[7] By reversing this strategy and counterintuitively representing celibacy as a seductress in Book I, Spenser wittily subverts

---

5 See Gordon Teskey, 'Allegory', in *SpE*, pp. 16–22 (p. 17).
6 See Chapter 4.
7 See Chapters 3 and 5.

Epilogue: Humour and allegory 197

our own literalising impulses as readers. Red Crosse's rejection of the body is an insidious form of literal-mindedness, and it is appropriate that we should be obliged to 'reject the letter' of his story in order to see the body rehabilitated.

Book III presents us with a different set of interpretative demands. As I argued in Chapter 4, Glauce's teaching that love is more than an abstraction – that her charge must seek 'No shadow, but a body' (III. ii.45.7) – coincides with our own obligation to attend to the literal level, the narrative intrigue, of Britomart's story. While it is still the occasion of rich social satire, body-centric thinking in this context accrues a positive connotation because it is aligned with the satisfaction as opposed to the suppression of desire. In effect, Chapters 3 and 4 together highlight humour's pliancy in *The Faerie Queene*: we laugh at the limitations of literal-mindedness, but we also take pleasure in the certainties it offers. Depending on the context, literal-mindedness can lead to prudery and pride, or it can militate against these things.

In its self-reflexivity and its capacity to reverse the rules of interpretation without notice, allegory intensifies the game-like nature of fiction, and holds an innate appeal for the poet inclined to reflect upon the tasks of writing and reading. It also discourages complacent and humourless reading practices. To attend to the spirit, not the letter, of Spenser's allegory is to resist the temptation to become dogged or fixed – to be able to negotiate the shifting relationship between the narrative and its allegorical suggestions. It may sometimes involve reading literally, in other words. But even as it requires us to be active, flexible interpreters, the game of allegory is designed to frustrate as well as reward our efforts. The chivalric romance of Book I may be an inadequate vehicle for divine truth, yet it is not one that we can 'see through' at will. Those who argue that Spenser's nostalgic, fantastical narrative presents a self-negating surface via which the Protestant poet disavows the seductive illusions of fiction have a point, but we need to replace the idea of negation and anxiety with something more playful and wilful – self-deflating, perhaps, but not self-negating. Our task is to see that it is not in our power wholly to discard the narrative terms, and so to attain the humility that their inadequacy is intended to invoke.

The reader's lesson in humility begins and ends with allegory's obstruction of authoritative interpretation. This obstruction consists not only of counterintuitive play that unsettles the reader's faith in appearances or oblique allegory that seems to veil contentious subject matter. In such cases, ambiguity can seem to be at the reader's expense,

198 *Comic Spenser*

as though the allegorist were claiming a superior vantage point or withholding a definitive interpretation. Allegory's multiplicity is not always under such close authorial control. As Gordon Teskey recognises, the sophisticated allegorist creates conditions for meaning, allowing for multiple interpretations, and in so doing reflects upon the absence of authoritative truth.[8] Both as an allegorist and as a humorist, Spenser is in the business of acknowledging how tempting, yet essentially impoverishing, it is to try to be definitively right about something. The best allegory, like the best humour, accommodates rather than eradicates moral grey areas, and exposes reductive and self-flattering habits of thought.

The Protestant moralist who is anxiously aware 'how doubtfully all Allegories may be construed' (LR, line 3) is a conventional and no doubt necessary authorial persona, but is also a wry one. The 'Letter to Raleigh', in its strangeness and inadequacy as a guide to the text, ought to be approached not as a serious attempt at clarity but as a joke at the expense of any reader who expects to 'as in a handfull gripe al the discourse' (LR, line 83). The same facetious pretence of transparency is found in the poem itself, when names such as Errour or Lust and morally polarised tropes (virgin, whore, monster) ostensibly do the work of interpretation for us, and when the narrator proffers easy moralising maxims. Spenser claims to sugar the pill of his moral discourse with an engaging 'historicall fiction' (LR, line 9), thereby making 'good discipline' (line 22) more palatable and accessible to the average reader. Yet to 'clowdily enwrap' bare 'precepts' with outward 'showes' (lines 22–4) is also wilfully to complicate the reader's task. We need to be alert to sophisticated allegory masquerading as the kind of naïve allegory that (like Prudentius's *Psychomachia*) renders abstractions tangible and distinguishes absolutely between good and evil. Relevant here is what I have described as the 'missability' of much Spenserian humour, the way it dips in and out of sight depending on the expectations and prerogatives we bring to the text. Critics wanting to find Prudentian clarity in the battle of Red Crosse and Errour have done so, while for others the wood is valuable (and funny) precisely because it 'Breedes dreadfull doubts' (I.i.12.4).

Allegory invites reflection on the limits of representation and interpretation. Even as it provides endless representational possibilities, allegorical narrative foregrounds our obligation to represent the non-spatial and non-temporal in terms of time and space, and, more generally,

---

8 See Teskey, 'Allegory', in *SpE*, pp. 16–22 (esp. pp. 16, 18).

Epilogue: Humour and allegory 199

the crudity and imperfection of all forms of representation. At a time when the created world was still thought of as God's book (one that, like all texts, is both revelatory and oblique) allegory could well offer, as it might for a postmodern world, a metaphor for temporal perception – for the hermeneutic deferral entailed not only by the visual arts and by language itself, but by sight.

Again, visual absurdity can be instrumental in articulating these limitations. In the *Mutabilitie Cantos*, allegory must call upon its most reductive and cartoon-like representational strategies: vast natural phenomena become wittily emblematic and naïve (time itself is an 'Old aged Sire, with hower-glasse in hand'; VII.vi.8.6) and, in the case of Mutability and the moon, subject to burlesque personification. Mutability's attempt to assert her dominance over Cynthia leads to a scuffle, cosmic in scale but comic in effect, in which the latter threatens to impale her opponent (vi.12). This pun-like allegory, with its playful literalisation of the moon's horns, shows the difficulty as well as the fun of dramatising a metaphysical debate.

The task of representing the unrepresentable was, of course, especially acute for Christian poets. Yet the challenge here could be artistically fruitful as well as limiting. As I argued in Chapter 2, when Spenser's narrator compares the '*well of life*' into which Red Crosse falls to 'th'English *Bath* and eke the german *Spau*' (I.xi.30.7), the terms of comparison are comically inadequate. Such analogies register the impossibility of fully comprehending, let alone expressing or representing, the mystery of salvation.[9] Here naïveté is not a façade that we are invited to see through, but a human condition. Insofar as it conveys this truth, the poet's inadequacy is a triumph.

I have argued that a fundamental example of bathos in *The Faerie Queene* is Spenser's fidelity to chivalric romance convention. The ironic disjunction between this popular, low-brow genre and the poem's status as national epic is often noted, but from a wide range of perspectives.

---

9 Nelson, *Fact or Fiction*, p. 83 interprets the 'striking' inadequacy of the well-of-life analogies as a playful acknowledgement of fiction's limitations. The claim for poetry's revelatory power implicit in the narrator's comparison of the Mount of Contemplation to Parnassus, and in Red Crosse's glimpse of the New Jerusalem (I.x.53–67) from that Mount, is tempered by the acknowledgement that Contemplation's 'earthly' eyes are 'both blunt and bad' (I.x.47.3), a point reiterated when the knight's sight fails (x.67.5–9). The jarring effect when the narrator juxtaposes Christ's meditation on the Mount of Olives to the muses making 'lovely lays' on Parnassus may, like the '*Bath*' comparison, be deflationary and affirmative in equal measure: in the words of the narrator, 'So darke are earthly thinges compard to things diuine' (x.67.9).

200   *Comic Spenser*

As discussed in Chapter 1, one perspective is that Spenser's outward mimicry of the ' "blotterature" of ignorant and misguided ages' is itself a moral lesson, in that he deliberately undermines his fictional surfaces in order to point up the morality they encode. In the words of Nuttall,

> [Spenser] has been comprehensively persuaded, at the level of ideology and belief, that art must be depressed in a certain manner. If art is to be allowed any place at all, it must first be drained of any pretended power to contain truth or value within itself. Rich poetry, poetry instinct with the beauty of the world apprehended by the senses ... is deeply mistrusted by Protestants.[10]

Freeman, by subtle contrast, locates Spenserian anxiety not in poetry's pretended power but in the restraints upon that power, insofar as allegory is 'an engine for truths that cannot be imaged directly'.[11] That is, her emphasis is not on Spenser's need to disavow his fictional surfaces, but on the final irreducibility of those surfaces. For Freeman, allegory offers a means of reflecting upon poetry's inability to access the divine – its crude approximations of truth. While I agree to an extent with both Nuttall and Freeman, it seems to me that humour has not been prominent enough in this discussion, and that there is an error of emphasis in the idea that limitation must always be wedded to anxiety or failure. If *The Faerie Queene* reveals Spenser's acute consciousness of poetry's 'pretended power', it also evinces delight in limitation.

Representational limitation, like interpretative ambiguity, takes away with one hand but gives with the other. I have suggested that representational failure can be an artistic triumph; it can also be an expression of faith. Book I's depiction of Satan as a dragon with 'flaggy winges' (I.xi.10.1) and comparison of the well of life to thermal springs may be said to *celebrate* the dark glass through which we see. Christ's triumph over sin allows us creatively to objectify evil in entertainingly inadequate fictions – an inadequacy that essentially says: 'Compared with the mercy of God, all the evil that man can do or think in this world, is as a spark quenched in the ocean.'[12] Conversely, our limited understanding generates anticipation of the unknown. Our worldly imaginations extend

---

10 Nuttall, 'Spenser and Elizabethan Alienation', p. 212. The term 'blotterature' was coined by John Colet; see Nelson, *Fact or Fiction*, p. 75. For discussion of this argument, see pp. 63–4 above.
11 Freeman, 'Vision', pp. 66–7.
12 Langland, *Piers the Ploughman*, trans. Goodridge, p. 70.

Epilogue: Humour and allegory   201

to the pleasures of a spa town; eternal life will render these pleasures absurd.

This is not to deny that there is something deeply sad and perplexing about limitation that is recognised but cannot be overcome, as the elegiac tone of the *Mutabilitie Cantos*' final two stanzas clearly registers. In them, the poet longs for the promised release from temporality and fallibility, from this life's incomplete, 'vnperfite' understanding of God (VII.viii.1– 2). This meditation on the defective present is, in *The Faerie Queene*, faith's bottom line. Yet, in recognition that limitation need not only be elegiac or chastening, the Faunus episode of Canto vii counters the poet's longing for transcendence with a wilful superficiality of vision, a merry fixation on the tangible and fleshly.

Faunus's laughter at Diana (VII.vi)

As Freeman has argued, the story of Faunus and Molanna is one of the places in *The Faerie Queene* where Spenser's thoughts on allegory seem particularly close to the surface. Indeed, almost all the points I have raised about allegory's overlap with humour are exemplified, if not consciously explored, in this episode. Assisted by the nymph Molanna, Faunus hides on Arlo Hill in order to watch the goddess Diana bathing, but betrays himself by laughing (specifically, at the sight of her 'some-what'; VII. vi.46.3). Invoking Diana's status during the Renaissance as a neoplatonic symbol of the 'beauty, knowledge, and truth of divinity that the intellect actively seeks', Freeman argues that the naked and laughter-provoking Diana 'becomes a figure for allegory divested of its power to signify'.[13] The goddess's higher meaning is displaced, or rather obscured, by the vehicle of that meaning – a female body. According to this reading, Faunus, a distinctly carnal beholder, may represent our lower earthly selves in their endless quest for gratification, or, if Diana is taken to represent a tran- scendent, inaccessible, truth, the limitations of temporal perception. In the first case, allegory is divested of its power to signify by a flawed, superficial reader: Faunus's sight stops at the husk of meaning, leaving the kernel unseen and turning the 'potentially exalted moment' into farce.[14] In the second case, allegory is divested of the power to signify in the more terminal sense that the subtlest reader will inevitably be frustrated in his or her search for definitive meaning, the search for which, in this

13 Freeman, 'Vision', p. 77.
14 *Ibid.*, 76.

202   *Comic Spenser*

life, must always be incomplete. Here we may interpret Diana's nakedness as the unclothed truth, the kernel without the husk (albeit represented allegorically, because we cannot really do away with the 'clothing' of secondary representation).[15] According to this reading, to see her and to laugh is to recognise that the extent to which we can know the truth is laughable – deflationary. In this light, the faun's laughter is not indicative of a failure of vision, but is, more ironically, a *response* to this failure.

What Freeman's very illuminating reading does not emphasise enough, in my opinion, is the circumstance that the naked Diana, by the same token that she represents the inaccessibility of transcendent truth, also represents human limitation in the full light of day. She is pride stripped of its trappings and shown in all its vulnerability and silliness. In other words, the faun's laughter is a response not only to the gulf between eternal truth and the defective present, but also to the gulf between the defective present and the fictions that we tell ourselves to make that present seem bigger, better, and more ideal than it is. Spenser is a self-aware creator of these fictions, and in this sense the episode constitutes an exercise in the kind of self-parody I explored in Chapter 5. Diana is Elizabeth without her clothes on, which is as much as to say Elizabeth without Gloriana. However, Faunus's laughter at the disjunction between ideals and reality is not, of course, limited to the exposed humanity of the queen. His laughter resonates back through the poem as far as Book I, which confronts us with the comic reality of the fallible Christian (with a prick instead of a some-what) beneath the heroic armour of Christ's saving act.

In *The Faerie Queene*, it is the comedy of representational inadequacy and of moral errancy that invites us to interpret these failings in a positive or redemptive light. That is, we are wrong to place humour in the service of anxiety and not the other way around. Humour attaches to the apprehension of limitation, but, as I have argued in each of the foregoing chapters, it also facilitates a sympathetic and redemptive interpretation of that limitation. Central to this study (and to comic theory more generally) is the understanding that comic recognition possesses an affirmative dimension, inextricable from the pleasure it entails, pertaining to the apprehension of limited negative consequences – from pain that is not too painful or ugliness that is not one's own, to sinfulness that is redeemed. Not coincidentally, there is a strong sense in the *Mutabilitie Cantos* that whatever limitation Faunus represents, and exposes, is to be celebrated

---

15 On clothing as a metaphor for allegory, see Walls, *God's Only Daughter*, pp. 8–9.

Epilogue: Humour and allegory   203

as well as condemned. His folly has undeniably serious consequences: he is violently punished and a curse is put on Arlo Hill (VII.vi.47–55). Superficially, this curse testifies to the faun's concupiscence and to Diana's vanity; at a deeper level, these sins testify to the curse – the fallenness of mankind. But it is significant that although the curse remains, Faunus is eventually let off the hook so that he might propagate his race. He is three times referred to as 'foolish', and indeed, he is folly itself: a thing to be mocked and punished but not, in this life, eradicated.[16] His crime is comically domesticated when Diana in her wrath is compared to

> an huswife, that with busie care
> Thinks of her Dairie to make wondrous gaine,
> Finding where-as some wicked beast vnware
> That breakes into her Dayr'house, there doth draine
> Her creaming pannes, and frustrate all her paine
> (VII.vi.48.1–5)

The things we deem to be of life-and-death importance are often petty, but while humankind's smallness in the universe is from one perspective disquieting, from another it is reassuring. The faun is described as 'silly' (vi.49.2), which could mean contemptibly foolish (a recent connotation in the late sixteenth century) but which also carried the older sense 'deserving of compassion' (*OED* II.2) and, as Freeman notes, 'good, innocent; blessed'.[17] The faun's pursuit of pleasure over wisdom (if the allegory may be thus interpreted) makes him bestial, but also an antidote to pride.[18]

The pleasurable dimension of Faunus's vision, and our own pleasure as readers of his story, prompts recognition that certain consolations attend – and are even exclusive to – fallibility. Although his laughter betrays his own limitation, it also registers the pleasure that inheres in that limitation. It is appropriate that the object of the faun's amusement is a body, that it should be the flesh that intervenes between perception and higher meaning (and that the sexual body in particular should epitomise

---

16 On the association of 'Faunus' with 'Fatuus' ('the foolish one') see Hamilton, VII. vi.42.7–9n, and, as cited by Hamilton, Nelson, *The Poetry of Edmund Spenser*, p. 300.
17 Freeman, 'Vision', p. 79. The definition is from the glossary to Geoffrey Chaucer, *The Tales of Canterbury*, ed. Robert A. Pratt (Boston, MA: Houghton Mifflin, 1966), p. 585. See also 'Seely', *OED* 3–5.
18 See Oram, 'Human Limitation', pp. 50–2. Although our approaches differ, my conclusions here complement Oram's interpretation. In an ingenious twist, Oram proposes we read Faunus as a 'stand-in for the author' (pp. 51–2) cf. Krier, *Gazing on Secret Sights*, p. 246.

204   *Comic Spenser*

the stripping away of worldly pretension), but also that the very thing circumscribing his vision is also the source of that vision's pleasure.

This circumscribing, pleasure-giving body is also the body of the text. As early modern moralists were well aware, fiction, like humour, depends for its existence upon temporality and fallibility: if there were no room for falsehood; no need for diversion, consolation, education; no grounds for crises (sin, error, vice), neither fiction nor humour would have any purchase (or purpose). If the concealment of the divine from human eyes divests poetry of its power to signify Truth, this limitation of vision is also the enabling condition of the partial truths poetry does contain, and of the pleasure their recognition affords.

Spenser's decision to make his Christian epic a chivalric romance may thus be approached not only as an in-joke or intimation of the child-like resources we have for thinking about spiritual things, but also as an invitation to make virtue of necessity, to access morality through a glass that is not only dark but consoling in its darkness. This approach to the allegory of *The Faerie Queene* is led by the poem's humour. Previous chapters have demonstrated that Spenser is at his most amusing when meditating on fallible human nature: our misled attempts to render morality black and white, our distorting subjectivity, our proud self-regard, and our equally proud mistrust of pleasure. It is surely no coincidence that Spenser chose to write chivalric romance, the archetypal entertaining fiction. Robert Burton in his *Anatomy of Melancholy* lists among the nation's favourite recreations 'merry tales of errant knights, queens, lovers, lords, ladies, giants, dwarfs, thieves, cheaters, witches, fairies'.[19] In the prologue to *Mother Hubberds Tale*, the sick narrator's friends relieve his discomfort with stories of 'Ladies, and their Paramoures', 'brave Knights, and their renowned Squires', 'Faeries', and 'Giaunts hard to be beleeved' (lines 28–31). The pains of the narrator's 'weake bodie' in *Mother Hubberds Tale* are evidently intended to be symptomatic of the malign aspect of the 'sinfull worlde' so relentlessly satirised in the poem – implying that fiction has something to offer by way of both corrective morality *and* sympathetic distraction from suffering and evil.

Harvey once commented in a letter to Spenser, 'you and I are wisely employed (are wee not?) when our Pen and Inke, and Time, and Wit, and all runneth away in this goodly yonkerly veine: as if the world had

---

19 Burton himself is not admiring of these things, however; Robert Burton, *The Anatomy of Melancholy*, ed. Holbrook Jackson, 3 vols (London: J. M. Dent, 1961 [1932]), Vol. II, p. 81 (2.2.4).

Epilogue: Humour and allegory 205

nothing else for vs to do: or we were borne to be only *Nonproficients* and *Nihilagents* of the world'. But an apologetical remark made by Chapman might be more incisively applied to the poet behind Colin Clout: 'true Poesie's humility, poverty and contempt are badges of divinity, not vanity'.[20] As Spenser himself says of *Mother Hubberds Tale*, 'Simple is the device, and the composition meane, yet carrieth some delight, even rather because of the simplicitie and meannesse thus personated' (Dedication to Lady Compton). In a Christian context, limitation is something to be disparaged as well as embraced: either response on its own fosters a problematic sort of humility. Could it be that the task of the 'gentleman or noble person' whom Spenser seeks to fashion in 'vertuous and gentle discipline' (LR, line 8) is not assiduously to reject the shows of fiction, or of temporal existence more generally, in fashioning a serious self, but humorously to accept life's smaller pleasures as proof of God's generosity? Such an acceptance, it seems to me, is common to Erasmus's Folly and Spenser's Faunus.

20 *Var* X, p. 473; 'The Preface to the Reader', in Homer, *Chapman's Homer*, p. 15.

Bibliography

Primary sources

Anon., 'A Sermon against Miracle-Plays', in *Reliquiæ antiquæ: Scraps from Ancient Manuscripts*, ed. Thomas Wright and James Orchard Halliwell, 2 vols (London: William Pickering, 1841), Vol. I, pp. 42–57

Anon., *The Three Parnassus Plays (1598–1601)*, ed. J. B. Leishman (London: Ivor Nicholson & Watson, 1949)

Apuleius, *The Golden Ass*, trans. W. Adlington (1566), rev. and intro. S. Gaselee (London: William Heinemann, 1965 [1915])

Ariosto, Ludovico, *Orlando furioso*, ed. Lanfranco Caretti (Milano: Riccardo Ricciardi, 1954)

Ariosto, Ludovico, *Orlando Furioso*, trans. Sir John Harington (1591), ed. Robert McNulty (Oxford: Clarendon Press, 1972)

Aristotle, *Problemata*, trans. E. S. Forster (Oxford: Clarendon Press, 1927). Retrieved from *Internet Archive*, https://archive.org/stream/worksofaristotle07arisuoft/worksofaristotle07arisuoft_djvu.txt (accessed May 2019)

Aristotle, *Poetics*, trans. M. E. Hubbard, in *Ancient Literary Criticism: The Principal Texts in New Translations*, ed. D. A. Russell and M. Winterbottom (Oxford: Oxford University Press, 1972), pp. 85–132

Ascham, Roger, *The Scholemaster* (Menston: Scolar Press, 1967 [1570])

Ashmole, Elias, *The Institution, Laws and Ceremonies of the Most Noble Order of the Garter* (London, 1672)

Augustine of Hippo, St, *The City of God against the Pagans*, ed. R. W. Dyson (Cambridge: Cambridge University Press, 1998)

Barclay, Alexander, *The Lyfe of St George*, ed. William Nelson, EETS, o.s. 230 (London: Oxford University Press, 1955)

Basil of Caesarea, St, *St Basil: Letters and Selected Works* (1895), trans. Blomfield Jackson, Vol. VIII of *Nicene and Post-Nicene Fathers*, second series, 14 vols, ed. Philip Schaff and Henry Wace (Buffalo, NY: Christian Literature, 1886–1900)

Bevington, David, ed., *Medieval Drama* (Boston, MA: Houghton Mifflin, 1975)

Boccaccio, Giovanni, *The Decameron*, 2 vols (London: J. M. Dent, 1963 [1930])

The Book of Common Prayer 1559: The Elizabethan Prayer Book, ed. John E. Booty (Charlottesville: University of Virginia Press, 2005)

Boorde, Andrew, *see Scoggins iests*

Brewer, Derek, ed., *Chaucer: The Critical Heritage*, 2 vols (London: Routledge & Kegan Paul, 1978)

Brewer, Derek, ed., *Medieval Comic Tales*, 2nd edn (Cambridge: D. S. Brewer, 1996)

Bullinger, Heinrich, *The christen state of matrimonye*, trans. Miles Coverdale (Amsterdam: Theatrum Orbis Terrarum, 1974 [1541])

Bunyan, John, *The Pilgrim's Progress*, ed. Roger Sharrock (London: Penguin, 1987)

Burton, Robert, *The Anatomy of Melancholy*, ed. Holbrook Jackson, 3 vols (London: J. M. Dent, 1961 [1932])

Byron, Lord [George Gordon], *Don Juan*, ed. T. G. Steffan *et al.* (London: Penguin, 1982)

Calvin, John. *Commentaries on the Book of the Prophet Jeremiah and the Lamentations*, trans. and ed. Revd John Owen, 5 vols (Edinburgh: Calvin Translation Society, 1850–5)

Calvin, John, *Institutes of the Christian Religion*, trans. Henry Beveridge, 2 vols (Edinburgh: T. & T. Clarke, 1863)

Castelvetro, Lodovico, *Castelvetro on the Art of Poetry: An Abridged Translation of Lodovico Castelvetro's 'Poetica d'aristotele vulgarizzata et sposta'*, trans, intro. and notes Andrew Bongiorno, Medieval and Renaissance Texts and Studies, Vol. 29 (Binghamton: State University of New York Press, 1984)

Castiglione, Baldassare, *The Book of the Courtier*, trans. Sir Thomas Hoby (London: J. M. Dent, 1974 [1928])

Cervantes, Miguel de, *The History of Don Quixote of the Mancha*, trans. Thomas Shelton, 2 vols (London: Navarre Society, 1923 [1612–20])

Chaucer, Geoffrey, *The Tales of Canterbury*, ed. Robert A. Pratt (Boston, MA: Houghton Mifflin, 1966)

Chaucer, Geoffrey, *The Riverside Chaucer*, ed. Larry D. Benson, 3rd edn (Oxford: Oxford University Press, 1988)

Chaloner, Sir Thomas, *see* Erasmus

208 *Bibliography*

Chapman, George, *see* Homer

Cicero, *De oratore*, trans. E. W. Sutton and H. Rackham, rev. edn, 2 vols (London: Heinemann, 1959–60 [1948])

Cummings, R. M., ed., *Spenser: The Critical Heritage* (London: Routledge & Kegan Paul, 1971)

Davenant, William, *Gondibert* (1651), ed. David F. Gladish (Oxford: Clarendon Press, 1971)

Davies, Sir John, *The Gullinge Sonnets* (*c.* 1596), in *The Complete Poems of Sir John Davies*, ed. Revd Alexander B. Grosart, 2 vols (London: Chatto and Windus, 1876), Vol. II, pp. 55–62; etext (created by Anniina Jokinen) in *Luminarium Editions*, www.luminarium.org/editions/gullingsonnets.htm (accessed May 2019)

Dives and Pauper, ed. Priscilla Heath Barnum, 3 vols, EETS, o.s. 275, 280, 323 (London: Oxford University Press, 1976–2004)

Donne, John, *Donne's Sermons: Selected Passages*, ed. Logan Pearsall Smith (Oxford: Clarendon Press, 1959 [1919])

Du Bellay, Joachim, *Defence and Illustration of the French Language*, trans. Gladys M. Turquet (London: J. M. Dent, 1939)

Du Bellay, Joachim, *La Deffence et illustration de la langue françoyse*, ed. Jean-Charles Monferran, Textes littéraires français, 543 (Geneva: Droz, 2001)

Erasmus, Desiderius, *A ryght frutefull epystle, deuysed by the moste excellent clerke Erasmns [sic], in laude and prayse of matrymony*, trans. Richard Taverner (London: Robert Redman, 1536)

Erasmus, Desiderius, *The Praise of Folie*, trans. Sir Thomas Chaloner (1549), ed. Clarence H. Miller, EETS, o.s. 257 (London: Oxford University Press, 1965)

Erasmus, Desiderius, *'Praise of Folly' and Letter to Martin Dorp, 1515*, trans. Betty Radice, intro. and notes A. H. T. Levi (London: Penguin, 1971)

Erasmus, Desiderius, *Enchiridion militis christiani*, trans. Charles Fantazzi, in *Collected Works of Erasmus*, Vol. LXVI: *Spiritualia*, ed. John W. O'Malley (Toronto: University of Toronto Press, 1988), pp. 1–127

Foxe, John, *The Unabridged Acts and Monuments Online* (Sheffield: Digital Humanities Institute, 2011), 1570 edn

Garret, Martin, ed., *Sidney: The Critical Heritage* (London: Routledge, 1996)

Gascoigne, George, *The Complete Works of George Gascoigne*, ed. John W. Cunliffe, 2 vols (Cambridge: Cambridge University Press, 1907–10)

Bibliography 209

Gascoigne, George, *A Hundreth Sundrie Flowres*, ed. G. W. Pigman III (Oxford: Clarendon Press, 2000)

Gower, John, *Confessio Amantis*, ed. Russell A. Peck (Toronto: University of Toronto Press, 1997 [1980])

Greenham, Richard, *The workes of the reuerend and faithfull seruant of Iesus Christ M. Richard Greenham, minister and preacher of the Word of God* (London, 1601)

Harington, John, *see* Ariosto, Ludovico

Hazlitt, William, *Lectures on the English Comic Writers* (London: Taylor and Hessey, 1819), pp. 1–53

Hobbes, Thomas, *The English Works of Thomas Hobbes*, ed. Sir William Molesworth, Bart, 11 vols (London: John Bohn, 1966)

Hobbes, Thomas, 'Hobbes's Answer to the Preface' (1650), in William Davenant, *Gondibert* (1651), ed. David F. Gladish (Oxford: Clarendon Press, 1971), pp. 45–55

Homer, *Chapman's Homer: 'The Iliad', 'The Odyssey', and the Lesser Homerica*, trans. George Chapman, ed. Allardyce Nicoll, 2nd edn, 2 vols, Bollingen Series, 41 (Princeton: Princeton University Press, 1956)

Homer, *The 'Iliad' of Homer*, trans. Alexander Pope, ed. Maynard Mack, 2 vols (London: Methuen, 1967)

Homer, *Homeric Hymns, Homeric Apocrypha, Lives of Homer*, trans. and ed. Martin L. West (Cambridge, MA: Harvard University Press, 2003)

Hooper, John, *Early Writings of Hooper*, ed. Samuel Carr, Parker Society Publications, 20 (Cambridge: Cambridge University Press, 1843)

Horace, *The Art of Poetry*, trans. D. A. Russell, in *Ancient Literary Criticism: The Principal Texts in New Translations*, ed. D. A. Russell and M. Winterbottom (Oxford: Oxford University Press, 1972), pp. 279–91

Hurd, Richard, *Letters on Chivalry and Romance* (1762), Vol. III of *Spenser's 'Faerie Queene': Warton's Observations and Hurd's Letters*, ed. David Fairer, 3 vols (London: Routledge, 2001)

Hurtado de Mendoza, Diego, *Lazarillo de Tormes*, trans. David Rowland (London: Abell Ieffes, 1586)

Jerome, St, *Select Letters of St Jerome*, trans. F. A. Wright (London: Heinemann, 1933)

Johnson, Samuel, 'Preface to Shakespeare' (1765), in *Johnson on Shakespeare*, ed. Arthur Sherbo, Vols VII–VIII of *The Yale Edition of the Works of Samuel Johnson*, 23 vols (New Haven: Yale University Press, 1968), Vol. VII, pp. 59–113

Jonson, Ben, *'The Alchemist' and Other Plays*, ed. and intro. Gordon Campbell (Oxford: Oxford University Press, 1995)

210 *Bibliography*

Joubert, Laurent, *Traité dv ris, contenant son essance, ses causes, et mervelheus effais, curieusemant recerchés, raisonnés & observés* (Paris, 1579)

Joubert, Laurent, *Treatise on Laughter*, trans. Gregory David de Rocher (Tuscaloosa, AL: University of Alabama Press, 1980)

Langland, William, *The vision of Pierce Plowman, nowe the seconde time imprinted*, ed. Robert Crowley (London: R. Grafton, 1550)

Langland, William, *Piers the Ploughman*, trans. and intro. J. F. Goodridge (Harmondsworth: Penguin, 1966)

Latimer, Hugh, *Sermons of Latimer*, ed. George Elwes Corrie, Parker Society Publications, 27 (Cambridge: Cambridge University Press, 1844)

Longinus, *On Sublimity*, trans. D. A. Russell, in *Ancient Literary Criticism: The Principal Texts in New Translations*, ed. D. A. Russell and M. Winterbottom (Oxford: Oxford University Press, 1972), pp. 460–503

Nashe, Thomas, *The Works of Thomas Nashe*, ed. Ronald B. McKerrow (Oxford: Basil Blackwell, 1958)

Malory, Thomas, *The Works of Sir Thomas Malory*, ed. Eugène Vinaver, 2nd edn, 3 vols (Oxford: Clarendon Press, 1973 [1967])

Mantuan, *see* Barclay, Alexander

Marx, Karl, *The Ethnological Notebooks of Karl Marx*, ed. Lawrence Krader, 2nd edn (Assen: Van Gorcum, 1974)

Milton, John, *Complete Prose Works of John Milton*, ed. Don Marion Wolfe, 8 vols (New Haven: Yale University Press, 1953–82)

Milton, John, *Paradise Lost*, ed. Christopher Ricks (London: Penguin, 1989)

More, Thomas, *A Dialogue of Comfort against Tribulation*, ed. Louis L. Martz and Frank Manley (1976), Vol. XII of *The Yale Edition of the Complete Works of St Thomas More*, 15 vols (New Haven: Yale University Press, 1963–97)

Mulcaster, Richard, *Positions wherein those primitiue circvmstances be examined, which are necessarie for the training vp of children, either for skill in their booke, or health in their bodie* (London: Thomas Chard, 1581)

Munday, Anthony, *A Second and Third Blast of Retrait from Plaies and Theatres* (New York: Garland, 1973 [1580])

Ovid, *Metamorphoses*, trans. A. D. Melville, intro. and notes E. J. Kenney (Oxford: Oxford University Press, 1987)

Bibliography

Parker, Matthew, *Correspondence of Parker*, ed. John Bruce and Thomas Thomason Perowne, Parker Society Publications, 33 (Cambridge: Cambridge University Press, 1853)

Perkins, William, *A Direction for the Governement of the Tongve According to Gods Word*, in *The Workes of That Famovs and VVorthie Minister of Christ, in the Vniversitie of Cambridge, M. W. Perkins*, 3 vols (London, 1608–37), Vol. I, pp. 439–51

Plato, *The Republic*, trans. Tom Griffith, ed. G. R. F. Ferrari (Cambridge: Cambridge University Press, 2008 [2000])

Pope, Alexander, *The Twickenham Edition of the Poems of Alexander Pope*, ed. Norman Ault and John Butt, 11 vols (London: Methuen, 1953–69)

Prudentius, *Prudentius, with an English Translation*, ed. and trans. H. J. Thomson, 2 vols (Cambridge, MA: Harvard University Press, 1949)

Puttenham, George, *The Arte of English Poesie* (1589), in *Elizabethan Critical Essays*, ed. G. Gregory Smith, 2 vols (Oxford: Oxford University Press, 1904), Vol. II, 1–193

Quintilian, *Institutio oratoria*, trans. H. E. Butler, 4 vols (London: Heinemann, 1953 [1921–2])

Rabelais, François, *The Complete Works*, trans. Sir Thomas Urquhart and Peter Motteux, 2 vols (London: John Lane, 1927)

Robinson, Hastings, trans. and ed., *The Zurich Letters*, 2 vols, Parker Society Publications, 50–1 (Cambridge: Cambridge University Press, 1842–5)

Russell, D. A., and M. Winterbottom, eds, *Ancient Literary Criticism: The Principal Texts in New Translations* (Oxford: Oxford University Press, 1972)

Schopenhauer, Arthur, *The World as Will and Representation*, trans. E. F. J. Payne, 2 vols (New York: Dover, 1969)

Scoggins iests, ed. Andrew Boorde(?) (London: Francis Williams, 1626)

Shakespeare, William, *The Riverside Shakespeare*, ed. Herschel Baker *et al.*, 2nd edn (New York: Houghton Mifflin, 1997)

Sidney, Sir Philip, *The Old Arcadia*, ed. and intro. Katherine Duncan-Jones (Oxford: Oxford University Press, 1999)

Sidney, Sir Philip, *The Defence of Poesy*, in *Sidney's 'The Defence of Poesy' and Selected Renaissance Literary Criticism*, ed. and intro. Gavin Alexander (London: Penguin, 2004)

Smith, G. Gregory, ed., *'The Spectator'*, by Addison, Steele and others, 8 vols (London: J. M. Dent, 1897)

212   *Bibliography*

Smith, G. Gregory, ed., *Elizabethan Critical Essays*, 2 vols (Oxford: Oxford University Press, 1904)

Smith, Henry, *A preparatiue to mariage* (London: Thomas Man, 1591)

Spenser, Edmund, *The Works of Edmund Spenser: A Variorum Edition*, ed. Edwin Greenlaw *et al.*, 11 vols (Baltimore: Johns Hopkins University Press, 1932–57)

Spenser, Edmund, *The Faerie Queene*, ed. A. C. Hamilton (London: Longman, 1995 [1977])

Spenser, Edmund, *The Yale Edition of the Shorter Poems of Edmund Spenser*, ed. William A. Oram, Einar Bjorvand, Ronald Bond, Thomas H. Cain, Alexander Dunlop, and Richard Schell (New Haven: Yale University Press, 1989)

Spenser, Edmund, *The Faerie Qveene*, ed. A. C. Hamilton, Hiroshi Yamashita, and Toshiyuki Suzuki (Harlow: Pearson Education, 2001)

Spenser, Edmund, *The Faerie Queene, Book I*, ed. and intro. Carol Kaske (Indianapolis: Hackett, 2006)

Spenser, Edmund, *The Faerie Queene, Books III and IV*, ed. Dorothy Stephens (Indianapolis: Hackett, 2006)

Spenser, Edmund, *'The Faerie Queene': Book Six and the Mutabilitie Cantos*, ed. Andrew Hadfield and Abraham Stoll (Indianapolis: Hackett, 2007)

Statius, Publius Papinius, *Statius, with an English Translation*, trans. J. H. Mozley, 2 vols (Cambridge, MA: Harvard University Press, 1967 [1928])

Stubbes, Phillip, *Anatomie of Abuses* (1583), ed. Frederick J. Furnivall (Vaduz: Kraus Reprint, 1965 [1877–9])

Tasso, Torquato, *Discorsi del poema eroico*, in *Prose*, ed. Ettore Mazzali (Milan: Riccardo Ricciardi, 1959)

Tasso, Torquato, *Discourses on the Heroic Poem*, trans. Mariella Cavalchini and Irene Samuel (Oxford: Clarendon Press, 1973)

Taverner, Richard, *see* Erasmus, Desiderius

Vickers, Brian, ed., *English Renaissance Literary Criticism* (Oxford: Clarendon Press, 1999)

Vida, Marco Girolamo, *The 'De arte poetica' of Marco Girolamo Vida* (1517, 1527), trans. and ed. Ralph G. Williams (New York: Columbia University Press, 1976)

Viret, Pierre, *The Christian Disputations*, trans. John Brooke (London: Thomas East, 1579)

Virgil, *Virgil, with an English Translation*, trans. H. Rushton Fairclough, rev. edn, 2 vols (London: Heinemann, 1950 [1934])

Voragine, Jacobus de, *The Golden Legend*, trans. William Granger Ryan, 2 vols (Princeton: Princeton University Press, 1993)

Webbe, William, *A Discourse of English Poetrie* (1586), in *Elizabethan Critical Essays*, ed. G. Gregory Smith, 2 vols (Oxford: Oxford University Press, 1904), Vol. I, 226–302

Wilson, Thomas, *Wilson's 'Arte of Rhetorique' (1560)*, ed. G. H. Mair (Oxford: Clarendon Press, 1909)

Zall, P. M., ed., *'A Hundred Merry Tales' and Other English Jestbooks of the Fifteenth and Sixteenth Centuries* (Lincoln: University of Nebraska Press, 1963)

Secondary sources

Adamson, Sylvia, 'Literary Language', in *The Cambridge History of the English Language*, Vol. III: *1476–1776*, ed. Roger Lass (Cambridge: Cambridge University Press, 1999), pp. 539–653

Adelman, Janet, 'Revaluing the Body in *The Faerie Queene* I', Hugh Maclean Memorial Lecture, *SR*, 36 (2005), 15–25

Allen, Don Cameron, *Image and Meaning* (Baltimore: Johns Hopkins University Press, 1968)

Anderson, Judith H., '"In liuing colours and right hew": The Queen of Spenser's Central Books', in *Poetic Traditions of the English Renaissance*, ed. Maynard Mack and George deForest Lord (New Haven: Yale University Press, 1982), pp. 47–66

Anderson, Judith H., '"A Gentle Knight was pricking on the plaine": The Chaucerian Connection', *ELR*, 15 (1985), 166–74

Anderson, Judith H., 'Arthur, Argante, and the Ideal Vision: An Exercise in Speculation and Parody', in *The Passing of Arthur: New Essays in Arthurian Tradition*, ed. Christopher Baswell and William Sharpe (New York: Garland, 1988), pp. 193–206

Anderson, Judith H., 'The "couert vele": Chaucer, Spenser, and Venus', *ELR*, 24 (1994), 638–59

Anderson, Judith H., *Spenser's Narrative Figuration of Women in 'The Faerie Queene'* (Kalamazoo: Medieval Institute Publications, 2017)

Aston, Margaret, *England's Iconoclasts*, Vol. I: *Laws against Images* (Oxford: Clarendon Press, 1988)

Auerbach, Erich, *Mimesis: The Representation of Reality in Western Literature*, trans. Willard R. Trask (Princeton: Princeton University Press, 1991 [1953])

214   *Bibliography*

Baker, David J., 'Spenser and Politics', in *The Oxford Handbook of Edmund Spenser*, ed. Richard A. McCabe (Oxford: Oxford University Press, 2010), pp. 48–64

Bakhtin, Mikhail, *The Dialogic Imagination: Four Essays*, trans. Caryl Emerson and Michael Holquist, ed. Michael Holquist (Austin: University of Texas Press, 1981)

Bakhtin, Mikhail, *Rabelais and His World*, trans. Hélène Iswolsky (Bloomington: Indiana University Press, 1984)

Barasch, Frances K., 'Definitions: Renaissance, Baroque, Grotesque Construction and Deconstruction', *MLS*, 13 (1983), 60–7

Beard, Mary, 'Ha Ha: What Made the Greeks Laugh? The Funny, the Peculiar, and a Possible Ancestor of Monty Python's Parrot', *TLS* (February 2009), 3–5

Bell, Bernard W., 'The Comic Realism of Una's Dwarf', *Massachusetts Studies in English*, 1 (1968), 111–18

Bennett, J. W., *The Evolution of 'The Faerie Queene'* (New York: Burt Franklin, 1960)

Benson, Larry D., 'The "Queynte" Punnings of Chaucer's Critics', *SAC*, 1 (1984), 23–47

Berger, Harry, Jr, *Revisionary Play: Studies in the Spenserian Dynamics* (Berkeley: University of California Press, 1988)

Berger, Harry, Jr, '"Kidnapped Romance": Discourse in *The Faerie Queene*', in *Unfolded Tales: Essays on Renaissance Romance*, ed. George M. Logan and Gordon Teskey (Ithaca: Cornell University Press, 1989), pp. 208–56

Berger, Harry, Jr, 'Displacing Autophobia in *Faerie Queene* I: Ethics, Gender, and Oppositional Reading in the Spenserian Text', *ELR*, 28 (1998), 163–82

Berger, Harry, Jr, 'Sexual and Religious Politics in Book I of Spenser's *Faerie Queene*', *ELR*, 34 (2004), 201–42

Berleth, Richard J., 'Heavens Favourable and Free: Belphoebe's Nativity in *The Faerie Queene*', *ELH*, 40 (1973), 479–500

Berry, Craig A., 'Borrowed Armor/Free Grace: The Quest for Authority in *The Faerie Queene* I and Chaucer's "Tale of Sir Thopas"', *SP*, 91 (1994), 136–66

Berry, Craig A., '"Sundrie Doubts": Vulnerable Understanding and Dubious Origins in Spenser's Continuation of "The Squire's Tale"', in *Refiguring Chaucer in the Renaissance*, ed. Theresa M. Krier (Gainesville: University Press of Florida, 1998), pp. 106–27

Bibliography 215

Bettelheim, Bruno, *The Uses of Enchantment: The Meaning and Importance of Fairy Tales* (London: Thames and Hudson, 1976)

Betts, Hannah, 'The Pornographic Blazon, 1588–1603', in *Dissing Elizabeth: Negative Representations of Gloriana*, ed. Julia M. Walker (Durham, NC: Duke University Press, 1998), pp. 153–84

Bieman, Elizabeth, '"Sometimes I ... mask in myrth lyke to a Comedy": Spenser's *Amoretti*', *SSt*, 4 (1984), 131–41

Blackburn, William, 'Spenser's Merlin', *Ren&R*, 4 (1980), 179–98

Blank, Paula, *Broken English: Dialects and the Politics of Language in English Writings* (London and New York: Routledge, 1996)

Bliss, Lee, 'Pastiche, Burlesque, Tragicomedy', in *The Cambridge Companion to English Renaissance Drama*, ed. A. R. Braunmuller and Michael Hattaway, 2nd edn (Cambridge: Cambridge University Press, 2003), pp. 228–53

Booth, Wayne, *A Rhetoric of Irony* (Chicago: University of Chicago Press, 1974)

Borris, Kenneth, *Allegory and Epic in English Renaissance Literature: Heroic Form in Sidney, Spenser, and Milton* (Cambridge: Cambridge University Press, 2000)

Bowers, R. H., 'Chaucer's *Troilus* as an Elizabethan "Wanton Book"', *NQ*, 7 (1960), 370–1

Brewer, Derek, ed., *Chaucer: The Critical Heritage* (1978), *see under* 'Primary sources'

Brewer, Derek, 'Comedy and Tragedy in *Troilus and Criseyde*', in *The European Tragedy of Troilus*, ed. Piero Boitani (Oxford: Clarendon Press, 1989), pp. 95–109

Brewer, Derek, ed., *Medieval Comic Tales* (1996), *see under* 'Primary sources'

Brewer, Derek, 'Prose Jest-Books Mainly in the Sixteenth to Eighteenth Centuries in England', in *A Cultural History of Humour: From Antiquity to the Present Day*, ed. Jan Bremmer and Herman Roodenburg (Cambridge: Polity Press, 1997), pp. 90–111

Briggs, Julia, *This Stage-Play World: Texts and Contexts, 1580–1625* (Oxford: Oxford University Press, 1997)

Broich, Ulrich, *The Eighteenth-Century Mock-Heroic Poem*, trans. David Henry Wilson (Cambridge: Cambridge University Press, 1990)

Burke, Charles B., 'Humour in Spenser', *NQ*, 166 (1934), 113–15

Burke, Charles B., 'The "Sage and Serious" Spenser', *NQ*, 175 (1938), 457–8

Burrow, Colin, *Edmund Spenser* (Plymouth: Northcote House, 1996)

216   *Bibliography*

Burrow, J. A., *Ricardian Poetry: Chaucer, Gower, Langland and the 'Gawain' Poet* (London: Routledge & Kegan Paul, 1971)

Burrow, J. A., ' "Sir Thopas" in the Sixteenth Century', in *Middle English Studies Presented to Norman Davis*, ed. Douglas Gray and E. G. Stanley (Oxford: Clarendon Press, 1983), pp. 69–91

Busby, Keith, and Roger Dalrymple, eds, *Arthurian Literature XIX: Comedy in Arthurian Literature* (Cambridge: D. S. Brewer, 2003)

Butler, Chris, ' "Pricking" and Ambiguity at the Start of *The Faerie Queene*', *NQ*, 253 (2008): 159–61

Callaghan, Dympna, 'Comedy and Epyllion in Post-Reformation England', *Shakespeare Survey*, 56 (2003), 27–38

Camille, Michael, *Image on the Edge: The Margins of Medieval Art* (London: Reaktion, 1992)

Campana, Joseph, '*Letters* (1580)', in *The Oxford Handbook of Edmund Spenser*, ed. Richard A. McCabe (Oxford: Oxford University Press, 2010), pp. 178–97

Carroll, D. Allen, 'The Meaning of "E. K." ', *SSt*, 20 (2005), 169–81

Carver, Robert H. F., *The Protean Ass: The 'Metamorphoses' of Apuleius from Antiquity to the Renaissance* (Oxford: Oxford University Press, 2007)

Cavanagh, Sheila T., *Wanton Eyes and Chaste Desires: Female Sexuality in 'The Faerie Queene'* (Bloomington and Indianapolis: Indiana University Press, 1994)

Cazamian, Louis, *The Development of English Humor* (Durham, NC: Duke University Press, 1952)

Cheney, Donald, *Spenser's Image of Nature* (New Haven: Yale University Press, 1966)

Cheney, Donald, 'Spenser's Parody', *Connotations*, 12 (2002), 1–13

Church, R. W., *Spenser*, 2nd edn (London: Macmillan, 1888)

Clark, Judith Petterson, 'His Earnest unto Game: Spenser's Humor in *The Faerie Queene*', *Emporia State Research Studies*, 15 (1967), 13–24, 26–7

Coles, Kimberly Anne, ' "Perfect hole": Elizabeth I, Spenser, and Chaste Productions', *ELR*, 32 (2002), 31–61

Cooper, Helen, *The English Romance in Time: Transforming Motifs from Geoffrey of Monmouth to the Death of Shakespeare* (Oxford: Oxford University Press, 2004)

Cooper, Helen, *Shakespeare and the Middle Ages: An Inaugural Lecture Delivered at the University of Cambridge, April 2005* (Cambridge: Cambridge University Press, 2006)

Cormier, Raymond, 'Humour in the *Roman d'Eneas*', *Florilegium*, 7 (1985), 129–44

Bibliography

Corrigan, Robert W., ed., *Comedy: A Critical Anthology* (Boston, MA: Houghton Mifflin, 1971)

Craig, Martha, 'The Secret Wit of Spenser's Language', in *Elizabethan Poetry: Modern Essays in Criticism*, ed. Paul J. Alpers (New York: Oxford University Press, 1967), pp. 447–72

Cross, Claire, *The Royal Supremacy in the Elizabethan Church* (London: Allen & Unwin, 1969)

Delany, Sheila, 'The Logic of Obscenity in Chaucer's *Legend of Good Women*', *Florilegium*, 7 (1985), 189–205

Dillon, Janette, 'Elizabethan Comedy', in *The Cambridge Companion to Shakespearean Comedy*, ed. Alexander Leggatt (Cambridge: Cambridge University Press, 2002), pp. 47–63

Dinshaw, Carolyn, *Chaucer's Sexual Poetics* (Madison: University of Wisconsin Press, 1989)

Dodge, R. E. N., 'Spenser's Imitations from Ariosto', *PMLA*, 12 (1897), 151–204

Duffy, Eamon, *The Stripping of the Altars: Traditional Religion in England c. 1400–c. 1580* (New Haven: Yale University Press, 1992)

Dundas, Judith, '"Muiopotmos": A World of Art', *Yearbook of English Studies*, 5 (1975), 30–8

Eastman, Max, *Enjoyment of Laughter* (London: Hamish Hamilton, 1937)

Eco, Umberto, *The Name of the Rose* (London: Minerva, 1992)

Edwards, Michael, 'A Meaning for Mock-Heroic', *Yearbook of English Studies*, 15 (1985), 48–63

Elias, Norbert, *The History of Manners*, trans. Edmund Jephcott (Oxford: Blackwell, 1978)

Erickson, Wayne, 'The Poet's Power and the Rhetoric of Humility in Spenser's Dedicatory Sonnets', *SLI*, 38 (2005), 91–118

Esolen, Anthony M., 'Irony and the Pseudo-Physical in *The Faerie Queene*', *SSt*, 8 (1987), 61–78

Esolen, Anthony M., 'The Disingenuous Poet Laureate: Spenser's Adoption of Chaucer', *SP*, 87 (1990), 285–311

Esolen, Antony M., 'Highways and Byways: A Response to Donald Cheney', *Connotations*, 13 (2003), 1–4

Evans, Robert O., 'Spenserian Humor: *Faerie Queene* III and IV', *Neuphilologische Mitteilungen*, 60 (1959), 288–99

Farnham, Willard, 'The Medieval Comic Spirit in the English Renaissance', in *Joseph Quincy Adams Memorial Studies*, ed. James G. McManaway *et al.* (Washington, D.C.: Folger Shakespeare Library, 1948), pp. 429–37

Fish, Stanley, *Surprised by Sin: The Reader in 'Paradise Lost'* (Basingstoke: Macmillan, 1997)

218   *Bibliography*

Foster, Verna A., *The Name and Nature of Tragicomedy* (Aldershot: Ashgate, 2004)

Freeman, Louise Gilbert, 'Vision, Metamorphosis, and the Poetics of Allegory in the *Mutabilitie Cantos*', *SEL*, 45 (2005), 65–93

Freud, Sigmund, *Art and Literature*, Penguin Freud Library, 14 (London: Penguin, 1990)

Froude, James A. *History of England*, 10 vols (London: Parker, Son, and Bourn, 1862–6), Vol. II, retrieved from https://babel.hathitrust.org/cgi/pt?id=hvd.hw20o3;view=1up;seq=6 (accessed May 2019)

Frye, Northrop, *Anatomy of Criticism: Four Essays* (Princeton: Princeton University Press, 1957)

Frye, Northrop, *Northrop Frye's Notebooks on Renaissance Literature*, ed. Michael Dolzani, Collected Works of Northrop Frye, 20 (Toronto: University of Toronto Press, 2006)

Fudge, Erica, 'Learning to Laugh: Children and Being Human in Early Modern Thought', *Textual Practice*, 17 (2003), 277–94

Gaisser, Julia Haig, *The Fortunes of Apuleius and the 'Golden Ass': A Study in Transmission and Reception* (Princeton: Princeton University Press, 2008)

Gibbs, Donna, *Spenser's 'Amoretti': A Critical Study* (Aldershot: Scholar Press, 1990)

Gilbert, Allan H., 'Spenserian Comedy', *Tennessee Studies in Literature*, 2 (1957), 95–104

Groves, Beatrice, 'The Redcrosse Knight and "The George"', *SSt*, 25 (2010), 371–6

Gurevich, Aron, *Medieval Popular Culture: Problems of Belief and Perception*, trans. János M. Bak and Paul A. Hollingsworth (Cambridge: Cambridge University Press, 1988)

Hackett, Helen, *Virgin Mother, Maiden Queen: Elizabeth I and the Cult of the Virgin Mary* (Basingstoke: Macmillan, 1995)

Hadfield, Andrew, 'Spenser and Jokes', *SSt*, 25 (2010), 1–19

Hadfield, Andrew, 'Spenser and Religion – Yet Again', *SEL*, 51 (2011), 21–46

Hamilton, A. C., ed., *The Spenser Encyclopedia* (Toronto: University of Toronto Press, 1990)

Hardin, Richard F., 'Spenser's Aesculapius Episode and the English Mummers' Play', *SSt*, 15 (2001), 251–3

Hecht, Paul J., 'Letters for the Dogs: Chasing Spenserian Alliteration', *SSt*, 25 (2010), 263–85

Bibliography 219

Heiges Blythe, Joan, 'Spenser and the Seven Deadly Sins: Book I, Cantos IV and V', *ELH*, 39 (1972), 342–52

Helgerson, Richard, *The Elizabethan Prodigals* (Berkeley: University of California Press, 1976)

Hendrix, Laurel, ' "Mother of laughter, and welspring of blisse": Spenser's Venus and the Poetics of Mirth', *ELR*, 23 (1993), 113–33

Herrick, Marvin T., *Comic Theory in the Sixteenth Century* (Urbana: University of Illinois Press, 1964 [1950])

Higgins, Anne, 'Spenser Reading Chaucer: Another Look at the *Faerie Queene* Allusions', *JEGP*, 89 (1990), 17–36

Hillman, David, *Shakespeare's Entrails: Belief, Scepticism, and the Interior of the Body* (Basingstoke: Palgrave Macmillan, 2007)

Hoffman, Donald L., 'Malory and the English Comic Tradition', in *Arthurian Literature XIX: Comedy in Arthurian Literature*, ed. Keith Busby and Roger Dalrymple (Cambridge: D. S. Brewer, 2003), pp. 177–88.

Holcomb, Chris, *Mirth Making: The Rhetorical Discourse on Jesting in Early Modern England* (Columbia: University of South Carolina Press, 2001)

Hopkins, David, 'Dryden and Ovid's "Wit out of Season"', in *Ovid Renewed: Ovidian Influences on Literature and Art from the Middle Ages to the Twentieth Century*, ed. Charles Martindale (Cambridge: Cambridge University Press, 1988), pp. 167–90

Hough, Graham, *Preface to 'The Faerie Queene'* (London: Duckworth, 1983 [1962])

Huizinga, J[ohan], *Homo ludens: A Study of the Play-Element in Culture* (London: Routledge & Kegan Paul, 1980 [1949])

Huston, J. Dennis, 'The Function of the Mock Hero in Spenser's "Faerie Queene"', *MP*, 66 (1969), 212–17

Jacobson, Howard, *Seriously Funny: From the Ridiculous to the Sublime* (London: Penguin, 1997)

Javitch, Daniel, *Proclaiming a Classic: The Canonization of 'Orlando furioso'* (Princeton: Princeton University Press, 1991)

Javitch, Daniel, 'The Advertising of Fictionality in *Orlando furioso*' in *Ariosto Today: Contemporary Perspectives*, ed. Donald Beecher *et al.* (Toronto: University of Toronto Press, 2003), pp. 106–25

Johnson, Paul, *Elizabeth I: A Study in Intellect and Power* (London: Weidenfeld and Nicolson, 1974)

Jones, Richard Foster, *The Triumph of the English Language* (Stanford: Stanford University Press, 1953)

Bibliography

Kahrl, Stanley J., 'The Medieval Origins of the Sixteenth-Century English Jest-Books', *Studies in the Renaissance*, 13 (1966), 166–83

Kaske, Carol, 'Review of Harold W. Weatherby, *Mirrors of Celestial Grace: Patristic Theology in Spenser's Allegory*', *SN*, 26 (1995), 15–19

Kaula, David, 'The Low Style in Nashe's *The Unfortunate Traveller*', *SEL*, 6 (1966), 43–57

Kay, Sarah, 'Courts, Clerks, and Courtly Love', in *The Cambridge Companion to Medieval Romance*, ed. Roberta L. Krueger (Cambridge: Cambridge University Press, 2000), pp. 81–96

Keach, William, 'Verbal Borrowing in Elizabethan Poetry: Plagiarism or Parody?', *Centrum*, 4 (1976), 21–31

Keach, William, *Elizabethan Erotic Narratives: Irony and Pathos in the Ovidian Poetry of Shakespeare, Marlowe, and Their Contemporaries* (New Brunswick: Rutgers University Press, 1977).

King, Andrew, '*The Faerie Queene* and Middle English Romance: The Matter of Just Memory* (Oxford: Clarendon Press, 2000)

King, Andrew, 'Spenser, Chaucer, and Medieval Romance', in *The Oxford Handbook of Edmund Spenser*, ed. Richard A. McCabe (Oxford: Oxford University Press, 2010), pp. 553–72

King, John, 'Spenser's Religion', in *The Cambridge Companion to Spenser*, ed. Andrew Hadfield (Cambridge: Cambridge University Press, 2001), pp. 200–16

King, Ros, 'In Lieu of Democracy; or, How Not to Lose Your Head: Theatre and Authority in Renaissance England', in *Early Modern Tragicomedy*, ed. Subha Mukherji and Raphael Lyne (Cambridge: D. S. Brewer, 2007), pp. 84–100

Kolve, V. A., *The Play Called Corpus Christi* (London: Edward Arnold, 1966)

Krier, Theresa M., *Gazing on Secret Sights: Spenser, Classical Imitation, and the Decorums of Vision* (Ithaca and London: Cornell University Press, 1990)

Kucich, Greg, 'The Duality of Romantic Spenserianism', *SSt*, 8 (1987), 287–307

Lamb, Mary Ellen, 'The Red Crosse Knight, St George, and the Appropriation of Popular Culture', *SSt*, 18 (2003), 185–208

Lamb, Mary Ellen, *The Popular Culture of Shakespeare, Spenser and Jonson* (Abingdon: Routledge, 2006)

Lehnhof, Kent R., 'Incest and Empire in *The Faerie Queene*', *ELH*, 73 (2006), 215–43

Bibliography 221

Leonard, Frances McNeely, *Laughter in the Courts of Love: Comedy in Allegory from Chaucer to Spenser* (Oklahoma: Pilgrim, 1981)

Lethbridge, J. B., 'The Poetry of *The Faerie Queene*', in *Spenser in the Moment*, ed. Paul J. Hecht and J. B. Lethbridge (Madison, NJ: Fairleigh Dickinson University Press, 2015), pp. 169–216

Levin, Richard, 'The Legende of the Redcrosse Knight and Una; or, Of the Love of a Good Woman', *SEL*, 31 (1991), 1–24

Lewis, C. S., *The Discarded Image: An Introduction to Medieval and Renaissance Literature* (Cambridge: Cambridge University Press, 1970 [1967])

Lewis, C. S., *The Allegory of Love* (Oxford: Oxford University Press, 1979 [1936])

Lindvall, Terry, 'Toward a Divine Comedy: A Plagiarized History, Theology and Physiology of Christian Faith and Laughter', *Lamp-Post of the Southern California C. S. Lewis Society*, 27 (2003), 12–31

Mack, Maynard, 'The *Second Shepherds' Play*: A Reconsideration', *PMLA*, 93 (1978), 78–85

Martin, Adrienne, 'Humor and Violence in Cervantes', in *The Cambridge Companion to Cervantes* (Cambridge: Cambridge University Press, 2002), pp. 160–85

Martin, Carol, A. N., 'Authority and the Defense of Fiction: Renaissance Poetics and Chaucer's *House of Fame*', in *Refiguring Chaucer in the Renaissance*, ed. Theresa M. Krier (Gainesville: University Press of Florida), pp. 40–65

Martz, Louis L., 'The *Amoretti*: "Most Goodly Temperature"', in *Form and Convention in the Poetry of Edmund Spenser*, ed. William Nelson (New York: Columbia University Press, 1961), pp. 146–68

Mason, H. A., *To Homer through Pope: An Introduction to Homer's 'Iliad' and Pope's Translation* (London: Chatto & Windus, 1972)

McCabe, Richard A., 'Ireland: Policy, Poetics and Parody', in *The Cambridge Companion to Spenser*, ed. Andrew Hadfield (Cambridge: Cambridge University Press, 2001), pp. 60–78

McCabe, Richard A., *Spenser's Monstrous Regiment: Elizabethan Ireland and the Poetics of Difference* (Oxford: Oxford University Press, 2002)

McCabe, Richard A., 'Parody, Sympathy and Self: A Response to Donald Cheney', *Connotations*, 13 (2003), 5–22

McFaul, Tom, 'The Butterfly, the Fart and the Dwarf: The Origins of the English Laureate Micro-Epic', *Connotations*, 17 (2007/8), 144–64

McKnight, George H., *Middle English Humorous Tales in Verse* (New York: AMS Press, 1972 [1913])

Miller, David Lee, *The Poem's Two Bodies: The Poetics of the 1590 'Faerie Queene'* (Princeton: Princeton University Press, 1988)

Miller, David Lee, 'Laughing at Spenser's *Daphnaida*', *SSt*, 26 (2011), 241–50

Miller, Henry Knight, 'The Paradoxical Encomium with Special Reference to Its Vogue in England, 1600–1800', *MP*, 53 (1956), 145–78

Miller, Lewis H., Jr, 'The Ironic Mode in Books 1 and 2 of *The Faerie Queene*', *PLL*, 7 (1971), 133–49

Montrose, Louis, 'Spenser and the Elizabethan Political Imaginary', *ELH*, 69 (2002), 907–46

Morreall, John, 'Philosophy of Humor', in *The Stanford Encyclopedia of Philosophy Archive* (Winter 2016 edn), ed. Edward N. Zalta, https://plato.stanford.edu/archives/win2016/entries/humor/ (accessed May 2019)

Murillo, L. A., '*Don Quixote* as Renaissance Epic', in *Cervantes and the Renaissance*, ed. Michael D. McGaha (Easton, PA: Juan de la Cuesta, 1980), pp. 51–70

Nadal, T. W., 'Spenser's *Muiopotmos* in Relation to Chaucer's *Sir Thopas* and *The Nun's Priest's Tale*', *PMLA*, 25 (1910), 640–56

Nelson, William, *The Poetry of Edmund Spenser: A Study* (New York: Columbia University Press, 1963)

Nelson, William, *Fact or Fiction: The Dilemma of the Renaissance Storyteller* (Cambridge, MA: Harvard University Press, 1973)

Nietzsche, Friedrich, *Beyond Good and Evil*, trans. R. J. Hollingdale (London: Penguin, 2003)

Nohrnberg, James, *The Analogy of 'The Faerie Queene'* (Princeton: Princeton University Press, 1976)

Norbrook, David, *Poetry and Politics in the English Renaissance*, rev. edn (Oxford: Oxford University Press, 2002)

Nuttall, A. D., 'Spenser and Elizabethan Alienation', *Essays in Criticism*, 55 (2005), 209–25

O'Callaghan, Michelle, 'Spenser's Literary Influence', in *The Oxford Handbook of Edmund Spenser*, ed. Richard A. McCabe (Oxford: Oxford University Press, 2010), pp. 664–83

Oram, William A., 'Spenser's Audiences, 1589–91', *SP*, 100 (2003), 514–33

Oram, William A., 'Human Limitation and Spenserian Laughter', *SSt*, 30 (2015), 35–56

Orange, Linwood E., ' "All Bent to Mirth": Spenser's Humorous Wordplay', *SAQ*, 71 (1972), 539–47

Bibliography

223

Orgel, Stephen, 'Spenser from the Gutters to the Margins: An Archeology of Reading', in *The Construction of Textual Identity in Medieval and Early Modern Literature*, ed. Indira Ghose and Denis Renevey, Swiss Papers in English Language and Literature, 22 (Tübingen: Narr, 2009), pp. 125–41

Parker, Patricia, *Inescapable Romance: Studies in the Poetics of a Mode* (Princeton: Princeton University Press, 1979)

Partridge, Eric, *Shakespeare's Bawdy*, 3rd edn (London: Routledge, 1990 [1968])

Peter, John, *A Critique of 'Paradise Lost'* (New York: Columbia University Press, 1960)

Pheifer, J. D., 'Errour and Echidna in *The Faerie Queene*: A Study in Literary Tradition', in *Literature and Learning in Medieval and Renaissance England*, ed. John Scattergood (Dublin: Irish Academic Press, 1984), pp. 127–74

Pieper, Josef, *Leisure: The Basis of Culture*, trans. Alexander Dru (London: Faber and Faber, 1952)

Potkay, Adam, 'Spenser, Donne, and the Theology of Joy', *SEL*, 46 (2006), 43–66.

Prescott, Anne Lake, 'Humour and Satire in the Renaissance', in *The Cambridge History of Literary Criticism: The Renaissance*, ed. Glyn Norton (Cambridge: Cambridge University Press, 1999), pp. 284–91

Pugh, Syrithe, *Spenser and Ovid* (Aldershot: Ashgate, 2005)

Pugh, Syrithe, 'Acrasia and Bondage: Guyon's Perversion of the Ovidian Erotic in Book II of *The Faerie Queene*', in *Edmund Spenser: New and Renewed Directions*, ed. J. B. Lethbridge (Madison, NJ: Fairleigh Dickinson University Press, 2006), pp. 153–94

Pugh, Syrithe, 'Reinventing the Wheel: Spenser's "Virgilian Career"', in *Spenser in the Moment*, ed. Paul J. Hecht and J. B. Lethbridge (Madison, NJ: Fairleigh Dickinson University Press, 2015), pp. 3–34

Quilligan, Maureen, *Milton's Spenser: The Politics of Reading* (Ithaca and London: Cornell University Press, 1983)

Quilligan, Maureen, 'The Comedy of Female Authority in *The Faerie Queene*', *ELR*, 17 (1987), 151–71

Ramachandran, Ayesha, 'Clarion in the Bower of Bliss: Poetry and Politics in Spenser's "Muiopotmos"', *SSt*, 20 (2005): 77–106

Rasmussen, Mark David, '*Complaints* and *Daphnaida* (1591)', in *The Oxford Handbook of Edmund Spenser*, ed. Richard A. McCabe (Oxford: Oxford University Press, 2010), pp. 218–36

Rhu, Lawrence F., 'Romancing Eliza: The Political Decorum of Ariostan Imitation in *The Faerie Queene*', *Renaissance Papers* (1993), 31–9

Rhu, Lawrence F., 'On Cheney on Spenser's Ariosto', *Connotations*, 15 (2005), 91–6

Richard, Terry, '"Meaner Themes": Mock-Heroic and Providentialism in Cowper's Poetry', *SEL*, 34 (1994), 617–34

Risden, E. L., 'Heroic Humor in Beowulf', in *Humour in Anglo-Saxon Literature*, ed. Jonathan Wilcox (Cambridge: D. S. Brewer, 2000), pp. 71–8

Robin, Diana, 'Review of David Marsh, *Lucian and the Latins: Humor and Humanism in the Early Renaissance*', *RQ*, 53 (2003), 559–60

Sanders, Andrew, *The Short Oxford History of English Literature*, 3rd edn (Oxford: Oxford University Press, 2004)

Screech, M. A., *Laughter at the Foot of the Cross* (London: Penguin, 1997)

Screech, M. A., and Ruth Calder, 'Some Renaissance Attitudes to Laughter', in *Humanism in France*, ed. A. H. T. Levi (Manchester: Manchester University Press, 1970), pp. 216–28

Sehmby, Dalbir, 'Comic Nescience: An Experimental View of Humour and a Case for the Cultural Negotiation Function of Humour', in *Developments in Linguistic Humour Theory*, ed. Marta Dynel (Amsterdam: John Benjamins, 2013), pp. 75–102

Shroeder, John W., 'Spenser's Erotic Drama: The Orgoglio Episode', *ELH*, 29 (1962), 140–59

Silberman, Lauren, 'Spenser and Ariosto: Funny Peril and Comic Chaos', *Comparative Literature Studies*, 25 (1988), 23–34

Smuts, Aaron, 'Humor', in *Internet Encyclopedia of Philosophy*, https://iep.utm.edu/humor/#SH2a (accessed May 2019)

Solomon, Robert, 'Are the Three Stooges Funny? Soitanly!', in *Ethics and Values in the Information Age*, ed. Joel Rudinow and Anthony Graybosch (Belmont, CA: Wadsworth, 2002), pp. 604–10

Stallybrass, Peter, and Allon White, *The Politics and Poetics of Transgression* (London: Methuen, 1986)

Steinberg, Glenn A., 'Spenser's *Shepheardes Calender* and the Elizabethan Reception of Chaucer', *ELR*, 35 (2005), 31–51

Steinberg, Glenn A., 'Chaucer's Mutability in Spenser's *Mutabilitie Cantos*', *SEL*, 46 (2006), 27–42

Stephens, Dorothy, 'Spenser's Language(s): Linguistic Theory and Poetic Diction', in *The Oxford Handbook of Edmund Spenser*, ed. Richard A. McCabe (Oxford: Oxford University Press, 2010), pp. 367–84

Bibliography 225

Sterne, Virginia F., *Gabriel Harvey: A Study of His Life, Marginalia, and Library* (Oxford: Clarendon Press, 1979)

Strong, Roy, *The Cult of Elizabeth: Elizabethan Portraiture and Pageantry* (London: Thames and Hudson, 1977)

Sullivan, Garrett, and Linda Woodbridge, 'Popular Culture in Print', in *The Cambridge Companion to English Literature, 1500–1600*, ed. Arthur F. Kinney (Cambridge: Cambridge University Press, 2000), pp. 265–86

Suttie, Paul, 'Edmund Spenser's Political Pragmatism', *SP*, 95 (1998), 56–76

Thomas, Keith, 'The Place of Laughter in Tudor and Stuart England', *TLS*, 21 (1977), 77–81

Tigges, Wim, 'Romance and Parody', in *Companion to Middle English Romance*, ed. Henk Aertsen and Alasdair A. MacDonald (Amsterdam: VU University Press, 1990), pp. 129–51

Tilley, M. P. *A Dictionary of the Proverbs in England in the Sixteenth and Seventeenth Centuries* (Ann Arbor: University of Michigan Press, 1950)

Trigg, Stephanie, 'Chaucer's Influence and Reception', in *The Yale Companion to Chaucer*, ed. Seth Lerer (New Haven: Yale University Press, 2006), pp. 297–323

Tuell, Anne Kimball, 'Note on Spenser's Clarion', *Modern Language Notes*, 36 (1921), 182–3

Tuve, Rosemond, *Allegorical Imagery: Some Medieval Books and Their Posterity* (Princeton: Princeton University Press, 1966)

Vaught, Jennifer C., 'Spenser's Dialogic Voice in Book I of *The Faerie Queene*', *SEL*, 41 (2001), 71–89

Vaught, Jennifer C., 'The Mummers' Play *St George and the Fiery Dragon* and Book I of Spenser's *Faerie Queene*', *LATCH*, 3 (2010), 85–106

Villeponteaux, Mary, ' "Not as women wonted be": Spenser's Amazon Queen', in *Dissing Elizabeth: Negative Representations of Gloriana*, ed. Julia M. Walker (Durham, NC: Duke University Press, 1998), pp. 209–25

Walls, Kathryn, 'The "Cupid and Psyche" Fable of Apuleius and Guyon's Underworld Adventure in *The Faerie Queene* II.vii.3–viii.8', *SSt*, 26 (2011), 45–73.

Walls, Kathryn, *God's Only Daughter: Spenser's Una as the Invisible Church* (Manchester: Manchester University Press, 2013)

Walls, Kathryn, 'Spenser and the "Medieval" Past', in *Spenser in the Moment*, ed. Paul J. Hecht and J. B. Lethbridge (Madison, NJ: Fairleigh Dickinson University Press, 2015), pp. 35–66

Bibliography

Watkins, W. B. C., *Shakespeare and Spenser* (Princeton: Princeton University Press, 1950)

Weinberg, Bernard, *A History of Literary Criticism in the Italian Renaissance*, 2 vols (Chicago: University of Chicago Press, 1961)

Weiss, Judith, ' "The Courteous Warrior": Epic, Romance and Comedy in *Boeve de Haumtone*', in *Boundaries in Medieval Romance*, ed. Neil Cartlidge (Cambridge: D. S. Brewer, 2008), pp. 149–60

West, Michael, 'Spenser's Art of War: Chivalric Allegory, Military Technology, and the Elizabethan Mock-Heroic Sensibility', *RQ*, 41 (1988), 654–704

Wiggens, Peter DeSa, 'Spenser's Use of Ariosto: Imitation and Allusion in Book I of *The Faerie Queene*', *RQ*, 44 (1991), 257–79

Wilson-Okamura, David Scott, *Spenser's International Style* (Cambridge: Cambridge University Press, 2013)

Wofford, Susanne Lindgren, 'Gendering Allegory: Spenser's Bold Reader and the Emergence of Character in *The Faerie Queene III*', *Criticism*, 30 (1988), 1–21

Wolfe, Jessica, 'Chapman's Ironic Homer', *College Literature*, 35 (2008), 151–86

Wood, Rufus, *Metaphor and Belief in 'The Faerie Queene'* (Basingstoke: Macmillan, 1997)

Woodcock, Matthew, *Fairy in 'The Faerie Queene': Renaissance Elf-Fashioning and Elizabethan Myth-Making* (Aldershot: Ashgate, 2004)

Index

Note: 'n.' after a page reference indicates the number of a note on that page. Literary works can be found under authors' names (excepting works by Spenser, works with multiple authors, and works of unknown authorship, which are listed by title alphabetically).

Adamson, Sylvia 40n.30
Addison, Joseph 58, 60, 99
Adelman, Janet 114–15, 117n.14,
 118–19, 127, 135
Adlington, William 43–4
allegory 16–17, 44, 54, 63–5, 81, 89,
 105, 115, 125–8, 139,
 154–5n.38, 193–205
Allen, Don Cameron 47n.47
alliteration 19, 25n.62, 27n.69, 74
Amoret 140n.8, 148, 154, 156n.42, 192
Amoretti 4, 139n.6, 142, 166, 173
Anderson, Judith H. 3, 114, 116,
 145n.21, 147–8, 171n.12,
 172n.15, 175n.23
Apuleius, Lucius 34, 37n.21, 40–4, 64,
 76–7
archaism *see* narrator, Spenser's
Archimago 39, 67, 69, 89–93, 102,
 103n.65, 109n.81, 122–3,
 126–7, 168, 176, 178, 186, 195
Argante 131, 156n.42, 158, 160–1,
 170, 172
Ariosto, Ludovico, *Orlando furioso* 2,
 3n.7, 57, 64–5, 83, 95, 97n.48,
 98n.51, 138–9, 143–4, 146,
 158, 165n.51, 179, 189n.53

Aristotle 7–9, 12, 33–4, 37n.21, 52,
 64n.100, 75n.137, 131
Arthur 3n.7, 92n.35, 106, 134n.52,
 142–9, 166, 174–5
Arthurian romance 62, 63n.95
 like Sir Thopas 18–19, 62, 140,
 145–8
 see also Malory, Sir Thomas
Ascham, Roger 63n.95
Aston, Margaret 90n.28, 124n.31
Auerbach, Erich 72n.125, 73, 74n.134,
 76, 77n.141
Augustine of Hippo, Saint 113, 142

Baker, David J. 171n.11
Bakhtin, Mikhail 9–10, 12n.30,
 13n.34, 32, 63n.96, 66–7, 78,
 189
Bale, John 55, 69
Barasch, Frances K. 20n.53
Barclay, Alexander 120–1
Basil, St 66
Beard, Mary 170n.9
Beaumont, Francis 51n.57, 61
Belphoebe 141, 170, 186–92, 196
Bennett, J. W. 147n.25
Benson, Larry D. 117n.13

228 *Index*

Berger, Harry, Jr 2, 23n.57, 89, 93n.38, 103n.65, 114–15, 129n.40, 162
Bergson, Henri 5, 7, 9n.24, 11n.28, 163
Berleth, Richard J. 141, 191
Berry, Craig A. 24n.59, 82–3, 138n.4, 148n.25, 179n.29
Bettelheim, Bruno 133n.50
Betts, Hannah 186n.45, 188, 190
Bevington, David 67, 68n.113
Bieman, Elizabeth 139n.6
Blackburn, William 178, 179n.31
Blank, Paula 25n.62, 25n.64
Bliss, Lee 58n.79
Blisset, William 149n.29
Boccaccio, Giovanni 43, 160, 188n.49
Boiardo, Matteo Maria 43
Book of Common Prayer 113n.2
Booth, Wayne 110n.84
Borris, Kenneth 81n.2, 101n.60
Bowers, R. H. 56n.73
Bracciolini, Poggio *see* jestbooks
Braggadochio 33, 39, 84, 86, 92, 94, 153, 186–9
Brewer, Derek 9n.24, 37n.22, 39n.26, 72, 149
Briggs, Julia 32n.6
Britomart 141–4, 152–7, 166, 170, 176–80, 197
Broich, Ulrich 85n.13
Brooks-Davies, Douglas 129n.42, 182
Bullinger, Heinrich 128n.36, 192n.59
Bunyan, John 104n.68
Burke, Charles B. 2n.4
Burrow, Colin 1n.3
Burrow, J. A. 56n.74, 72n.125, 74n.134, 141n.9, 147n.25, 151
Burton, Robert 204
Busirane 141, 154, 156n.42, 176, 178
Butler, Chris 117n.13
Byron, Lord [George Gordon] 130

Cain, Thomas H. 36n.18
Calder, Ruth 66n.105

Calidore 101n.62
Callaghan, Dympna 51n.59
Calvin, John 49n.54, 69–71, 102n.64, 128n.36
Camille, Michael 72n.125
Campana, Joseph 35n.16
Carroll, D. Allen 36n.18
Carver, Robert H. F. 43n.40
Castelvetro, Lodovico 34n.9
Castiglione, Baldassare 26, 34–7
Cavanagh, Sheila T. 147n.23, 153n.36
Cazamian, Louis 1
Cecil, William (The Lord Burghley) 24–5, 47, 138
Cervantes, Miguel de 32, 39, 43, 52, 61, 65, 103, 130, 179
Chaloner, Sir Thomas 32n.3, 90n.27
Chapman, George 58–60, 77, 99n.57, 205
Charissa 135
Chaucer, Geoffrey 2, 24–7, 53, 55–6, 72, 83, 118n.16, 119n.19, 166
  House of Fame, The 175–81
  'Knight's Tale, The' 57, 72
  'Merchant's Tale, The' 39, 61n.90, 158
  'Miller's Tale, The' 61n.90, 112
  'Nun's Priest's Tale, The' 46n.46, 61n.90
  'Tale of Sir Thopas, The' 19, 27n.69, 83n.9, 95n.45, 116, 145–8
  Troilus and Criseyde 55n.65, 56, 72–3, 140, 149–52
Cheney, Donald 3, 82–3, 88n.23, 94n.41, 97n.50, 110n.85, 117n.15, 143n.14, 144n.16, 152
chivalric romance 3, 18–19, 55, 60–6, 120, 124n.30, 145, 184, 197, 199, 204
Christianity and humour 72–7, 101–2
  in the Middle Ages 57, 66–9, 71
  after the Reformation 31–4, 63, 69–71, 99–100
Church, R. W. 2n.4, 103, 170

Index

Cicero, Marcus Tullius 8, 25n.63, 35
Clark, Judith Petterson 2n.6
Clark, Sandra S. 155n.39
Coles, Kimberly Anne 171n.12
comic theory 5–7
  ambiguity 10–12
  bias against humour 4, 8–9n.24–5,
    11–12, 14–15, 77–8
  play 12–16
  reduction 7–10
  see also Bakhtin, Mikhail
Cooper, Helen 54, 60, 61n.91,
  116n.10, 175
Cormier, Raymond 61n.91
Cowley, Abraham 19
Craig, Martha 2n.6
Crane, Walter 192
Cross, Claire 169n.6
Cupid 42–3, 44n.41, 52, 64, 140–2,
  155
  in Amores 53

Daphnaida 36n.19
Davenant, William 19
Davies, Sir John 166
Dedicatory Sonnets see
  Faerie Queene, The
Delany, Sheila 119n.19
Deloney, Thomas 13
Democritus 9
Diana 20, 42, 130n.45, 133, 141, 201–4
Dillon, Janette 33n.8, 58n.79
Dinshaw, Carolyn 118n.16
Dives and Pauper 68–71
Dodge, R. E. N. 144n.16
Donne, John 75n.137
dragon see Red Crosse
Dryden, John 39, 57, 166
Du Bellay, Joachim 82–3
Dudley, Robert (Earl of Leicester)
  47–8
Duessa 27, 88, 96–7, 101–2, 113,
  115–16, 119, 126–34, 194–5
Duffy, Eamon 129n.43

Dundas, Judith 48n.52. 86n.14
dwarf 133–4

E. K. 4, 25–6, 36, 39–41, 62, 118n.16
Eastman, Max 14
Eco, Umberto 129–30
Edward VI 90
Edwards, Michael 49n.54
Elias, Norbert 33n.6
Elizabeth I 3, 37, 62, 130n.45, 154,
  168–78, 180–1, 202
  and Belphoebe 170, 186–92
  and Gloriana 83, 169n.4, 170,
    174–5, 180, 184–6, 202
  and Lucifera 171, 173, 181–6
epic poem 3n.7, 16, 18, 20–1, 29, 31,
  57, 59, 62, 75–6, 79–111, 138,
  199
  trumpet metaphor 27, 29, 82–3,
    86, 101, 105–6, 110, 176–7,
    180–1
  see also mock-epic; narrator,
    Spenser's; neoclassical
    criticism
Epithalamion 114, 121
epyllion 32, 50–1, 166
Erasmus, Desiderius 36–7, 75–7,
  114
  Moriae encomium (Praise of
    Folly) 32, 35, 42n.35, 44,
    47–8, 74–5, 78, 100n.59,
    137, 141n.11, 152–3,
    173n.19, 180n.33, 205
Erickson, Wayne 23–5
Errour see Red Crosse
Esolen, Anthony M. 3n.7, 4n.11,
  24n.59, 26–8, 56, 86n.15,
  89n.25, 92n.35, 104n.69, 110,
  171n.11, 174n.23, 195n.4
Evans, Robert O. 2n.4

fabliauesque humour 18, 27, 33, 39,
  55, 61n.90, 112, 153, 158–9,
  165–6

230 *Index*

Faerie Queene, The
Book I
Proem I, 1 24, 26, 52, 64, 83, 86,
101, 101n.62, 138; **Proem I,
2** 82; **Proem I, 3** 141; **Proem
I, 4** 168, 180; **I.i.1** 40, 71, 82,
116–17, 194; **I.i.2** 80–1, 85,
86n.15, 87; **I.i.3** 83–4, 108n.79;
I.i.4 194; **I.i.6** 117, 117n.15,
121; **I.i.9** 83; **I.i.11** 85; **I.i.12**
88, 117, 198; **I.i.17** 88; **I.i.19**
87–8, 123; **I.i.21** 119, 191n.58;
I.i.22 96, 119; **I.i.23** 95–6, 105;
I.i.27 89; **I.i.28** 88; **I.i.30** 88,
122n.27; **I.i.31** 89, 98; **I.i.32**
89; **I.i.35** 102; **I.i.45** 124; **I.i.48**
97n.50; **I.i.49** 122; **I.i.51–3**
116; **I.i.53–4** 119; **I.ii.*Arg.*** 124;
I.ii.4 95n.45; **I.ii.6** 122, 127,
87; **I.ii.7** 87, 124; **I.ii.10–11**
91–2, 109n.81; **I.ii.12** 91; I.
ii.16 96, 98, 104; **I.ii.21–2** 97;
I.ii.24 129; **I.ii.26** 97; **I.ii.27**
97n.49; **I.ii.28** 97, 101; **I.ii.30**
97, 101; **I.ii.31** 98; **I.iii.24** 92;
I.iii.26–7 92–3; **I.iii.32** 93;
I.iv.5 185, 195; **I.iv.8** 173;
I.iv.10 180, 183; **I.iv.11** 182; I.
iv.14 185; **I.iv.15** 184–5; **I.iv.16**
183; **I.iv.18–35** 184; **I.iv.37**
94, 183, 185; **I.v.1** 106; **I.v.2–3**
105–6; **I.v.6** 105; **I.v.8–9** 23,
105; **I.v.12** 145n.19; **I.v.16** 106,
184–5; **I.v.26** 129; **I.v.46** 185;
I.v.51–3 169, 185–6;
I.vi.11 140; **I.vi.21** 95n.45;
I.vi.22 159; **I.vii.4–7** 130–3;
I.vii.6–18 131–2n.48; **I.vii.11**
131, 196; **I.vii.14** 145n.19; I.
vii.19 133; **I.vii.32** 92n.35; I.
viii.5 132; **I.viii.10** 106–7; I.
viii.11 108; I.viii.13 95n.45; I.
viii.16 106; **I.viii.22** 106; I.
viii.24 106; **I.viii.46–8** 195;

I.ix.**10–12** 134n.52, 139; I.
ix.**12–15** 145; I.ix.**24** 98n.52;
I.ix.**35** 98n.52; I.ix.**38** 90; I.
ix.**53** 86, 100; **I.x.17** 103n.65;
I.x.18 101; **I.x.29** 135; **I.x.31**
135; **I.x.35** 101n.60; **I.x.47**
199n.9; **I.x.53–67** 199n.9;
I.x.60 110; **I.x.60–2** 101n.62;
I.x.65–6 83, 88n.24, 91n.31,
94; **I.xi.4** 108; **I.xi.5** 111; **I.xi.7**
29n.75, 110; **I.xi.9** 111; **I.xi.10**
108, 200; **I.xi.13** 108; **I.xi.15**
92n.35, 109n.81; **I.xi.16–17**
111; **I.xi.18** 110–11; **I.xi.19**
110; **I.xi.20** 108, 111; **I.xi.22**
107–8; **I.xi.25** 111; **I.xi.29** 111;
I.xi.30 109, 199; **I.xi.39** 104,
106; **I.xi.41** 111; **I.xi.46** 111; I.
xi.51 135; **I.xi.55** 111 n. 86; I.
xii.4 102; **I.xii.8** 101; **I.xii.11**
101, 109; **I.xii.7–12** 100; I.
xii.14–15 102; **I.xii.16** 102; I.
xii.27 129; **I.xii.32–3** 103 n.
65; **I.xii.40–1** 136
Book II
Proem II, 4 176; **II.i.33** 184; II.
iii.4–21 186; **II.iii.9** 188; II.
iii.22–31 186; **II.iii.33** 188; II.
iii.35 187; **II.iii.37–8** 188; II.
iii.40 189; **II.iii.42** 186, 189;
II.iii.5 157; **II.vi.6** 140; **II.x.72**
40, 88n.24; **II.xii.68** 119n.19
Book III
Proem III, 2 170; **III.i.4** 153; **III.i.6**
143; **III.i.11** 143; **II.i.13** 143,
144n.16; **III.i.17** 144; **III.i.19**
152; **III.i.42–62** 153–4; **III.i.65**
155; **III.ii.*Arg.*** 176; **III.ii.1–2**
176; **III.ii.3** 176, 178, 180; III.
ii.5–16 154; **III.ii.7–8** 177;
III.ii.9 178; **III.ii.15** 176; III.
ii.18 178–9; **III.ii.19** 177–8,
180; **III.ii.20** 177–8; **III.ii.21**
177–8, 181; **III.ii.22** 157, 180;

Index

231

III.ii.26 141, 155; III.ii.27 153;
III.ii.30 155; III.ii.30–3 156;
III.ii.35 157; III.ii.36–8 156;
III.ii.40–2 154–6; III.ii.45
155, 197; III.ii.50 156; III.ii.52
156; III.iii.1–2 139; III.iii.5
157; III.iii.19 154; III.iii.24
155n.40; III.iv. 8–11 154; III.
iv.26 139; III.iv.46–50 144–5;
III.iv.53–61 145–8; III.v.11
145; III.v.51 65, 190, 196; III.
vi.1 189; III.vi.2 141, 191n.57;
III.vi.7 191; III.vi.8 141; III.
vi.15 140; III.vi.19–25 42, 141;
III.vi.26 141; III.vi.34 114;
III.vi.41 113; III.vi.49–51 43;
III.vii.17 145; III.vii. 27–31
158; III.vii.38–44 158; III.
vii.47–50 156n.42, 172; III.
vii.55–61 159; III.vii.57–8
140, 159; III.viii.1 165; III.
viii.5–9 162–3, 196; III.viii.14
164; III.viii.23 119n.19, 162;
III.viii.23–4 161–2; III.viii.27
159–60; III.viii.28 160–1; III.
viii.33–4 164; III.viii.35 163;
III.viii.35–41 42; III.viii.37
164; III.viii.43 165; III.viii.44
116; III.viii.47 158; III.viii.51
160; III.ix.6 140, 159, 165; III.
ix.11–17 154; III.ix.27–52
154; III.ix.35 161; III.ix.53
160; III.x.5 141; III.x.12 141;
III.x.44 160; III.xi.29–46
156n.42; III.xi.32 119n.19,
140; III.xi.44 42, 139; III.xi.54
173; III.xii.23 141; III.xii.38
174; III.xii.47 83n.6
Book IV
Proem IV, 1–2 138; IV.i.7 154; IV.
ii.25–7 160; IV.ii.32 56; IV.
iv.13 86; IV.v.18–19 140, 159;
IV.vi.32 140; IV.vii.*Arg.* 192;
IV.vii.6 192, 196; IV.vii.8–9

186n.44, 192; IV.vii.20 156; IV.
vii.24 140; IV.vii.32 192; IV.
vii.35–6 192; IV.vii.40 192; IV.
viii.14 192; IV.viii.21–2 148;
IV.viii.23–4 149; IV.viii.29
148; IV.viii.30 149; IV.x.47
140, 142; IV.x.56 140n.7,
140n.8; IV.xi.5 139, 142
Book V
Proem V, 9 101n.62; V.ii.10 194; V.
vii.1–24 44; V.vii.38 157
Book VI
VI.ix.36 102n.62; VI.x18 102;
Book VII
VII.vi.8 199; VII.vi.12 199; VII.
vi.31 42; VII.vi.38–55 194,
201–5; VII.vi.46 191; VII.vii.9
56n.71; VII.viii.1–2 201
Dedicatory Sonnets
DS 2 24; DS 8 184; DS 14 26
Faunus 20, 194, 201–5
Fish, Stanley 98–9, 125n.32, 128
Florimell 3n.7, 42, 144–8, 156n.42,
157–65
false Florimell 162–4, 196
Foster, Verna A. 67n.108
Foxe, John, *Acts and Monuments*
55n.67, 90, 126, 130
Fradubio 97–8
Freeman, Louise Gilbert 4n.11,
193n.1, 194, 200–3
Freud, Sigmund 5, 7n.18, 12–14, 168,
192
Froude, James A. 15n.39
Fry, Christopher 12
Frye, Northrop 11–13, 118n.17, 121,
125
Fudge, Erica 10n.27, 34n.11, 70n.119,
71n.124

Gaisser, Julia Haig 43n.40
Garden of Adonis 65, 113, 134, 145, 195
Gascoigne, George 34, 40, 70n.121,
173, 180

232 *Index*

George, Saint
 post-Reformation 90–1, 110, 183n.37
 Saint George's Day 183–4
 see also Red Crosse
Gibbs, Donna 139n.6
Gilbert, Allan H. 2n.4, 89n.25, 135n.54, 144n.16
Gill, Roma 51n.59
Glauce 39, 140, 152–7, 197
Gloriana 83, 140, 148, 174
 see also Elizabeth I
Golding, Arthur 50
Gower, John 140–1
Greene, Robert 56
Greene, Thomas 25–6
Greenham, Richard 71
Grindal, Edmund (Archbishop of Canterbury) 169, 192n.59
grotesquerie 20–1, 57, 60, 63, 67, 73–6, 103–6, 170–3, 181, 192, 195
Groves, Beatrice 90, 121n.24
Gurevich, Aron 13n.34, 67, 72n.125, 73n.131, 74n.134
Guyon 115n.5, 142–4, 149, 152, 186

Hackett, Helen 169n.4, 169n.6, 171n.11, 184n.40
Hadfield, Andrew 4, 28, 38, 40n.29, 91n.32, 102n.64, 116, 125n.33, 136n.55, 161n.45, 163–4
Hamilton, A. C. 84, 92n.35, 95n.45, 97, 105n.71, 107, 134n.51, 135n.52, 140n.7, 144n.16, 145n.21, 146n.23, 147n.24, 153n.36, 154–5, 155n.39, 156, 172, 183–4, 187, 192, 203n.16
Hardin, Richard F. 91n.29, 91n.30
Harington, John 31n.1, 32n.3, 45, 55n.68, 143n.15, 173n.19
Harvey, Gabriel 35, 38, 41, 45
 Letters, Spenser-Harvey 18, 35–7, 62n.95, 204–5

Hazlitt, William 142
Hecht, Paul J. 27n.69
Helgerson, Richard 24n.59, 101n.62
Hellenore 33, 39, 141, 158–61, 165
Hendrix, Laurel 140
Heraclitus 9
Herrick, Marvin T. 8n.20
Higgins, Anne 147n.25
Hillman, David 33n.6
Hobbes, Thomas 5, 8n.21, 13, 57, 60
Hoffman, Donald L. 63, 85n.11
Holcomb, Chris 35n.13
Homer 34, 42, 58–9, 82–3, 99, 103
 Pseudo-Homer 37n.21, 44–5
Hooper, John (Bishop) 90, 124
Hopkins, David 52n.61
Horace 93
Hough, Graham 20, 158n.43, 163
House of Alma 195–6
House of Holiness 101n.60, 125, 134–5
House of Pride 94, 169, 172, 181–6
Huizinga, Johan 12n.30, 14n.38, 15n.40
humanist wit 34–54, 75–9
humility topos *see* narrator, Spenser's
Hunt, Leigh 20n.52, 21
Hurtado de Mendoza, Diego 38n.24
Huston, J. Dennis 2 n. 6, 84n.10

Iambicum trimetrum 36
idolatry 123–34, 169n.4, 169n.6
Incarnation 73
invisible Church 87, 126n.34
Ireland 103n.67, 170, 173
Isis Church 44

Jacobson, Howard 80
Javitch, Daniel 32n.3, 95n.46, 165n.51
Jerome, Saint 142n.13
jestbooks 31, 37–9, 43
Johnson, Paul 186n.44
Johnson, Samuel 32, 39–40, 58
Jones, Richard Foster 25n.63, 94n.43

Index

233

Jonson, Ben 15–16, 25, 39–40, 45, 76
Joubert, Laurent 10, 70–1, 78

Kahrl, Stanley J. 37n.20
Kant, Immanuel 5, 13, 14n.36
Kaske, Carol 109, 132n.49, 134,
  191n.57
Kaula, David 76n.138
Kay, Sarah 61n.91, 65n.102
Keach, William 41n.32, 51n.57–9
Kenney, E. J. 50
King, Andrew 124n.30, 147n.25
King, John 91n.31
King, Ros 58n.79, 60, 76
Kolve, V. A. 13n.34, 67–8, 72n.125,
  108n.78
Krier, Theresa M. 187, 188n.51,
  203n.18
Kucich, Greg 20n.52, 21

Lamb, Mary Ellen 18n.45, 90n.27
Langland, William 55, 74, 76, 87n.20,
  104n.68, 200n.12
Latimer, Hugh 129n.41
Lehnhof, Kent R. 170n.11
Leicester, Earl of see Dudley, Robert
Leonard, Frances McNeely 96n.48,
  154n.38
Lethbridge, J. B. 107n.76, 154–5 n.38
'Letter to Raleigh' 16–18, 29n.75, 62,
  83–5, 128n.37, 190, 198, 205
Levin, Richard 114, 119n.20, 136n.55
Lewis, C. S. 4n.11, 20, 22, 125–6,
  175
Lindvall, Terry 66n.105
Lodge, Thomas 51n.57, 188
Longinus 42n.36, 82
Lord Burghley see Cecil, William
Lucian of Samosata 32, 34, 38, 41–2,
  44, 51–2, 76–7
Lucifera 94, 169–72, 180–6, 195
Lust ('greedie lust') 131, 140, 156n.42,
  192, 196, 198
Lydgate, John 56

Mack, Maynard 68
McCabe, Richard A. 3n.7, 16, 23n.57,
  45n.44, 86, 91n.32, 98n.53,
  103n.67, 147–8, 170, 171n.12,
  173–4
McFaul, Tom 47n.48, 49n.54
McKnight, George H. 55n.66
MacLachlan, Hugh 94n.42
Malbecco 27, 33, 39, 158–9, 165
Malory, Sir Thomas 60n.89, 63–4,
  85n.11
Mantuan (Baptista Mantuanus)
  see Barclay, Alexander
Marlowe, Christopher 50–1, 188
marriage 113–16, 121, 130, 134,
  136, 138, 142n.13, 144, 170,
  185n.44, 192
Martin, Adrienne 103n.67
Martin, Carol, A. N. 181n.34
Martz, Louis L. 139n.6, 166n.53,
  173n.18
Marx, Karl 169
Mason, H. A. 85n.13
medieval drama 55, 57, 67–9, 108n.78
'Sermon against Miracle-plays, A'
  66–8
melancholy, danger of 71, 102, 204–5
  see also Red Crosse, sadness
Meredith, George 11n.29
Merlin 154, 157, 176–80
Miller, David Lee 36n.19, 171n.11
Miller, Henry Knight 44n.42
Miller, Lewis H. 2–3n.6, 23n.57
Milton, John 1, 4, 98–9, 125n.32
mock-encomium 32, 44–9, 78
  see also Erasmus
mock-epic 3n.7, 4, 32, 44–9, 85n.13,
  86, 98
  see also violence, comic
Montrose, Louis 171n.12
More, Sir Thomas 14–15, 36–7, 69, 75
Morreall, John 5n.13, 14n.36–8
Mother Hubberds Tale 4, 39, 41, 204–5
Motteux, Peter 32n.3

Index

Muiopotmos 4, 44–9, 85–6
Mulcaster, Richard 70n.122
Munday, Anthony 66n.105
Murillo, L. A. 65n.103
Musaeus Grammaticus 51

Nadal, T. W. 49
narrator, Spenser's 3, 17, 22–7, 105–6,
    110, 166, 176–7, 179
  archaic and rustic diction 25–7
  epic ambition 29–30, 82–6
  humility 23–7, 86n.15, 178,
    180
  pathos 23, 53, 165
  reductive moralising 20, 23, 54,
    105, 139, 148, 149, 160–1, 176,
    195, 198
  unreliable praise 23, 85, 89, 123,
    138, 143–4, 152, 159, 170,
    178–80, 184, 189
  see also Spenser, Edmund
Nashe, Thomas 39–41, 43, 45, 52,
    62n.95, 76–7
Nelson, William 3n.6, 24n.59, 47n.47,
    63–4, 91n.29, 199n.9, 200n.10,
    203n.16
neoclassical criticism 57–60, 62, 72,
    77, 79, 85n.13, 166
  satirical reception of Spenser
    19–21
Nietzsche, Friedrich 112
Nohrnberg, James 107n.76
Norbrook, David 108n.77, 170–1n.11,
    174, 175n.24
Nuttall, A. D. 24n.59, 63–4, 200

O'Callaghan, Michelle 96n.47
Oram, William A. 4n.11, 23n.57,
    24n.59, 41n.33, 137n.1,
    159n.44, 161n.45, 190n.55,
    203n.18
Orange, Linwood E. 3n.6
Orgel, Stephen 168n.2

Orgoglio 106–8, 131–4, 196
Osselton, Noel 25n.62, 27
Ovid (Publius Ovidius Naso) 42, 46,
    49–54, 64, 97n.48, 106n.72,
    132–3, 137, 166
  Pseudo-Ovid 44

Paglia, Camille 156n.42
Paridell 112, 116, 141, 154, 157–8,
    160–1
Parker, Matthew 185n.44
Parker, Patricia 83n.9, 165n.51
Partridge, Eric 119n.19
pastoral 26–7, 48, 60–2, 81, 83,
    93–103, 158
Paul, the Apostle 48, 91, 112, 122
Perkins, William 69, 70n.119
Peter, John 98
Petrarchism 4, 33, 51, 57, 160, 163–4,
    166n.53, 188–9
Petronius 37n.21
Pheifer, J. D. 118n.18
Pieper, Josef 9n.25
Plato 42n.36
  Neoplatonism 148, 174, 201
play, literary 3n.7, 15n.40, 17–18
  see also comic theory; wordplay
Pope, Alexander 21, 58–9, 85n.13,
    96n.47, 99
Potkay, Adam 71n.123
Prescott, Anne Lake 41n.32,
    77n.142
Preston, Thomas 33n.8
Prudentius 105, 195
Pugh, Syrithe 52n.60, 114–15,
    179n.31
puns *see* wordplay
Puttenham, George 8, 31n.1,
    62n.93, 153

Quilligan, Maureen 40n.29, 91n.33,
    147n.25, 186–7, 191n.58
Quintilian 8, 35

Index

Rabelais, François 22, 32, 39–40, 43, 52, 76
Raleigh, Sir Walter 26, 186n.44, 192
  see also 'Letter to Raleigh'
Ramachandran, Ayesha 47n.48
Rasmussen, Mark David 146n.23
Rastell, John 37
Red Crosse
  analogy with poet 82–6, 185
  and Archimago 91–3, 102, 103n.65, 109n.81, 122–3, 126–7
  and Braggadochio 84, 86, 92, 94
  clownishness, rusticity 81, 83–6, 88, 94–103
  defeat of dragon 100–11
  defeat of Errour 80–1, 87–9, 95–7, 104–5, 117–23, 135, 198
  and Duessa 96–7, 101–2, 113, 115–16, 119, 126–134
  sadness 71, 80–1, 89–90, 98n.52, 100–2
  as Saint George 90–2, 94, 97, 110–11, 120–3, 183–4
Rhu, Lawrence F. 3n.7, 138n.4
Richard, Terry 98n.54
Riley, Anthony W. 169n.7
Risden, E. L. 106n.72
Roberts, William 20n.52
Robin, Diana 42n.35
Roche, Thomas P., Jr 146n.22, 148n.27
Roman de la rose, Le 65, 155, 189, 190, 196
Romantic criticism 20–1, 58

salvation 21, 68, 100, 102–3, 133, 109, 199
Sanders, Andrew 143–4
Sansfoy 96–7, 104–5, 116
Satyrane 140, 157–61, 164–5
Schopenhauer, Arthur 5, 11n.28, 13–14, 193n.1
Screech, M. A. 66n.105, 75n.137
Sehmby, Dalbir 9n.25, 11–12

Shakespeare, William 12, 14, 19–20, 32, 39–41, 43, 50–51, 58, 67, 76, 106n.73, 146, 150, 164, 187n.47
Shelton, Thomas 32n.3
Shepheardes Calender, The 4, 25–7, 39n.27, 41n.31, 83–4, 137, 146, 149, 191
  see also E. K.
Shroeder, John W. 97n.48, 131–2, 134
Sidney, Sir Philip 8n.20, 39–40, 43, 54–55, 56n.73, 60–2, 171, 180, 185
Silberman, Lauren 2–3, 144n.16, 144n.18
Silenus 75
Skelton, John 37–8
Smith, Henry 115
Smuts, Aaron 13n.35, 14n.36, 14n.38
Socrates 75, 77n.141
Solomon, Robert 13n.35
Spenser, Edmund
  Colin Clout 83n.6, 84, 102n.62, 205
  'Immerito' 36
  letters see Harvey, Gabriel; 'Letter to Raleigh'
  self-satire 48, 82–6, 174, 180, 185
  see also narrator, Spenser's
Squire of Dames 140, 157–9, 161, 165
Stallybrass, Peter 192n.60
Statius, Publius Papinius 45
Steadman, John M. 87n.19, 118n.18
Steinberg, Glenn A. 24n.59
Stephens, Dorothy 25n.62, 165
Sterne, Virginia F. 35n.13, 38n.23
Stoll, Abraham 28
Strong, Roy 62n.93, 183–4
Stubbes, Phillip 69n.117
Sullivan, Garrett 33n.7, 38n.22
Suttie, Paul 28n.73, 102n.65, 110n.83, 171, 172n.14

Tasso, Torquato 34n.9, 138
Teskey, Gordon 196n.5, 198

236   *Index*

Thomas, Keith 70n.119
Tigges, Wim 61n.91
Tilley, M. P. 106n.73
Timias 95n.45, 190, 192
tragicomedy 9, 12, 14–15, 32–3, 49,
    50–2, 57–8, 60, 67, 72, 76, 100,
    133–4, 149, 151, 158
Trigg, Stephanie 55n.68
Trompart *see* Braggadochio
Troyes, Chrétien de 65
Tuell, Anne Kimball 47n.48, 86n.18
Tuve, Rosemond 194n.3

Una 87–8, 92–3, 97n.50, 100–3,
    111n.86, 116, 123–7, 135–6,
    175n.23, 194
Upton, John 20, 101
Urquhart, Sir Thomas 32n.3

Vaught, Jennifer C. 90n.29, 98n.51,
    108n.79, 109n.81, 184n.42
Venus 42, 140–2, 191n.57, 195
    in *Venus and Adonis* 50–1
Vida, Marco Girolamo 45
Villeponteaux, Mary 171n.12, 172n.16
violence, comic 38–9, 43–6, 52–3,
    67, 88–9, 96, 98–9, 103–11,
    106n.72, 118–20
Viret, Pierre 69n.118, 70
Virgil 29, 34, 83, 98n.51–2, 117n.15,
    179n.31
    pseudo-Virgil 44–6, 155, 156n.41
    see also Virgils Gnat

Virgils Gnat 4, 45–9, 85, 95–6, 147
Virgin Mary 129–30
virginity 74, 119, 126n.34, 163, 167,
    171n.12, 173, 182, 191, 196
Voragine, Jacobus de 90n.28, 120

Walls, Kathryn 40n.29, 44n.41,
    85n.12, 87–8, 89n.26, 92n.36,
    93n.38–9, 102n.64, 111n.86,
    115n.7, 123–5, 136n.55,
    202n.15
Warton, Joseph 57–8
Watkins, W. B. C. 2n.4
Webbe, William 25, 26n.65, 70
Weinberg, Bernard 138n.2
Weiss, Judith 61n.91
West, Michael 104n.69, 111n.86
White, Allon 192n.60
Wiggens, Peter DeSa 138n.4
Wilson, R. Rawdon 15n.40
Wilson, Thomas 35, 55, 107
Wilson-Okamura, David Scott 29–30,
    110n.85
Wofford, Susanne Lindgren 155n.38,
    165n.52
Wolfe, Jessica 59, 99n.56–7
Wood, Rufus 96n.47
Woodbridge, Linda 33n.7, 38n.22,
    38n.24
Woodcock, Matthew 63n.95, 175
wordplay 2n.6, 33, 39–41, 43, 99, 113,
    116–19, 131–2, 135, 161–3,
    174, 187–8